What on Earth Is the Church?

What on Earth Is the Church?

An Exploration in New Testament Theology

Kevin Giles

InterVarsity Press
Downers Grove, Illinois 60515

Published in the United States of America by
InterVarsity Press, Downers Grove, Illinois,
with permission from the
Society for Promoting Christian Knowledge,
London, England.

InterVarsity Press® is the book-publishing division of
InterVarsity® Christian Fellowship, a student movement active
on campus at hundreds of universities, colleges and schools of
nursing in the United States of America, and a member
movement of the International Fellowship of Evangelical Students.
For information about local and regional activities, write
Public Relations Dept., InterVarsity Christian Fellowship,
6400 Schroeder Rd., P.O. Box 7895, Madison, WI 53707-7895.

ISBN 0-8308-1868-5

Typeset and printed in Great Britain.

Library of Congress Cataloging-in-Publication Data
has been requested.

15 14 13 12 11 10 9 8 7 6 5 4 3 2 1
02 01 00 99 98 97 96 95

Contents

Foreword   vii

Preface   ix

1   Opening the Door: What on Earth Is the Church?   1
    The word *ekklēsia* – a brief comment   23

2   Jesus and the Founding of the Church   26

3   Matthew, Mark, Luke, and John   46

4   The Church in the Book of Acts   74

5   The Church in Paul's Earliest Epistles   98

6   The Church in the Middle and Later Paulines   125

7   The Church in the Non-Pauline Epistles and the Book of Revelation   152

8   Drawing the Threads Together and the Invisible–Visible Church   182

9   The Denomination as Church   196

10   Deficiencies in Past Ecclesiology and the Promise of Trinitarian Ecclesiology   212

Excursus 1   The Meaning of the Word *Ekklēsia*: Old Testament and Intertestamental Background   230

Excursus 2   Translating the Greek Word *Ekklēsia*   241

Abbreviations   244

Notes   246

Select Bibliography   288

Index of Names and Subjects   300

Index of Biblical References and Ancient Sources   303

Foreword

When teaching the New Testament, I have become increasingly aware that one of the major obstacles that confronts Western Christians in understanding its message is the individualism that pervades present-day society. Individualism, the perception of the world in relation to 'me' (or 'my group') rather than 'us', may be seen as one of the determining features of our culture. It leads to a selfish concern with the interests of our own immediate circle rather than those of society as a whole – indeed, in its more extreme forms it may lead to the denial that such a thing as 'society' even exists.

Our politics and economics in the post-war period have increasingly moved in this direction, and our religious perceptions tend too easily to follow suit. Where the New Testament speaks in corporate terms, we instinctively see it as addressing the individual believer. Yet the New Testament, no less than the Old, focuses on the people of God in its corporate identity. It is the body of Christ growing towards that maturity which Paul calls 'the full stature of Christ', a stature that is seen not in any *one* outstanding individual or even *one* local group, but as 'all of us come to the unity of the faith and of the knowledge of the Son of God' (Eph. 4.1–16).

Evangelical Christians, with their robust concern for personal salvation, have been particularly prone to lose sight of the corporate dimension of New Testament Christianity, and so have often been slow to play an effective part in the life of the wider church. These days, such individualism even seems to be on the increase in some evangelical circles, and it can all too easily lead to the type of isolationism that a generation ago threatened to deprive the church of the evangelical contribution that it both needed and valued.

It is therefore a pleasure to be asked to commend an evangelical study of the New Testament doctrine of the church that tackles head-on the issue of modern Western individualism. Disturbed by such trends in the Australian church, the author decided to go back to the New Testament. He has studied it with academic rigour, but all the time with an eye to what it may have to contribute to the life of the church today.

Kevin Giles brings together in this book some of the most widely respected expressions of current New Testament scholarship, and has judiciously selected his material in order to provide an essentially 'mainstream' overview of the issue. Consequently, New Testament theologians will be in his debt; however, he is a churchman and pastor as much as he is an academic, and concerned church members may turn to him with confidence for a well-grounded but accessible guide to this centrally important – and yet strangely neglected – aspect of biblical theology.

R. T. France
Principal of Wycliffe Hall, Oxford

Preface

For nearly thirty years, the doctrine of the church has held my attention. I first became interested in this topic in my undergraduate days at Moore Theological College, in Sydney, Australia, in the mid-1960s, and time and time again I have come back to this issue in my reading and writing. I owe this interest in the doctrine of the church to the stimulating influence of my most formative theological teachers, Drs Broughton Knox and Donald Robinson, who persistently argued that this matter demanded more serious study, clarification, and reformulation. Over the years they developed a distinctive doctrine of the church, which is essentially congregational in nature,[1] and this has captured the minds of a whole generation of clergy and informed lay people in the diocese of Sydney. It has also gained currency in the wider church through their writings, and also the writings of a number of their students who have gone on to become theological teachers themselves. They have since taken up their ideas and promoted them.[2] This book is in part a critique of their ecclesiology, though it is much more than this. However, it is not a critique of Dr Knox or Dr Robinson, who as great teachers made it their highest aim to encourage students to think for themselves.[3]

After five years in parish ministry, following ordination, I had the opportunity to undertake post-graduate study at Durham University in England, under Professor C. K. Barrett. I remember well his smile when I told him at our first meeting that I wanted to write a thesis on the church in the New Testament. He suggested that I concentrate on something less ambitious, as the research project needed to be quite specific. A week later I saw him again and nominated my topic – the church in the theology of St Luke – which he was happy to accept. Thus began my own search to understand how the apostolic writers conceived of the community called into existence by the ministry, death, and resurrection of Jesus Christ. Some years later, when I was again in parish ministry, I became involved in the ongoing debate about the ministry of women, and in writing about this I found ecclesiological issues were always close at hand.[4] The most pressing of these was the question of leadership structures in the early church. Was there one given form? Were comments about leaders in the New Testament prescriptive or descriptive? Was there development? What importance was placed on the laying on of hands, later called ordination? In seeking to answer these questions, I wrote *Patterns of Ministry Among the First Christians*.[5] In many ways, this book is its sequel, in that I return to answer the more fundamental question: How should we understand the community called into being by Jesus Christ?

What started off as a modest project has turned out to be a complete survey of communal ideas in the New Testament and a discussion of related theological questions. The first draft of the book was written in spare moments in a busy parish, and then completed in an intense spell of writing in England at Bristol and Oxford. As I found myself dealing with almost every book in the New Testament, the study of the meaning of the word *ekklēsia*/church in the Old Testament and intertestamental writings, and the development of a theology of the church, I called on my friends and acquaintances to read chapters, or parts thereof, on which they are specialists. I greatly value their comments, which in almost every case I took up. Nevertheless, all the failings in this book are entirely my own.

Bill Dumbrell and John Pryor read the first draft before I left Australia, and encouraged me to finish the project. In the three weeks I was in Bristol, Robert Forrest read the first two chapters; and in the seven weeks in Oxford, David Wenham went the extra mile and read each chapter as I finished a draft. John Kleinig, Gordon McConville, and Hugh Williamson read the excursus on the Old Testament background to the Greek word *ekklēsia*; John Nolland, the material on Luke-Acts; Andrew Lincoln, the chapter on the church in the middle and later Paulines; Alan Cadwallader, the section on Hebrews; Tim Bradshaw, the opening chapter and the last one on the Trinity – which Alister McGrath and Duncan Reid read as well; while Bruce Kaye, Graham Cole and Charles Sherlock read the chapter on the denomination as church. I would also particularly like to thank John Nolland, who made me welcome at Trinity College, Bristol, and Dick France, who made me welcome at Wycliffe Hall, Oxford. In addition, I gratefully acknowledge financial assistance for the three months of study in England from a scholarship fund of the Diocese of Adelaide which paid my air fare and the Australian Research Theology Foundation which made a grant towards living expenses. Finally, I mention my wife Lynley, who supports me in all that I do – and made our time in England such a happy one.

Chapter 1

Opening the Door:
What on Earth Is the Church?

Nothing in the Christian life impinges on us so forcefully and so pervasively as our membership of the church to which we belong. Week by week we meet in 'our church' with other Christians whom we get to know by name, and with whom we share a part of our life and faith. Yet equally important is our membership of the world-wide Christian community, which at this time is divided into the differing denominations. Our membership of this community links us with all other believers in Christ throughout the world. We can travel to a great city such as London, New York, or Moscow, or to a little village in Cambodia, Tanzania, or Argentina, and meet up with other Christians in the fellowship of the church – and immediately sense our unity in Christ. However, despite the importance of the church in Christian experience, and despite the fact that we confess in the Nicene creed that 'we believe in one holy catholic and apostolic church', uncertainty continues as to what is meant when we speak of 'the church'. The major reason for this is that there is no agreed formal definition of what constitutes 'the church'. The early Christians debated many things, and on fundamental matters – such as the person of Christ and the Trinity – they formulated definitive answers, but the church as an experiential reality was taken for granted. It was only in the sixteenth century, as a consequence of the Reformation, that Protestants and Roman Catholics attempted to define the church. Yet the result was not an agreed definition, but a number of competing assertions.

Because there is not an agreed understanding of the doctrine of the church, despite its ever-present reality, and because Christians remain divided over this issue, books continue to be written on

1

this topic. So why yet another volume, you may ask. A number of reasons can be given. First, I write with the somewhat optimistic hope that I can say something not already in print. This is a possibility because real advances have been made by critical scholars in the understanding of the Bible in recent years, and these insights can now be utilized by those who take the Bible as the starting point in building a theology of the church, and because the ongoing debate on the doctrine of the church has clarified many issues – thereby making possible a better methodological approach. Secondly, I write to bring attention to the fact that after centuries of debate and acrimony between Christians over the doctrine of the church, things have gradually changed at a scholarly level. There is now a general consensus among biblical scholars of differing confessional backgrounds on the exegesis of many of the passages that once divided Christians when they came together to discuss the church. To illustrate this point, I admit that although I am an Anglican, the books that I found closest to my own conclusions on the New Testament data and in theological method were written by Roman Catholics.[1] I attempt to utilize this consensus as succinctly and clearly as possible in what follows.

This comment about the contribution of Roman Catholic scholars leads me to give yet a third reason for writing. It is not only that Roman Catholics have produced the best books on the doctrine of the church in recent years, but they have produced *most* of what has been written on this topic. I know of no detailed biblical and theological study on the doctrine of the church, written recently, from the pen of a Protestant – other than those that are an attempt to justify a confessional position, or to explore one particular issue. The innumerable Roman Catholic books on the church are important, but despite our agreements on so much, a Protestant contribution is still needed. Fourthly, I write to establish the contours of a contemporary *theology* or *doctrine* of the church. Most of what is written about the church by Protestants either assumes a particular point of view, or concentrates on practical aspects of church life. A few years ago the most popular topic was church reunion, but nowadays it seems to be church growth. As valuable as such literature may be, it must, says Professor Macquarrie, 'be guided and correlated by a theological understanding of the church'.[2] Fifthly, I write at a particular time and place to address particular problems and questions, as has every theologian who has ever written.

Although this book is mainly concerned with New Testament teaching, arising almost two thousand years ago, the aim is to address the present. The questions constantly in mind are how should we understand the church as it is now after two millennia of history and development, and how should we seek to transform it? Writing as an Australian Anglican, I also own up to some quite specific but diverse concerns which arise out of my own ecclesial context. Two contrasting but related opinions seem to capture Christian thinking on the church in Australia. On the one hand, many play down the thought of a separation between the church and the world. They stress so strongly that Christians should be involved in the world, that, as a consequence, the implication seems to be that church membership is no longer an issue of any great importance. Belonging to a worshipping community of Christians is secondary to Christian social action. On the other hand, many so concentrate on the church as a gathering of believers where people minister to one another that Christians' responsibilities in the world, and in particular to the wider church, are minimized. The church on this view is basically a local congregation where 'my' spiritual needs are met. In the first case, membership of a specific and localized community of Christians is discounted; in the second, membership of the world-wide Christian community is discounted. Although the two positions may seem unrelated they are not. Both are predicated on modern individualism. In each instance the profoundly communal nature of Christianity is eclipsed. I was interested to come to England and be told that these two inadequate ecclesiologies were also well supported in Britain.

Methodology

The major problem with most books on the church is that they begin as if everyone is agreed as to the nature of the church, how this topic should be approached, and the issues to be addressed; yet, in reality, this is far from the truth. When it comes to discussions about the church, there is in fact more disagreement than agreement, more confusion than clarity, despite the fact that scholars today are agreed on so much as far as biblical teaching is concerned. Only one approach will cast light on the path and overcome these problems. It is one that begins by defining the terms and issues in question; clearly outlines the methodology to be used; and recognizes the difference between biblical theology, which gives us an overview of what is in the Bible, and systematic theology (or doctrine), which is an attempt to address the present building on the Bible, but drawing in other insights as well.[3]

A problem word

The English word 'church' is the first point where confusion and misunderstanding occur. We use this term in many ways in everyday speech. When we speak of 'going to church', we are usually thinking of entering a building called a 'church'. On the noticeboard at the front of these buildings there is often wording that reads 'The Anglican Church', 'The Uniting Church', 'The Presbyterian Church', or something similar. In this case, the word 'church' is used of what we today call a 'denomination'. When I was in my twenties, I told people I was about to start theological studies, and the reply sometimes came, 'So you are going into the church, are you?' In this usage, 'the church' means the clerical profession. While I was at theological college, the Vietnam war was raging. I often heard people say then, 'Why doesn't the church do something about the war?' The idea seemed to be that the church was a united institution that could act decisively and speak with one voice on complex issues. In the course of my studies, one of the subjects I had to master was 'church history'. This dealt with the life and work of significant individual Christians of the past, and the impact of momentous debates and great movements within Christendom. There are other uses of this English word 'church', but these examples are sufficient to make the point. In everyday English, the word 'church' is not a technical term with an agreed meaning. Yet it is no better when we turn to theological textbooks. Theologians are not agreed as to what constitutes the church or how it should be defined, as we will see in what follows. Despite this fact, biblical and theological scholars often write tomes on 'the church' without telling the reader exactly what is their understanding of the subject under discussion.[4] Some even argue that the church cannot be defined – that it is a true mystery, a completely supernatural reality.[5]

Does the Greek help?

A common solution to this terminological confusion created by the varied uses of the English word 'church', often advocated by

Protestants,[6] is to appeal to the word it translates from the Greek –
namely, *ekklēsia*. This seems a very plausible solution, and continues to find supporters, but in fact it is a seriously flawed approach.
James Barr, in his important book entitled *The Semantics of Biblical
Language*,[7] published in 1961, convinced the scholarly world that
it was not possible to build theology on the basis of biblical word
studies. There are two main reasons why this is so. First, the word
study approach builds on the premise that key biblical terms have
a fixed technical meaning, but this is simply not true. All biblical
words are in the first instance ordinary words that were used in
everyday speech, and as such have a range of meanings. To presume that a particular biblical word has one technical meaning
leads to what Barr calls 'illegitimate totality transfer' – the reading
into each use of a word a predetermined content. Secondly, the
word study approach to theology confuses words and concepts.
Words represent ideas or concepts, and therefore they can be
replaced in any sentence by other words, groups of words, or
metaphors that can bear the same meaning. If all attention is
given to the study of a particular word, then the bigger picture,
of which any one word is but a part, may be missed.

Yet to make these points is not to deny the place and importance of technical terms as such. We are arguing that a study of
how the one Greek word, *ekklēsia*, is used in the Bible cannot produce a basis for a theology of the church, not that technical terms
as such have no part to play. Every science needs technical terms
if clarity and precision in discourse is to be achieved, and systematic theology is no exception. The creation of technical theological
terms by theologians is quite legitimate and necessary, and often
these take up biblical words, but the technical term and biblical
word usage should not be confused. A couple of examples may
make this clearer.

For the theologian, 'salvation' is a technical term that refers to
the deliverance of the individual from the consequences of sin and
guilt made possible by the death of Christ. The biblical usage of
the noun 'salvation' (Greek *sōteria*) or the verb 'to save' (Greek
sōzō), however, are far less precise. The verb basically means to
rescue or to deliver from some threat. In the New Testament, it
can be used of deliverance from immediate physical danger (Matt.
8.25, 14.30; Acts 27.20, 31, 34, etc.), of miracles of healing (Mark
10.52; Luke 8.48, 17.19, etc.), and of the forgiveness bestowed by
Christ (Matt. 1.21; Mark 8.35; Luke 1.27, etc.). The imprecision

of the word usage in the Bible is, however, only one point of contrast with the technical theological term. The technical theological term 'salvation' embraces far more than the theological uses of the words 'save' or 'salvation' in the Bible. It is a general concept. Under this category, the theologian also discusses intimately related ideas such as eternal life, redemption, and justification by faith. If the theologians could only speak about salvation when the term was present in the Bible, then they would have to conclude that the fourth evangelist was not greatly interested in salvation – for he only uses the noun once and the verb four times in his Gospel, whereas the opposite is the truth: salvation, understood as eternal life, is central to Johannine theology. Similarly, it could be argued on this premise that Paul was not interested in salvation when he wrote to the Colossians, for the noun or the verb do not appear in this epistle. Again the reverse is the truth: the epistle highlights the uniqueness of the salvation found in Christ. The specific word, salvation, is not used, but the concept undergirds the epistle.

Another instructive example is the word 'sanctification'. In Protestant theology, sanctification is an important technical/ theological term used of the progressive growth in love, Christian maturity, and holiness that should take place in the life of the believer. However, in the New Testament, the Greek verb, *hagiazein*, 'to sanctify' (or its cognate forms) *seldom* carry this meaning. When applied to people, the most common usage of the *hag*—word group is in fact not to describe a process, but rather the changed status given to those who believe in Christ, which Paul usually calls justification by faith, and the Reformation theological tradition contrasts with sanctification![8] (cf. Acts 20.32, 26.18; 1 Cor. 1.2; 1 Thess. 5.32; Heb. 2.11, 10.10, 29, 13.12). The idea that Christians should grow in Christ-likeness is, nevertheless, an entirely biblical idea (cf. Rom. 12.2; 2 Cor. 3.18; Eph. 4.15; 1 Pet. 2.2, etc.), and some technical term is needed to designate this. 'Sanctification' may be chosen as it is 'sanctified' by history, but the point to note is that the theological concept and the biblical usage of this one word must be differentiated.

With the difference between biblical word usage and technical theological terminology explained, we return to the word *ekklēsia/* church. A study of how this word is used in the New Testament discloses that, like all words of everyday usage, it can have a range of applications.[9] In Acts 7.38, it is used of the Jewish people gathered at Mount Sinai. In Acts 19.32, 39, 41, it is used in the secular sense of an unruly gentile mob actually assembled. In a similar way, Paul uses the word to refer to Christians actually assembled when writing to the Corinthians (1 Cor. 11.18, 14.19, 28, 34, 35), but he usually uses the word in a more developed Christian sense: sometimes of the believers who regularly meet in a particular home (Rom. 16.5, 23; 1 Cor. 16.19; Col. 4.15); sometimes of all the Christians in one city or location (1 Cor. 1.2; 2 Cor. 1.1; 1 Thess. 1.1; 2 Thess. 1.1), and sometimes of all those in Christ (1 Cor. 10.32, 12.28, 15.9; Eph. 1.22, 3.10, 21).[10] When Christians appeal to the biblical usage of the word *ekklēsia* as the basis for their doctrine of the church, they invariably disclose their already formulated doctrine of the church by adopting one of these uses as the basic meaning of the word *ekklēsia*. Protestants of congregational conviction usually begin with the references in Acts 19, arguing that *ekklēsia* only means assembly (or, possibly, those who regularly assemble), and conclude that the church is but a gathering of believers. Other Protestants who believe that the universal church is the primary reality often argue that *ekklēsia* is a technical term taken over from the Old Testament, meaning 'the people of God', and this sense of the word is always to be presupposed. Finally, Catholic theologians tend to argue that the word *ekklēsia* is to be defined, as it is in Colossians and Ephesians, as the body of Christ; and, they add, this is more than a metaphorical turn of phrase. The problem with all these positions is that not only do they posit one fixed meaning for the word in question, drawn from their prior convictions, but in concentrating on just one word they miss so much else in the New Testament, which speaks of the reality for which the word *ekklēsia* is but one designation.

A more theologically aware and critical approach is needed if the New Testament is to provide a starting point for a doctrine of the church. This demands first of all an agreed understanding of what we would call 'the church idea', or 'the church concept'. In other words, what is needed is a technical term or description that encapsulates what Christians should understand to be the reality summed up in the English word 'church' understood theologically. Ideally, this should take up the more developed uses of the Greek word *ekklēsia*, exclude others, and embrace related ideas not necessarily signified by this one Greek word. In contrast to those who say that the church is such a profound reality, no one definition can be given; only contrasting images or models can be enumerated:[11] we seek one concept that will allow for the integration of other key ecclesiological terms and metaphors. In searching for this, we proceed by enumerating and evaluating suggestions that others have made.

1 *The church, the divinely constituted institution called into being by Christ himself*

In the Vatican II documents, the church is described in a number of ways, but the primary definition is given in chapter 1 of 'The Dogmatic Constitution on the Church'. After a lengthy preamble, the conclusion is reached that the church is at one and the same time 'a visible structure' and 'the mystical body of Christ'.[12] It is, however, the former that in this section is of most importance, for the document then goes on to say: 'After his resurrection our Saviour handed her [the church] over to Peter to be shepherded (John 21.17), commissioning him and the other apostles to propagate and govern her. . . . This church, constituted and organized in the world as a society, subsists in the Catholic Church, which is governed by the successor of Peter and by the Bishops in union with that successor.'[13] In chapter 3 of this document, the ordering of this divinely created institution is explained. Christ appointed the apostles with Peter as their leader, giving them special powers. They then appointed 'successors in this hierarchically structured society',[14] the first bishops, who were to ordain their successors in turn 'down to our own day'.[15] To assist them, the bishops ordained men as priests and deacons. The priests 'share in the sacerdotal dignity'[16] of the bishops and have exclusive powers, the most important being the power to re-present the sacrifice of Christ in the Mass.[17] This conception of the church as a divinely established institution, the Jesuit scholar Avery Dulles points out, 'has been a standard feature of Roman Catholic ecclesiology from the late middle ages until the middle of the present century'.[18] When an orthodox Roman Catholic hears the word 'church', these are the ideas that first come to mind.

In turning to the New Testament, the data is not read inductively; but instead through a pair of spectacles created by this framework of thought that, almost all contemporary New Testament scholars (including many who are Roman Catholics) would agree, distorts what is before the eye. In what follows, we will see that the New Testament does not suggest that Jesus called into being the church as a hierarchically ordered and clearly structured institutional society, but at this point it is to be noted that the most fundamental assertion in this position – namely, that Jesus appointed the twelve apostles as the font of all priestly ministry – is not based on any evidence stemming from the New Testament. Neither Jesus nor any of the apostolic writers ever suggests that the twelve were appointed to fulfil this role. Except for their involvement in the appointment of the seven in Acts 6.1–6, we have no indications that they were at all concerned with the ordering of the leadership of the early church. At no point do we find them appointing bishops. Much more could be said, but it is not needed, for in a paradoxical turn of events the most strident critics of this understanding of the church, as a dominically constituted and hierarchically ordered society, now come from within the Roman Catholic Church. Appealing first to the Bible and then to the record of history, scholars such as Edward Schillebeeckx,[19] Bernard Cooke,[20] and Kenan Osborne,[21] just to mention three of the most important contributors to this debate, have shown that this picture of the original constitution of the church is historically untrue. If this is the case, then it cannot be a viable way to define the church.

However, before leaving this particular conception of the church, it is important to note that this position is not only assumed by Roman Catholics. Almost word for word, apart from the claim for the Papacy, Anglo Catholics conceive of the church exactly in these terms. It is a divinely constituted institution established by Jesus and ordered by apostolic succession. The classic expression of this point of view is seen in Charles Gore's *The Church and the Ministry*, first published in 1886, but followed by a number of revised editions – the last being in 1936.[22] Many believe Gore was the most influential Anglican theologian of the late nineteenth and early twentieth century. For the Anglo Catholic, even more so than the Roman Catholic, the threefold form of the ministry (i.e. bishops, priests, and deacons) is constitutive of the being of the church.

2 The church, the body of Christ

Closely allied to the conception of the church as a divinely constituted institution, but not dependent on it, is the view that the church is to be defined exclusively, or pre-eminently, as the body of Christ. This approach can be expressed in more than one way, but common is the belief that the church is in some sense ontologically and literally the body of Christ on earth. In Roman Catholic theology, this understanding of the church was given classic expression in the influential book by the Belgian Jesuit, Emile Mersch, *The Whole Christ*, first published in 1933.[23] He defines the church as 'the mystical body of Christ', the 'physical' presence of Jesus in the world. It then gained official endorsement in the 1943 encyclical of Pius XII, *Mystici Corporis Christi*. In the Anglican Church, the same teaching also gained prominence at this time. Lionel Thornton, an Anglo Catholic, writing during the Second World War, concluded: 'We are members of that body which was nailed to the cross, laid in the tomb, and raised to life on the third day.'[24] Yet it was the book by J. A. T. Robinson, *The Body: A Study in Pauline Theology*, published in 1952, that popularized these ideas among Anglicans.[25] He argued that Paul viewed the church as literally Christ's resurrected body. When the church is understood to be in the first instance the actual body of Christ present in the world, this conclusion determines how everything the New Testament says about the church is understood. When the Christian community comes into view, or the word *ekklēsia*/church is used, it is presupposed that the entity envisaged is nothing less than the embodiment on earth of the risen Christ.

In due course, Paul's ecclesiological use of the body of Christ motif will be considered in some detail, but at this point three criticisms of the argument that this is the primary way in which the church should be understood (because only this image is to be taken realistically and ontologically) are raised. First, it is unconvincing to argue that this is the most fundamental way the New Testament understands the church, when only one contributor, Paul, mentions it – and then in only four of his epistles (Romans, 1 Corinthians, Ephesians, and Colossians). Secondly, nothing Paul says suggests that this one motif should have precedence over all the other metaphors he uses for the Christian community, and only this one be understood literally. If the church is literally the body of Christ, is it also literally his bride (Eph. 5.25ff), a field (1 Cor. 3.9), a temple (1 Cor. 3.16), or a building (Eph. 2.20ff)? Most would think not. And thirdly, to argue that the church on earth is literally the body of the risen Christ negates Paul's clear belief that Jesus now reigns in heaven.

The understanding of the church as the body of Christ, we may agree, is one of the most profound insights of St Paul, but it would seem to be but one metaphor among several he uses – with each one making its own distinctive contribution to the overall picture, and none on its own providing a comprehensive definition of the church.

3 *The church, the people of God*

More common in Protestant circles is the view that the church is pre-eminently the people of God, but this interpretation is also to be seen in the Vatican II discussion on 'The Constitution of the Church'.[26] This title is first used in the Old Testament, where Israel is called by Yahweh almost three hundred times, in an exclusive sense, 'my people'. Thus in the *LXX* (the Greek translation of the Old Testament), the Greek word *laos*, translated into English as 'people', is almost another name for Israel. In the New Testament this word continues to be used of the Jewish people, but it is accepted that gentiles are, through faith in Christ, included among the people of God; and gradually the title itself is applied to Christians, irrespective of their national origins (Acts 15.14, 18.10; 2 Cor. 6.16; Titus 2.14; 1 Pet. 2.9–10). Yet as the primary church concept, this designation has certain limitations. First of all, it does not sufficiently bring out the radical newness of the community brought into existence by the ministry, death, and resurrection of Christ, because it obscures the radical breach between historic Israel as the people of God and the Christians as the people of God, for the one term is used of both. When this designation is used, the church is defined apart from its head and source of life. What is most distinctive about the church – its filial relationship with Christ and complete dependence on him – is not mentioned or implied.[27] In Matthew's Gospel, Jesus speaks not of gathering the people of God, but of 'building *my* church' (16.18). A second limitation that this title has is that while it was a meaningful way to describe Israel, which was both an ethnic entity and a religious community, it is less meaningful when applied to Christians who are the latter but not the former. Most of the contributors to the New Testament, if not all of them, claim in one way or another, as we will see, that Christians have become the (new) people of God; yet this is a theological claim, not an ethnic one. Christians are not the people of God in the same sense as Israel was. They are in reality many peoples united only by their common faith in

Christ. This point raises a third and final limitation inherent in this title as a possible definitive church concept. The title 'people of God' makes a quite specific claim; namely, that Christians are true Israel. For this reason, many of the other titles and metaphors used of the church cannot be integrated by it. For example, the people of God and the body of Christ are two very different images of the church, pointing to very different truths, and one cannot be subsumed under the other.

4 *The church, Christians working in the world*

The fourth option assumed by some is difficult to formulate, as it has many variations and is often held more in spirit than as a clearly enunciated doctrine. Those who take this approach usually want to avoid a clear line of demarcation between the church and the world; insist that what really counts in Christian living is identification with the poor and needy; and allow that in the end all will be saved.[28] In recent years, this position is predicated sometimes on creation theology – God made the whole world and we are all his children without distinction, the church being but the community who at this present time acknowledge this – at other times, it is predicated on liberation theology.[29] Just before his death at the hands of the Nazis, Dietrich Bonhoeffer, in his *Letters and Papers from Prison*, eloquently prepared for this ecclesiology. He wrote, 'The church is only the church when it exists for others. To make a start it should give away all its property to those in need and the clergy should . . . engage in some secular calling.'[30] Later, Harvey Cox was to write, 'The church's task in the secular city is to be the *diakonos* of the city, the servant who bends himself to struggle for its wholeness and health.'[31] Similar views were expressed by Gibson Winter in *The New Creation as Metropolis*,[32] by J. A. T. Robinson in *The New Reformation*,[33] and this model of the church is also to be found in the Vatican II documents.[34]

This preconception of the essential nature of the church has an element of truth to it. It is a needed correction to those ecclesiologies that imply that the church exists for itself, and is a challenge to self-centred discipleship. Yet to claim that this view captures the essence of the apostolic understanding of the church is unconvincing. The New Testament defines Christian communal existence theologically. It is not what the Christians do individually or corporately that sets them apart as the church, but what God in Christ has done for them. Furthermore, this view discounts the communal nature of the Christian faith, which theologians generally have seen as foundational. Meeting together, the celebration of the sacraments, the hearing of God's word, and corporate prayer all fade into insignificance as involvement in the world comes on to centre stage. Finally, we note Dulles's trenchant criticism. He says, 'One serious objection to this theory is its lack of any biblical foundation. While service is often extolled, the Bible does not seem to envision the task of the church as service.'[35]

5 *The church as congregation*

In Catholic theology, the word 'church' invariably calls to mind first of all the whole company of the faithful, but in much Protestant theology the same term calls to mind first of all the local community of believers. In fact, in a not insignificant strand of Protestant theology, the congregation is the church manifested in a local setting, and no other structured group of believers on earth should rightly be called 'church'. This fundamental conception of the church finds its origins in the sixteenth-century Anabaptist tradition.[36] It developed among the separatist Puritans, and came to fruition as a doctrine of the church known as 'congregationalism' in the mid-seventeenth century in England and North America.[37] Today it is held by many Baptists, most Pentecostals, and most of the Brethren – along with those who belong to the independent churches that are such a common feature of American life. Yet besides these groups where congregationalism is explicitly endorsed, this understanding of the church is very common in the Protestant mainline churches. One lecturer at a large evangelical Anglican theological college in England told me that in discussion in class, most students admit to being convinced congregationalists. Usually those who hold this view argue that all the universal uses of the word *ekklēsia*/church in the New Testament refer to believers generally, on earth and in heaven, but not to what is commonly called a denomination.

A variation on this particular explanation of the universal uses of the word *ekklēsia*/church is common in Brethren theology, American dispensationalism,[38] and, surprisingly, among Moore College-trained evangelical Anglicans in Australia. The cord linking these three disparate groups is dependence (usually indirect and unrecognized) on the writings of J. N. Darby, one of the founding fathers of the Brethren, who seems to be the first in modern times to have advocated this alternative. Little did Darby realize that his earthly–heavenly ecclesiology owed more to Plato than to the Bible. On this view, the universal uses of the word *ekklēsia*/church are taken to refer solely to a heavenly assembly. Moore College theologians who have sought to give this position a better exegetical foundation argue first of all that the word *ekklēsia* means no more and no less than 'assembly', and in the New Testament it is used only for: (1) local assemblies of Christians on earth; or (2) the great assembly of all believers in continuous session in heaven, in which Christians on earth even now are participants in a spiritual sense. Thus Drs Knox and Robinson, who introduced this theology into Sydney Anglicanism, argue that the so-called 'Anglican Church' is a misnomer.[39] No earth-bound association other than the local congregation may be called 'church'; it is better to speak of 'the Anglican denomination' or 'the Catholic denomination'.

Both variants of congregational ecclesiology appeal to the more conservative of evangelical Christians, because these ideas 'feel' right to the modern mind imbued with the prevailing popular philosophy of individualism, and because it is thought to be the 'biblical' position – as this is what the great evangelical teachers claim. In the congregational ecclesiology, the thought that the church is basically a locally specific 'aggregation' of believers who have decided to form a church, or to belong to it, is invariably close at hand. This individualistic way of thinking is one serious flaw in this conception of the church, as the New Testament is not predicated on such a view of life. Those who suggest this, or base their ecclesiology on this premise, are mistaken – for in the ancient world, communal thinking was pervasive. Another very significant weakness in this approach is that too much is built on the presupposed meaning of the word *ekklēsia*, and this one word is taken in isolation from other communal ideas in the New Testament as if it alone provided the basis for a complete ecclesiology. In what follows, it will be shown that in the New Testament the word is used more widely than this ecclesiology allows, and that the meaning 'assembly' in most cases is missing, the word referring quite clearly to a community called into existence by God. The apostle calls three groups the *ekklēsia*/church: a congregation, all the Christians in one city or town, and all Christians on earth. Nevertheless, it is conceded, in the New Testament age, that the wider church, alluded to for instance in Matthew 16.18, is not an organized structured association such as the Roman Catholic Church or any other denomination known today. Whether or not such groupings of Christians may be called 'church' is a complex question, to which we will return much later, but most Christians allow this theological legitimating of the present form of the church. But whether or not the word 'church' is used of a denomination today, the congregational concept of the church is seriously flawed. As we will demonstrate in what follows, the church is primarily that world-wide community that confesses Jesus as Lord and is enlivened by the Holy Spirit.

6 The church, the Christian community

Having given these alternatives, we now suggest that the best solution to the quest for the fundamental church concept, under which all other titles and descriptions of the church can be subsumed, is 'the Christian community'. In other words, I am arguing for what is commonly called today a 'communio' ecclesiology, but one defined very carefully.

In the Vatican II discussions on the church there is nothing specifically said about the church as the Christian community, although communal ideas are present; however, in the subsequent thirty years, the church, defined as *koinonia* in Greek, or as *communio* in Latin, has become the most important category in Roman Catholic ecclesiology. Kilian McDonnell, in his survey of this period, argues that both at the 1979 conference of Latin American Bishops in Pueblo, Mexico, and at the 1985 Synod of Bishops in Rome, 'the church as *communio* eclipses all other ways of speaking of the church'.[40] A parallel interest in the usually equated terms *communio/koinonia*, understood as the primary concept to capture the essence of the church idea, is also evident in the writings of theologians from other traditions and in ecumenical texts. Paul Avis, a well-known Anglican theologian, has written *Christians in Communion*, in which the term *koinonia/* communion is seen as the key to an ecumenical, contemporary ecclesiology,[41] while the Greek Orthodox Bishop, John Zizioulas, has written an important study entitled *Being as Communion*.[42] He argues that *communio* is a word that reflects the very nature of the triune God, and as such can be seen as the ontological basis for human existence as *communio* – a reality sacramentally realized on earth in the church. The concept has also featured prominently in almost all the bilateral talks between the churches in the last ten years – at times being the controlling theme of the whole document.[43] For this reason, the report of the 'Fifth Forum on International Bilateral Conversations', held in 1990, concludes, '*Koinonia* is the fundamental understanding of the church emerging from bilateral dialogues.'[44] Finally, we mention that the 1993 Fifth World Conference on Faith and Order, held in Santiago, Spain, made '*Koinonia*: Towards Communion in Faith, Life and Witness' the theme of the whole conference.

There is, however, a problem with this now pervasive *koinonia/communio* ecclesiology, despite its great promise. The terminology lacks precision. The Greek noun *koinonia* is found nineteen times in the New Testament, thirteen of these being in the Pauline epistles, four in 1 John, and one each in Acts and Hebrews.[45] It is often translated 'fellowship', but whereas the English word brings to mind first of all convivial relationships, the Greek carries the meaning of 'participation' or 'to share in'. It is built on a root that means 'common', and it is used to denote many kinds of sharing: sharing with others in suffering (2 Cor. 1.7; Phil. 3.10), in giving money or possessions (Rom. 15.26; 2 Cor. 8.4, 9.13), in the gospel (Phil. 1.5), in the body and blood of Christ (1 Cor. 10.6), etc. The uses with the most ecclesiological content are found in the four examples in 1 John 1.2–3, 6–7. These passages speak of the fellowship we have 'with the Father and his Son, Jesus Christ', and of the fellowship we have with one another as believers. This is often called the vertical and the horizontal aspects of *koinonia*. As Christians, we are related to Christ as we share in his divine life, and to one another through our common participation in the Spirit. The word is thus used of the relationships that constitute the Christian community, the church – but, we add, never of the social reality thereby created. The word *koinonia* is always used as an abstract noun (of relationships and activities), and never as a concrete noun (of a group of people or an institution). It is therefore not a church concept.[46]

Yet having noted how the word *koinonia* is used in the New Testament, it must be added that in ecumenical literature the word is most commonly taken as a *concept* that speaks of what we participate in as Christians. This is a much broader matter. It is argued that this idea is also alluded to, for example, by the Pauline 'in Christ' and 'with Christ' terminology, the body of Christ metaphor, and in the Johannine vine and the branches imagery, 'the abiding in' symbolism, and in the teaching on the believer as being 'one' with Christ and 'one' with other believers.[47] This reminds us yet again that any concept is more comprehensive than any one word. In this conceptual use of the word *koinonia*, there can be no question that the church as a concrete social reality comes into view – for many of the terms and metaphors subsumed under this category are ecclesiological in nature.

The Latin *communio* is an acceptable translation of this New Testament word *koinonia*, for – like the Greek – its root alludes to that which is held in common, but the Greek word could also be translated equally well by the Latin *participatio* (participation). The problem, and the benefits, of adopting the translation *communio* is that, unlike the Greek noun it translates, it has both abstract and concrete force. It can be used to speak of the relationship that Christians have with Christ and with each other, and of the social reality called the church. In the latter case, *communio* (communion) is used as a synonym of *communitas* (community).[48] We see this usage in the Apostle's Creed, in the words 'I believe in . . . the communion of saints', which stands in apposition to the clause 'one holy, catholic church'.[49] However, *communio* has yet a third meaning. It is also a term to speak of the Eucharist – or, to be more exact, of receiving the elements. In this it follows Pauline usage of the word *koinonia* (1 Cor. 10.16). In many books and documents that adopt this terminology, all three usages are in play, often without any distinctions being made. Acceptance of this may further ecumenical discussion, but it does not clarify what is of the essence of the theological concept: the church. I am not criticizing the widespread use of the *communio* motif in ecclesiology (which has basically been a very positive development), but simply trying to see its particular relevance for our purposes.

All three meanings of the word *communio* are legitimate, but only the meaning *communitas*/community has promise as a fundamental church concept. This meaning does not reflect the Greek word *koinonia*, but rather – as we will see in due course – the more theologically developed Christian meaning of the word *ekklēsia*/church. Luther clearly saw this, for he insisted that the right translation for the Greek *ekklēsia* was the German word *Gemeinde*, which is best rendered into English as 'community'.[50] In this century, Karl Barth has followed him by consistently translating *ekklēsia* by *Gemeinde,* which in the English text of the *Church Dogmatics*[51] becomes 'community'. Furthermore, Roman Catholic and Protestant theologians, in writing or speaking about the church, almost invariably come to identify this reality as the Christian community. Even if there is no reflection or comment on this matter, as is usually the case, the equating of the concept of 'the church' with the Christian community is extremely common. This suggests that today this expression is the most widely held definition of the church. However, we want to go further than this. It is our argument that the concept 'the Christian community' is the reality implied by the more developed uses of the word *ekklēsia*/church, this expression profoundly captures the essence of our communal existence in Christ, and all other ecclesiological terms and metaphors can be subsumed under this one category.

The strength of this definition of the concept of the church is that it reflects the basic corporate thought of the Bible, which is given new direction and new dimensions through the ministry, death, and resurrection of Christ. It is a reminder that God's work in history, as it is presented in the biblical drama, involves the gathering together of a people who are united to him and to each other. This has been admirably underlined in Paul D. Hanson's important book, *The People Called,* which traces 'the growth of the notion of community over the entire history of the Bible'.[52] In the Old Testament, God reveals himself to the nation Israel, who are chosen as his own people, but who fail time and again in their calling to be a holy people and a witness to the nations, so that in the end the prophets look to the gathering together of a holy remnant and the making of a new covenant. In various ways, the New Testament sees these prophecies coming to pass in Christ, who gathers together the holy remnant and inaugurates the new covenant, and the new covenant community. From the beginning, this community is given form by incipient institutional structures; St Paul argues that it is nothing less than the body of Christ, and gradually it is perceived that those who belong to this community are the true people of God. They have supplanted the Jews. There is but one Christian community, and wherever this is found, Christians form local worshipping communities to express their oneness in Christ and to encourage one another.

In coming to study the New Testament, the matter of chief interest will be the communal thinking of Jesus and the apostolic writers, and its outworking in the life of those who form this new community. We are not attempting to prove that Jesus established an institution with an ordered ministry; nor trying to show that one metaphor such as the body of Christ gives definitive content to the nature of the church; nor wanting to relate the Old Testament and the New Testament by designating the church as the people of God; nor working to involve Christians in the world by defining the church as the servant of Christ; nor desiring to limit the church to the local congregation of believers. Our goal is much wider. It is to subsume all these ideas and others under the one basic concept, the Christian community. No other category, we argue, offers the possibility of an integrated ecclesiology of such breadth and depth.

Communalism versus individualism

Why, it might be asked, has this communal understanding of the church so often been missed, or minimized, if it is so basic to the New Testament? The answer to this question, to a large degree, depends on the age in which it is asked, but why this has been so for well over a hundred years is clear. Modern Western culture is thoroughly individualistic, and theologians have all too often read the New Testament in the light of their own cultural experience. They have imagined Jesus and Paul to be evangelists like Billy Graham, calling on people to make a personal and individual response of faith, and suggested that the church is where they will get help in living out their Christian life.[53] This church is, of course, the local church as a voluntary association. The wider church is of no interest, because it in no way helps the individual. Surprisingly, the two groups most guilty of this misreading of the Bible are conservative evangelicals and fundamentalists – who so often claim their theology is based solely on the Bible – and theologically liberal Christians, who unashamedly interpret their faith in terms of the prevailing culture.[54]

In the ancient world, the cultural setting of both Old and New Testaments, and still in those parts of the world less influenced by Western individualism, the wider community is always more important than the individual, or even the individual family unit, the nuclear family. In this situation, people find their identity in relation to, and as part of, an interconnected social world. The following are the more important communal identity markers:[55]

1 *The extended family or clan.* In a traditional culture, the 'family' to which one belongs is of most importance. The nuclear family is but a unit within this larger grouping. Thus in the Old Testament the word most commonly translated 'family' (Hebrew, *mispaha*) normally refers to a tribe or a clan, and in the New Testament, the Greek word *patria*, which can be translated by the word 'family', only appears three times (Luke 2.4; Acts 3.25; Eph. 3.15), and in each case refers to lineage or extended family.

2 *Place of origin.* The town or city of birth (Jesus of Nazareth, Paul of Tarsus) is also of great importance. It is a fundamental personal identity marker, but it can also bestow honour (Tarsus, no mean city), or question it ('Can anything good come out of Nazareth?'), depending on the public perception of the place.

3 *Nationality.* One's country – or, more importantly, what we call today ethnicity – was also highly significant. According to this category, people were stereotyped as Jews, Samaritans, Greeks, Barbarians, etc.

4 *Religion or sect.* In the ancient world and in traditional societies today, religion is of such importance that it is hard for modern secularized Westerners to appreciate even dimly its social impact. The religion or sect (taken as a sub-group of the parent religion) of which one is a part determines much of life, and places the individual in a special relationship with all others of the same religion.

It is against the backdrop of this social world where people are identified by others, and identify themselves by the communal solidarities to which they belong, that the New Testament must be set. Jesus and all the New Testament writers would not have understood modern individualism. For them, the individual was always part of a larger social world and this social world was primary. To become a follower of Jesus by necessity meant joining a community, becoming part of a new spiritual family.

In English, the word 'community' is built on the word 'common'. Thus by inference a community is any group of people who hold certain things in common.[56] What is common may be the most personal of relationships such as in a nuclear family, or something less personal such as involvement in a common locality or pursuit, or simply national identity – 'I belong to the Australian community'. Yet what differentiates modern attitudes to community and ancient attitudes is that for the former, communal allegiance as a general rule takes second place to individual self-realization, rights, and freedoms. In the latter, the reverse is true. Many contemporary social commentators point out that modern individualism is a novel doctrine, inherently deceptive, and inimical to the ultimate well-being of the person.[57] Robert Bellah, in his book *Habits of the Heart: Individualism and Commitment in American Life*, highlights its deceptive powers. He says:

> There are truths we do not see when we adopt the language of radical individualism. We find ourselves not independently of other people and institutions but through them. We never get to the bottom of ourselves on our own. We discover who we are face to face and side by side with others in work, love, and learning. All of our activity goes on in relationships, groups, associations, and communities ordered by institutional structures and interpreted by cultural patterns of meaning. . . . Finally, we are not simply ends in ourselves, either as individuals or as a society. We are parts of a larger whole that we can neither forget nor imagine in our own image without paying a high price.[58]

In contrast to our modern Western way of thinking, the Bible is predicated on the belief that human beings at every level are bound together in communities of various sorts. To suggest that the Bible is ultimately about individual salvation, or that the church is but a local assembly of individuals who are bound together only by their personal associations, or that each individual congregation is in no profound way linked with other congregations, introduces ideas alien to biblical thinking. Those who suggest such things reflect their own cultural values, not the values of the biblical writers.

From what has been said it should be clear that in speaking of the church as the Christian community we are not suggesting that the church is but a sociological phenomenon, a community of people with like religious convictions who have created their own institution. The sociological is naturally present and important, but the Christian community, the church, is God's creation in Christ. Christians are united in a common fellowship because they are united to Christ. The horizontal and the vertical both play their part in the church, but the vertical, our relationship with God in Christ, is always primary. This theological basis for our common life as Christians also calls into question right from the beginning individualism or radical congregationalism. Our unity cannot be reduced to anything less than a 'truly catholic'[59] understanding of Christianity. As important as the local church is in the experience of the believer and in the purposes of God, the common union with Christ shared by all must take priority, and be of ultimate importance. Another matter that the integrating church concept, the Christian community, helps explain is the relationship between the theological reality and its human manifestation(s). As Bellah reminds us in the quote above, communities *always* develop institutional forms, no matter how rudimentary. The Christian community without any institutional form, local or para local, is an impossibility.

The goal and presuppositions of this study

Finally, in this rather long introductory chapter we come to say something about the particular approach to be taken and how we will proceed. Most of what follows will be a study of the communal ideas in the teaching of Jesus and in the writings of the various New Testament authors. We will begin by trying to work out what Jesus intended by calling disciples, and then consider the question 'Did Jesus found or institute the church?' This will be preparatory to a somewhat detailed study of all the major writings in the New Testament. It will involve the *exegesis* of relevant texts, the attempt to articulate what the author intended the original readers to understand by his words, and the systematizing of the information gleaned so as to come to some conclusions as to how each writer understood the community brought into existence by the Christ event. In doing this, we will often appeal to sociology to help us conceptualize what is described in the text.[60] This synthesis of the communal thought of particular New Testament authors that builds on exegesis and is historical and descriptive in nature is called *biblical theology.* It is to be distinguished from *systematic theology,* or doctrine as it is commonly called – a prescriptive discipline that seeks to address the church in the present. This draws

in other data besides biblical teaching, such as earlier answers to the same question being considered, philosophical or sociological insights that may help clarify issues, and such like. Most of this study will be biblical theology as we have defined it, but as we progress the questions of our age will be addressed from time to time in passing. However, this changes in chapters 8, 9 and 10 where the present becomes the primary focus and the discussion thus becomes systematic theology by definition.[61]

Most of the writings of the New Testament will be studied, but questions of date and authorship of individual books will generally be left to one side, mainly because entering these debates would demand too much time. The almost certain fact that the canonical books were written over several decades and reflect changing perspectives is, however, not ignored. As far as authorship is concerned, the names given with each book are taken as the name of the person responsible, but again where authorship may bear on exegetical conclusions, such as in the case of some of the Pauline epistles, critical distinctions are carefully made.

The word *ekklēsia* – a brief comment

We have already mentioned the Greek word *ekklēsia* a number of times, and as this term will reappear time and time again in what follows, a brief comment will be helpful. This is the word all English translations render as 'church'. This particular word must be used frequently because, as has already been noted, the English word 'church' has become the primary term to designate the 'church concept', the Christian community. This can be designated or described in the New Testament by other words than *ekklēsia*, while in a few instances in the New Testament *ekklēsia* does not refer to the church but to a gathering of unbelievers (Acts 19.32, 39, 41). When we are speaking explicitly about the use or force of the word *ekklēsia* in a particular context, the word itself is best used to make sure it is perfectly clear what is being discussed.

In considering how the New Testament writers understood this Greek word, no prior commitment as to its meaning controls the discussion. It is in fact allowed that the word is used in more than one way by the apostolic writers. The meaning in each instance discussed will be pursued in the context of the passage in which it is found and in the light of the writer's overall thinking. Scholars do, however, have diametrically opposed opinions as to why the early Christians chose the word *ekklēsia*, and what it meant to them in the first instance. As there is a limited amount of objective data, this suggests that prior commitments about the nature of the church may determine the conclusions reached. In a detailed excursus at the end of this book, the debate, the evidence, and my conclusions are set out in full. At this point I want to summarize very briefly this information to help make sense of some of what follows.

In classical Greek, *ekklēsia* was the word used of the citizens of the state in assembly. It was an abstract noun that spoke of those actually gathered. When the people went home, the *ekklēsia* ceased to exist. In the Greek Old Testament, known by the Latin number *LXX*, as there were supposed to have been seventy (or seventy-two) translators, *ekklēsia* renders the Hebrew word *qahal* about a hundred times, although thirty-five times it is translated by the Greek word *synagōguē*, which comes into English as 'synagogue'. In earlier parts of the Old Testament, *qahal* clearly means virtually the same as *ekklēsia* in classical Greek. It speaks of Israel, or some group of people, actually in assembly. The key word used in the early parts of the Old Testament for Israel as God's covenant people, as an ongoing community, is *edah*, which is translated by *synagōguē*. At Qumran, *qahal* can be used of any gathering, and Philo and Josephus, two Jewish writers who lived close to the time the New Testament was written, can use *ekklēsia* in the classical sense. On this evidence, some scholars conclude that the early Christians took over the word *ekklēsia* because it was a neutral term to speak of their assemblies, and from this usage the word developed so that those who regularly assembled could also be thought of as an *ekklēsia*. The basic meaning 'assembly' continued, but the abstract noun became a concrete noun, referring to an ongoing group of people.

In complete contrast, many scholars have argued that *qahal* is a synonym of *edah*, and refers to Israel as the covenant community. Thus when Christians used the word *ekklēsia* they were claiming to be true Israel. Our examination of the evidence set out in the excursus already mentioned, indicates that neither opinion is correct. What seems to be the case is that *qahal* changed its meaning, and in later parts of the Old Testament, especially in Deuteronomy and Chronicles, came to approximate in meaning to *edah*. In these texts where *qahal* in fact refers to Israel as the people of

God, this meaning was carried over in translation to the word *ekklēsia*. Added semantic content for the word *ekklēsia* was also provided by the fact that it was used to translate both *edah* and *qahal*. This meant it came to be seen as a word that could carry the meaning of both Hebrew words. At Qumran, *qahal* is usually used to speak of people assembled with no theological content implied, but in a few examples it is used of Israel as God's covenant community. Similarly, Philo, a Greek-speaking Jew of the early first century AD, usually uses *ekklēsia* in the classical sense to refer to people assembled, but he can also use it to designate Israel as a substantive entity.

This suggests, then, that while *ekklēsia* was not a technical term for Greek-speaking first century Jews, always understood to mean Israel the people of God, this meaning was known. It was a word with theological potential. The early Christians generally found the word *synagōguē* uncongenial because this was a name for Jewish communities, and the buildings they met in, and so its close associate, *ekklēsia*, was preferred, but the Book of Acts shows that at first many other collective titles were also used to designate the Christian community. It is uncertain whether the early Christians' use of the word *ekklēsia* to designate themselves collectively originated among Greek-speaking Jewish converts, or in the Pauline mission to the Greco-Roman world; however, this is not a crucial issue.

Chapter 2

Jesus and the Founding
of the Church

At the beginning of this century, Alfred Loisy, the radical Roman Catholic scholar who was excommunicated by Pope Pius X in 1908 for his 'modernist' teachings, succinctly expressed the two most fundamental questions that modern critical study raises in relation to speaking of Jesus as the founder of the church. In the oft-quoted maxim he said, 'Jesus foretold the kingdom, and it was the church that came.'[1] These words imply two things. First, Jesus' proclamation of the Kingdom of God speaks of the imminent inbreaking of a completely supernatural order that will happen either during his ministry or immediately afterwards, and result in a transformed heaven and earth.[2] From this it follows that if this was the heart of the proclamation of Jesus, it is inconceivable that he would have given himself to establishing a community, let alone an organization, to continue for an indefinite period into the future. And secondly, the fact that such a community with developing organizational features did emerge shows how the early Christians responded to the non-fulfilment of the proclamation of Jesus. As the radically new order to be established solely by God's action did not eventuate, they created the church. To answer Loisy, one has to show that Jesus did not proclaim the almost immediate coming of the Kingdom of God, and that the community created by his summons to follow him is in fact related to what we call the church today. Yet this is not as easy as it may sound, for the Gospels seem to suggest that Jesus did proclaim the nearness of the inbreaking of the Kingdom of God, and that he said very little about the structuring of an ongoing institution called 'the church'.

26

Eschatology in the teaching of Jesus

1 *End-time expectations*

Loisy was absolutely right in making the proclamation of the Kingdom of God central to the ministry of Jesus.[3] The frequency of the expression in the synoptic tradition is the most compelling evidence in support of this contention. There are 76 independent Kingdom sayings, or 103 if the parables are included. Jesus' understanding of this reality builds on Old Testament ideas of God's rule over his people, and contemporary Jewish expectations that God would definitively intervene in human history on behalf of Israel. In using this expression, Jesus' hearers would have understood him to be speaking of God's dynamic rule over the whole universe, which would vindicate Israel as God's chosen people. This eschatological conception of the Kingdom of God remains central in Jesus' usage, but, as we will see, he also gives it new content. Often Jesus speaks of the Kingdom as something about to break into human history. It is to be anticipated in the near future, and so Jesus tells the disciples to pray, 'Your kingdom come' (Matt. 6.10; Luke 11.2). One picture that Jesus uses more than once to speak of this future reign of God over his people is that of a banquet (Luke 13.22–30, 14.15–24; Matt. 22.1–14), a familiar figure in Jewish end-time expectations (Isa. 25.6, 1 Enoch 62.14; Syr. Bar. 29.5). The invitation is, 'Come; for everything is ready now' (Luke 14.17). This orientation to the future in the teaching of Jesus, seen in his proclamation of the Kingdom, is nevertheless much wider than this one motif. The parables, many of which speak of the impending coming of the Kingdom, often are related to end-time warnings.

The need to be ready, since the eschatological climax of history may come at any moment, is underlined in parables such as the ten maidens (Matt. 25.1–12); the nocturnal burglar (Matt. 24.43–50; Luke 12.39–40); the doorkeeper (Mark 13.33–7; Luke 12.35–8; cf. Matt. 24.42), and the servants entrusted with supervision (Matt. 25.14–30; cf. Luke 19.12–27).[4] In many vivid metaphors, Jesus makes the same point. The end will come suddenly like lightning (Luke 17.24), like a flood (Luke 17.26), like the fire on Sodom and Gomorrah (Luke 17.28–33). The axe is ready to be put to the root of the unfruitful fig tree (Luke 13.37–9). In the light of the impending inbreaking of the Kingdom of God in judgement and salvation, Jesus calls on all Israel to repent (Mark 1.15; Luke 13.1–5). It is the last hour.

This note of urgency that runs through the Gospels cannot be missed, but the number of texts that can be quoted to suggest that Jesus expected the end to come almost immediately, or directly after the completion of his ministry, are few in number and not as clear as Loisy and others have claimed. It can be accepted that when Jesus said, 'Truly I tell you, this generation will not pass away until all these things have taken place' (Mark 13.30 par.), he was speaking about his own generation, but the context suggests that 'these things' refers to the fall of Jerusalem, an event that must take place before the Kingdom of God breaks into history.[5] The earlier saying, 'Truly I tell you, there are some standing here who will not taste death until they see that the Kingdom of God has come in power' (Mark 9.1; both Matthew and Luke omit 'come in power' – cf. Matt. 16.28; Luke 9.27) is more problematic. It is noted first that in these words nothing is said of pressing imminence, for it allows that some must die before those remaining 'see' the Kingdom; and secondly, what will be seen when the Kingdom comes in power is not specified. Many suggestions have been made: the transfiguration that follows, the resurrection, the coming of the Holy Spirit, the fall of Jerusalem, etc.[6] Lastly, we mention Matthew 10.23, where Jesus is reported as saying to the disciples as he sends them out on mission, 'Truly I tell you, you will not have gone through all the towns of Israel before the Son of Man comes.' Much has been made of this comment on the assumption that Jesus was mistaken. He predicted that he would return as the Son of Man before the twelve had finished their mission to Israel, and yet this did not happen. On this interpretation, Matthew included a prophecy of Jesus that he knew did not eventuate. A more plausible view is that Matthew understood Jesus to be saying that the mission to Israel would continue until the Son of Man returns.[7] This is in fact exactly what Matthew understands Jesus to have commanded after his resurrection. I am assuming the most common view that the 'all nations' of Matthew 28.19 includes Israel.[8]

Loisy, and those who insist that Jesus taught that the Kingdom of God was about to erupt into history, are correct in underlining the eschatological nature of the ministry of Jesus, but they are wrong in arguing that Jesus expected this to happen almost immediately. The small number of problematic texts that can be appealed to in support of this view have to be balanced against a large body of teaching that allows that both the Kingdom of God is already present in some way, and that a period of grace was anticipated by Jesus. In this regard, Mark 13.32 is important. In words almost universally taken as coming from the lips of Jesus, speaking of the end he says, 'But about that day or hour no one knows, neither the angels in heaven, nor the Son, but only the Father. Beware keep alert . . .' The meaning is clear: the end is not fixed by an apocalyptic timetable, but is entirely a matter of the Father's choice – he can lengthen or shorten the days – and no one, not even the Son, knows when the Father will act in judgement and salvation.[9] Jeremias writes, 'All human existence, hourly threatened by the catastrophe, lives in the interval of grace.'[10]

The pressing imminence of the end matched by an uncertain period of grace, which we have argued characterizes the teaching of Jesus, allows for the possibility that Jesus did call disciples with the intent of establishing a community that would continue after his death. His insistence that the end is near, rather than counting against this idea, substantiates it. To quote Jeremias again:

> Precisely because Jesus believed that the end is near, it had to be his purpose to gather God's people of the time of salvation. For the people of God belong to the one whom God has sent; the group of disciples belongs to the prophet. Indeed we must put the point even more sharply: the *only* significance of the whole of Jesus' activity is to gather the eschatological people of God.[11]

2 Present reality

Yet Jesus not only allows for an interval before the end, he also insists that end-time expectations are already being realized in the present. Again, the Kingdom sayings are important. In many of these, the point is made that the Kingdom has already come in some sense, and even now is impinging on the present. In a dispute about the power by which he performs exorcisms, Jesus says, 'But if it is by the Spirit of God that I cast out demons, then the kingdom of God has come to you' (Matt. 12.28; Luke 11.20). It is now generally agreed that the Greek verb *ephthasen*, translated here as 'has come to you', means 'to come in the sense of to arrive'.[12] Jesus is claiming that his triumph over demonic forces shows that the reign of God is now operative in this world. There are other sayings that also speak in a similar way of the presence of the reign of God in and through the ministry of Jesus (e.g. Matt. 11.5–6/Luke 7.22–3; Matt. 13.16–17/Luke 10.23–4; Matt. 11.12/Luke 16.16; Matt. 11.11/Luke 7.28; Mark 4.10–12; Luke 4.16–30, 17.20–1), but to discuss each one of these would involve detailed exegetical work that is not necessary here.

Another rich source of comment on the presence of the Kingdom is found in many of the parables.[13] Yet for our purposes what is more to the point is the way in which Jesus makes the Kingdom of God a present soteriological possibility. The proclamation of the Kingdom is an offer of salvation. In the synoptic Gospels, salvation includes deliverance from many kinds of oppression (cf. Luke 4.18) – exclusion from being numbered among the people of God, sickness, demon possession, and sin. Jesus' one explicit claim that the casting out of the demons showed that the Kingdom of God was present (Matt. 12.28/Luke 11.20) must not be taken in isolation. The ongoing conflict between Jesus and the demonic forces, which is so prominent in the synoptic Gospel narratives and the frequent healing miracles, speaks of the present triumph of the reign of God that brings salvation to the oppressed. Repeatedly, the casting out of demons and the working of miracles are associated together (e.g. Matt. 4.23, 9.35; Mark 1.34, 6.13). When John the Baptist sent messengers to Jesus to ask him, 'Are you the one to come?' – that is, are you the Messiah? – Jesus replied in words reflecting Isaiah 35.5–6, 61.1, 'Go and tell John what you hear and see: the blind receive their sight, the lame walk, the lepers are cleansed, the deaf hear, the dead are raised, and the poor have good news preached to them' (Matt. 11.2–6; Luke 7.22–3). In Isaiah, the fulfilment of these things heralds the advent of the saving reign of God.

However, it is not just the exorcisms and the miracles that speak of the saving presence of the Kingdom. Equally important is the gathering of the people of God. It has been pointed out that the term, the Kingdom of God, primarily speaks of the dynamic rule of God, but as the thought of God ruling implies a people he rules over, the expression also can involve, in a secondary sense, the idea of 'realm'. Thus Jesus not only proclaims the Kingdom of God – that is, God's dynamic reign – but also invites people to 'enter' the Kingdom of God (Matt. 18.3; Mark 9.47; Luke 16.16, etc.), which must mean deciding to recognize God's rule over one's life.[14] Those who do this constitute a new community where the rule of God is of utmost importance, and life transforming. Yet the reign of God is not limited to this sphere. God is King over all, even if unbelief at this time does not recognize this fact. Schnackenburg notes the contrast: 'the disciples . . . remain attached to earth whereas God's reign, despite its penetration into this realm on earth, is never absorbed in it, at least in the present era'.[15] This means that the Kingdom, and the community called into being by the preaching of the Kingdom, are not to be equated. This gathering of a community through the preaching of the Kingdom takes up the idea common in Jewish intertestamental writings that the coming of the Messiah would involve the formation of a Messianic kingdom, a reconstituted Israel (*LXX* Bar. 4.36–7, 5.5–9; Philo *Praem.Poen.* 28; 4 Ezra 13.39–47).

If, then, the disciples are those who have 'entered' the Kingdom of God, and as such experience something of end-time reality, this means that they cannot be seen simply as those waiting for eschatological salvation, or as those who prefigure the Christian community, the church. They are rather as 'the community of salvation', the church as it existed provisionally before Easter. In this brief period, the divine presence, one of the hallmarks of the life of the church, was experienced in the presence of Jesus. After Easter, this would be known through the presence of the Holy Spirit.

The twelve

The Gospels agree that Jesus called people to be his disciples, thereby distinguishing between those who responded to his invitation and those who did not.[16] The invitation was extended to all who heard him, and in this sense we can think of his ministry to all Israel, but nowhere does Jesus promise salvation without a response. This means that division within Israel was not only a consequence of his ministry, but also an inherent aspect of it. At some early point in his ministry, Jesus selected from a larger number of followers a small group, twelve in number, to be the nucleus of his work. They were to be with him, hearing what he said and seeing what he did (Mark 3.13–19 pars.). The existence of this inner core of twelve disciples is well attested at all levels of the Gospel tradition, and commentators agree that the number twelve has profound theological significance. It was a sacred number for the Jews. Historic Israel had been constituted on the basis of twelve patriarchs, sons of Jacob, who was also called Israel. The prophetic hope alive and well at the time of Jesus was that the twelve tribes, which had long since ceased to exist, would be reconstituted in the last days when the Messiah appeared (Ezek. 37.1–28, 39.23–9, 40–8; Baruch 4.37, 5.5; Ben Sira 36.11; Ps. Sol. 17.28–31, 1QM. 2.2, 7, etc.).[17] The appointment of the twelve was thus a *symbolic prophetic action*. It announced that Jesus was recreating Israel. As the nucleus and foundation of restored Israel, the twelve were the patriarchs of a reconstituted people of God; but as a circumscribed group, with whom only some identified, they were also a warning to recalcitrant Israel. In a sense, the twelve were witnesses to both the salvation and judgement now close at hand for the historic people of God, the Jews. This thought is spelt out by Jesus when he says to the twelve: 'Truly I tell you, at the renewal of all things, when the Son of Man is seated on the throne of his glory, you who have followed me will also sit on twelve thrones, judging the twelve tribes of Israel' (Matt. 19.28; cf. Luke 22.30). Lohfink says, 'at the last judgement they will testify against Israel if Israel does not repent'.[18]

Because Jesus had come to reconstitute Israel, his mission had to begin with the house of Israel. All the Gospels agree that with one or two special exceptions, Jesus directed his ministry only to Jews. Matthew makes the point explicit. He has Jesus say, 'I was sent only to the lost sheep of the house of Israel' (Matt. 15.24; cf. 10.6, 23). The imagery of the sheep and the shepherd that Jesus frequently used (Mark 6.34, 14.37; Luke 12.32, 15.3–7; John 10.1–30, etc.) underlines that the mission, at least in the first instance, was to Israel. This imagery would have been clear to those who heard him speak. In the Old Testament, Israel is God's flock (e.g. Num. 27.17, Ps. 74.1, 79.13, 100.3; Jer. 13.20; Zech. 11.27), a flock often led astray and scattered by false under-shepherds (Ezek. 34.1–31; Zech. 10.2–12), and needing to be purified and reassembled by *the* shepherd himself (Isa. 40.11; Ezek. 34.23; Jer. 23.1–8, Mic. 4.6–7). In speaking of his hearers as sheep or a flock and by calling himself the shepherd, Jesus was claiming to fulfil these prophecies. He was gathering the lost sheep of Israel, reconstituting the flock, the 'remnant' of which Jeremiah spoke (Jer. 23.3).

By introducing the word 'remnant', we return again to the divisive nature of Jesus' ministry. He came as the Jewish Messiah and invited all Israel to respond, but it seems that gradually he came to see that only some of Israel would accept the salvation he offered. The Gospels are in fact a story of a separating process, and the conflict within Israel that this created. The disciples who follow the good shepherd are 'a little flock' (Luke 12.32) who stand apart from the leaders of the nation who reject Jesus and eventually organize his death, and the Jewish crowds who are either hostile or indifferent to him. The thought that true Israel would consist of a holy remnant finds its origins in the Old Testament (1 Kings 19.18; Isa. 10.21, 28.16; Jer. 23.3; Zeph. 3.12, etc.), but became a major theme in the intertestamental writings.[19]

Both the Pharisees and the Essenes, each in their own way, reflect this remnant theology. Some have denied that this was so with the Pharisees, but the evidence certainly points strongly in this direction.[20] The most distinctive feature of the Pharisaic movement was its adherence to a body of traditional teaching, handed down 'from the fathers' which represented both an interpretation and a supplement to the Pentateuchal laws (Josephus *Ant.* 13.106; Mark 7.6–13). These traditions the Pharisees sought to keep with the utmost exactness and rigour. Both Paul and Josephus speak of their 'strict' observance of their laws (*War* 1.108–9, 2.162, *Ant.* 20.200–1; Acts 22.3, 26.6). Jews who did not keep the law with such 'strictness' they regarded as 'sinners' outside of the covenant made with Israel (Mark 2.16).[21] In contrast, they liked to think of themselves as 'the righteous' (Mark 2.17; Matt. 23.28, 29; cf. Matt. 5.20; Luke 18.14; Gal. 2.21). In essence, they were a purity sect who bound themselves to keeping in their daily life the laws governing access to the temple and participation in the cult. By doing this as laymen, they were claiming to represent the priestly eschatological people of salvation (Exod. 19.6). Neusner sees this concern for purity focused particularly on the meal table. Even ordinary meals had to be eaten in a state of purity, as if one was a priest serving in the temple.[22] The depth of hostility between Jesus and the Pharisees arises because both are making exclusive claims to represent the will of God for Israel.

With the Essenes, there is no debate. Without reserve they claim to be (true) 'Israel' (1QS 5.22, 8.4; 1Qsa 1.6; 1QM 10.9), 'the remnant' (CD 1.4f, 2.6; 1QH 6.8; 1QM 13.8), 'the elect' (CD 4.3f), 'the sons of grace' (1QH 7.20), 'the members of the new covenant' (CD 6.19), etc., to make the point that they alone are the community of salvation to the exclusion of other Jews. They too considered themselves to be a priestly community (CD 3.12—4.12; 4Q Flor. 1.1–7),[23] but they rejected the existing priesthood and the temple – arguing that God has placed both under judgement. Whereas the Pharisees sought to express priestly purity in everyday life, the Essenes of Qumran thought this could only be done by withdrawing into the wilderness; no compromises could be allowed.

It is within this social and theological context that Jesus' ministry, especially his calling of disciples, must be understood. He chose a different path than that of the Pharisees and the Essenes, but he too sought to gather a holy remnant, the elect within Israel. What was special about Jesus' gathering of a community was that the offer was one of free forgiveness, and it was extended to those rejected by others.

Salvation by grace

Meyer says, 'the theme of salvation as pure gift runs through the whole of Jesus' public proclamation'.[24] In proclaiming the Kingdom of God, Jesus makes an open invitation to his hearers to receive the salvation God offers. This is a gift freely given; there are no prerequisites. Neither law keeping, rules of purity, nor withdrawal from this world are expected. Jesus' comment, 'I came to call sinners not the righteous' (Mark 2.17), takes us right to the heart of his message. In contrast to the Pharisees and the men of Qumran, Jesus welcomed sinners – those who the rigorists excluded: those who knew they needed the grace of God. The Gospels consistently maintain that it was such people who made up most of his following. The divergence from Qumran could not be starker. In their writings, the lame, the blind, the deaf, the ceremonially unclean, and the gentiles were excluded on principle. *The Community Rule* says: 'No one who is afflicted with any human impurity may come into the assembly of God. . . . Anyone who is afflicted in his flesh, maimed in hand or foot, lame or blind, or deaf or dumb or with a visible mark on his flesh . . . may not enter to take their place in the midst of the community' (1Qsa 2.3–9).

Jesus, on the other hand, said, 'When you give a banquet, invite the poor, the crippled, the lame, and the blind' (Luke 14.13), the very ones proscribed at Qumran. For him, it was the outcasts and the despised who were singled out to be invited to the messianic banquet and to be included in his community. What was most upsetting for the Pharisees was that Jesus even ate with such people; in doing this he broke in the starkest way their rules of purity (Mark 7.1–8). In the social world of that time, eating with someone symbolized acceptance and mutual recognition. As Jeremias says, 'It was an offer of peace, trust, brotherhood and forgiveness; in short, sharing a table meant sharing life.'[25] That the Gospels frequently mention Jesus eating with tax collectors and sinners (Mark 2.15–17; Matt. 11.19; Luke 15.1–2, etc.), confirms the claim that Jesus made an open invitation and was ready to accept those whom others rejected.

The inclusion of gentiles in the restored people of God was foreshadowed by the prophets (Isa. 2.2–3; 60.2–3; Mic. 4.1–2), but their summons was not part of Jesus' own ministry. He did not suggest gentiles were not to be included, far from it, but he himself as Israel's Messiah directed his mission to Israel. When the Syro-Phoenician woman, a non-Jew, asked Jesus to heal her daughter, he initially refused saying, 'Let the children first be fed' (Mark 7.27). Only because of her persistence and faith did he relent. He did, however, envisage a future inclusion of gentiles in the restored Israel, the community of salvation. In the two versions of the banquet parable (Matt. 22.1–10; Luke 14.16–24), the second group invited after the refusal of the first group are to be understood as gentiles.[26] Jesus' words found again in Matthew and Luke, 'I tell you, many will come from east and west and sit at table with Abraham, Isaac, and Jacob in the kingdom of heaven, while the sons of the kingdom will be thrown into the outer darkness' (Matt. 8.12–13; Luke 13.28–9), also foreshadow the gentile mission. The 'many' are opposed to the Jewish listeners, so they must be gentiles. This expression, 'the many', has an Old Testament background and means an immense number.[27] Jesus anticipates a great multitude of gentiles coming to sit at the messianic banquet with those Jews who have entered the Kingdom of God. His ministry would involve a sifting of Israel: judgement for some, salvation for others, and the inclusion of large numbers of gentiles in the future (Mark 13.10, 14.9). Sanders concludes, 'the overwhelming impression is that Jesus started a movement which came to see the gentile mission as the logical extension of itself'.[28]

In welcoming the outcasts of Jewish society and anticipating the inclusion of gentiles, Jesus rejected the entirely Jewish nationalistic understanding of the Kingdom of God. He interpreted it in a thoroughly universal way. The proclamation of the Kingdom was an offer of salvation to all.[29]

Jesus: the builder of the church

In two places in the Gospel tradition, Jesus is reported as speaking of building a new community (Matt. 16.18; Mark 14.58). The two texts are united by their common use of the Greek verb *oikodomeō*, to build. The authenticity of both texts has been questioned, but the case that Jesus spoke words to this effect is strong and has good scholarly support. In the case of Matthew 16.13–20, the evidence includes the following facts: (1) Simon was known as Peter in the early church, so at some point he had a name change; (2) he was recognized as the leader of the early Christians; (3) there are many semitisms in this passage, which set it at the very least in a Palestinian context; (4) many close parallels with the thought of Qumran are evident, and (5) what is said is consistent with Jesus' teaching seen elsewhere in the Gospels.[30]

In Matthew 16.18, in response to Peter's confession, 'You are the Christ', Jesus says, 'You are Peter, and on this rock I will build my church.' These words are only found in Matthew's Gospel. Although Jesus almost certainly knew some Greek,[31] commentators are generally agreed that because Jewish ideas and terminology control this section, the original wording was Hebrew or Aramaic. What we have is a translation of Jesus' words. If this is the case, the question then becomes, what did Jesus actually have in mind when he spoke of building what is translated as 'my church/*ekklēsia*'? As with so much in the New Testament, the Old Testament supplies the background for interpretation. This whole passage reflects themes common to Davidic messianism that have their roots in Nathan's prophecy that one of David's descendants would build a house for God (2 Sam. 7.4–16; 1 Chron. 17.1–15). Peter's confession 'You are the Messiah, the Son of the living God', Jesus' reply, 'I will build my church' (new temple?), and the giving of the keys of the Kingdom to Peter all reflect Davidic motifs.[32]

At the time of Jesus, Davidic messianic hopes were alive and well. Nathan's prophecy was taken as referring to the coming Messiah, understood as Israel's eschatological king, who would rebuild the temple, conceived of metaphorically as a new community.[33] The men of Qumran, for example, had as part of their messianic hope the establishment of a new eschatological community based on a rock foundation, safe from the ravages of evil (see 1QH 6.26f, 7.8–9).[34] In later Jewish texts, which probably take up ideas from this period and earlier, it is claimed that the temple had as its foundation a great rock (the *eben settiyya*) that was the centre of the world. It linked heaven and the underworld, being the gate to the former as well as the entrance to hades, the realm of the dead.[35] Exactly what word Jesus used of this community he was to establish cannot be settled with any finality. Elsewhere it is said that he spoke of building a temple not made with hands (Mark 14.58).[36] Did he use a Hebrew or Aramaic word for temple that Matthew, or the source he is using, render by the word *ekklēsia*? This is one possibility. Another possibility, well supported on the basis of the Qumran parallels mentioned above, is that he used the Hebrew word *edah* – the community of Israel, or its Aramaic equivalent, *edta*.[37] Yet another possibility is that Jesus used the Aramaic word *kenista*, which could be used either of a local Jewish community, or more generally of the Jewish people. This would parallel the local and universal use of the word *ekklēsia*/church. This Aramaic word could be used to translate either the Hebrew *edah* or *qahal*.[38] Finally, it is possible that Jesus used this word *qahal*, which in the later parts of the Old Testament had taken over the meaning of *edah* – the community of Israel. In the *LXX*, *qahal* is always translated by *ekklēsia*.[39] But whatever the word Jesus used, he here speaks of 'building' a new community. Peter has confessed Jesus as the Messiah, and the Messiah is the one who gathers together the eschatological people of God, the church.

We will return to Matthew 16.13–19 in the next chapter when considering how Matthew himself thinks of the church and of the role of Peter, but one final point needs to be made before leaving this passage for the moment. In verse 18 ('I will build') and in verse 19 ('I will give you the keys'), the future tense is used. This could mean that these promises are either to be fulfilled later – that is, after Easter – or from now on. Both are possibilities, but the second option seems more likely for a specific future point is not mentioned.

The building imagery appears again in the narrative of Jesus' trial, where we are told 'false witnesses' claimed he had said, 'I will destroy this temple that is made with hands, and in three days I will build another, not made with hands' (Mark 14.58). The parallel in Matthew 26.61 omits 'with and without hands'.[40] In what sense these witnesses were 'false' is perplexing. Mark is quite certain that Jesus spoke of the destruction of the temple (13.1–2; cf. 15.9).[41] The promise that the present temple would be replaced by another is more difficult, but as this was expected when the Messiah came, as noted above, Jesus may well have claimed that he would do this. In John's Gospel this prophecy is actually found on the lips of Jesus, although John gives the words another application (John 2.21).[42] Some suggest Mark calls the witnesses 'false' because of their intent; they spoke only to destroy Jesus. Juel suggests that a note of irony is also present.[43] What these men say from an evil heart proves to be a true prophecy. More recently, R. H. Gundry has returned to this question. He argues that the witnesses are called 'false' because they claim Jesus said *he* would destroy the temple, when in fact he only spoke of its destruction – not that he personally would destroy it.[44] Yet the more important question is, what did Jesus mean when he spoke of rebuilding the temple 'after three days' – that is, after his resurrection?[45] Jewish expectations that the Messiah would rebuild the temple and that this temple would be a community of people dedicated to Yahweh suggests the answer. The Qumran parallels, we have already noted, which anticipate a new temple seen as a new people, are striking – and such teaching would reiterate the thought of Matthew 16.18.[46] If this interpretation is correct, then we have two passages in the Gospel tradition where Jesus himself actually speaks of 'building' a community, the community that later would be called in Greek *he ekklēsia tou theou*, or, in English, 'the church of God'.

In speaking about the destruction of the temple and its rebuilding, Jesus is yet again indicating that the kingdom of God is even now breaking into history and the community of the end time is being gathered. Sanders says the meanings of these sayings, 'is to be found in his [Jesus'] eschatological expectation. The kingdom was at hand, and one of the things which that meant was that the old temple would be replaced by a new.'[47] The unique feature of Mark's account of this saying, the contrast between the temple 'made with hands' and the one to come 'not made with hands', highlights the contrast between the two temples, which brings out the meaning of the saying even more clearly.

The Last Supper

The synoptic evangelists agree that on the night of his betrayal Jesus ate a final meal with his disciples, and that in some way this meal was related to the Passover celebration. This incident is of particular importance for our study because it both confirms the view that Jesus envisaged a continuing community, and explains something of how Jesus himself understood his own death.

The Last Supper narratives, like other important Gospel passages, have been the subject of much critical study and some have concluded the accounts have been so modified by repeated liturgical use that the original wording can no longer be determined.[48] This opinion is not compelling. We have four separate accounts (Matt. 14.22–5; Mark 14.22–5; Luke 22.15–20; 1 Cor. 11.23–6); they differ in some details, but agree in the overall presentation. Liturgical repetition, moreover, does not exclude careful preservation of oral tradition; instead, it favours it.

Scholarly debate as to what Jesus actually said and did at this meal continues, but that he gave special significance to the bread and wine – which would have been part of every meal – seems certain. One unusual feature of this particular meal was that, contrary to custom, Jesus shared his cup with his disciples, instead of letting them drink from their own cups. This suggests Jesus was indicating that, just as they shared in the blessing attached to the bread that he broke, so also they shared in the blessing attached to the cup. A comment by Jesus on his actions must have followed; not to have said anything would have left the disciples perplexed. Mark has Jesus saying as he passes the cup, 'This is my blood of the covenant, which is poured out for many' (14.25). Luke and Paul add the word 'new' to covenant, and have 'for you' instead of 'for many' (Luke 22.20; 1 Cor. 11.25). Mark's 'for many' reflects a semitic expression meaning an immense number, and may be taken as original. We can understand Luke and Paul changing this for something more comprehensible for a gentile audience. In these words, Jesus interprets his death in the light of the servant songs of Isaiah, where God's servant gives his life as atonement for the sins 'of many' (Isa. 53.11–12). The addition of the word 'new' to qualify the word covenant in Luke and Paul's account is not of great significance, for the adjective is implied in the Marcan narrative. Mark and Matthew's reference to the covenant calls to mind first of all the old covenant sealed in the blood of animals

(Exod. 24.8), but as Jesus is renewing this covenant by the shedding of his own blood the inauguration of the new covenant, promised by Jeremiah (31.31–4), is to be understood.[49]

In the context of Jewish eschatological expectations, the renewal of the covenant was fundamental.[50] The Jews generally believed that the age to come would commence only when God made a new covenant with his people. This would symbolize the rebetrothal of Yahweh and Israel after their apparent divorce;[51] it would bring the forgiveness of sins;[52] it would involve the giving of the Spirit to all God's people, so that they could keep the Torah properly,[53] and bring about the 'circumcision of the heart'.[54] In claiming to establish this covenant, Jesus is announcing the fulfilment of these hopes. By implication, those who enter into this new covenant are true Israel, the community of the last days. No higher status could Jewish theology bestow, and it is bestowed by Jesus on his disciples, those now called the church. In our earliest account of the words of institution found in 1 Corinthians 11.23, and in the longer text in Luke's Gospel (cf. 22.19), widely taken to be authentic, the command is given, 'Do this in remembrance of me.' By giving this command, Jesus clearly envisages the disciples continuing as a community after his death, and meeting together regularly. The Book of Acts and the epistles show that this is exactly what happened.

Organization

Our study so far indicates that Jesus did anticipate some delay before the end, and he gave himself to gathering a community who in the final analysis proved to be a remnant of Israel. This 'little flock' experience in some measure the blessings of the age to come, they know the forgiveness of sins, they enjoy the divine presence in the person of Jesus, and they are seen as those with whom God has made a new covenant. Yet very little is said about how they are to organize themselves after Jesus has departed. This is a point traditional Catholic theologians have been very reluctant to concede, but it is a conclusion hard to avoid. As noted in the introduction, the Catholic definition of the church is predicated on the view that Jesus instituted the church by appointing Peter as the first head of the church, and the apostles as the first pastors who were to ordain subsequent leaders.

It is true that Jesus makes Peter pre-eminent amongst the

twelve,[55] and the early chapters of the Book of Acts indicate that in the period after Easter he continued in this role. Matthew also has Jesus give Peter the ministry of 'the keys' (Matt. 16.19–20), which is taken to mean the giving of authority to regulate doctrine and discipline, but then later Matthew has Jesus give this ministry to the whole church (Matt. 18.18).[56] We do not know how this ministry was exercised, for nowhere in the New Testament is anything like this mentioned. Furthermore, neither Peter's leadership nor his responsibilities with the 'keys' are said to be transferable. The contribution of the twelve is even more problematic. It is clear that they fulfilled a typological or symbolic role, indicating that Jesus was restoring Israel; in the age to come, Jesus promised that they would sit in judgement with him (Matt. 19.28; cf. Luke 22.30), and it may be inferred that Jesus set them apart to hear what he said and see what he did, so that they could authenticate the gospel to be proclaimed after his death, but nothing more can be claimed. It seems that Jesus did not regularly call them 'apostles'. Mark and Matthew only record Jesus giving them this title on the one occasion when he sent them out two by two on a mission to Israel (Mark 6.30; Matt. 10.2), while John never calls them apostles.[57] Matthew and Luke have Jesus commission them as preachers (Matt. 28.19; Luke 24.47–8; cf. John 20.19–23[58]), but not as church leaders with a specific office; nor as those who were to select and appoint others such as the first presbyters or bishops; nor as those who were to preside at the Eucharist. So hazy was the early Christians' remembrance of the twelve, except for the more prominent members of the group, that the four lists of their names differ as to who should be included (cf. Matt. 10.2–4; Mark 3.16–19; Luke 6.13–16; Acts 1.13).

There are nevertheless some indications of a minimal communal rule. As we have just seen, the disciples were to meet and break bread and drink wine in remembrance of Christ and his death; those who joined this fellowship were to be baptized (Matt. 28.19);[59] and in this community, leaders would play an important part. Peter would in some sense be 'first', but other leaders are also envisaged. This is indicated by the frequent comments Jesus makes about how leadership is to be exercised in this community. In the Gospels, on no less than six occasions in varying formulations, Jesus makes the point, 'Whoever wishes to become great among you must be your servant' (Mark 10.44 par.; Matt. 20.26; Matt. 23.11 par.; Luke 22.26; Mark 9.35 par.; Luke 9.48). The model that leaders are to emulate is provided by Jesus himself who said, 'I am among you as one who serves' (Luke 22.27; cf. Mark 10.45; John 13.1–20).

Alfred Loisy once more

We have agreed with Loisy that the near advent of the Kingdom of God was at the heart of Jesus' proclamation, but not that he understood this to be an almost immediate event. This proclamation therefore does not exclude the thought that Jesus believed that in calling disciples he was gathering the community of the last days. In fact, we have argued that the eschatological nature of Jesus' ministry presupposes this. Yet we have found nothing that suggests that Jesus founded a structured institution such as the word 'church' implies today. Our brief consideration of the organization of this community came up with modest conclusions. Thus again, Loisy's provocative maxim is seen to be partly true. Jesus proclaimed the Kingdom of God, and, we would argue, called disciples who formed a community, but the church that followed in later centuries was something very different. This is a problem we will consider in some detail in a concluding chapter, but to make a preliminary response to this observation we need the help of modern sociology.

The emergence of groups and their consolidation

Historical reconstruction and theological definition can tell us only so much about the first disciples of Jesus, and the kind of community they formed. To understand another dimension, the social reality and how this developed, we need the help of sociology. It is this science that explains group formation, group development, and provides models to categorize diverse social phenomena. A number of sociological insights open up possibilities of a more holistic understanding of the first disciples. For our purposes, we need only briefly touch on these. Their importance lies in their explanatory potential.

The use of the words 'church' and 'sect' as technical sociological terms originates in the work of Max Weber, the pioneer sociologist of the earlier part of this century, but it was his student, Ernst Troeltsch, who established their common usage by sociologists.[60] For Troeltsch, these terms characterize two radically different social manifestations of Christianity. 'The church' represents the established, organized church as he knew it earlier this century in Germany. It accepts the world in which it finds itself; it is a conservative upholding of the values of the ruling class, and provides salvation to all through the sacrament of baptism. 'The sect', in contrast, is typified for him by the Anabaptists of the Reformation period. It is a small group of people, set apart from the world, holding distinctive values that one can only join by conversion. The sect recruits its members mainly from the lower classes, is egalitarian, and antisacramental. Often it comes into being as a protest movement against 'the church', which it considers to be worldly and unregenerate.

These ideas are very evocative, but they have their limitations. Can Judaism be equated with the twentieth-century church, and Jesus and his disciples with the radical wing of the Reformation? Some think there are more differences than similarities. One important corrective has been offered by the English sociologist Bryan Wilson. He argues that in fact there are many kinds of sects, and offers a sevenfold typology. His work is cross-cultural, not related to Christianity in particular, and not at all focused on the early Christians.[61] Another corrective has come from Robin Scroggs, who has sought to reformulate the technical concept 'sect' so that it can be used more accurately to study early Christianity. He argues that sects are defined by seven major characteristics, all of which Christianity exhibited.[62] The debate continues. A helpful working definition is offered by J. Blenkinsopp:

> A sect is only a minority, and not only characterized by opposition to norms accepted by the parent-body, but also claims in a more or less exclusive way to be what the parent-body claims to be. Whether such a group formally severs itself, or is excommunicated, will depend largely on the degree of self definition attained by the parent-body and the level of tolerance obtaining within it.[63]

Using this definition, we can conclude that Jesus and his followers may be called a 'sect'. Yet this sociological usage of the term must be distinguished from the use of the Greek work *hairesis* – usually translated 'sect' – in the New Testament, which means a party or sub-group,[64] and from modern colloquial usage where 'sect' and 'sectarian' carry a pejorative sense. To avoid this confusion

in meaning and other limitations of the concept 'sect', other terms
have been preferred by some scholars. G. Thiessen, for example,
uses the term 'movement'.[65] In one of the more recent discussions
of this matter, Anthony Blasi explores this option. He concludes
that early Christianity would best be called 'social movement',
which he sets in opposition to a 'formal organization'.[66] He makes
some good points, but in the end it would seem that the alternatives he suggests are more terminological than substantive. Yet
whether we think of Jesus and his followers as a sect or a movement, it is agreed that the terminology designates an initial stage
in group life. To a greater or lesser degree, sects usually move
towards the church type, and social movements usually become
formal organizations if they do not die out. This introduces our
second key sociological term: 'institutionalization'.

Explaining how sects, movements, and groups develop and
evolve is also an area that sociology can profoundly elucidate. The
term used to describe this is 'institutionalization'. This is taken to
be 'not a process that may arise after a time but a process that
inevitably starts almost as soon as human interaction begins and
continues for as long as the group, association or society exists'.[67]
It is something dynamic, a continuous spiral. Not infrequently, a
primary and a secondary stage are clearly evident. In the first
phase, behaviour becomes 'routinized'; beliefs are formalized;
the task (or mission) enunciated; and authority (leadership) legit-
imized. In the second stage, which often commences after the
initial founder of the group has departed, these social constructs
take on a life of their own and are built upon. The Gospels obviously reflect the primary stage. Yet the point to stress is that this
process called institutionalization began from the moment Jesus
called the first disciples and they came to see themselves as a
distinct group, with a specific mission. In every word Jesus taught
them, every direction he gave them for living, every description
by which he identified them and by everything he said about
leadership, he encouraged the development of institutional form
to structure their life together. This process entered the second
stage after his death, and has continued over the centuries – sometimes to such a degree that the gospel that gave life to the institutional form seemed to get lost. In what follows, we will see how
this initial beginning in the process of institutionalization develops
in the apostolic age.

Did Jesus found the church?

Now to return again to this question. From what has just been said, the answer becomes clearer. It is to some degree a matter of definition. Jesus did not establish what Troelsch and later sociologists define as 'church', which is what Loisy had in mind, but Jesus did call into being the Christian community, the church theologically defined. Then and now he forgives the sins of those who repent and believe and makes them members of his family. He calls them a flock, is present with them as their shepherd, sends them into the world on mission, sustains them with spiritual food, and provides them with leaders. If these things constitute the church then Jesus is most certainly the founder of the church. The sociological form of the church has changed, and changed dramatically over the centuries, moving in different directions at different times and in different places, but the constituent elements remain the same. The continuity to be seen lies at the theological level, not the sociological. Jesus and his first followers, we may agree, were a 'sect' or a 'movement' in the sociological sense of these words, but this was how the church had to begin. Institutional forms are never given *in toto* from the beginning; and, in choosing to accept the path of lowly service, Jesus chose to begin with a small band of ordinary people in simple circumstances. To the outward eye, they seemed so insignificant, but for Jesus, those who responded to his preaching were God's family (Mark 10.29–30 par.; Matt. 10.25, 11.25, 23.9); God's flock (Luke 12.32; Mark 14.27 par.; Matt. 10.16; John 10.1–29); God's field (Matt. 13.24, 15.13); the elect (Mark 13.32 par.; 13.27 par.; Matt. 24.22) – all titles once reserved for historic Israel. They were those with whom he had established the new covenant promised by Jeremiah (Luke 22.20; 1 Cor. 11.25; Mark 14.24). They were, he said, 'my church', against which the gates of hell will not prevail (Matt. 16.18).

Chapter 3

Matthew, Mark, Luke, and John

The four Gospels all came to their final form several decades after the earthly ministry of Jesus. Each of the evangelists recounts the story by keeping to the historical setting of Jesus' lifetime, but at the same time each reflects to some degree individual interests, concerns, and theology, and the problems and beliefs of the Christian community for whom they wrote. As the experience of Christian community life forcefully impinges upon every believer, we should expect that the evangelists would at times betray something of their own church life and seek to address it, and this seems to be the case. It is most noticeable in Matthew's Gospel, but there is something of this to be seen in each of the four Gospels. As four inspired interpreters of the Jesus story, the evangelists speak in their own right. The material each writer includes, emphasizes, or adds makes their Gospel what it is – namely, one of four personal accounts of the ministry, death, and resurrection of Jesus. The distinctive emphases to be seen in each Gospel can be called the 'theology'[1] of the evangelist, and this theology should be considered as significant as that of St Paul, or any other New Testament author. In recent years, New Testament scholars using 'redaction criticism' have made the delineating of these Gospel theologies a major area of study.

In regard to ecclesiology, Matthew and John's Gospel are the most important because of their more developed understanding of the identity of the Christian community, and for this reason they will be given more attention; however, Mark and Luke cannot be forgotten.

The disciples and discipleship

In the previous chapter, we argued that Jesus created a distinct

46

community, which we now identify as 'the church', when he gathered a group of followers called disciples, who accepted the salvation he offered and then shared in his life and ministry. In this chapter, our major concern is to discover how the evangelists develop the stories about these disciples, and how they depict them as a paradigm of the Christian community.[2] We proceed with the premise that each of the evangelists tells the stories about the disciples gathered around Jesus in such a way that they speak to the church community addressed. This relative blurring of the historical horizons came easily, because by the time the evangelists wrote, the title 'the disciples', had become a common ecclesiological term.[3] Thus except for Peter, the spokesman of the twelve, and occasionally one or two of the others, generally the individual disciples are not singled out. Instead, the Gospel writers characteristically speak of the disciples as a group. Several New Testament scholars in their discussion of this phenomenon have spoken of the 'transparency' of the disciple stories.[4] By this, they mean that they are like a window allowing the reader to see the church of the evangelist.

The Gospel writers thus present the disciples as a paradigm of individual and corporate Christian existence. In the hearing or reading of each of the Gospels, believers are invited to identify with the disciples in the presence of Jesus. The way each Gospel writer does this varies, but the goal is the same. When Jesus speaks of the cost of discipleship, or of the mission of the disciples, or of the frailties of the disciples, or of the love they should have for one another, Christians of every age have realized that the Lord of the church is not only speaking to those actually before him, but to all believers. The Gospel stories about the disciples are correctly understood when they are read, not only as accounts of those who actually followed Jesus, but also as texts intended to address the reader. This suggests therefore that the stories about the disciples are an important avenue in discovering not only the evangelists' understanding of the church, but also what they believe should be normative for church life.

Mark's Gospel

Christology and discipleship are the twin themes around which Mark develops his narrative. The evangelist says nothing directly about the church of his own day, but the way in which he presents the disciples, especially in relation to Jesus, discloses something of Mark's own beliefs about the post-Easter Christian community.[5] This community confesses Jesus as the Christ (1.1, 8.31), interpreting his messiahship mainly in terms of divine sonship (1.1, 11, 12–13, 8.27–32, 14.61–4, 15.39); to this community Jesus has disclosed truths otherwise unknown (4.34, 6.31, 9.28), and this community expects that Christ as the Son of Man will soon return (13.28–30, 35–7), although no one knows exactly when this will be (13.32).[6] While Mark allows that many responded to Jesus' call to repentance and faith, he usually has the twelve in mind when he speaks of 'the disciples'. They are the Jesus community in the telling of his story.[7] Between the disciples gathered around Jesus and the Jewish crowds who listen to his teaching, there is a clear line of demarcation (4.34, 6.7, 30), and often antagonism. Jack Kingsbury has well described Mark as a story about 'conflict'.[8] Jesus' main opponents are the Jewish leaders who represent the people of Israel; they oppose him at every point and eventually have him put to death. Yet this is not the end of the story. In this final drama he makes atonement for sins, replaces the temple as the place of salvation, 'and becomes the founder and ruler of God's end-time people'.[9]

Entwined with Mark's account of the conflict between Jesus and the Jewish authorities is his account of the disciples. In the opening chapter of the Gospel, we are told of the call of the first four disciples who leave everything to follow Jesus (1.16–20). This explains the nature of Christian discipleship. It is a call to total allegiance to Christ, which is to be lived out in community. The chief responsibility of the disciples is announced in the call of Simon and Andrew: 'Follow me and I will make you fish for people' (1.17). What this involves is seen later when Jesus sends out the twelve to do what he is doing. Mark says, 'they went out and proclaimed that all should repent. They cast out many demons, and anointed with oil many who were sick and cured them' (6.12–13). Yet even with the disciples, Mark introduces a note of conflict. He consistently draws them as frail human creatures who regularly fail and oppose Jesus. They are uncomprehending of his teaching (4.34, 6.51–2, 7.18, 8.17–18); fearful (4.40, 9.5–6); status-conscious (9.13–14, 34); exclusive (9.38–40); attracted by wealth (10.27–31); desirous of power (10.28–31), and anxious about the future (10.28–31). Worst of all, Mark insists, they fail to grasp that the essence of Jesus' ministry, and therefore the essence of all discipleship, is suffering. After each of the three passion predictions (8.31, 9.31, 10.33–4), Mark points out that the disciples did not really understand what Jesus was saying. After the first prediction, Peter, as spokesperson for the twelve, 'rebukes' Jesus for what he has said (8.32); in the second instance, Mark simply says the disciples did not 'understand' (9.31), and in the third case, Mark places the unflattering story of the dispute about pre-eminence in the Kingdom as the sequel to the prediction (10.35–44). In his final hour, Judas betrays Jesus (14.17–21, 42), the others flee (14.50), and Peter denies him (14.60–72). Mark's persistence in stressing the frailties of the disciples suggests that he is attempting to make these stories speak afresh to the church of his own day.[10] He is in effect saying, if you find following Jesus difficult and costly and you often fail, then it was the same with the first disciples.[11] Mark depicts the disciples, to use Kingsbury's vivid terminology, as sometimes 'thinking the things of God' and at other times 'thinking the things of humans'.[12]

However, discussion about the disciples is only one way in which Mark alludes to the church. Professor Kee makes the important observation that, 'in every case the images employed in Mark to represent Christian existence are corporate'.[13] The call to follow is made to individuals (1.15, 17, 20), but the followers then assume a collective identity. They become members of the eschatological family (3.20f, 31–5, 10.28–31); sheep in God's flock (6.34, 14.27); part of the new vineyard (12.1–11); the community of the new covenant (14.24). Kee concludes from the uses of these titles that the 'central feature' of the Marcan understanding of the identity of Jesus' followers is that they are 'the people of God'.[14] Mark is clear that any leadership given in this community must be modelled on that of Jesus himself, and involve humble self-giving (10.43–5); but apart from this principle, virtually nothing can be discovered about the organization or communal life of the Marcan church.[15] From a sociological perspective, Kee concludes that Mark's community may be described as an 'apocalyptic sect': a small group of Christians seeing themselves as God's family and true Israel, anticipating the end in the near future, firm in the belief that divine truths not known to others had been revealed to them, and active in evangelism.[16]

Luke's Gospel

Luke's understanding of the church will be covered in detail in the subsequent chapter on Acts, but at this juncture a few comments on the ecclesiology of the third Gospel are given. Luke is far less critical of the disciples than Mark.[17] He deletes most of the sayings about the disciples' incomprehension (e.g. Mark 7.18, 8.21, 9.20), and attributes others to the fact that 'the meaning was hidden from them' (9.45, 18.34), or that it was due to the prophetic ordering of things (Acts 1.6). He also makes a clear distinction between the inner core of disciples whom he regularly calls 'the apostles' (6.15, 9.10, 17.5, 22.14, 24.10), and a much larger outer circle of disciples (6.13, 17, 19.37), something not spelt out in Mark. By doing this he prepares for the Acts narrative where 'the twelve apostles' become the chief witnesses of the life, ministry, death, and resurrection of Jesus and the founding nucleus of the new Jesus community. The Marcan Christological titles are found with some additions in Luke, but he differs from Mark by allowing the characteristic post-Easter confession of Jesus as Lord to define discipleship (2.11, 24.34, etc.). The Christian community comprises those who recognize Jesus as the Lord (*Kurios*).[18]

In Luke's Gospel, the disciples are clearly differentiated from those who do not respond to Jesus. They are depicted as a distinct community who confess Jesus as Lord, and are called to suffer with him. However, Luke does not suggest that a clear breach with Israel has occurred. Thus he does not have Mark's emphasis on Jesus as the teacher only of the twelve. In Luke, Jesus' proclamation is in 'the hearing of the people' (7.1). In this Gospel, the designation *laos* – the people of God – remains the special preserve of the Jewish people, whether they be followers of Jesus or not. Yet this 'pro-Jewish orientation' is not the full picture. In a carefully nuanced discussion of Luke's understanding of the identity of the Christian community, Robert Maddox points out that in the third Gospel there is also to be seen an 'anti Jewish orientation' and 'a gentile orientation'.[19] Thus he notes that right from the beginning of his Gospel (1.5—2.40), Luke has Israel being divided in the light of its response to God's visitation in Jesus.[20] This is seen to be taking place in the travel narrative (9.51—19.27), where the recurring theme is the judgement of Israel for its hardness of heart. More recently, Kingsbury has come to a similar conclusion. He writes, 'Luke's story is primarily a story of conflict between Jesus and Israel, made up of the religious authorities and the people. Jesus' conflict with the people is to win their allegiance. Jesus' conflict with the authorities is over "authority" and who will rule God's (reconstituted) people.'[21] It has often been suggested that Luke's Gospel betrays a 'universalistic outlook', not found in the other synoptic Gospels, that is welcoming of gentiles, but this claim needs to be critically examined. It is true that Luke begins his Gospel by anticipating their inclusion within the people of God, Israel (2.32), concludes with the command to the disciples to preach repentance and forgiveness of sins 'to all nations' (24.47), and has a few hints of a positive attitude to the gentile mission.[22] Yet it is not true to say that Luke has Jesus initiating the gentile mission before Easter. He leaves this matter until he writes the Book of Acts. If there are these three 'orientations' to be detected in Lucan thought – one apparently affirming the continuing place of Israel in the purposes of God, one speaking of the rejection of historic Israel, and one open to the salvation of gentiles – then the relationship between Israel as a national identity and the followers of Jesus as another distinct entity is a complex one. In our discussion of this in the next chapter, we conclude that Luke sees the church emerging out of Israel, with the truly devout Jews who recognize Jesus as the Messiah forming the initial membership of the new community. It is only as Israel hardens its heart and opposes the gospel that Luke has God directing the mission to the gentiles. As a consequence, a new entity emerges that transcends the old division between Jew and gentile, 'the Church of the Lord' (Acts 20.28). This conception of the church as 'restored Israel', Jervell maintains, takes us right to the heart of 'Luke's unique ecclesiology'.[23]

Before leaving the third Gospel, two special Lucan themes are to be noted. First, the suffering of the disciples in this life, and the reversal to be enjoyed in the life to come; and secondly, the dignity of women. Luke emphasizes the suffering involved in discipleship, but then balances this with his reversal motif.[24] What is lost or denied in this age will be restored many times over in the age to come. All the synoptic evangelists record sayings about the cost of discipleship, but Luke adds to these and often accentuates the point. Luke takes over Mark's one extended discussion on the cost of discipleship (Mark 8.34–8), making several important modifications to make it more generally applicable (9.23–7),[25] and he adds a second and longer discussion of this matter (14.25–33), which ends with two little parables found only in Luke about counting the cost – implying that one should think twice before becoming a disciple. The reversal motif, so common in this Gospel, is closely related to this teaching.[26] It first of all stresses the lowly lot of the disciple, but then balances this with the rewards to come in the Kingdom of God. Luke introduces this matter in the Magnificat (2.50–5), returns to it in 'the sermon on the plain' (6.20–6), and illustrates it in such parables as the rich fool (12.13–21), Dives and Lazarus (16.19–31), and the Pharisee and the publican (18.9–14). Both in accepting suffering and in future reward, Luke sees Jesus as the great exemplar. He takes the path that his disciples must also take. For Luke, the Christian community, the church, is a community called to follow in the steps of their Lord, 'taking up the cross daily' (9.23).

It has long been noted that Luke gives greater prominence to women in his Gospel than the other synoptic evangelists, and that he always draws women in a very positive light.[27] Mary is presented as a model disciple who believes without doubt and never falters; Mary, the sister of Martha, is commended for taking the role of a man by sitting down and listening to the teaching of Jesus when he visits their home (10.38–42); and hearing and obeying the word of God is made the highest calling for man and woman (11.27–8). Luke also often pairs men and women together – Zacharias and Elizabeth, Joseph and Mary, Simeon and Anna, are just a few examples. Flender concludes from this that it is Luke's intent to remind his readers that, 'man and woman stand together and side by side before God, they are equal in honour and grace; they are endowed with the same gifts and have the same responsibilities'.[28]

Matthew, the ecclesiastical Gospel

The most distinctive feature of Matthew's Gospel is its 'Jewishness', which is somewhat surprisingly matched by a fierce antipathy to the Jewish leaders. This is generally explained by arguing that this Gospel reflects a community of conservative Jewish Christians who have broken away from a larger group of Jews with whom they are now in conflict.[29] No more needs to be said on these matters at this point, but as we proceed, the particular context from which Matthew speaks will be constantly relevant and must be kept in mind.

Matthew's Gospel has often been called 'the ecclesiological Gospel', not only because it alone uses the word *ekklēsia*/church (16.18, 18.17), and gives the triadic formula for baptism (28.19), but also, and importantly, because in a number of places the evangelist quite boldly makes the words of Jesus address issues that were of interest to Matthew's church, and because one of his central concerns was to theologically define the community Jesus had called into existence in distinction from historic Israel.[30] In this last matter, the way he presents Jesus as the fulfilment of the hope of Israel brings ecclesiology and Christology together in a manner only paralleled by John among the Gospel writers. Indeed, J. P. Meier says, 'the nexus between Christology and ecclesiology is one of the most typical characteristics of Matthew's Gospel'.[31]

The term 'church' in Matthew

It is only in Matthew's Gospel, and not the other three, that the word *ekklēsia*/church appears. The first use of the word is in the famous saying following Peter's confession, 'You are the Christ, the Son of the living God' (16.16). In reply, Jesus says that this insight has been given by God, and then adds, 'You are Peter, and on this rock I will build my church, and the powers of death shall not prevail against it' (16.18). The second time Matthew uses the word *ekklēsia*/church is in the context of a discussion about what to do 'if your brother sins against you' (18.15). After speaking personally to the brother Christian, and then along with two or three witnesses and finding no resolution to the matter, Matthew advises, 'tell it to the *church*, and if he refuses to listen even to the *church*, let him be to you as a gentile and tax collector' (18.17). In discussing Matthew's theology, the question of whether or not Jesus actually said these things – and, if he did, what Hebrew or Aramaic words he used – does not concern us. The only question of interest to us at this point is what ideas did Matthew intend to convey by these words: what meaning do they hold in the context of Matthew's Gospel?

In Matthew 16.18, almost all scholars are agreed that here the word *ekklēsia*/church is used in what is called 'the universal sense' – the totality of Christians. In this context, the word *ekklēsia* has completely lost its classical meaning, 'assembly'. The possibility that *ekklēsia* simply means 'those who assemble together' is excluded. Matthew has Jesus speak rather of building a community, not

based on national origin, or the keeping of the law, but on the
confession of Jesus as the Christ – a confession first enunciated by
Peter. It is not human association that constitutes this church, but
divine action. Jesus as the Messiah is the builder.[32] Whether or not
the following words, 'and on this rock', refer to Peter's confession,
or to Peter himself as the leader of the church, remains a matter
of debate, but the majority of scholars these days prefer the latter.[33] However, a clear line between the two interpretations should
not be made. It may be agreed that the rock is Peter, but Peter is
the rock on which the church is built because he makes this confession. If this is the case, then this church is made up of all those
who make the same confession as Peter. Jesus goes on to promise
that 'the powers of death (hades) shall not prevail' against this
church/community (16.18). The threat of death by martyrdom or
attack by the forces of the underworld are both possibly in mind.
In this community, Peter as the leader is given the 'keys of the
kingdom of heaven' (16.19–20). This means that he has been
conferred with authority to regulate doctrine and discipline.[34]

In all of the Gospels, Peter is depicted as the leader and
spokesman of the twelve, and in the early chapters of Acts this
continues; but only Matthew has this commissioning of Peter.[35]
The leadership of Peter in the early church raises no problems
today for a non-Roman Catholic, because it is agreed that the text
says nothing about successors. In speaking about Peter, Matthew
makes him simply first among equals. He does not idealize him or
give him unique powers. 'The keys' to bind and to loose are later
given to the whole church (18.18). He is in fact presented as a
typical disciple with strengths and weaknesses.[36] This second
giving of 'the keys' can be read either as a democratization of the
office, or as the provision for the continuation of this ministry
when Peter is gone.

The two uses of *ekklēsia*/church in Matthew 18.17 raise other
issues. Here, in contrast to Matthew 16.18, a local community of
believers must be in mind. Such a congregation, Matthew implies,
has a unitary collective identity. This church can be *told* what has
taken place and can *speak* to the offender. Again it would seem
that Matthew has introduced the term *ekklēsia* into this narrative,
the original wording being less specific.[37] This use of *ekklēsia* for
the local community of believers parallels Matthew's frequent
disparaging comments about 'their synagogues' (4.32, 9.35, 10.17,
12.9, 13.54), and 'your synagogues' (23.34) when speaking about

Jewish communities. Stanton concludes on this evidence that when Matthew writes, '*ekklēsia* and *sunagōgē* are separate rival institutions'.[38] The basic difference is that in one Jesus is confessed as the Christ, and in the other the law still holds pride of place.

The theological status of the Christian community

In the first Gospel, as in the other Gospels, the disciples are a mirror reflecting the life of the Christian community of Matthew's day.[39] This merging of the horizons between the two groups of disciples is most clearly seen in the final words of the Gospel, where Jesus commands his followers to make *disciples*, baptizing and teaching them (28.19). The importance of the disciples for Matthew is demonstrated by the fact that in the first Gospel, the collective term 'the disciples' appears 73 times, 45 of these without parallel in Mark or Luke. Matthew emphasizes that Jesus is the teacher of the disciples and they are good learners. For this reason, he plays down the negative comments about the disciples that is so much part of Mark's picture, and on three occasions says they understood what Jesus had taught them (13.52, 16.12, 17.13), words not found in Mark. Luz says, 'in Matthew the disciples are men who have heard and understood all that Jesus taught in his lifetime; they are ear-witnesses'.[40] As good learners they are being prepared to be teachers; the wording of the final commission comes therefore as no surprise. The disciples are not sent out to preach, to heal and to cast out demons, but rather to make disciples . . . *teaching* them to obey everything I have commanded you' (28.19, cf. 5.19).

Particularly striking are a number of Matthean passages where the disciples are promised that Jesus will be with them in their community life as God was once present in temple and synagogue (1.23, 18.20, 28.20).[41] Matthew knows that Jews had long thought that God was present in the temple (23.21), but as he writes the temple is 'desolate and forsaken' (23.38). It has been replaced by 'something greater' (12.6), namely Jesus, who is now dwelling with his people. This Matthean motif explains the authority invested in the disciples, another distinctive feature of the way the first Gospel presents the disciples. In Mark and Luke, forgiveness is something bestowed by Jesus himself, but in Matthew it is the disciples who are to forgive sins (6.15, 9.8, 16.19, 18.18). What they forgive 'on earth' will be forgiven 'in heaven' (16.19, 18.18). In a sense they embody the kingdom of heaven on earth. Thus in Matthew's version of the Lord's prayer, the disciples pray not only 'your kingdom come', but also 'your will be done, *on earth* as in heaven' (6.10, cf. Luke 11.2).

In Matthew, the followers of Jesus are designated by a number of titles, all of which were used in the Old Testament of Israel. In some cases, the evangelist takes over designations found in Mark, such as the flock (26.31, cf. 10.6, 16, 15.24, 25.32), the elect (24.22, 24, 31), the children (of God) (3.9, 15.26, 23.37), and brethren (5.22, 23, 24, 47, 7.3, 4, 5, 18.15, 21), but he also adds some very important ones. In the Beatitudes, the disciples are called 'the poor in spirit', 'the meek' and 'the righteous' (5.1–10), all titles used of the holy remnant in the Old Testament, especially in the Psalms. 'Righteousness' in fact sums up Matthew's ethical demand for the disciples. This righteousness must exceed that of the scribes and Pharisees (5.20).[42] Its goal is nothing less than to be 'perfect, as your heavenly Father is perfect' (5.48), a command that echoes a refrain in the Book of Leviticus, 'You must be holy for I am holy' (11.44–5, 19.2, 20.7, 20.26). This demand was basic for the distinctiveness of Israel, the historic people of God, as Leviticus 20.26 makes clear by quoting God as saying, 'I have separated you from the peoples, that you should be mine.' In making the same demand on those who would become disciples, Matthew depicts Jesus as gathering the true people of God, a separate community, distinguished by holy living.

In Matthew's Gospel, the special term to designate Israel, '*laos*' – God's people – is usually used of the Jewish leaders and those they represent who are hostile to Jesus, but in the programmatic announcement of the angel in the opening chapter, 'You shall call him Jesus, for he will save his people (*laos*) from their sins' (1.21), many commentators suspect the word is used prophetically to include all who believe in Christ, the whole church, Jews and gentiles.[43]

Prophetic fulfilment

This community of disciples finds its identity as far as Matthew is concerned in relation to Jesus and in distinction from the historic Israel. This is made clear by noting how Matthew views the time of Jesus' ministry as the time of fulfilment of Old Testament prophecies. For Matthew, all that has taken place is foreshadowed in the Jewish scriptures. He thus speaks of the prophets and the law prophesying until John (11.13): that is, anticipating, or pointing to, a time of fulfilment. The term *pleroun*, 'to fulfil', is one of the key terms in Matthew's vocabulary, and the idea, which is wider than this one word, is possibly the central Matthean motif.[44] It is developed in a number of ways, the two most important for our study being:

1   Jesus as the fulfilment of the messianic hope

All the Gospels present Jesus as the hoped-for Messiah of Israel, but Matthew accentuates this, making the claim in a distinctive way.[45] He takes over most of Mark's uses of the title *Christos* (the Greek translation of the Hebrew Messiah), but adds many more. In the opening chapters of the first Gospel, a cluster of occurrences of this title are found. The opening words of the Gospel refer to 'Jesus Christ, the son of David, the son of Abraham' (1.1), and twice in drawing his genealogical introduction to a close, Matthew speaks of Jesus as 'the Christ' (1.16, 17). The royal connotations to this title are made explicit in the story of the coming of the wise men who ask about the 'birth of the king of the Jews', to which Herod responds by asking about the birthplace of 'the Christ' (2.1–4). Matthew's understanding of this title is further brought out in his wording of Peter's confession, 'You are the Christ, the Son of the living God' (16.16). By adding 'Son of the living God', Matthew equates the titles Son of God and *Christos*. Another cluster of occurrences of this title appear in the narrative leading up to, and associated with, Jesus' death. At this juncture, the title 'son of David', equated from the first verse in the Gospel with *Christos*, comes to the fore (20.30, 31, 21.9, 15, 22.45). It is thus clear that Matthew is presenting Jesus as the anticipated Davidic Messiah, the fulfilment of prophecy, who announces that the kingdom of heaven is at hand, and who gathers a people who recognize him as their king. A messianic king without subjects would have made no sense. The Matthean definition of Jesus as the Davidic Messiah necessitates the corollary, the reconstitution of Israel, the people of God.

2 The rejection of unbelieving Israel as the fulfilment of the prophetic warnings

The Old Testament prophets constantly warn Israel that if she does not repent and live a life pleasing to God, the coming day of the Lord will bring judgement not salvation (Isa. 48.1–11; Jer. 9.7–11; Ezek. 7.1–14; Joel 2.1–30; Amos 5.18–20, 8.9–12; Mal. 4.1–6). Matthew is quite certain that this judgement has begun because most of Israel has rejected the Messiah sent by God. He accentuates the condemnation of Jewish unbelief found in the synoptic tradition, and makes an unremitting and bitter condemnation of Jewish leaders who exemplify this (see particularly, chapter 23). Twice Matthew quotes Isaiah's condemnation of the hardness of heart of the Jews of his day (Isa. 6.9–10, 29.13), and applies it to the Jews of Jesus' day. He makes his point forcefully by the introductory formulae, 'With them is fulfilled the prophecy of Isaiah' (13.14), and, 'Well did Isaiah prophesy of you' (15.7). But the contemporizing of the judgement of the past shortcomings of Israel finds its clearest expression in a number of denunciations of 'this generation'. This generation, says Matthew, is like a group of unresponsive children (11.16); it is an 'evil and adulterous generation' (12.39, 16.4; cf. 12.45); a generation destined for judgement (12.41–2); a 'perverse generation' (17.17); a generation led by hypocritical leaders (23.29–36) and doomed to destruction with the pending fall of the temple (24.34). S. Van Tilborg writes, 'The judgement is definitive. . . . The measure is full, Israel has been rejected. Under the guidance of its leaders Israel has let the opportunity to repent go by.'[46]

This conclusion is supported by the three parables of rejection and replacement that Matthew locates together. The leaders of Israel are addressed (21.23), but, as these parables show, they are but the representatives of the Jews who reject Jesus. The first is the parable of the man with two sons, one who refuses at first to work in his father's vineyard and then repents; and the other who agrees, but then does not do so (21.28–32). The latter is to be equated with unbelieving Israel, as is made clear by the concluding words on the lips of Jesus, 'Truly I say to you, the tax collectors and the harlots go into the kingdom before you.' The second parable is that of the wicked tenants (21.33–43), which Luke and Mark also record, but Matthew makes the application more pointed by adding two other parables – one before and one after on the same theme – and by including two important additions, one in verse 41 and one in verse 43. In the first instance, the Matthean version of the parable speaks of what the owner of the vineyard (God) will do to those who murdered his son: 'He will put those wretches to a miserable death, and let out the vineyard to other tenants who will give him the fruits in their due season.' In the second addition, Matthew envisages the transfer of the vineyard to other owners: 'Therefore I tell you, the kingdom of God will be taken away from you and given to a nation producing the fruits of it.' The word translated 'nation' is *ethnos*. It refers to a new entity that is neither Jew nor gentile. The replacement motif cannot be missed. In this parable, the vineyard metaphor is drawn from Isaiah 5.1–7 where the vineyard is said to be 'the house of Israel'. Matthew is saying in the clearest of terms that the Christians, not the Jews, are now God's vineyard, his elect people, true Israel.[47] The third parable is about a royal wedding feast to which those invited refuse to come and the king then opens the invitation to all (22.10). The invited guests who refuse to come and treat the king's servants shamefully are destroyed at the king's command and their city is burned (22.6). Almost certainly, this is an allusion to the destruction of Jerusalem, the clearest possible indicator that God has rejected historic Israel.

The new community

Matthew's point is clear: Jesus is the long-awaited Jewish Messiah who comes to call Israel to repentance, and thereby reconstitute the people of God; however, Israel's leaders and those who identify with them reject him. Jesus thus gathers together all who respond, a holy remnant, and as a consequence those who refuse him are excluded. In this monumental step, the old order is drawn to a close. For Matthew, the way of entrance into the Jesus community is not by birth, or law keeping, or circumcision, but by grace: a theme explicated in Matthew's parable of the two debtors (18.23–35), which insists that the disciple's forgiveness flows solely from the mercy of God. In affirming this, Matthew cuts right across Jewish beliefs – and in effect endorses a new understanding of how one becomes a member of the people of God.

During the ministry of Jesus, Jews are called to repentance (Matt. 4.17, 11.20–4, 12.38–41, 21.29, 32), but the importance of faith as the post-Easter response to Christ is foreshadowed in the

story of the healing of both the gentile centurion's servant
(8.5–13) and the Canaanite woman's daughter (15.21–8) (each of
whom are said to believe), and possibly indicated also in the story
of Peter's walking on the water (14.22–33).[48] The universal mission
is clearly seen by Matthew as the sequel to the death and resurrection of Jesus. His final command to the disciples is: 'Go therefore and make disciples of all nations, baptizing them in the name
of the Father and of the Son and of the Holy Spirit . . . and
remember, I am with you always' (28.19). In this new community
founded by Christ, what in Matthew Jesus calls 'my church', God
is present with the disciples as he once was in the temple.

Continuity and discontinuity with historic Israel is thus for
Matthew the hallmark of the church that Jesus founded. For
Matthew, God's promise to Israel is fulfilled in Jesus who comes
as the Jewish Messiah and invites all Israel to repent. It is only
the continuing hardness of heart and hostility of so many in Israel
that leads to the rejection of the Jewish people as God's elect, and
their replacement by those who believe, whether Jew or gentile.
Matthew underlines that Jesus' historic mission was to Israel
(10.5–6, 15.24), but he insists that after the resurrection the disciples have a mission to 'all nations' (28.19).[49] This new community so constituted is, for Matthew, true Israel in all but name. It
is a 'nation' (*ethnos*), producing the fruits of the Kingdom (21.43),
what Jesus calls 'my church' (16.18).

The church as a 'corpus mixtum'[50]

Matthew insists that the Christian community will contain true
and false disciples until the final day when judgement is made. At
the end of the sermon on the mount, this theme is introduced.
Jesus warns that false Christian prophets will come 'in sheep's
clothing'; 'not everyone who says "Lord, Lord", will enter the
kingdom of heaven', and to hear but not do is to build one's house
on sand (7.15–27). In chapter 13, the same teaching is given in the
parables of the wheat and the weeds (vv. 24–30) and the net (vv.
47–50). These two parables, only found in Matthew, remind the
reader that the final separation will come only at the end of the
age. Matthew's version of the parable of the wedding banquet
(22.1–14, cf. Luke 14.15–24) adds the little scene at the end
where the king notices a guest without a wedding garment and
has him thrown out (vv. 11–14). He is there as one who replaced

those originally invited – that is, as one of the new people of God – but despite being present among this select group, when the king appears he is not accepted. Two and possibly three of the eschatological parables in chapter 25 can be read similarly. The ten bridesmaids all start off with lit lamps, but the five who took no extra oil were not ready when the bridegroom came suddenly, and were not included in the nuptial banquet (vv. 1–13). This is surely a warning to Christians to be ready for the return of Christ. On the last day, some will be ready and be saved, and some will not and be lost. The parable of the talents (vv. 14–30) is another warning to the Christian community. Each man is given a number of talents to be used wisely; the disciple who wastes what he is given is thrown into 'outer darkness'. The meaning of the parable of the sheep and the goats (vv. 31–46) is more difficult, and continues to be debated. One interpretation with a long exegetical history is that the sheep are to be identified as true disciples, those whose lives are characterized by compassionate and practical care of the needy.[51] The goats, on the other hand, are those who have been outwardly members of the church, but on the last day are not recognized by the Lord of the church because faith has not shown itself in works. If this is the case, then this parable also warns that one can be 'in the church but not of it'.

Communal organization

We have already argued in our comments on the two Matthean passages that speak of 'binding and loosing' (16.19, 18.16) that these sayings indicate a concern for church discipline in this community. This ministry involved deciding on matters of behaviour and doctrine. It is a responsibility first given to Peter, and then later to each congregation (cf. 18.18). However, besides this issue there are other aspects of internal church life that can be detected. In Matthew's community there appear to have been some who were designated prophets who were active in teaching.[52] Matthew calls them 'prophets and *righteous people*' (i.e. teachers above reproach) (10.41, 13.17, 23.29),[53] or 'prophets, sages and scribes' (23.34).[54] Yet it would seem that a prophetic ministry was not restricted to these leaders. As elsewhere in the New Testament, prophecy is a possibility for every believer.[55] Thus the disciples are also described in prophetic terms (5.12, 10.4), and the problem of false prophecy is raised. Matthew adapts the unspecific saying found in Luke about knowing a tree by its fruit (Luke 6.43–4) so as to make it a test by which a true prophet can be known (7.15–23). Matthew also introduces a warning against teachers claiming lofty titles for themselves (23.8–12). Debates about leadership in Matthew's community were obviously a live issue.

The pattern of communal life that Matthew wants to encourage in the churches is given extended treatment in chapter 18, the so-called 'Matthean church order'. All disciples are first encouraged to think of themselves with humility. In their own estimation, they should see themselves as 'little ones' (1–4),[56] their brothers and sisters as the personification of Christ (5–9), and each without exception as of infinite value to God (10–14). When a brother sins, every opportunity should be given for him to repent. Only after he has refused three attempts, should he be excluded from the community (15–20). The ideal is, however, to continue to forgive (21–34).[57]

In the communal gatherings known to Matthew it seems that the worship of Jesus by those assembled was designated by the cultic term *proskunein*. Matthew uses this word some ten times, more than any other New Testament writer, always with Jesus as the focus (2.2, 8, 11, 8.2, 9.18, 14.33, 15.25, 20.20, 28.9, 17). Yet the term is obviously used metaphorically, for nowhere in Matthew is there any suggestion of a continuation of the Jewish cult, and nowhere is there any hint of the existence of an order of priests, and much to the contrary. In this worship it would seem the celebration of the Lord's Supper was important (26.26–9),[58] while prayer (6.9–13) and singing (26.30) almost certainly had a part. Matthew seems to envisage every disciple as having a teaching ministry (5.19, 28.19), but we presume the prophetic scribes took particular responsibility for teaching the faith when the community assembled. Here we should recall that Minear argues that Matthew was written as a teaching manual.[59]

The sociological window

From a sociological perspective, what Matthew says about the church is particularly instructive. A number of important studies have given consideration to this, but here we can only touch briefly on a few matters. Overman, along with most scholars, locates Matthew in the period sometime after the fall of Jerusalem in AD 70. He sees him defining the church against 'formative

Judaism', which was also defining itself before evolving into Rabbinic Judaism. It is Matthew's claim that the Christian community is true Israel, the fulfilment of Old Testament prophecies, and conversely that Israel represented by its leaders has been rejected by God. In sociological terms, Matthew is involved in 'legitimating' the Christian claim. This involves a bitter struggle because Matthew and his community wish to stand in continuity with much of Israel's faith – the pursuit of righteousness, commitment to prayer, fasting and alms giving, and the study of the (Old Testament) scriptures – yet be different. Always the feelings are strongest when spiritual brothers break with each other. Matthew's church still must be considered a 'sect', hostile to its parent, but it is a sect with a missionary vision, but now much more structured and well established than at first.[60]

The picture of church life that emerges from a study of Matthew's ecclesiology speaks of development. It is clear that institutionalization has progressed many steps from the incipient forms left by Jesus. The one church founded by Christ is now meeting in individual churches that have as their counterpart synagogue communities; disputes about doctrine and discipline have agreed procedures to resolve them; certain people are recognized as leaders; and what takes place when congregations meet is seen as the worship of Jesus.

John's Gospel

Two distinctive features of John's Gospel bear upon the ecclesiology reflected in this document. The first is the dialectical relationship with Israel. Like Matthew, John is thoroughly conversant with Jewish life and institutions. It has even been claimed that John is the most Jewish of all the Gospels. However, again, like Matthew, there is in John an antagonism to Judaism that leads him to argue, in his own characteristic manner, that Israel has lost its status as the people of God – this honour now being the preserve of those who believe in Christ. The second is its multi-faceted presentation of the gospel story.[61] John merges the past and the present, and frequently gives to seemingly straightforward narratives a symbolic meaning. In John, says Beasley-Murray, 'the historical ministry of Jesus in Palestine is set in indissoluble relation to the ministry of the risen Lord in the world'.[62] As a result, the gospel story is frequently to be understood on two levels. At one level, there is an account of Jesus' words and actions, but at another level the reader is supposed to see a spiritual or symbolical dimension to the story or words. The narrative of John, chapter 9, has been taken as a good example. Jesus heals the man born blind, and then he speaks of himself as the 'light of the world'. The point is not made explicit, but the reader is to deduce from this that true sight is found in recognizing Jesus for who he truly is: the risen Lord who gives light to the world.[63]

Christ and the individual

In John's Gospel, Christ is the main theme, the central motif. He is the Son sent to reveal God the Father. He says what the Father gives him to say (3.34, 8.28, 12.48–9, 17.8, 14), and he does what the Father asks him to do (4.34, 5.36, 9.4, 10.37). In this sense, he and the Father are one (10.30, 17.22). His special role for which he has been sent by the Father is to save the world (3.17, 4.42, 12.47), or, to put it in another way, to give eternal life (3.14–16, 36, 5.21, 10.10, 28, 17.2). The means of receiving this salvation or eternal life is through believing in Jesus, or knowing Jesus. The importance of these parallel ideas is seen in the frequency of the expressions. Over 120 times, the two verbs translated as 'knowing' are found (*ginoskein* 40 times, *eidenai* 85 times). These verbs carry the meaning of 'knowing personally'. They speak of an intimate relationship. The verb to believe (*pisteuein*) is found ninety-six times.[64] John insists that, 'everyone who believes . . . may have eternal life' (3.16). Thus there is a universal offer of salvation. Yet those who do not believe in Christ are said to be in darkness (3.19, 8.12, 12.35, 46), and under judgement (3.18, 5.22, 27). This salvation comes 'from the Jews' (4.22) and Jesus is 'the king of Israel' (1.49, 19.19–22), but John does not allow any special privileges for the Jews. Schweizer says, 'The antithesis is always between faith (which responds to God's call) and unfaith (which closes its ears to God).'[65] This focus on the personal response to Christ as the key to receiving eternal life has led scholars to speak of John's soteriological 'individualism'. Yet while this trait is to be recognized, it should not be taken to imply that John is not interested in the communal dimension of Christianity.[66] He is simply insisting that the basis of membership in the community called into being by Jesus rests entirely on a personal faith response to him as revealer and Lord.

The disciples in John

The word 'disciple' appears in John seventy-eight times, more than any other Gospel, and in the majority of cases the noun is in the plural.[67] This is not by accident. In the presentation of his Gospel narrative, the disciples play a very important role. They are those who positively respond to the invitation to believe and form the community in which Jesus is confessed as Lord.[68] Yet in John, as is often the case, the picture given is multi-dimensional. Sometimes the historic disciples seem to be primarily in view; sometimes it is the disciples of John's day (his community); and often it is those who read the Gospel in whatever age. The narratives of John frequently mention particular disciples. In some cases, they are only introduced as partners in a dialogue with Jesus (e.g. 6.1–14, 14.1–14), but in other cases they are drawn as flesh and blood persons. The opening chapter gives two examples of the latter. Here we read of the call of Andrew and Simon Peter (1.35–42) and of Nathaniel (1.43–51). The story of Thomas, who will not believe until he sees the risen Christ, is another example (20.24–9). At one level, historic events and people are brought to mind, but John also speaks at another level. The call of the first disciples and the Thomas story are in fact paradigmatic; they say something of what is involved in discipleship in every age. In the call of these first disciples, the key words are 'seeking' (v. 38b), 'seeing' (vv. 38a, 39, 46), 'following' (vv. 17, 43), and 'staying' (v. 39), and the key motif, confessing Jesus as 'the Son of God and the king of Israel' (v. 49), which at the symbolical level makes the narrative become timeless comment about true discipleship.[69] This two-level communication is also well illustrated in the story of 'doubting Thomas'. The literal story evokes identification, and the concluding words make it clear that John intends this story to continue to speak about discipleship: 'Blessed are those who have not seen yet have come to believe' (20.29). A number of women are also singled out: Mary the mother of Jesus (2.1–12, 19.25–7); the Samaritan woman (4.7–42); Mary and Martha (11.1–44, 12.1–8), and Mary Magdalene (20.1–18). These women all show exemplary faith. They are model disciples.[70]

It is in fact this timeless call to follow, and thereby become part of the Jesus community, that is John's major interest as he speaks about discipleship. In John, a disciple is one who believes that Jesus is the Christ, the Son of God (1.49, 6.69, 11.27, etc.), which means that every comment about believing in John's Gospel is in fact a comment about discipleship. Sometimes this is made explicit as, for example, in 8.31 where Jesus says: 'If you continue in my word, you are truly my disciples,' and in 8.12: 'Whoever follows me will never walk in darkness but will have the light of life', but mostly the point is implicit. If a distinction between the past and the present needs to be made, John speaks to both contexts. Thus in chapter 17, the Johannine Jesus prays, 'not for these only [the disciples in the upper room] but also for those who are to believe through their word' (v. 20). And in chapter 20, Thomas is commended for believing because he has seen the risen Jesus and his wounds, but then the latter believers come into focus in the added commendation: 'Blessed are those who have not seen and yet believe' (v. 29).

Yet besides speaking of the historic disciples and of discipleship in every age, John seems to speak also to the disciples of his own day (his church). These are thought to be in mind in many of the passages where he mentions the conflict between the disciples and the Jews. Thus in John, Jesus predicts, 'they will put you out of the synagogues . . . and kill you' (16.2, cf. 9.22, 12.42), which most commentators think reflects a post AD 70 situation. These disciples, or some of them, seem to be in mind also when John speaks of followers of Jesus who live 'in fear of the Jews' (7.13, 12.42, 13.41, 19.38, 20.19). Many recent commentators also think John's own church situation is in mind in the way stories about Peter and 'the beloved disciple' are told. It is argued that at a symbolic level, the fourth evangelist makes these stories speak to a tension between Johannine and Petrine expressions of the faith known in his own day.[71]

Communal imagery

The picture of Jesus as the good shepherd who lays down his life for the sheep brings to the fore John's profound communal understanding of discipleship (10.1–18, 26–9, cf. 6.37, 39, 17.6–11). The background to this imagery is principally Ezekiel 34, where Israel's leaders are condemned for neglecting the sheep, allowing them to be the prey of wild beasts and be slaughtered. The Lord declares he will be their shepherd and pasture them on the mountains of Israel, and set over them 'my shepherd David', i.e. the

Messiah. In the words, 'I am the true shepherd', Jesus claims to be fulfilling this prophecy. The unique feature of John's picture of the shepherd is his willingness to die for the sheep. The claim being made is that Jesus is Israel's Messiah and that his disciples are the flock of God, true Israel. Christology and ecclesiology are thus brought together. The shepherd and the sheep belong to each other; into the care of the good shepherd God has entrusted the flock. The good shepherd leads and protects them; he directs them to the pastures of life; and he lays down his life for them. He and they are united in a bond of mutual knowledge and trust (10.14, 27). But in this passage, the post-Easter mission also comes into view. Jesus speaks of 'other sheep that do not belong to this fold. I must bring them also, and they will listen to my voice. So there will be one flock, one shepherd' (10.16). An echo of the same thought appears in the following chapter in Caiaphas' prophecy that Jesus must die 'not for the nation only, but to gather into one the dispersed children of God' (11.52). The good shepherd as Israel's saviour begins his ministry among the Jews, but as the saviour of the world his vision is far wider. The inclusion of gentiles is also part of the good shepherd's work.[72]

The 'parable' of the vine and the branches (15.1–17) is another strongly communal passage. The Old Testament again provides the background for interpretation. The prophets frequently spoke of Israel as a vine (Isa. 5.1–7; Jer. 2.21; Ezek. 15.1–5, 17.1–21, 19.10–15; Hos. 10.1–2), always in the context of judgement and unfaithfulness. In the Johannine discourse, Jesus is the *true* vine and the disciples are the branches. Their responsibility is 'to bear fruit', but they cannot do this unless they 'abide' in the vine. Ten times in verses 4 to 10 John speaks of the believer abiding in (*menein eis*) Christ or his love. Here Jesus is true Israel, but not simply by himself. He represents Israel together with his disciples. The vine and the abiding branches are bound together in a living union. In this passage, the point is also made that loving one another is of the essence of Christian communal life. God has shown his love in sending his Son, and now those who believe in him are to love each other (15.9, 10; cf. 13.34, 14.15, 21, 23, 24, 17.26).

Emphasis on the essentially communal nature of discipleship also comes through clearly in chapter 17, where the departing Jesus prays for his followers and their life together. He speaks of them as 'mine' (vv. 6, 10; cf. 10.3, 12, 14, 13.1), and asks that the Father might 'protect them' (vv. 11, 15), 'sanctify them in the truth' (v. 17), and make them 'one' (vv. 11, 21, 22, 23; cf. 10.16, 30, 11.52). This oneness or unity would seem to have two aspects: (1) it is contemporary (i.e. the unity of disciples at any one time) and (2) it is historical (the unity between the first disciples and all who follow them). The separation between the disciples and the 'world' is stressed in chapter 17. The disciples are to recognize that they are a community set apart in truth and love. The word 'world' (*kosmos*) is used by John some seventy-eight times. Occasionally it can be used neutrally of people generally (3.16, 12.19), but in most cases it alludes to human beings hostile to Christ and his message (12.31, 14.30), who are in darkness (12.35–6) and under judgement (9.39, 12.31). The world and the church stand diametrically opposed, but Jesus prays not that the disciples may be taken out of the world (17.15), but that the Father will protect them as they are sent into the world (v. 18). Again it is the missionary mandate, as the primary responsibility of the Christian community, which was spoken of in terms of 'bearing fruit' in chapter 15, that is stressed.

The Holy Spirit

Another very important indicator of John's communal understanding of the Christian faith is seen in his treatment of the Holy Spirit. John can think of the Spirit as present with the disciples during the earthly ministry of Jesus (6.63b), but when speaking historically he insists that the Holy Spirit, identified as the *paraclete* – the helper, advocate, counsellor – will only be given when Jesus is glorified (7.39, 14.16–26, 15.26–7, 16.7–15).[73] He will then take the place of Jesus (14.16). His special work in the life of the church will involve four things: (1) He will make Christ present in the believing community (14.18–20). (2) He will teach the disciples and remind them of all that Jesus has said (14.26). This teaching will take place as the Spirit calls to mind Jesus' words.[74] (3) He will guide them into all truth (16.13), but he will only reveal what Christ has given him to say (v. 14). Most recent commentators take these words to refer to the ongoing prophetic ministry in the church.[75] (4) He will convict the world of sin and righteousness and judgement (16.8). This is not something the Spirit will do independently. He works through Jesus or through the disciples. This rich theology of the Spirit's activity after Jesus is glorified, Burge argues, reflects the rich experience of the Spirit in the Johannine community.[76]

The work of the Holy Spirit in the life of the post-Easter church again comes to the fore in the account of the corporate giving of the Holy Spirit to the disciples after the resurrection (20.19–23). Here Jesus commissions the disciples to continue his mission; 'As the Father has sent me so I send you' (v. 21). As he utters these words, he breathes on them and says, 'receive the Holy Spirit'. How this story relates to Luke's account of giving of the Spirit on the day of Pentecost is difficult to decide. It is perhaps best to see it as John's counterpart to this story, but using different symbolism. John's use of the Greek verb *emphusaō*, 'to breathe on', betrays the ideas he has in mind.[77] This word reflects the Genesis account of God breathing on Adam to give him life (Gen.2.7), and the prophecy of Ezekiel where God promises to breathe his Spirit on Israel to give the nation new life (Ezek. 37.9). In both texts, the Greek Old Testament has the verb *emphusaō*. John is thus indicating that in the gift of the Holy Spirit the anticipated age to come has dawned, the promised new creation has eventuated and a Spirit-filled Israel, the end-time people of God, has been established. Those who are part of this eschatological community, John insists, are to continue Jesus' mission in the world in the power of the ever-present Spirit. In making the gift of the Spirit the constituting principle of the post-resurrection church, John is in fact indicating that the Spirit is the co-founder of the church – alongside Jesus.[78]

The final words in this narrative, 'If you forgive the sins of any, they are forgiven them; if you retain the sins of any they are retained' (v. 23), are also problematic. However, what must be noted is that this is not an ordination scene in which the apostles as the font of all future ministry are given special powers. John never calls the disciples 'the apostles'. Here, as elsewhere in John, the disciples represent the whole Christian community. With Raymond Brown, a Roman Catholic scholar, we agree that what seems to be meant by this concluding statement is that, 'Working through the disciples, the Paraclete, like Jesus before him, divides men [sic] into two groups: those who believe and can recognize and receive him, and the world which does not recognize or see him and which he will prove wrong.'[79]

John and Judaism

If in Matthew's Gospel the idea is that the Christian community
is all but in name true Israel, this is also the case in John's Gospel,
but the ways in which the two evangelists express this thought are
very different. In John's Gospel, historic Israel is viewed entirely
negatively. Jesus came as the Jewish Messiah, but as the Jewish
rejection was so pervasive, the Jews have now been rejected by
God. They are no longer the children of God: this honour is now
given to those who believe in Christ. This viewpoint is first introduced in the prologue. John writes, 'He came to his own home,
and his own people received him not. But to all who received him,
who believed in his name, he gave power to become children of
God' (1.11–12). The Jews have not only lost their privileged status,
according to John, but they are in fact now children of the devil
(8.44, 47). Some seventy times John mentions 'the Jews', com-
pared to five or six references in each of the synoptic Gospels, and
in most instances in John the note of hostility is present. In most
of these examples where Jesus speaks against the Jews, the Jewish
leaders are the audience; and so some have suggested that it is only
they who are negatively considered, but in some places the crowds
are in mind (6.41, 52, 7.15, 35, 10.31, 33), and it is doubtful
whether a distinction between the leaders and the Jews in general
is possible. For John it would seem that the Jewish leaders represent the Jewish people.[80] That a complete break with Judaism has
occurred is also suggested by the way John speaks of 'your law'
(8.17, 10.34, 15.25), of 'the feast of the Jews' (5.1, 6.4, 7.2), and of
the breach with the synagogue (9.22, 12.42, 16.2). This wording
implies that these institutions are no longer of concern to
Christians.

Of particular importance is the wording of Caiaphas' prophecy
in John 12.50–2. In classic Johannine irony the high priest
declares, 'It is better for you to have one man die for the people
than to have the whole nation perish.' The evangelist then
explains: 'He did not say this on his own, but being high priest
that year he prophesied that Jesus was about to die for the nation,
but not the nation only but to gather into one the dispersed children of God.' At one level, the words speak of Jesus' death for
Israel termed as the people/*laos* (of God), the nation/*ethnos*, and
the children of God. Yet at another level, these terms all apply to
the church which, when John writes, is the people of God, the

nation, and the children of God.[81] In support we note that elsewhere in John's Gospel the purpose of Christ's death is always the
salvation of all those who believe, whether they be Jew or gentile
(3.14f, 10.1–21, 13.23–4, 32–3, 19.37).

What we see in the fourth Gospel is a profound linking of
Christology and ecclesiology. Jesus as the Jewish Messiah comes
to his own people, but they reject him and so he calls all those who
believe to become children of God (1.11–12). Into a bond of
personal communion, knowledge, and love, those who respond are
united with Christ. They are the new people of God. In an important study on the narratives and themes in John's Gospel, Pryor
argues that these themes reflect Jeremiah's prophecy of the new
covenant (Jer. 31.31–4), indicating that the evangelist is claiming
that Jesus has inaugurated this, and thereby brought into existence
the new covenant community. The word 'covenant' is not used by
John, but Pryor is able to demonstrate that covenant ideas pervade
this Gospel. He concludes that John presents the Christian
community as 'The true, eschatological people of God gathered
by their covenant Lord, Jesus.'[82] For Pryor, this claim to be 'true
Israel' means that 'John wants to show that the Christian community has displaced the old.'[83] It is 'now claiming for itself the
exclusive status of the people of God'.[84]

The inner life of the Johannine church

Because John's Gospel says nothing directly about Christian
leaders, does not mention the institution of baptism or the Lord's
Supper, and seems to suggest that the Holy Spirit is the only
teacher Christians will need after Easter (14.26, 16.13), it has
been argued that we see in John an entirely charismatic community where there are no publicly authorized leaders, no interest in
the sacraments, and no appreciation of the church as a corporate
entity.[85] Just the reverse picture has often been painted by traditional Catholic scholars, who have found in John allusions to all
seven sacraments and an emphasis on baptism and the Lord's
Supper, plus an ordered ministry instituted directly by Christ
himself. Neither picture seems to capture what is there to be seen.

The fact that we find nothing in John explicitly about Christian
leaders is not surprising. Although John certainly speaks to the
church of his own day, he does so indirectly. He does, however,
seem to indicate a special pastoral role for Peter in 21.15–19 as the

shepherd of the flock,[86] and if John allows for this, we may infer
he was open to others assuming leadership in the Christian community. The existence of community leaders may be implied also
by the account of the footwashing (13.1–20), which can be read at
least in part as speaking to those in authority in the church.
Nevertheless, it has to be admitted that in John the stress falls on
what would be called today 'lay ministry'. The disciples represent
the whole Christian community and it is they who are commissioned by Jesus to 'go'. This thought is reiterated many times. 'You
did not choose me but I chose you. And I appointed you to go and
bear fruit' (15.16). 'As you sent me into the world [Father], so I
have sent them into the world' (17.18). 'As the Father has sent me,
I also send you' (20.21).[87] For John, the whole Christian community is called to mission and ministry.

In relation to communal assemblies it seems that John understood that Christians were to continue to 'worship' (*proskunein*)
God, but that the new worship was not to be restricted to any one
holy place (4.21), nor follow the old material and cultic forms
(4.23).[88] Because 'God is spirit, those who worship him must worship in spirit and truth' (4.24). We are not told at this point how
such worship will be expressed. In 9.38, the man born blind who
has been healed by Jesus first confesses, 'Lord, I believe', and then
'worshipped him'. The Greek verb *proskunein* means 'to prostrate
one self before', or 'to do obeisance'. The word does not appear in
20.24–9 where Thomas confesses Jesus as 'my Lord and my God',
but the idea is present. In both narratives, Jesus is given the
honour due to God. John is thus suggesting that true worship is
rightly focused on Jesus, who reveals the Father.

Despite arguments to the contrary, it does seem that John
mentions Christian baptism at least in 3.5, where he speaks of the
need to be born of water and the Spirit,[89] and possibly alludes to
it in such passages as 4.13–14, 7.37–9.[90] The Lord's Supper also
seems to be reflected in 6.35–59, most explicitly in verse 53: 'Very
truly, I tell you, unless you eat the flesh of the Son of Man and
drink his blood, you have no life in you.' Beasley-Murray says
that 'neither the evangelists nor the Christian readers could have
written or read this saying without conscious reference to the
eucharist'. Catholics and Protestants may continue to debate the
force of these words, the former wanting to take them more literally and the latter more spiritually, but they should agree that
chapter 6 does allude to the Eucharist, or the Lord's Supper. We

may assume therefore that in the Johannine community the celebration of the Eucharist was an important part of their corporate life.

A sect?

Again in a strictly sociological sense, it can be agreed that John's church was a sect.[91] It had broken sharply with the parent body, denying that it was the heir of the promises of God, insisting that the child now was true Israel. It is also true that in John there is a clear demarcation between the world and the church – another common sectarian characteristic. Yet here it should be noted that this does not imply withdrawal from the world. Rather, John's Gospel stresses the disciples' ongoing mission to the world. It is strongly evangelistic in tone, as has been noted.

Perhaps what is more significant is the apparent minimal development of institutionalization. It is often argued that, in its final form at least, John's Gospel and the Pastoral epistles (1 and 2 Timothy and Titus) should be dated at much the same time; but if this is so, the contrast in ecclesiological organization should be highlighted. The Pastorals, as we will see, reflect the most developed church structures to be observed in any writing in the New Testament, and John possibly the least. This is a reminder that institutionalization does not simply evolve on a steady curve upward with the passing of time. There are forces that can promote it and those that can hinder it. In the Johannine community it would seem that institutionalization was limited by the emphasis on the activity of the Holy Spirit and by the belief that every disciple had been sent out by Christ, matters that are constantly stressed in John's Gospel.

Chapter 4

The Church in the
Book of Acts

The Book of Acts makes a very special contribution to the development of a theology of the church because Luke writes both as a *theologian* (in the non-technical sense of the word) and as a *historian*. As a historian, he sets out to tell his readers the story of the first decades of the Christian mission, and as a theologian he deliberately brings his own views to the fore. We thus have both a selective account of what took place in the years following the first Easter, and comment on what Luke thought about this. In putting pen to paper, Luke hopes to confirm the faith of those who have become part of the Jesus community, and to help others make the decisive step demanded of those who would be members of this community.[1] The Jesus community, which we call the church, is a prime concern of Luke's writing. He highlights its post-Easter beginnings on the day of Pentecost, emphasizes its empowerment by the Holy Spirit, describes its corporate life, shows how its leadership emerged and developed, and struggles to define it in relation to historic Israel from which it sprang.

Setting the scene

Chapter 1 of Acts prepares for what takes place in chapter 2. The ascension for Luke signals that Jesus' earthly ministry is completed and that he now reigns in heaven (1.9–11).[2] The 120 in the upper room (which includes some women), praying for the promised Holy Spirit, is the church in a transitional stage (1.12–15).[3] The disciples have known the divine presence of Jesus while he was on earth, and now await the divine presence to come in a new way to

74

empower them. However, before the Spirit can be given, the sacred number twelve has to be completed. The apostasy of Judas has caused the problem, not his death, for when James is martyred he is not replaced (12.2). Luke does not envisage successors to the apostles, for eyewitnesses cannot pass on their ministry to others. After the casting of lots to make sure that the man of God's choice is selected, Matthias is numbered among the twelve.

As far as Luke is concerned, the twelve have two fundamental roles. First, they symbolize that God is reconstituting Israel: they are the patriarchs of the restored people of God.[4] And, secondly, they are the authenticating witnesses of what is proclaimed. Time and time again Luke says everything proclaimed is based on the apostles' testimony (2.22f, 3.12f, 4.8f, 5.29f, 10.34f, etc.). Thus the necessary qualifications for inclusion among the twelve are: (1) to be a man (v. 21);[5] (2) to have been with Jesus throughout his earthly ministry; (3) and, in particular, to have seen him after his resurrection (1.22). The oft-heard argument that church leaders must be men because the twelve apostles were all men, does not follow from anything Luke says. In Acts, the twelve are not depicted as congregational leaders: they are proto church, not proto ministers, and this role cannot be passed on. Their maleness is necessitated by the implied symbolism (the first patriarchs were men, and so their counterparts have to be men), but cultural factors also were important. In the first-century Mediterranean world men were the natural leaders; and when it came to being a witness, the testimony of women was usually discounted in Judaism.[6]

The central focus

The location and length of the Pentecost narrative, which includes Peter's sermon and what follows, indicates the importance of this story for Luke. Whatever is of fundamental significance for the author of Acts, we should suspect it will be disclosed in this chapter. The coming of the Spirit is described in terms of an Old Testament theophany – an appearing of God – such as when the law was given to Moses (Exod 19.16–19), or God spoke to Elijah (1 Kings 19.11–12). Suddenly from heaven there came a 'rush of violent wind', the whole house shook, fire appeared on each one present, and 'they began to speak in other languages' (2.1–4). This led the crowd of Jewish pilgrims 'from every nation under heaven', present in Jerusalem for the feast, to cry out, 'what does this mean?' (v. 12). Peter then stands and interprets these events in terms of the fulfilment of Old Testament prophecy.

This mighty outpouring of the Spirit, Peter explains, comes as the direct fulfilment of the prophecy of Joel 2.28–32, which he quotes in full (2.17–21), adding his own introduction, 'And in the last days, it will be God declares' ('that I will pour out my Spirit'). The Greek adjective translated 'last' is *eschatos*, from which the term eschatology is derived. This expression, 'the last days', is frequently found in the Old Testament, where it refers to the time when a prophecy will be fulfilled (cf. Isa. 2.2; Jer. 23.20; Ezek. 38.16; Mic. 4.1, etc.), and at Qumran, where it commonly introduces a prophecy the Essenes believed had been fulfilled in their age. By introducing the Joel quotation with these words, Luke is boldly claiming that the end-time has broken into history with the coming of the Holy Spirit on the day of Pentecost. Yet even if Luke had not used this introduction, those at home in Jewish culture would have understood that this spectacular outpouring of the Spirit of God signified nothing less than the arrival of 'the last days', for in the Old Testament, the intertestamental writings, and at Qumran, the Spirit's coming, characterized the age of final redemption (Ezek. 36.27, 37.14; Isa. 32.15; Zech. 12.10; 4 Ezra 5.22; T.Job. 1.23; T.Levi 18.11; 1QH 7.6, 17.26, etc.).

The word 'Pentecost' is derived by transliteration from the Greek word meaning 'fiftieth'. It was the name given to the Jewish feast that came fifty days after Passover. In the Old Testament, it is a harvest festival (Exod. 23.16; Lev. 23.15–21; Deut. 16.9–12), but after the fall of Jerusalem, Jewish texts describe it as the festival to celebrate the giving of the law to Moses on Mount Sinai (e.g. B. Pes. 68b). It would seem that this understanding of Pentecost was well known much earlier, but some dispute the evidence.[7] If, however, Luke does associate Pentecost with the giving of the law, and the evidence seems to indicate this, then Luke is saying a new epoch has begun, which is characterized by the presence of the Holy Spirit in the lives of all God's people. Moses is the giver of the law: Jesus is the giver of the eschatological Holy Spirit.

This gift of the Spirit was, as the prophets had foretold, for all God's people. It was a universal gift to restored Israel. The promise therefore had a communal dimension, and this is highlighted in Acts 2. Luke begins his narrative by noting that '*they* were all together in one place' (we presume he means the 120 that he has just mentioned in 1.15); they were '*all* filled with the Holy Spirit', and *all* began to speak in other tongues (2.1–4). Then Peter stands and proclaims to the perplexed crowd that Jesus of Nazareth whom they crucified is in fact the promised Messiah whom God raised from death, and is now reigning in heaven as Lord and Christ (2.36). When they cry out 'what then should we do?', Peter calls on them to 'Repent and be baptized every one of you in the name of Jesus Christ so that your sins may be forgiven; and you will receive the gift of the Holy Spirit' (2.38). Luke then adds that about 3,000 'welcomed the message' and were baptized. This indicates that they were all forgiven of their sins, all received the Spirit, and all were then numbered among the reconstituted people of God. He descriptively names this new community as 'those who believed' (2.44). Not surprisingly, therefore, commentators and theologians frequently speak of this climax to the Pentecost narrative as 'the birthday of the church'. Luke then goes on to speak immediately of the communal life of these first believers. 'They devoted themselves to the apostles' teaching, and fellowship, to the breaking of bread and the prayers' (2.42). Whether or not these four activities recall the sequence of early Christian worship, or simply list the most important aspects of their life together, is not important for our purposes.[8] What is important is that Luke intimately connects conversion and communal life. The mutual dependence of these early believers is highlighted by Luke's comments about how they 'had all things in common', so that there were no needy among them (2.44–5; cf. 4.32–7). The chapter ends with the words 'and every day the Lord was adding those who were being saved to the community'.[9]

This giving of the Holy Spirit to all who are baptized in Acts 2, in characteristic Lucan parallelism, is drawn as the counterpart of the coming of the Spirit on Jesus at his baptism in Luke 3. Peter's sermon that follows likewise parallels Jesus' sermon at Nazareth at the commencement of his Spirit-filled ministry.[10] This gives the clue to what otherwise could be a perplexing problem: two points at which the Christian community comes into being – once during the ministry of Jesus, and again on the day of Pentecost. In his Gospel, Luke depicts the birth and ministry of Jesus as the commencement of the new age, and his calling of disciples as the commencement of the Jesus community.[11] The Pentecost story is at one level its sequel, but at another it is for

Luke a parallel commencement of the new age and the new community. In both epochs this community is characterized by the forgiveness of sins and the divine presence. In the Gospel story, this divine presence is known in the company of Jesus, and in Acts by the gift of the Spirit, whom Luke can call 'the Spirit of Jesus' (16.7).

However, while it seems clear that Luke intends his readers to understand Acts 2 as speaking of 'the birthday of the post-Easter church', it is to be noted that he does not use the word *ekklēsia/* church in this context; in fact, it does not appear until 5.11. In the immediate post-Pentecost situation, Luke prefers to use descriptive terms. The Christian community is designated as 'those who received the word' (2.41); 'those who believed' (2.44, 4.32); 'those who are being saved' (2.47), and the 'community' (2.47).[12] Almost certainly nothing should be made of the omission of the word *ekklēsia* at this point. Luke loves to vary his terminology, including or omitting words in different sections of the Gospel or Acts. Thus, for example, not only does *ekklēsia* not appear until 5.11 and then disappear after 20.28, but also *hoi mathētai* (the disciples) is not used until 6.1, and then ceases to be used after 21.16, while *hoi hagioi* (the saints) is used three times in chapter 9 (vv. 13, 32, 41) and then only once again in chapter 26 (v. 10).[13]

The community of the new age

In Luke's understanding, the coming of the Holy Spirit brings a whole new world. It has often been noted that Luke says very little in Acts about the return of Christ, or of the imminence of the end. These things are mentioned (cf. 1.11, 3.20, 17.31, 28.31), but Luke's attention is so captured by the eschatological events already present that the future fades somewhat into the background.[14] The Spirit has been given to all God's people, prophecy long silent is now present possibility, 'wonders and signs' are taking place, and gentiles are being included among the people of God, as the prophets had foretold. As a result, a divinely given 'gladness' fills the believers' hearts.[15] More frequently than any other writer in the New Testament, Luke speaks of the Holy Spirit. Some seventy times the word *pneuma* (Spirit) occurs in Acts, which is almost one-fifth of the total use of the word in the New Testament. Many have suggested that this book could have been named 'the Acts of the Holy Spirit'; and it is this dominant interest in the Holy Spirit that leads Raymond Brown to conclude that 'the distinguishing feature of Lucan ecclesiology is the overshadowing presence of the Spirit'.[16]

Luke also believed that a profound sense of unity prevailed among the first Christians. He speaks of them being 'united' together (*homothumadon*). This Greek word is found in the New Testament only in Luke's writings; he uses it to describe either the spiritual unity of the Christian community (2.46, 4.24, 5.12, 8.6, 15.25), or of the opponents of the gospel (7.57, 12.20, 18.12, 19.29). The oneness of heart of the disciples is for Luke most clearly seen in that they held 'all things in common' (2.44, 4.32), so that 'there was not a needy person among them' (4.34).

The community of believers Luke speaks about is also a persecuted minority. The pressure, Luke suggests, mainly comes from Jews hostile to those who are proclaiming Jesus as the Jewish Messiah (5.17–42, 6.8—7.60, 8.1–4, 9.23, 14.19, 17.5, etc.). The Romans, in contrast, are generally presented favourably, which many think betrays an apologetic motive in Luke's writings.[17] Luke seems to be suggesting that Rome has a benevolent attitude to the Christian community. The thought that being a Christian by definition involves suffering is stressed in Paul's exhortation to the Christians of Asia Minor, 'It is through many persecutions that we must enter the Kingdom of God' (14.22).

Collective titles for Christians in Acts

One of the special features of the Book of Acts is the numerous collective titles for Christians used by Luke. H. J. Cadbury, in a famous study of these, listed and discussed nineteen terms.[18] A few of them hardly qualify as titles, but there still remain a large number of significance. Some of these are largely descriptive, and may have been developed by Luke building on popular usage of his own day. Possibly 'those who believe' (in various Greek participial forms: cf. 2.44, 4.32, 15.5, 16.34, 18.27, 19.18, 21.20, 25, 22.19), 'those who call on the name' (9.14, 21, 22.16), and 'those who are being saved' (2.47; cf. Luke 13.23) fall into this category. The most important of these is 'those who believe', for it is not only the most commonly used of the above mentioned titles, but it is also indicative of what Luke sees as essential for membership in the Christian community. On the day of Pentecost, 'those who received the word' and were baptized (2.41) are described by Luke as 'those who believed' (2.44). The necessity of believing in Christ or the word is made clear in Peter's sermon in the house of Cornelius. The apostle declares, 'everyone who believes in him [Christ] receives forgiveness of sins' (10.43; cf. 13.39, 48, 15.7). Belief in Christ is demanded of Jew and gentile: this is the only way to find forgiveness and to become part of the Christian community, restored Israel.

Some of the other collective titles, on the other hand, seem to reflect terminology used in the earliest Jerusalem community. 'The disciples', 'the brethren', 'the saints', and 'the church' are four clear examples, and probably 'those belonging to the way' (9.2, 19.9, 23, 24.22) is another example.[19] These are collective titles for the post-Easter followers of Jesus, which would seem to witness to a period of some fluidity in nomenclature before Paul's favoured term, the church, gained precedence. A detailed study of the background and force of each of these titles is not needed, but some comment is demanded because several of them provide important information on how Luke understood the Christian community.

The brethren

The title 'the brethren' (*hoi adelphoi*) is a good example to illustrate Luke's understanding of Christians viewed collectively. This was a title Jews used of themselves and Luke reflects this usage throughout the Book of Acts. In his account of Peter's sermon on the day of Pentecost, the Jewish crowd is addressed as 'brethren' (2.29), Stephen uses the same term of his audience (7.2), as does Paul in his sermon in the synagogue at Pisidian Antioch (13.26, 38). Even in the last chapter of Acts, Jews are still called 'brethren' (28.21). However, without any apology, Luke also calls those who belong to the Christian community 'brethren' some twenty-three times. This suggests that Luke did not think of the Jews as outside the family, but he was aware that a new 'brotherhood' (which included women) had emerged alongside the Jewish one, and this new family was made up of believing Jews and gentiles (cf. 14.2, 15.1, 22, 36). The Christian usage would seem to go back to Jesus himself (Matt. 12.46–50 par., etc.). If the descriptive title 'the believers' highlights what is essential for admission to the Jesus community, then the title 'the brethren' underlines the familial nature of the association enjoyed by those who believe in Christ.

The disciples

The collective title 'the disciples/*hoi mathētai*' is equally of interest. It is the next most common title to the brethren, being used at least twenty-one times. Like 'the brethren', it almost certainly originated with Jesus. For Luke, 'those who believe', 'the disciples' (Acts 6.7, 9.26, 11.26), and 'the brethren' (cf. 9.26 and 9.30, 11.29, 18.27) signify the same group of people. The absolute form, 'the disciples', is usually used without any qualification, but in one instance Luke explicitly relates the title to Christ by speaking of 'the disciples of the Lord' (9.1), and this is always what is meant.[20] Three times Luke uses the word in the singular of an individual Christian (9.10, 36, 16.1); in the second instance, the person so designated is a woman, a usage with no parallel in Judaism. In all the Gospels, as was noted in the previous chapter, the title 'the disciples' transcends the historic followers of Jesus, and is to be read as a designation of the church, the post-Easter Christian community.[21] In Acts, this is explicit.

The developed way in which Luke uses this title makes this clear, for he often speaks of the disciples as one corporate entity. In 15.10, Peter warns of those who would put a 'yoke' (singular) around the neck of the disciples; later he speaks of summoning the disciples as a group (18.27, 9.30). And in 20.30, Paul prophesies that false teachers will draw away the disciples (as a whole) from the apostolic faith. It seems certain that the early believers called themselves 'the disciples', but Luke says that, 'In Antioch the disciples were first called Christians' (11.26). The verb is in the passive tense. This was a name others gave them; it was a title coined by outsiders for the disciples. Little did Luke realize that this novel designation, used in scorn by the enemies of the followers of Christ, would one day eclipse the title 'the disciples'.

The term 'the disciples' is a constant reminder that those who believe in Christ are his personal followers. They know his presence in the person of the Holy Spirit; they are for ever learners dependent on his guidance and direction; and they are a community bound together by a common faith and life.

The saints (or holy ones)

When the Israelites reached Mount Sinai, after their deliverance from Egypt, Yahweh bound himself to them by covenant, and on this basis designated them 'a holy nation' (Exod. 19.5–6). The Old Testament writers thus speak of the people of Israel collectively as 'the saints' (Deut. 33.3; Num. 16.3; Ps. 34.9, 89.6). In later Jewish apocalyptic texts, the saints are the elect of Israel who will enjoy the rewards of the messianic Kingdom (Dan. 7.18–27; Ps. of Sol. 17.1; Enoch 51.5, 8, 62.6, 8, etc.). At Qumran, the community is described as 'the saints of his people' (1QM 6.6; cf. 1QM 14.22; 1QS 8.13, 21), and Paul takes over this term and uses it repeatedly to designate the Christian community (Rom. 1.7, 16.15; 1 Cor. 1.2; 2 Cor. 1.1, 13.12; Phil. 1.1, etc.). It is also used in this way in Hebrews 6.10, 13.24, Jude 3, Revelation 8.4, and Acts 9.13, 32, 41, 26.10. In these Christian uses of this title, the claim is made implicitly that the Christian community has taken the place of Israel in the purposes of God.

Because the four Acts references all apply to Jewish Christians in Jerusalem, the argument has been made that this title originally applied only to Christian Jews, or even that it always carries this meaning. Such arguments are not convincing.[22] In the next chapter, we will see that this does not explain Paul's usage, but two strands of evidence in Acts show that Luke also understood that this title could be used of all Christians, even if initially it was used of Jewish Christians, as would be expected. First, it seems certain that 'the saints' is but one of the many collective titles used in Acts of believers generally. Acts 9 is instructive; in verse 1, Luke introduces the title 'the disciples', which appears again in verses 25, 26, and 38; in verses 26 and 30, he uses the title 'the brethren'; in verses 13 and 32, 'the saints'; in verses 14 and 21, 'those who call on the name', and in verse 2, those 'who belong to the way'. Luke's penchant for stylistic variation accounts for the multiplication of terms: no other explanation is needed. The various collective titles are to be read as virtual synonyms. Secondly, Luke's use of the plural, passive participial form of the cognate verb *hagiazo* for Christians, irrespective of their race, in 20.32 and 26.18 shows that the term is not restricted to Jewish Christians. It is through faith in Christ that men and women are 'sanctified' or, more literally, 'made saints'.

In calling Christians collectively 'the saints', Luke indicates that he believed this new community had a theologically defined status given by God. The Christian community is restored Israel.

The church

After the brethren and the disciples, the term *ekklēsia*/the church is the next most common collective title for believers in Acts. Some nineteen times it is used of Christians. In classical Greek, this word was used only of an actual 'assembly' of citizens. An *ekklēsia* existed while the people were gathered. In Acts 19.32, 39, 41, Luke uses the word in this way to speak of an unbelieving mob who have (unlawfully) assembled in the stadium at Ephesus. When they went home, this gathering or assembly ceased to exist. The fact that Luke can use this important theological term, *ekklēsia*, in a secular context in its classical sense is not at all surprising, for Luke and other New Testament writers frequently use words that have rich Christian meaning non-theologically. This means we should no more derive Luke's Christian meaning of the term *ekklēsia* from the Acts 19 uses than we should derive the Christian meaning of *sōdzō*/save from his usage of this term in Acts 27.20 and 31, where it refers to rescue from drowning.

This matter is raised, because – as has been noted – many Protestants appeal to these references in Acts to show that the early Christians were well aware of the classical meaning of the word *ekklēsia*. On this basis, they argue, that in all probability the Christian usage finds its origins in classical usage. The early Christians first used the word *ekklēsia* simply to refer to their assemblies, and only with the passing of time did the word develop so as to mean those who assemble, a local community, and then later, the world-wide community of Christians.[23]

One special feature of Lucan theology should be noted at this point. Luke has what many have called an 'absentee Christology'.[24] This idea must be carefully qualified because Luke insists that Christ is present through his Spirit (16.7) and by his word, but it is true that Luke emphasizes that Jesus is now reigning in heaven. He is the ascended Lord who rules over and directs the church on earth. Luke certainly believed that Christians went to heaven when they died (Luke 23.43, 7.54–60, 14.27), but he has no conception whatsoever of a heavenly church. Indeed, his theology of the risen Christ as the ascended Lord of the church excludes such an idea. For him, Christ is in heaven and the Christian community is on earth. This reminds us that each New Testament writer must be understood in terms of his own framework of thought.

The force of the use of *ekklēsia* in Acts 7.38 is debated. The

word is found on the lips of Stephen when he alludes to the giving
of the law to the Israelites at Mount Sinai 'in the church in the
wilderness' (RV). Modern commentators tend to see this use of the
word at this point as but a reflection of the Old Testament story,
but Cerfaux argues that this passage betrays the origins of the
Christian usage as a title for an ongoing, theologically defined
community, and Luke is indicating this in Stephen's sermon. For
the early Christians, he argues, the assembly at Sinai was thought
of as 'a permanent assembly that had become a community, a type
of the messianic people'.[25] In our excursus on the Old Testament
background to this word and its use in Philo, the possibility of
Christians reaching this conclusion is seen to be a possibility.[26] In
support of this interpretation, the Moses–Jesus typology implied
in this passage, and already seen in the story of the giving of the
Holy Spirit on the day of Pentecost, should be noted.[27] In
Deuteronomy 18.16, immediately after Moses tells the people of
Israel that God will raise up another prophet like him, he speaks
of 'the day of *assembly*' (*LXX ekklēsia*) at Horeb when the law
was given. As Luke seems to make the gift of the Holy Spirit the
counterpart or fulfilment of the Sinai events (2.1–36), and identifies Jesus as the second Moses, the prophet of the last days (3.22–3),
the implication would seem to be that in this instance he is saying,
just as Moses was with the people of Israel, the *ekklēsia* in the
wilderness, so now Jesus is with restored Israel, the *ekklēsia* in this
eschatological age.[28]

The first time Luke uses the word *ekklēsia* of Christians in
5.11, he qualifies it with the adjective 'whole' (*holos*), as he does in
15.22. The word *ekklēsia* in 5.11 is introduced to make a contrast
between those who were assembled and *saw* the judgement on
Ananias and Sapphire take place, a small group in a household
setting in all probability, with the whole church – that is, all the
Christians in Jerusalem who Luke numbers in the thousands
(2.41, 4.4), who later *heard* about what had happened.[29] The *holos*
is emphatic, as it often is in Luke's writings.[30] It does not add anything to the meaning of the word *ekklēsia* in this sentence. 'The
whole church' mentioned in 5.11 is the same entity that Luke calls
'the whole group of those who believed' in 4.32 at the commencement of this section of Acts.[31] When Luke speaks of the
severe persecution 'against the church in Jerusalem' (8.1), he is
again using the word to refer to all the Christians in the city. This
is made plain by the words that follow. Using the plural Luke says,

'they were all scattered except the apostles'. All the Christians – that is, the church except the apostles – were forced to flee Jerusalem. This persecution of 'the church' proceeded as Saul 'entered house after house; dragging off both men and women' (8.3). 'The [whole] Christian community' would also seem to be the force of the word in 11.22 and 12.5. Acts 12.1 is of special interest; here Luke says, 'Herod the king laid violent hands on some who belonged to the *ekklēsia*/church' (*tinas tōn apo tēs ekklēsias*). A parallel is found in Acts 15.5, where Luke speaks of 'some who belonged to the party of the Pharisees'. In each case, Luke alludes to a substantive group of people who form an identifiable community. As the mission moves beyond Jerusalem, Luke continues to use the word *ekklēsia* in the singular (11.26), or the plural when speaking of believers in a number of cities or towns (15.41, 16.5) to mean the Christians in that place. Thus in 14.27, he says that Paul and Barnabas gathered (*sunagagontes*) the *ekklēsia*; a specific group of people, which the context identifies as the Christians in Antioch, were brought together. The same verb is used in 15.30, but in this parallel those gathered together at Antioch are called '*to plēthos*' – 'the whole community'.[32] This evidence makes it clear that Luke understood the word *ekklēsia* to be a term to designate the Christian community as it was found in particular places. In 7.38, he suggests that this community in its entirety is restored Israel, called into being by the new Moses, Jesus.

Two references where the word *ekklēsia* appears are to be singled out for special comment: 9.31 and 20.28.[33] In the first passage, little can be concluded with certainty; for although the textual evidence favours a singular reading, the plural *ekklēsiai* may be the original. This possibility is to be seriously considered, because nowhere else in Acts, or for that matter in the New Testament, do we find the word *ekklēsia* used in the singular to speak of Christians in different cities. The plural is what would be expected. Most commentators prefer the singular reading, arguing that it is hard to imagine why a scribe would change the singular *ekklēsia* to a plural, and yet leave the plural at 15.41 and 16.5. Seldom, if ever, is any comment made of the fact that the textual evidence not only has the singular and the plural of the noun *ekklēsia*, but also the singular and the plural of the verbs and participles that follow. As Luke can use the singular *ekklēsia* with a plural verb following (cf. 8.1), at the beginning of the section

that 9.31 concludes, it may be that he used the singular *ekklēsia* in
9.31 with plural verbs and participles following. This must be considered as a distinct possibility. Indeed, such a reading makes the
best sense of the text. On this reading, what Luke is saying is that
the *ekklēsia* (singular) of Jerusalem, understood as the disciples or
the Christians (plural), was dispersed by the persecution 'throughout all Judea and Galilee and Samaria [and they] had peace and
[they] were built up; and [they] walking in the fear of the Lord
and in the comfort of the Holy Spirit were multiplied'. If this is
the case, then here the word *ekklēsia*/church refers to a body of
believers that can be called 'church', although they are dispersed
in many places. It seems that the word carries the same meaning
as our use of the words 'the Christians'. Yet even if the singular
readings are preferred, we still have a distinctive usage of the word
ekklēsia in Acts 9.31. Thus in this one instance, in the New
Testament, the word would be used of Christians spread over a
larger area than one city, who continue to be thought of as 'the
church' in the singular. In either case, the word carries the same
meaning. The church is Christians – or, more specifically, the
Christian community in this world.

The use of *ekklēsia* in 20.28 is significant, because this is the
only place where Luke explicitly indicates that the word can refer
to a universal reality without geographical limitations. In Paul's
sermon at Ephesus, the apostle speaks of the church of God,[34]
which the elders as guardians of the flock are to feed – that is, the
local community of Christians – but he then adds 'for whom Christ
shed his blood'. As Christ certainly did not die only for the
Christians of Ephesus, all Christians come into view. This is also
indicated by the fact that these words reflect the language of Psalm
74.2, where the Hebrew *edah* is found.[35] Although the Hebrew
word *qahal*, meaning assembly, is always translated by *ekklēsia* in
the Greek Old Testament, the more theologically weighty
Hebrew word *edah*, meaning the covenant community, or the
people of God, lies behind 20.28. Hort, who discusses the implications of using *ekklēsia* as a translation of *edah*, in this verse says,
'this helped directly or indirectly to facilitate the use of *ekklēsia* to
denote God's people'.[36] The fuller expression 'the church of God'
takes up a designation Paul himself uses (1 Cor. 15.9; Gal. 1.13,
etc.), but in Paul, the 'of God' does not seem to add anything not
implied by the word 'church' on its own.[37] It is hard to conceive

that Luke intended readers to think that at this point the word *ekklēsia* meant something more than it did elsewhere in Acts.[38]

The fully communal and substantive meaning of the word *ekklēsia*/church in Acts is also seen in that Luke makes this word a virtual synonym of other key ecclesiological terms, especially 'the disciples'. In the latter case, this is indicated by parallel usage. Luke can speak of the church in a particular city (8.11, 11.2, 13.1), or of the disciples in a particular city (6.7, 9.19, 21.16); he can call the Christians in several cities or locations 'all the disciples' (18.23) or 'the churches' (15.41, 16.5); twice he says the missionaries strengthened 'the disciples' (14.22, 18.23), and once that they strengthened 'the churches' (15.41); twice he speaks of the disciples 'multiplying' (6.1, 7), and once of the church 'multiplying' (9.31). It has been seen already that the titles of the 'believers', the 'brethren', the 'disciples', the 'Christians', and the 'saints' can be used interchangeably, and now the word *ekklēsia*/church must be included in this list.

It is true that in 5.11, 8.1, 3, and 9.31 that 'the church' is the church in Jerusalem, as 11.22 makes explicit, but for Luke this is the whole Christian community at this time. The only examples where Luke would appear to have a specific congregation in mind is when he uses *ekklēsia* of the church in Antioch (11.26, 13.1, 14.27, 15.3). This usage is possibly in mind in 14.23, where Luke speaks of Paul and Barnabas appointing elders 'in each church' in the towns of Iconium, Lystra, and Derby, but if elders are more communal overseers than congregational ministers, as we would argue, then he is alluding to the appointment of elders for each city-wide community of Christians. The parallel in Titus 1.5 is significant. Titus is told to 'appoint elders *in every town*'.

Therefore we find in Acts no Christian use of the word *ekklēsia* in the classical sense to refer to the event of assembling,[39] a few references where it designates a particular congregation, and a large number where it means the Christian community in its entirety. In one instance (7.38), the suggestion is made that the Christian *ekklēsia* is the counterpart of that community to whom Moses gave the law. Most commentators speak of Luke's local and universal uses of the word *ekklēsia*, but we must remember that these are post-New Testament categories. It is doubtful whether Luke could have made sense of this dichotomous approach. Instead, it would seem that for him there was but one Christian

community, which sometimes he thought of as all the Christians
on earth; sometimes as all the Christians in one town or city; and
sometimes as the Christian community who met regularly together
in one location. In each case, people are called 'the church' because
by their faith they are related to Christ and therefore to one
another.

The importance of this word to designate Christians collectively lies in its breadth. In this one word, Christians collectively
considered are defined as a theological entity, the new people of
God led by the Moses of the last days, as those who are related to
Christ and those who are related to one another because of their
common faith and common experience of the Holy Spirit. What
is implied in the titles the brethren, the disciples, and the saints is
summed up in one term: the *ekklēsia*.

The people (of God)

One final collective name for Christians found in Acts must also
be discussed, '*ho laos*' – the people (of God). In the Old Testament,
this was one of the most distinctive and exclusive designations for
Israel. Luke repeatedly uses it of Jews in his Gospel, and in Acts
he twice dares to transfer this weighty theological title for Israel
to Christians who are definitely not Jews. In 15.14, Luke has
James speak of gentiles becoming 'a people [*laos*] for his name',
and in 18.10 he has 'the Lord' tell Paul that he has 'many people
[*laos*] in this city' – and the city is pagan Corinth. These two
references must be associated with 3.23, where Peter, speaking to
Jews, says that all those who do not recognize Jesus as the (eschatological) prophet like Moses 'shall be destroyed from the people'
(*laos*). Just as gentiles can be included among God's people, so
Jews can be excluded. Luke does not cease to call Jews *ho laos* (as
late as the last chapter of Acts he is still calling them by this title:
cf. 28.17, 26, 27), but that he can transfer the title to Christians,
irrespective of their nationality, shows that a theological transition
in his thinking on the status of Christians is well under way.

Each of these collective titles for Christians evokes certain ideas
but they describe one reality, the Christian community called into
being by Christ and empowered by the Holy Spirit. The overlapping, but not exactly synonymous, meaning of each word can
be diagrammatically illustrated to clarify the point.

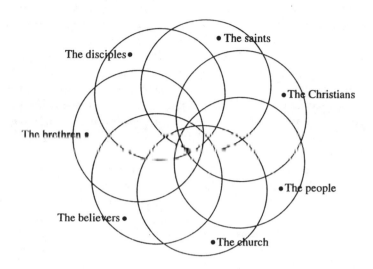

One reality, the Christian community, designated by different terms

Restored Israel, new Israel, true Israel, the church?

Our discussion of Luke's use of the term *ho laos* of Christians introduces one of the most complex and debated issues in the quest to understand Luke's ecclesiology. Hans Conzelmann, who began the relatively recent debate about Lucan theology, argued that as far as Luke was concerned the Jews were no longer of any interest to God; their day had passed. After Easter, a new epoch had begun, 'the age of the church'. As Luke writes, the Christian community is predominantly made up of gentiles, and this new reality is the true people of God in an exclusive sense.[40] Ernst Haenchen, who published a large commentary on Acts soon after Conzelmann's important study, assumed a similar position. He boldly states, 'God has written the Jews off.'[41] He makes much of the three declarations on Paul's lips that he is now turning to the gentiles (13.44–6, 18.5–6, 28.23–8). The last of these, strategically situated at the end of Acts, is seen as the most important. The reader is left with the impression that the Jews have been offered the gospel, but as they have consistently refused it, their privileged place in the purposes of God has ended. These scholars suggest that Luke is underlining the discontinuity between Israel and the church. On their view, Luke thinks a radical breach in salvation history has occurred. The Christian community is a new work of God; in other words, the Christians are 'true Israel'.

Jacob Jervill's book, *Luke and the People of God*, published in 1972,[42] surprised the scholarly world by taking a diametrically opposed position to that of Conzelmann and Haenchen, which had once seemed so convincing. He argued that as far as Luke was concerned, there could only ever be one people of God, the Jews. Jesus is presented as the Jewish Messiah who had come to redeem Israel. Those who respond to his preaching, or later to that of the apostles, are seen as the restored people of God – that is, a reconstituted or new Israel. Unbelieving Jews are excluded, but large numbers of Jews respond. Luke emphasizes the success of the Jewish mission (2.41, 4.4, 5.14, 9.42, 14.1, 17.10ff, 21.20), and that these believing Jews kept the law (2.46, 3.1, 16.3, 21.20). Gentiles are included in the restored Israel, as the prophets had foretold, but they are not obligated to keep the Jewish law. In Jervell's opinion, there is no sharp breach with the past, the church is restored Israel, or new Israel. Salvation history has moved forward, but Israel has remained in the centre of God's plan. Here the emphasis is on continuity. On this view, Luke sees the Christian community as purified Israel, brought to life by the Spirit that now allows for the inclusion of gentiles.

These two approaches capture details of Luke's thought, but as overall perspectives they are inadequate. Each only sees half the picture, but this is understandable because, to extend the metaphor, Luke never quite completes the picture. As he writes, Luke himself seems to be struggling with these issues, having not fully formulated his thoughts. Of the various attempts to sort out what Luke is attempting to say on the relationship between Israel and the Christian community, two stand out, but the conclusions are not the same. They each come to the question from a different perspective. Robert Maddox, in *The Purpose of Luke–Acts*,[43] argues in effect that both Conzelmann and Jervell are right in what they affirm, and wrong in what they deny. Luke has both a positive and a negative orientation towards historic Israel. He stresses that Jesus was the Jewish Messiah who came to call Israel to repentance, and that the apostles took the gospel first to Jews, and then only to gentiles when the Jews hardened their hearts. The Christian community grows out of Israel, finding its beginnings in a restored Israel that allowed for the inclusion of gentiles. Thus for Luke, there is continuity with the past. Yet Maddox also points out that Luke underlines God's rejection of Israel as a totality (always excepting that many individual Jews believed). After the initial offer of the gospel to Jews, it is then offered to gentiles apart from the law. This means that, for Luke, Israel is no longer the same: it is no longer simply identical with the community based on law. Because Luke allows for this radical breach with law keeping, it means discontinuity with Israel is also a motif to be seen in Luke–Acts. Luke is saying that the church arose out of Israel, the people of the law, but is now something altogether new. It is that community of people who confess Jesus as Lord and are empowered by the Holy Spirit.

The other important study is by the German Catholic scholar Gerhard Lohfink.[44] He agrees with Jervell that Luke underlines continuity between Israel and the Christian community, the church, but he holds that Luke–Acts describes a progressive parting of the ways. He argues that Luke does not write as a systematic theologian, but as a Christian historian who sets out to show how the church of God evolved out of historic Israel. Implicitly, Luke describes how this breach took place in seven steps that lead from Israel being the true people of God to the church being the true people of God. Step one is seen in the Old Testament, where through the ministry of the prophets a gathering and separating of true Israel begins; key aspects of this are described in Stephen's speech in Acts 7. A second step takes place through the ministry of John the Baptist, who calls on all Israel to repent and prepare for the coming of the Messiah. The third step is taken in and through the ministry of Jesus, who seeks to gather all Israel – as the appointment of the twelve so clearly shows. They are representative Israel. The fourth step follows from the death and resurrection of Jesus; the gospel is now to be offered to all nations (Luke 24.47; Acts 1.8). The fifth step is the most important, but not the last. It comes with the gift of the Holy Spirit on the day of Pentecost. The new community is now empowered by the Spirit; but even at this point, Luke does not think of the church as true Israel, for to do so would imply that the Jews had been left outside; that they were no longer the people of God. The sixth step takes place through the gentile mission, which Luke insists fulfils the prophecy of Amos (Acts 15.16–18). The end of the process, step six, comes when Luke looks back and sees that it was the death of Christ that made salvation possible for all, irrespective of birth or law keeping, and created a new people of God – 'the church of God' (20.28). In so designating the Christian community, Luke is saying that the church is not simply restored Israel, but a new reality.

Both Maddox and Lohfink arrive at the same conclusion, but by different routes. The Lucan writings bear witness to a point in history where the Christians are coming to see themselves as a distinct new entity, having their roots in Israel, but now independent of Israel. They are the community of salvation, the 'church of God'. Entry is through faith in Christ, not through descent from Abraham or by keeping of the law; however, time-honoured titles for Israelites such as 'brethren' or 'the people of God' are not denied to Jews as yet, but they are being taken over by Christians.

Communal life

The Book of Acts suggests that the usual practice was for Christians to meet in homes (2.46, 5.42, 10.2, 11.14, 12.12–17, 16.15, 31–4, 18.8).[45] This social setting determined to some degree the nature of the gatherings; it would have encouraged informal sharing, mutual care for one another, and interactive ministry.

Baptism

Water baptism is frequently mentioned in Acts (2.38, 41, 8.12, 13, 16, 36, 38, etc.). It is administered as a general rule following repentance or believing, and in association with the reception of the Holy Spirit (2.38, 41), but there is no fixed pattern. In the various conversion narratives in Acts, the Spirit comes sometimes before water baptism (9.17, 10.44–8), sometimes after (2.38, 19.5ff), and sometimes the two are quite unrelated in time (2.4, 8.16).[46] This suggests that Luke does not have what moderns would call a sacramental understanding of baptism, where the Spirit is bestowed in the sacramental action. Who does the baptizing is of no concern to Luke. An otherwise unknown disciple baptizes Paul (22.16), but in most cases Luke uses the passive form of the verb 'to baptize', which means it is impossible to tell who performed the act.

The Eucharist

Communal meals at which Jesus is present are given great prominence in the Gospel of Luke (5.29, 7.36–50, 10.38–41, 11.37, 15.1–2, 19.1–10); even the Last Supper (22.14–23) is such a meal, albeit a special one. Despite the fact that we call the meal Jesus had with his disciples before his betrayal 'the Last Supper', it was not the last meal that Jesus took with his followers as far as Luke is concerned. He mentions a number of meals Jesus had with the disciples between his resurrection and the ascension. In Acts 10.41, he says the apostles 'ate and drank with him [Jesus] after he rose from the dead', and he gives three examples of these meals (Luke 24.13–35, 42; Acts 1.4). The meal scene in the Emmaus narrative is particularly instructive. Here we find for the first time in Luke's writings the expression 'the breaking of bread' (24.35 and Acts 2.42; cf. Luke 24.30; Acts 2.46, 20.7, 11, where the equivalent 'to break bread' is found). Many echoes of both the Lucan version of the feeding of the 5,000 (9.11–17) and the Last Supper (22.15–23) can be seen. The meal is preceded by teaching (vv. 25–7); as they sit down to eat, Jesus naturally assumes the role of the host, and as he breaks the bread, 'their eyes were opened and they recognised him' (v. 31).

These meal scenes provide the background and the meaning of the cryptic references to the 'breaking of bread' found in 2.42, 46, 20.7, 11.[47] Luke is saying that communal meals continued to be a very important part of the shared life of the disciples, even after Jesus had ascended. As the early believers met and ate together, listened to the apostles' teaching and prayed (cf. 2.42), they sensed that Jesus was powerfully present in their midst. Luke displays a profound and integrated understanding of the meaning of communal meals at which Jesus is present, but in different terms to those of John and Paul.

Preaching and teaching

However, it is the preaching and teaching of the word of God that stands at the heart of the life of the Christian community as far as Luke is concerned. The risen Christ commissions his followers to proclaim repentance and forgiveness of sins in his name to all nations (Luke 24.47), and in Acts we see this happening. Professor Kee says, 'Throughout Acts, the proclamation of the

word is a central concern and a major factor in the spread of the
new community.'[48] When the apostles find their responsibilities
too great, they insist that they must concentrate on prayer and the
ministry of the word (6.2, 4); yet it is not just the twelve who
preach the word, but leaders such as Philip and many unnamed
believers as well (8.4). Luke insists that this ministry of the word
has both an evangelistic focus and a teaching focus. There is a
preaching to outsiders calling for a faith response, and a preaching
to those who believe within the Christian community. The twelve
apostles are the first teachers of the early Christians (2.42); Paul
obviously took his teaching ministry very seriously (11.26, 14.22,
15.35, 20.7–12, 17–35), and the prophets seem to be active in
teaching. Luke calls them 'leaders among the brethren' (15.22),
and he conjoins the titles 'prophets and teachers' (13.1).[49]
However, those involved in this ministry of teaching seem to be
quite extensive. In Antioch, Luke says, 'many others' besides Paul
and Barnabas 'taught and proclaimed the Lord' (15.35).

Leadership

In the early chapters of Acts, the apostles are presented as the
evangelists and teachers of the first post-Easter believers, but as
the numbers increase and consolidation begins, the apostles gradually relinquish this role.[50] The appointment of the seven (Acts
6.1–6) to care for the Hellenist widows is a difficult incident to
understand, for Luke says so little about it. He probably mentions
the story mainly to introduce Stephen. It seems that it tells of the
appointment of seven men as leaders of Greek-speaking Jewish–
Christians in Jerusalem. If this is so, then these men should be
considered as 'elders' – senior men – entrusted with the oversight
of their community.[51] Luke frequently speaks of Jewish elders who
functioned in this way (Luke 7.3; Acts 4.5, 6.12, 23.14, etc.), and
without any explanation commences speaking of Christian elders
(11.30, 14.23, 15.2ff, 20.17) who we must presume were their
counterparts. In Judaism, elders were laymen without any given
liturgical or teaching role in the synagogue. Luke presents Christian
elders in a similar way. He does not depict them as individual
'ministers' of churches (the 'ministers of the word' are the apostles
and prophets), but as those entrusted with the general pastoral
'oversight' (*episkopos*) (20.28) of local communities of Christians.

The giving of the Holy Spirit to all God's people makes

prophecy a possibility for every believer, young and old, men and women (Acts 2.17–18); but Luke, along with Paul, considers some, both men and women, to be prophets in a distinct sense.[52] These people regularly exercised a prophetic ministry. A prophet can be defined as one who proclaims the word given directly by God, but Luke allows for some overlapping of the ministry of the prophet and the teacher in the period he describes. Thus in speaking of those leading the worship (*leitourgein*) at Antioch, he calls them 'prophets and teachers', as we noted earlier (13.1–3). He also calls prophets 'leading men among the brethren' (15.22), which gives us some idea of their importance in the early church. These people were recognized as prophets not because of ordination, but because it was acknowledged that God regularly spoke through them in various ways.

Commissioning/ordination

The public and prayerful recognition of at least some Christian leaders (later called 'ordination' and given weighty theological meaning) was nevertheless something that emerged very early. There are two, or possibly three, accounts of the laying on of hands with prayer to publicly mark out Christian leaders in Acts (6.6, 13.3, cf. 14.23). In the first two instances, the people set apart in this way are explicitly depicted as Spirit-filled leaders, who have already had a significant ministry. The laying on of hands by those assembled therefore does not signify the bestowal of a ministry, or of the Spirit, but rather that from now on their ministry is no longer an individual one: they are from this point on representatives of their community. What they do, they do not undertake in their own name, but in the name of the community that has set them apart as its representatives. The laying on of hands on the 'elected' (*chierotonein*) elders in 14.23 is not mentioned: only their prayerful commendation, which may, however, have involved this outward act as well (cf. 1 Tim. 5.22).[53]

Community organization

Luke's comments about the decision-making processes among the first Christians are of particular interest. He depicts the early Jerusalem community as what could be called a 'guided democracy'. A problem arises, the apostles come up with an answer, the church

endorses it, and then is involved in its implementation (see
1.15–25, 6.1–6). This communal leadership, which Luke considered the twelve provided initially, is eventually taken over by a
group of elders who are first introduced in 11.30, when they accept
the gift for the poor on behalf of their whole community. In 21.18,
James appears as the chairman of a council of elders, and although
Luke shows no knowledge of monarchical episcopacy, it is not
surprising that later writers thought of James in these terms.[54] If
we can take Jewish models as a parallel, this council of elders
would have been responsible for the general pastoral oversight of
the Christians in Jerusalem who met in many house-churches.

The story of 'the council of Jerusalem' in chapter 15 is particularly important, because it illustrates an attempt to decide on an
issue involving churches in different geographical locations.[55] It is
the prototype of later church councils and synods, even if it was a
one-off event. In this narrative, the apostles and elders are depicted
as the leaders of the Jerusalem community; and it is they who
meet with the delegation led by Paul and Barnabas (15.6, 12).
These two groups represent the churches involved. After the
meeting, the apostles and elders decide to send a group back with
the visitors to pass on the decision, and Luke says 'the whole
church' consented to this (15.19). We take it he is saying that all
the Christians in Jerusalem endorsed this proposal, probably in
some very general and informal sense.

Locating Lucan ecclesiology

Anyone attempting to describe sociologically the ecclesiology seen
in Acts faces the same problem as anyone who attempts to explain
theologically the relationship between Israel and the church as
seen in Acts. In both cases, historical description and Luke's own
views are so intertwined that a distinction is not always possible.
Although Luke believes that the dynamic presence of the Holy
Spirit determines the life of the Christian community, the ecclesiology that emerges in Acts is more structured than that seen in
the early Paulines. With the exception of the Pastorals, Paul's
epistles do not mention the office of the elder, nor the laying on
of hands on Christian leaders. Both of these things have Jewish
roots, and so in all probability they arose first in a Jewish setting;
however, this does not challenge the case that the ecclesiology
seen in Acts is more structured than that described in the early

Paulines. Nevertheless, Luke does not mention the office of deacon or bishop,[56] and prophets appear as the main 'ministers of the word' (after the twelve and Paul). Office bearers are emerging, but the charismatic dimension to ministry is still very much alive. The impression gained therefore is that Luke is describing a church where institutionalization has progressed further than in the early Paulines, but is not as advanced as it is in the Pastorals.

Chapter 5

The Church in Paul's Earliest Epistles

In the Pauline epistles there is to be seen a developed and clearly thought-out understanding of Christian communal existence. Paul nowhere spells out a systematic theology of the church, for all his writings are occasional letters answering particular problems facing the Christians to whom he writes; but time and time again we find him explaining to his converts what it means to be one with Christ and one with each other, and to be a distinct community in a hostile world. Men and women received the gospel as individuals, but this always involved, as far as Paul was concerned, a crossover from one community to another. Communal thinking pervades Paul's writings and is expressed in many ways. One key term the apostle uses when speaking of this community is *ekklēsia*/church, but a study of this word in isolation would miss a great deal, and result in a very inadequate account of the apostle's communal theology. Paul's theology of the church has to be set in a wider context before particular terms are considered. However, before going any further, a critical framework for this study of Paul's ecclesiology needs to be established.

Thirteen epistles are ascribed to St Paul in the New Testament, but there is debate about whether or not he personally wrote all of these. Scholars have noted a marked development in thought, especially in relation to the church, from what have been taken as his earliest epistles to the latest, and have raised the question of how one man could have so changed in his views. A development in outlook and theology in the Pauline writings is conceded without reservation, but as the focus of this study is solely on the communal ideas reflected in these epistles, the question of who wrote them and when is not a major concern for us. Nevertheless,

98

the recognition of differences demands an approach that ensures that this critical advance in understanding of the epistles is preserved. It is generally accepted that the Pauline epistles can be divided into three groups on the basis of broadly based agreement in thought and outlook in each case. Thus we will proceed by studying separately these three groupings: the earliest epistles – Romans, 1 and 2 Corinthians, Galatians, Philippians, 1 and 2 Thessalonians,[1] and Philemon; the middle Paulines – Ephesians and Colossians; and the late Paulines – 1 and 2 Timothy and Titus, the so-called Pastoral epistles.

Frequently, the development to be seen in the Pauline epistles has been discussed solely in terms of changing theology, but in recent years the importance of considering these changes from a sociological perspective has also been highlighted. This has been done in a number of studies in different ways, but one study particularly relevant to our quest is Margaret MacDonald's *The Pauline Churches: A Socio-historical Study of Institutionalization in the Pauline and Deutero-Pauline Writings*.[2] She argues that the three groups of Pauline epistles reflect not only a development in theology, but also in the social structuring of the church. In the early Paulines, she finds 'community-building institutionalization'; in the middle Paulines, 'community-stabilizing institutionalization', and in the late Paulines, 'community-protecting institutionalization'. I came to very similar conclusions independently in *Patterns of Ministry*. This schema provides a model with great potential to elucidate Pauline ecclesiology, and we will use it as an added dimension to our basically theological discussion.

The early Paul

There are various suggestions as to what stands right at the heart of Paul's theology, the doctrine of justification by faith, being 'in Christ', reconciliation, the salvation of Jews and gentiles, etc., but the argument that it is his belief that end-time realities have broken into history through the death and resurrection of Christ is compelling.[3] This one theme explains and integrates almost everything in the apostle's writings; the other suggested central motifs can all be subsumed under this particular category. Paul's eschatology especially illuminates his communal thinking. It is the great apostle's conviction that Jesus is the long-awaited Jewish Messiah, through whom God has ushered in the end-time, and who now reigns as Lord in heaven. It follows from this that a new community is to be called into existence. The Messiah must have a messianic community, an end-time must have a people of the end-times. The invitation to become part of this new entity goes first to Jews and then to gentiles, but the same demand is made on both. They must desist from striving after a righteousness of their own, and accept the righteousness that is freely bestowed on those who believe in Christ (Rom. 10.1–13). Paul sees his mission not only in terms of the winning of individuals for Christ, as might a modern evangelist, but also as the gathering together of the community of the last days. Those who respond to the preaching of the gospel do so as individuals, but Paul sees this mainly in terms of a 'transfer' from one community to another.[4] The eschatological and the communal are inextricably intertwined. If this is all too often missed by modern-day students of the Bible, it is not because Paul does not underline this, but because our cultural glasses, heavily tinted by Western individualism, hinder us from seeing what is in the text.

The two communities

Paul considers humankind to be identified with one of two communities, and salvation, as just noted, involves changing sides. He speaks of these communities in different ways, using different images, but possibly the most important is the Adam-Christ motif. In 1 Corinthians 15.20–9 and in Romans 5.12–21, Paul explicitly contrasts Adam and Christ, and many scholars see allusions also to Adam typology in Romans 1.18ff, 7.1–12, and Philippians 2.5–11.[5]

For Paul, Christ is 'the last Adam', the counterpart of the first Adam. The two are set in juxtaposition. They are not just individuals, but representative leaders of two communities. As far as Paul is concerned, every human being is in solidarity with one leader or the other. So complete is this union that Paul uses the language not only of identification, but also of incorporation.[6] Those who belong to the community identified with Adam are spiritually dead (Rom. 5.12ff; 1 Cor. 15.22ff), and those belonging to the community identified with Christ are spiritually alive (Rom. 5.18ff; 1 Cor. 15.20ff).

The background of Paul's understanding of Adam is found in a number of related Old Testament ideas. First, that Abraham and his descendants fulfil the promises made to Adam; secondly, the corporate understanding of the Son of Man, the true Adam, in Daniel 7.13; and thirdly, on Jewish intertestamental speculations where Adam is not humankind in general, but Israel, the people of God – an idea developed in the rabbinical writings.[7] Christ as 'the last Adam' is thus depicted by Paul as true Israel, and to him, and those identified with him, belong all the blessings promised to Adam. The framework of thought is therefore thoroughly eschatological. Adam and those in union with him belong to that order that is doomed to pass away; Christ and those in union with him belong to the age to come that is now breaking into human history.

The prepositions 'in', 'with', and 'into'

Paul also uses a number of Greek prepositions to stress the close identification between Christ and his followers that bonds them together in union as a distinct community. The first of these to be briefly discussed is 'in Christ', an expression Paul uses over one hundred times in the epistles we are considering if we include the equivalents such as 'in the Lord' or 'in him'.[8] The frequency of usage indicates the importance of this motif for Paul. The apostle uses the expression in a number of ways, not all of them being of equal theological significance; but even when those with no communal significance are left to one side, there remain a large number of examples that speak of believers' common oneness with Christ – some of which suggest that this oneness is in fact best described as 'incorporation' into Christ. The Good News Bible's translation captures well what this means by rendering the expression as 'in union with Christ'. On a number of occasions, this common oneness in Christ is made explicit: 'we who are many, are one body in Christ' (Rom. 12.5); 'the churches of Judea that are in Christ'; there is 'no condemnation to those in Christ Jesus' (Rom. 8.1). The individual has this status, but it is a status indicative of belonging to a new community related in a distinctive way to the risen Lord. Several suggestions have been made as to how Paul understands the believer to be 'in Christ', but the linkage with the Adam–Christ typology, which contrasts those 'in Adam' (1 Cor. 15.22) and thus 'in the flesh' (Rom. 7.5, 8.9), with those 'in Christ' (Rom. 8.9; Gal. 3.28; Phil. 3.8) and thus 'in the Spirit' (Rom. 8.9), would seem to indicate what is in mind. Those who are 'in Christ'

belong to the new age. They are identified with 'the last Adam' in
his resurrected life, and they experience something now of end-
time existence. This means we have here again the conception of
the Messiah as a corporative figure who includes within himself
the messianic community.[9] As the 'last Adam', the representative
leader of God's people, Christ and those who believe in him are
one. So Paul declares, 'If anyone is in Christ, there is a new creation: everything old has passed away; see, everything has become
new' (2 Cor. 5.17). 'The new creation' is a Jewish idiom that
speaks of the eschatological age.[10] All those 'in Christ' are the
community of the last days.

Reinforcing this identification between Christ and his people,
expressed in some uses of the preposition 'in' (*en*), is Paul's use of
the preposition 'with' (*sun*), most commonly in compound words
beginning with *sun*. Christians are described as living with Christ
(Rom. 8.17), suffering with Christ (Rom. 8.17), crucified with
Christ (Rom. 6.60), and being glorified with Christ (Rom. 8.17).
Some forty examples can be found. In speaking of people becoming
Christians, Paul uses the preposition 'into' (*eis*), characteristically
in relation to baptism. 'Do you not know', he asks the Christians
in Rome, 'that all of us who have been baptised into Christ were
baptised into his death?' (Rom. 6.3). In writing to the Galatians
he is emphatic: 'As many of you as were baptised into Christ have
put on Christ' (Gal. 3.27); and to the Corinthians he says, 'For in
the one Spirit we were all baptised into one body' (1 Cor. 12.13).
The point is that although baptism is an individual act, it results
in incorporation into the body of Christ, the church.

The communal dimensions of this language cannot be missed.
Baptism 'into Christ', following a decision to believe in Christ,
signifies entry into the eschatological community; those belonging
to this community are 'in Christ', and they live their lives 'with
Christ'.

The body of Christ and the new temple

Closely allied with these fundamental communal categories are
two more readily recognizable ecclesiological and communal
motifs, the body of Christ and the new temple. In three important
instances in his earlier epistles, Paul calls Christians collectively
the body (*soma*) of Christ.[11] In writing to the Corinthians, he first
speaks of the Christian community as the body of Christ in

arguing for the complete incompatibility of taking part both in the Christian Eucharist and the worship of idols (1 Cor. 10.14–22). He says: 'The cup of blessing which we bless, is it not a participation [*koinonia*] in the blood of Christ? The bread which we break, is it not a participation in the body of Christ? Because there is one loaf, we who are many are one body' (vv. 16–17). Although this passage mainly concerns the exclusive nature of belonging to Christ, it also introduces the idea that because Christians 'participate' in Christ, they are bound together, forming a corporate entity that Paul calls 'the body of Christ'.

Later in this same epistle, when combating the elitism of the pneumatics, who seem to have suggested that they were in some way superior to the ordinary Christians at Corinth, Paul again calls the Christian community at Corinth 'the body of Christ'. He says: 'For just as the body is one and has many members, and all the members of the body, though many are one body, so it is with Christ. For by one Spirit we were all baptised into one body' (1 Cor. 12.12–13).[12] Into this one body 'we all' (*hemeis pantes*), says the apostle, which seems to suggest he means all Christians, a wider group than the 'you' (*humeis*) of verse 12, were 'baptized into one body', presumably by Christ (cf. Mark 1.8 par.). Christians are one body not because they meet together, but because of divine initiative. Yet although this body is one, the apostle then goes on to insist that it has many members (v. 13); each of these has a part to play and each is of equal value (vv. 15–26) So he concludes, 'Now you are the body of Christ and individually members of it' (v. 27).

The third passage in Romans 12.3–8 also affirms that believers are one body and that this body has a diversity of ministries; but Paul expresses himself slightly differently. In verse 5 he says: 'So we, who are many, are one body in Christ, and individually we are members one with another.' In describing the church 'as one body in Christ', the apostle points to the fact that Christians are united together because they share a common incorporation in Christ. Ridderbos concludes, 'the distinguishing feature of the idea of the "body", therefore, is that these many in virtue of this common belonging to Christ form in him a new unity with each other. They are not each one individually, but as a corporate unity, all together in him.'[13]

These are the only passages in the early Paulines where Paul explicitly speaks of the church as the body of Christ, but many other passages convey in different terminology the thought that Christians are one with Christ, and therefore one with all other Christians. Becker discussing this fact says, 'Although Paul uses the body motif rarely, it belongs to a field of interrelated metaphors and images that express the reality of communal participation in Christ through incorporation in him.'[14] Thus, for example, the very important text Galatians 3.27–8 is clearly related in thought to 1 Corinthians 12.12–13, but does not use the word *soma*/body. Paul states: 'For as many of you were baptised into Christ have put on Christ. There is neither Jew nor Greek, there is neither slave nor free, there is neither male nor female: for you are all one in Christ.' So profound is our oneness as believers that even the most indelible of differences among human beings are transcended 'in Christ'. Once this communal dimension in the apostle's thinking is noted, it can be seen at almost every point in his epistles.[15]

What exactly Paul has in mind when he calls the church the body of Christ continues to be debated.[16] Some suggest that the expression 'the body of Christ' is to be taken literally, or, as it is sometimes expressed, realistically and ontologically. The church is at this present time Christ in the world; but as Paul himself clearly distinguishes between the glorified, risen Christ in heaven and the Christian community on earth, and as he does not single out this one communal image as the definitive definition of the church, this view is untenable. Others suggest that the language is *mere* metaphor, but this explanation is also inadequate. Paul's realistic language cannot be read as if he is simply using an illustration likening the Christian community to the body of Christ. Metaphor, nevertheless, is the term that best describes Paul's thought. It is no 'mere metaphor', but a metaphor (like all powerful metaphors) that conveys something of the reality indicated by the words.[17] It is analogical in nature. This means that there is some correspondence between the metaphor and the truth to which it points. In speaking of the church as the body of Christ, Paul is boldly affirming that Christians are one with Christ and one with each other by divine agency, and the church on earth is an expression of Christ's presence in the world.

In this body there is a diversity of ministries that promotes the unity already given in Christ by building up and drawing together the members of the body. In other words, this unity is a gift and a goal to be achieved. Faith in Christ sealed in baptism constitutes not an aggregation of Spirit-filled believers, but 'the body of

Christ', the church, in which every member has a part to play. A more profound communal metaphor is hard to imagine.

The new temple

Lastly, to complete this section on Paul's essentially communal understanding of Christian eschatological existence, we note his use of the building and new temple motifs. In seeking to combat the disunity among the Corinthians, Paul first of all speaks of them as 'building' (1 Cor. 3.9), and then more specifically as 'God's temple . . . in which God's Spirit dwells' (3.16). This is a highly significant comment, for both the Old Testament and the intertestamental writings anticipated the creation of a new temple in the age of eschatological fulfilment (Ezek. 37.26ff, 40.1ff; Hag. 2.9; 1 Enoch 90.28–9, 91.31; Jub. 1.17, 29), and at Qumran these prophecies were taken as having been fulfilled in the establishment of their community.[18] Developing these ideas, and possibly the teaching of Jesus along similar lines (cf. Mark 14.58 par.), Paul insists that it is the Christians at Corinth as a community who make this temple. In 3.17b he says: 'For God's temple [*naos* singular] is holy, and you [*humeis* plural] are that temple.' In this personal, corporate temple, the divine presence abides through the Holy Spirit. McKelvey says, 'God's dwelling on earth is no longer a thing apart from his people; it is the people themselves.'[19]

The same idea again appears in 2 Corinthians 6.16, where the apostle declares, 'we are the temple of the living God'. In this case, the assertion is supported by a number of Old Testament quotations,[20] which are linked together by allusions to the themes of the new covenant and the new exodus.[21] Appealing to these texts, Paul sees God dwelling among the Corinthian Christians as he did among the Israelites, and having the status once the sole preserve of Israel. They are now God's people (*laos*), and sons and daughters of the Lord Almighty (vv. 16–18). Only one conclusion can follow: Paul is affirming that Christians collectively are the redeemed community of the new covenant, true Israel.

The identity of this new community

As a young man Paul had found his personal identity primarily as a Jew, as a son of a Jewish family with an impeccable lineage, and as a Pharisee (Phil. 3.3–6). Being part of these interconnected collectives for Paul, as a first-century Jew, was what gave meaning to life. When Paul became a Christian, he set himself adrift from these social certainties; and his theology is in part an exercise in recreating a new collective identity for himself and other Christians. In developing his essentially eschatological and communal theology, Paul struggles with the reality of historic Israel's continuing existence in unbelief, despite the fact that many individual Jews have believed in Jesus as Christ and Lord. Nevertheless, in seeking to identify the new community, his basic approach is to bestow on it the lofty collective titles once the sole preserve of Israel.

Paul's use of the title 'the saints' illustrates his practice well.[22] In the establishment of the covenant at Sinai, God set apart Israel as his holy people (Exod. 19.6; Lev. 11.44, 45, etc.). It thus follows that in the Old Testament, historic Israel can be called 'the holy ones' or, as the Hebrew is usually translated, 'the saints' (Num. 16.3; Deut. 33.3; Pss. 16.3, 34.9, 89.5; Isa. 4.3, etc.). In later Jewish apocalyptic texts, the saints are the elect of Israel who will share in the rewards of the messianic Kingdom (Dan. 7.18, 21, 22, 25, 27, 8.24; Ps. of Sol. 17.1; 1 Enoch 51.5, 8, 62.6, 8, etc.); and at Qumran, the community called itself 'the saints of his people' (1QM 6.6, 14.12; 1QS 8.13, 21). Without hesitation, Paul designates the new community in Christ 'the saints' at least twenty-three times in his earlier epistles (e.g. Rom. 1.7, 8.27, 12.13, 15.25; 1 Cor. 1.2, 6.1, etc.). By doing this, he is claiming that collectively those in Christ are now in a unique way God's holy people, set apart for his service.[23] Paul always uses this title collectively, viewing it as a status given by God, not earned.

It is much the same when Paul calls Christians 'the elect' (*hoi eklektoi*), 'the beloved' (*agapēmenoi*), or 'the called' (*klētoi*). These are communal titles, like the saints, drawn from the Old Testament where they are used of the community of Israel, God's own people. Frequently these terms appear together in a cluster. Romans 8 has the Christian community in mind throughout, as the consistent use of the plural indicates. It is in this community, Paul insists, that the Holy Spirit is at work, where the promises made once to historic Israel are now being fulfilled,[24] and those who belong to it are 'the saints' (8.27) and 'the elect' (8.33). In calling the followers of Jesus collectively 'the elect', Paul uses terminology Jesus himself used of his disciples (Matt. 20.16, 22.14, 24.24, 31; Mark 13.20, 22, 27), and takes over a central element in Jewish self-understanding (1 Chron. 16.13; Pss. 89.3, 105.6; Isa. 42.1, 45.54, etc.). Earlier in Romans, in his introductory address, Paul calls the Christians in that city 'the beloved' and 'the saints' (1.7), using the terms synonymously (cf. 1 Thess. 1.4; 2 Thess. 2.13). 'The beloved' again is a designation of Israel (Pss. 60.5, 108.6; cf. Deut. 7.6–9; Hos. 11.1–4), as Paul himself recognizes (Rom. 11.28). Finally, closely associated with all of these titles is 'the called'. This expression reflects the fundamental basis of Israel's status as God's elect people – those whom he has called (Exod. 12.6; Isa. 41.9, 42.6, 43.1, 45.3, etc.). Writing to the Corinthians, Paul addresses them as 'the church of God which is at Corinth, to those sanctified in Christ Jesus, called to be saints together' (1 Cor. 1.2; cf. 1 Cor. 1.24; 2 Cor. 1.1; Rom. 1.6, 7, 8.28).[25] In this instance, *ekklēsia*, *klētoi*, and *hagioi* appear as parallel expressions describing the one reality. In designating those who belong to the church as those 'called', Paul is again transferring language once the special preserve of Israel to the Christian community.

Paul is more restrained in his transferral to Christians of the title *ho laos* (the people of God), as this was how the apostle and other Jews commonly designated historic Israel, but even in this case we see the same pattern.[26] The most telling example is found in 2 Corinthians 6.16–18. In seeking to support his identification of the Christian community as 'the temple of the living God' (v. 16), Paul appeals to a number of Old Testament texts that he sees fulfilled in the emergence of the Christian community. He applies these to the largely gentile Corinthian church as if God himself is speaking. 'God said, I will live in them and move among them, and I will be their God and they shall be my people [*laos*]' (2 Cor. 6.16b).

A similar application of an Old Testament promise in which this term is used is found in Romans 9.25. In this case, Paul sees God anticipating the inclusion of gentiles, in the words of Hosea, now being fulfilled. God says, 'Those who were not my people [*laos*], I will call my people [*laos*].'[27] In these two instances, the word *laos* is unambiguously used of Christians. Later, in Romans 15.7ff, Paul appeals to the Old Testament to show that from the time of the patriarchs, God intended to include gentiles within the covenant community. One of the texts drawn into the argument is Deuteronomy 32.43 (Rom. 15.10), which is read to anticipate gentiles *and* Jews praising God together as the one people of God/ *laos*. In 1 Corinthians 14.21, Paul again applies an Old Testament text that uses the word *laos* to the Christian community, but as his reason to quote Isaiah 28.11 is not concerned with the theological status of the Corinthians, but with their interest in tongue speaking, this passage is not so significant.

The church and Israel

The application of these theologically pregnant terms (once the sole preserve of historic Israel) to the Christian community sharply raises the question: has God now abandoned the Jews as his chosen people? In Galatians and Romans we find the great apostle struggling with this difficult theological problem: the relationship between Israel as the elect people of God called to obey the law, and the new community brought into existence by the death and resurrection of Christ, and entered by faith. These two discussions of this problem must be studied separately, because we must not presume that in Galatians and in Romans Paul follows exactly the same line of reasoning. All Paul's letters speak primarily to those addressed, and deal with particular issues facing a particular church. Thus J. Christiaan Becker insists that Paul be read not as a dogmatic theologian who has a worked-out answer to every major issue, but rather as 'an interpreter of the Gospel who is engaged in a hermeneutic that fits the occasion'.[28] In both epistles Paul is agreed that faith in Christ alone is the basis for salvation and incorporation into the new community, not circumcision or observance of the law. In Galatians, because of the problems raised by the Judaizers, he stresses discontinuity between Israel and the Christian community. In Romans, where he is mainly concerned with the faithfulness of God in relation to the promises made to historic Israel, he stresses the interrelationship between the two communities, and the continuity of God's electing purposes.[29]

Galatians

In Galatians 3 and Romans 4, Abraham features prominently in the argument about the priority of faith, but the logic follows differing paths in these two epistles. In Galatians, Paul's object is to identify believers in Christ as the true children of Abraham and to exclude those who hold that law keeping is demanded of the true children of Abraham.[30] As far as Paul is concerned in Galatians, it is only 'those who believe [who] are the descendants of Abraham'

(3.7). These people are 'blessed', but 'all who rely on the law are under a curse' (v. 10). He undermines the value of the law by showing that it belongs to a different and inferior order to that of the Abrahamic promise, and as such was of temporary importance (vv. 15–18).[31] The boldly stated conclusion to his argument is reached when he declares, 'There is no longer Jew or Greek, there is no longer slave or free, there is no longer male and female; for all of you are one in Christ. And if you belong to Christ, then you are Abraham's offspring, heirs according to the promise' (3.28–9). The apostle is of course not arguing that ethnic, social, and sexual differences are obliterated in Christ, but that these distinctions are no longer of primary importance. The Hagar allegory accentuates the breach with historic Israel even more forcefully (4.21–31). Jews obedient to the law are said to be descendants of the slave girl and in bondage, and to be thrown out (v. 30). In chapter 5, the apostle again insists that Israel's privileges have come to an end when he declares that the essential mark of commitment to the covenant – circumcision – is now of no importance: 'For in Christ neither circumcision nor uncircumcision counts for anything' (v. 6; cf. v. 15).

Paul draws his argument to an end in a final benediction: 'As for those who follow this rule, peace be upon them, and mercy, and upon the Israel of God' (6.16). Those who are concerned to harmonize Paul's teaching and hold that he consistently maintains a special place in the purposes of God for Israel argue that the apostle is blessing two groups, Christians and Jews of one kind or another,[32] the latter alone being called 'the Israel of God'; but this is unlikely. Grammatically it is possible to divide the blessing so as it is addressed to two groups,[33] but it is hard to believe in an epistle where Paul has vehemently argued that being a Jew by birth, keeping the law, and circumcision are of no importance for salvation that he gives a special blessing on Jews and thus recognizes that they stand apart from gentile believers. It is much easier to read this comment rather as the climax of Paul's whole argument against the Judaizers in Galatia.[34] Longenecker suggests that this unusual expression 'the Israel of God', not used elsewhere in the Pauline corpus, and not known in the writings of second temple Judaism, was how the Judaizers described themselves. In his final blessing, Paul bestows this title on all who are part of 'the new creation' (6.16) in Christ by faith. They are the true children of Abraham, who can be properly called 'the Israel of God'.

Romans

It is tempting to begin the discussion of Paul's understanding of
the relationship between the Christian community and Israel in
Romans by turning immediately to chapters 9–11, but some preliminary comment is needed because these chapters are integral to
the whole argument of this epistle; and are in fact an attempt to
answer the questions Paul himself has raised by insisting that the
righteousness of God is now bestowed by faith in Christ and not
earned by works of the law. The indictment of all people as under
the wrath of God because of sin (1.18–3.20) leads Paul to ask as
early as 3.1, 'What advantage has the Jew?' The answering of this
question is not the only reason why Paul wrote this epistle, but it
must be understood as one of his major concerns as he put pen to
paper. In attempting an answer, Paul writes reflectively – in contrast to his impassioned style in Galatians – as he confronts those
whom he sees to be undermining the gospel. He now expresses
himself very carefully. What troubles his mind is the following
question: if God has proved unfaithful to the promise he made to
the descendants of Abraham that they were to be his people, then
can his promise made in Christ to those who believe be trusted?

In Romans 4, Abraham is not introduced to show that believers
in Christ are the true descendants of Abraham as in Galatians, but
to prove that righteousness has always been given on the basis of
faith – thereby showing the continuity of God's workings. In this
argument, the true Jew is one who, like Abraham, accepts the
promises of God by faith. Much more could be said about the
reasoning leading up to chapters 9–11, but this is not demanded
for our purposes. In his argument, in these three chapters of
Romans Paul comes to his basic questions in more than one way:

1 First of all, Paul claims in 9.6–29 that God's word of promise
   to Israel has not failed because 'not all who are descended from
   Israel belong to Israel, and not all are the children of Abraham
   because they are his descendants' (9.6–7). God has always chosen and blessed only a remnant; he never intended the salvation
   of every member of the family of Abraham. Salvation has
   always been a gift of God's grace.

2 He then argues in 9.30–10.21 that as the offer of righteousness
   by faith is to all, if some or many of the people of Israel reject
   this offer, preferring rather to seek their own righteousness

based on law, and they are excluded from receiving the promise, then it is their own fault, not God's. He concludes this section with the question, 'Have they not heard?', to which he replies, 'Indeed they have' (10.18).

These two answers are then followed by two more:

3 He now claims the rejection of the gospel by Jews is only partial (11.1–10), for a remnant has believed (v. 5).

4 And it is only temporary, as the salvation of the gentiles will make Israel jealous and they will then believe (11.11–24). To make this point, the apostle introduces the illustration of the olive tree. The relation of the believing gentiles to Israel is like an olive tree that has had unfruitful branches pruned off, only to have these replaced by grafted-on wild olive branches. The life of the grafted branches comes from the original root, so there is no room for gentiles to boast.

5 Finally, the argument in relation to Israel is drawn to a conclusion by appeal to a revealed 'mystery' (11.25–32). Despite the present 'hardening' that has come upon 'part of Israel, until the full number of the gentiles has come in . . . all Israel will be saved' (11.26). What does Paul mean by this claim? Many answers have been given. Some see this as a promise that the Jewish people will be saved apart from the gospel; others see it as a prediction that through the preaching of the gospel all Jewish people will eventually turn to Christ; and yet others see it as a prophecy that there will be a national turning to Christ when he returns. Most modern commentators, Dunn says, agree that 'Israel', in this statement, 'must mean Israel as a whole, as a people whose corporate identity and wholeness would not be lost even in the event there were some (or indeed many) individual exceptions'.[35] When this will happen is not indicated. Of the various options as to how this will happen, Paul's own Christocentric theology would favour the view that he thought this would come about through the Jews recognizing Jesus as the Messiah, and thus coming to faith.

This conclusion raises the question as to how Paul can still speak of the Christian community as the inheritor of the titles and privileges once belonging to historic Israel, and then in Romans argue that historic Israel as a distinct entity still has a special place in the eternal plan of God. The simplest solution is to suggest that in Romans 11.25–32, Paul allowed his concern to uphold the faithfulness of God and the privileges of Israel to better his logic,[36] but this is not a satisfactory answer. Paul's thinking can be explained more charitably to show its consistency. In these chapters in Romans, Paul sees the drama of salvation history working out sequentially. First, the gospel goes to the Jews and a remnant believe, then it is offered to gentiles and many believe; this eventually provokes the Jews to jealousy, and as a result, sometime in the future 'all Israel' believe – thereby showing that God's electing grace in favour of Israel is in fact irrevocable. This allows Paul to see the Christian community as endowed with all the blessings and privileges of Israel and occupying the place of historic Israel in this present time, and yet to expect that in the end an eschatological salvation of all Israel will take place.[37]

Paul's use of the word church/*ekklēsia*

With this outline of Pauline eschatological and communal thought spelt out, we are now in a position to study Paul's use of the word *ekklēsia*/church. If what has been said is correct, then it is impossible to conceive that Paul thought either that local groups of believers were the primary corporate expression of the Christian faith, or that individual churches were but an aggregate of justified sinners, as many Protestants seem to believe.

The word *ekklēsia* is found 114 times in the New Testament, and 46 of these are in early Paulines. Exactly how Paul understood this term is a difficult question to decide, because competent scholars come to diametrically opposed conclusions. One suspects that all too often prior theological beliefs about the church determine the position taken. These divergent opinions are invariably rooted in competing claims as to what the word *ekklēsia* meant in the *LXX*. Some claim that in the *LXX* it is a technical term meaning 'the eschatological people of God': others that it is a non-technical term, and means no more than 'assembly'.[38] The position taken on this matter invariably sets the agenda for the study of Paul's usage. Those who see the word pregnant with theological content tend to start with texts that speak of the church as a world-wide community (Acts 20.28; 1 Cor. 12.28, 15.9, etc.), and those who take the word simply to refer to Christians who form a local community by regularly assembling together, start with the texts that use the word *ekklēsia* of an actual gathering of believers (1 Cor. 11.18, 14.19, etc.).

In a detailed excursus at the end of this book, I argue that neither understanding of the word *ekklēsia* as given above can be supported by Old Testament and intertestamental writings. It seems that by New Testament times, Greek-speaking Jews usually used this word to refer to an actual assembly of people, but a more theological usage was well established. It had become a term that could designate Israel as God's covenant community. *Ekklēsia* was thus a word with theological potential rather than a technical term. In seeking to let Paul speak for himself, we do not begin with any fixed view of what the word meant for him, or how he used the word. It may well be that even the frequently made distinction between the local and the universal usages are foreign to Paul's own thinking. What we must try to do is let Paul speak for himself. In regard to the starting point, which is so critical if objectivity is to be achieved, the best place to start would seem to be where Paul himself starts.

In recounting his past life as a persecutor, Paul speaks of his attacks on the 'church of God' (Gal. 1.13; 1 Cor. 15.9; cf. Phil. 3.6). Whether this is how the earliest Christians designated themselves, or how Paul designated them, is not a fundamental issue. The important thing to note is that Paul himself calls those whom he persecuted 'the church of God'. He starts with the belief that those before him in Christ were rightly called 'the *ekklēsia*/church'. If this is where Paul begins, then this is where we should begin if we want to understand his usage accurately.

Yet before we turn to this matter it needs to be noted that the early Christians, as a general rule, met in houses.[39] It was not until the middle of the third century that the Christians began to own property in which to meet. The size of the homes of that day determined the maximum number of Christians able to gather together at any one time. Murphy O'Connor argues that even the largest of homes would have been stretched to the limit to accommodate fifty people.[40] The most likely number for most home gatherings, therefore, was between twenty and thirty. Thus once the number of Christians multiplied in any given city or location, the number of house groups would also have multiplied. At Corinth we can identify at least three 'house churches', led respectively by Stephanas, Crispus, and Gaius, but there are hints of several others as well, and at Rome a number of house churches can also be identified.[41] The long list of people greeted by Paul in the last chapter of his epistle to the Romans almost certainly includes many who were leaders/hosts of house churches.

The earliest Jewish believers as the church of God

On a number of occasions, Paul speaks of those before him in Christ as 'the church'. Twice he says he 'persecuted the church of God' (1 Cor. 15.9; Gal. 1.13), and once 'the church' (Phil. 3.6). He also speaks of 'the churches of Judea' (Gal. 1.22) and, with some variation in expression, of 'the churches of God in Christ Jesus that are in Judea' (1 Thess. 2.14; cf. 1 Cor. 11.16; 2 Thess. 1.4). Paul obviously held that the Christian community in Jerusalem, and the other Jewish Christian communities in Palestine,[42] were rightly called 'church' or 'church of God'. Some scholars argue that here the apostle is using the title that the earliest Jewish believers used of themselves,[43] but others are not convinced by this argument.[44] The former seems very likely, but as the argument cannot be proved we make nothing of it. Our case is simply that this is how Paul designated the earliest Jewish believers.

In calling those whom he persecuted 'the *ekklēsia*/church [of God]', Paul makes it clear that for him this term refers to an identifiable group of people with an ongoing existence. 'The church' is what we would call a community. When Paul speaks of persecuting 'the church', he means he persecuted Christians. This understanding of the word is dictated by the context. 'Persecuting the church' stands in opposition in each case to faithfulness to 'Judaism'.[45] Those persecuted were not one congregation designated 'a church' because they met together. Luke suggests that by the time Paul began as a persecutor, there were many thousands of believers – they would have needed St Peter's Basilica to assemble together! What is more, those whom Paul persecuted were not only the Christians in Jerusalem, as the apostle himself makes clear (Gal. 1.23) and Luke explains (Acts 9.3). Paul's usage also indicates that no distinction should be made between the expression 'the church of God' (1 Cor. 15.9; Gal. 1.13) and the abbreviated form 'the church' (Phil. 3.6).[46] The same rule as used in reading the synoptic Gospels applies. 'The Kingdom of God' and 'the Kingdom' mean exactly the same thing. Little should be made also of the use of the singular and plural forms of the word *ekklēsia*; grammar rather than theology explains this. When Paul is thinking of Christians generally, one entity, he uses the singular: when he is thinking of particular communities in more than one location, several entities, he uses the plural. However, these conclusions only allude to how Paul used the term *ekklēsia* when speaking of the earliest Jewish believers. This does not determine how he uses the word in every other instance. A survey of examples of other uses in the early Paulines therefore follows.

Pauline usage

1 All the Christians in one location

When addressing a specific group of Christians, Paul can locate them geographically and theologically. Thus he writes to 'the church of God that is in Corinth . . . in Christ Jesus' (1 Cor. 1.2), and to 'the church of the Thessalonians in God the Father and in the Lord Jesus Christ' (1 Thess. 1.1; cf. 2 Thess. 1.1). In this latter case, Donfield argues that both 'ins' should be given their full incorporative force.[47] The Christians of Thessalonica are not those called to a temporary assembly, but to a permanent union with God the Father and Jesus Christ. In some cases, however (e.g. 2 Cor. 1.1; Rom. 16.1), Paul only mentions a geographical marker. The theological status of those called the church is possibly brought out most clearly in 1 Corinthians 1.2. In writing to the Corinthians, he gives this one group of people three titles. They are 'the church of God in Corinth', 'those sanctified in Christ Jesus', and 'saints by God's call'. As we have already noted, the last two titles were once the sole preserve of Israel. In designating these Christians in this way, Paul is identifying them as true Israel. If this is the case, then the first title, 'the church of God', must surely bear the same force. In this address to the Corinthians Paul is calling this believing community the (true) people of God. In the two epistles to the Corinthians, the two epistles to the Thessalonians, and in the epistle to the Galatians, those addressed are called 'the church', but when writing to the Christians in Rome and in Philippi Paul changes the terminology and addresses them as 'the saints' (Rom. 1.7; Phil. 1.1). Nothing should be made of this change in wording, for, as we have just seen, Paul can use this title as a synonym for 'the church of God'.[48] To be saints, or those called, depends solely on God's initiative. It is a status given by

God. There is no reason to suggest any difference for the word *ekklēsia*.

Whether or not those called 'the church' in a particular location ever 'assembled' together in their entirety is of no consequence. What has been noted so far does not suggest that it was by human association that the church was constituted in one place, but by divine action. As the largest of homes held no more than fifty people, and several house churches are envisaged in Corinth, combined meetings seem unlikely.[49] To read the address as if Paul has in mind one medium- to large-sized congregation who regularly assemble together is to impose our contemporary understanding of the parish church on to the text.

Many discussions of Paul's usage of the word *ekklēsia* list the plural occurrences as a separate category, but this is not helpful in clarifying his thought. When the apostle thinks of Christians in one specific location, he uses the singular; when he thinks of Christians in more than one specific location, or of various churches with something in common, he uses the plural. The plural *ekklēsiai* is only found once in the *LXX* (Ps. 26.12), but Paul uses it regularly. He adopts the plural most frequently to designate separate groups of Christians, each one residing in a particular city or town, but within a specific area. Thus he speaks of 'the churches of Galatia' (1 Cor. 16.1; Gal. 1.2), 'the churches of Asia' (1 Cor. 16.19), 'the churches of Macedonia' (2 Cor. 8.1), and 'the churches of Judea' (Gal. 1.22). However, he also uses the plural to refer to a number of churches that in each case have something in common other than geographical location. Thus he speaks of: 'the churches of the gentiles' (Rom. 16.4), 'the churches of the saints' (1 Cor. 14.33), and 'the churches of God' (1 Cor. 11.16; cf. 2 Thess. 1.4) – the last two examples are probably references to Jewish churches.

2 *All Christians on earth*

In a number of places Paul simply speaks of 'the church' or 'the church of God', without any geographical marker or other circumscription. Often he is addressing those to whom he is writing (e.g. 1 Cor. 6.4, 14.5, 12), but this is not always the case. One particularly important verse is 1 Corinthians 10.32, where the apostle says, 'Give no offence to Jews or Greeks or to the church of

God.' The 'church of God' in this context must refer to something analogous to 'Jews or Greeks'. Paul is therefore speaking of three recognizable groups of people found dispersed in the world.[50] If he had said, 'Give no offence to Jews or Greeks or to Christians' (a word he never uses), then the meaning would be much the same. The main difference is that the expression 'the church of God' is potentially more theologically pregnant with meaning, for it can imply that believers are in fact the people of God. F. F. Bruce quite correctly sees Paul here defining the church in such a way that second-century writers drew the right conclusions when they described Christians collectively as a 'new race', or a 'third race', which is neither Jew nor Greek.[51] It would seem that 1 Corinthians 12.28 implies much the same thing. Paul says, 'God has appointed in the church first apostles, second teachers, third prophets' (the plural is used in each case). As these are ministries given to the whole Christian community on earth, not just to the Christian community in Corinth, the word *ekklēsia* must imply the so-called universal meaning in this context. The point Paul is making is that God 'appointed' these leaders 'in the church': their ministry is God's gift to the whole Christian community, not just for the Christians in Corinth.[52]

3 *A small Christian group who regularly meet together in a home*

Just as ten or more male Jews meeting in a home could form a synagogue, so too Paul considered a group of Christians meeting in a home an *ekklēsia*/church (Rom. 16.5; 1 Cor. 16.19; Philem. 2). A home setting was the normal context for the early Christians to meet; here, teaching, prophecy, and mutual ministry took place and the Eucharist was celebrated. There were no doubt fraternal relationships with those in other house churches in the one city, and possibly when numbers were small, combined meetings may have taken place; but these house churches were not sub-groups of some larger organized church, like home groups may be today. In Paul's epistles this use of the word *ekklēsia* refers to what Protestants would call today 'the local church' or 'the congregation'. Certainly those who belonged to these house churches gained a sense of corporate identity by the fact that they were all Christians, and because they regularly met together, but Paul saw the unity of each of these house church congregations in far more profound terms than this. They were an expression of the body of Christ, corporately united with their Lord and united together by the Spirit. This assertion is based on Paul's own teaching on the church as the body of Christ, but we see in small measure this corporate identity being expressed in the way Paul speaks of particular house churches when he has cause to mention them. Each small group he envisages as a unitary entity. He can thus address the church as if it is a person, or speak of it as acting like a person. For example, he sends a greeting to the church that meets in the home of Priscilla and Aquila (Rom. 16.3–4), and passes on a greeting from the church hosted by the same couple at an earlier period when they were in Corinth (1 Cor. 16.19), and he writes to 'the church in your house' in the epistle to Philemon (Philem. 2).

4 *A Christian gathering*

In a limited number of examples, all in the later chapters of 1 Corinthians, Paul uses *ekklēsia* in almost a classical Greek sense, alluding to Christians actually assembled (11.18, 14.19, 28, 34, 35). He speaks of what they should do when they come together 'in church' – that is, 'in assembly'. Those who minimize the theological content in the word *ekklēsia* usually find here the key to Paul's use of this word.[53] It is argued that from this usage Paul comes to think of the church as 'those who assemble'. This argument is not convincing. Already in 1 Corinthians, Paul has identified the church as true Israel (1.2), as a distinct people in this world (10.32), and as the body of Christ (12.12–13). These verses therefore mean 'when you gather together as God's people, when the body of Christ is actualized . . . this is how you should behave'.[54]

The one and the many

How these different uses of the one word relate to each other has generated a lot of discussion. Basic to the various competing opinions is the thought that Paul conceives of the *ekklēsia*/church essentially in two forms, the local church and the universal church. In Roman Catholic dogma, the absolute, 'the church', the so-called universal usage, is taken to refer to the 'one holy Catholic Church' over which the Pope presides, and that can be distinguished from local or national (Roman Catholic) churches presided over by a bishop, which consist of many parishes. Not surprisingly, non-Roman Catholics have rejected this opinion, because it denies that they can be church in any sense of the word. Paul's own writings give no support to this view; nowhere does he define the church as an organized, hierarchically structured institution broken up into geographical areas under the leadership of one person. In Protestant theology, the most widely accepted view is that 'the church', while referring to all Christians on earth, is somehow an almost Platonic reality as well. Each local church can be thought of as a particular manifestation of the one ultimate and eternal church.[55] A variant on the mainstream Protestant position, mentioned already in the first chapter, is that the universal uses of *ekklēsia* refer entirely to a heavenly church in continuous session.[56] Behind this heavenly interpretation lies a radical congregational and individualistic view of Christianity. Nothing on earth but the local congregation can be considered church, and this church is but an assembly of believers. It has no reality when not meeting; is not manifest on earth in any form but the congregation; and cannot act corporately. Thus, for example, Donald Robinson argues that only individuals can evangelize, and that the church as church has no evangelistic function.[57]

It is quite obvious that even in his earliest epistles Paul has a clear sense of Christians as citizens of heaven. He assumes the common Jewish eschatological belief that what lay ahead in the age to come already existed 'above'.[58] The present heavenly status of the Christian was an expression of Paul's realized eschatology always held in tension with his futuristic eschatological expectations, closely connected with the return of Christ. Yet it is altogether another thing to argue that all the so-called universal uses of *ekklēsia* refer exclusively to a continuous assembly of believers in heaven. Such an argument confuses two distinct strains of thought in the apostle's mind: the church on earth and the believers' true home in heaven. The heavenly perspective first appears in Galatians 4.21–31, where Paul speaks of the heavenly Jerusalem, but in this context he does not use the word *ekklēsia*; and, what is more, he sets in contrast believers on earth and the Jerusalem above that is their 'mother' (v. 26). In Philippians 3.20–1, the present heavenly status of believers comes into focus more clearly. In speaking to Christians, Paul says, 'our commonwealth is in heaven, and from it we await a saviour, the Lord Jesus Christ'. The present tense of the Greek verb *huparchei*, translated 'is', underlines that this heavenly citizenship is a reality here and now; but again there is no mention of the word *ekklēsia* anywhere in this context, and no suggestion that Christians are *assembled* in heaven. The only point made is that believers on earth, who are awaiting the return of Christ from heaven, should view the world above as their true home. The impossibility of this exclusively heavenly understanding of the universal uses of the word *ekklēsia* is, however, most clearly seen via a study of the actual usage in Paul. The church of God to which offence must not be given (1 Cor. 10.32); the church in which God has appointed apostles, prophets, and teachers (1 Cor. 12.28), and the church that Paul persecuted (1 Cor. 15.9; Gal. 1.13; Phil. 3.6), simply cannot be an entirely other-worldly reality. The Jews and the Greeks to whom offence must not be given are on earth, and so too must be the church in this triad; church leaders are not appointed to serve in a heavenly church, but in an earthly church, and Paul did not persecute a church in heaven, but one on earth, by 'entering house after house' (Acts 8.3). This is not to deny that the church may have a heavenly dimension made up of those in Christ who have already died, though little is said about this by Paul; however, it is a complete rejection of the thesis that all the so-called universal uses of *ekklēsia* refer exclusively to a heavenly assembly.

One community, expressed in more than one way

How, then, can the distinctive and varied Christian uses of *ekklēsia* in Paul's earliest epistles be understood and related to one another? The answer lies in giving the most appropriate modern English equivalent to this Greek word. In contemporary English it corresponds most closely to the word 'community'. Community is a word that designates people who hold something in common, but not necessarily with the same level of personal involvement, and *ekklēsia* seems to parallel this almost perfectly. Thus we can speak of a nuclear family as a household community; or of all the people who live in one area as the 'Kensington' (or whatever) community; of all Australians as the Australian community; and even of all men and women as the human community. If several different concrete examples of any of these communities are in mind, then the plural is used. Thus it is proper to speak of the Italian community in Australia (singular), but of the Italian communities (plural) in particular locations in Australia. Likewise, Paul can speak of a household (Christian) community/*ekklēsia*, or of a city-wide (Christian) community/*ekklēsia*, or of all believers on earth as *the* (Christian) community/*ekklēsia*. There is only one Christian community called into being by God in Christ that Paul sometimes speaks of generally (in its entirety), or more specifically as it is seen in particular places, or as it is personally experienced in a household setting. If he wants to speak of this community as it is realized in several locations, he uses the plural. Institutional, Platonic, or heavenly categories are not needed to explain Paul's varied usage of the word *ekklēsia*, and all of these suggestions actually misrepresent the apostle's thought. So also do the categories 'universal' and 'local' (church). Paul simply does not make this distinction.[59] For him, there was but one Christian community. Sometimes he thought of it as that ever-growing number of believers throughout the Roman empire; sometimes he thought of it as all the Christians in one town or city; and sometimes as those who formed a house church. Believers were the *ekklēsia* (the Christian community) by definition because they shared a common life in Christ. Paul expected that those in Christ would meet together to express their communal life, but assembling together did not make them church. Indeed, most of the uses of the word *ekklēsia* in Paul are used of Christians generally, with no thought that they all met face to face at least sometimes. This means, then, that the meaning 'assembly' in these instances has completely disappeared.

Church life

The point has been made already that Paul's converts generally met in small groups in the homes of (mainly) better-off believers whose dwellings could accommodate them.[60] This setting determined to a large degree the nature of their communal meetings. The owners of such homes in most cases would have continued to exert some leadership because of their social status, and because they were the 'head' of the extended family that formed the nucleus of this little community. It is probably such people Paul has in mind when he tells the Thessalonians, 'to respect those who labour among you and are over you in the Lord' (1 Thess. 5.12), and the Corinthians, to 'be subject' to Stephanas and others like him. In due course, it seems as if those in charge of home groups, who at first had no title, were called overseers (*episkopoi*) and their assistants, servants (*diakonoi*) (Phil. 1.1). This structured leadership obviously did not provide all that was needed for the edification and direction of the churches, for prophecy was encouraged (1 Thess. 5.19–20; 1 Cor. 14.1ff), and when the group met, Paul says, 'each one has a hymn, a lesson, a revelation, a tongue, or an interpretation' (1 Cor. 14.26). The picture thus emerges of small house church meetings where there was some formal leadership, but participation by everyone present was a possibility. In these early epistles of St Paul, elders and ordination are never mentioned.

The involvement of women seems to have been welcomed, but apparently it raised certain strains. Paul's argument that the local church is like a human body suggests that each member, man or woman, had the freedom to contribute and was given equality of consideration. This is matched by his praise of a number of women involved in active Christian leadership (Rom. 16.1, 3, 6, 7, 12, 15; Phil. 4.2–3), and his acceptance of women prophesying in church (1 Cor. 11.5). Yet 1 Corinthians 11.2ff suggests that guidelines for the contribution of women needed to be worked out. Paul's argument seems to be in this very difficult passage that women could lead in prayer and prophecy when the church met, but they had to maintain cultural norms and be seen as women.[61] Even more difficult is the command in 1 Corinthians 14.34–6 that women keep silent in church. There is some doubt as to the authenticity of these words – a case can be made that they were added by a later scribe[62] – and much uncertainty as to what exactly is being asked of wives. If Paul wrote this paragraph it may be that he was only forbidding married women from asking disruptive questions in church: 'Let them ask their husbands at home,' he says.

In this home setting, the Eucharist was celebrated in the context of a meal (1 Cor. 11.21–2). This recalled the death of Christ (1 Cor. 11.24–6), and the apostle says that it is a participation (*koinonia*) in his body and blood (1 Cor. 10.14–16). In Romans 6.3, he speaks of believers being baptized into (*eis*) Christ, which is a reminder that, for Paul, Christ is understood corporately, as the representative head of the new community now being called into existence. Baptism is thus to be seen in Paul as more than the outward demonstration of faith in Christ made by an individual. It signifies rather incorporation into Christ, and therefore into the body of Christ. In 1 Corinthians 12.13, it is explained as nothing less than drinking of the one Spirit given to every believer.[63]

For Paul, the gathering together of the church was of great importance, for this was the main means of 'building up' the body of Christ. Some seventeen times he uses the noun *oikodomē*, or the verb *oikodomeō*, which literally means 'to build up', but is generally translated as 'edification'.[64] This took place mainly as Christians ministered to one another. In English we call such gatherings 'worship', but Paul avoids using any of the cultic terminology of the Old Testament when speaking of Christian assemblies. He wants to emphasize that Christian 'worship' is altogether different from temple worship. When he does use Jewish cultic terminology, he applies it to the whole of the Christian life (Rom. 12.2; Phil. 3.3), or to his own ministry for the gospel (Rom. 1.9, 15.16).

The first urban Christians

Paul more than anyone else was responsible for the movement of Christianity from the world of Judaism to the Greco-Roman world.[65] It was he who had to work out strategies not only for evangelism in the cities he visited, but also for the nurturing, leadership, and group life of his converts. He utilized the homes of more affluent converts, so that believers would be able to meet together and build one another up in the faith. He affirmed the leadership of those responsible for each group, and he continued to give supervisory direction by personal visits, sending delegates and by letters. Where there were disciplinary or doctrinal problems, he acted swiftly and decisively. He clearly saw that an ordered communal life, unity in diversity, and a growing understanding of what it meant to be a Christian, would further the work of the gospel.

In doing these things, Paul was encouraging institutionalization. He was deliberately promoting the consolidation of the beliefs and social structures of these early Christians. This he did because he saw clearly that institutional form would give stability to the communal life and witness of his converts. In these early Paulines, we see the process in its infancy. Charismatic freedom in communal meetings is still to the fore and doctrinal and ethical issues are still being worked out. It is here that Margaret Mac-Donald's schema illuminates, for she categorizes this stage as 'community building institutionalisation'.[66] What we see in these early Pauline epistles is a reflection of the Christian community in the initial period; further development was still to take place.

Chapter 6

The Church in the Middle and Later Paulines

It has been accepted as a premise that a development in thought, especially in relation to the church, can be seen in the epistles ascribed to the apostle Paul. Colossians and Ephesians (what we have called the middle Paulines) expand on what is found in the epistles just considered (the early Paulines) by highlighting the unity and universality of the church, and the Pastorals (what we have called the late Paulines) on the structure and permanence of the church as an institution. These epistles may be grouped into these categories because in each case the letters bracketed together reflect a marked degree of homogeneity in theology and outlook. In studying these writings, it is important to let them speak for themselves.

Colossians and Ephesians

Colossians and Ephesians are very closely related in language, style, and content. Both are written to gentile converts (Col. 2.11, 13; Eph. 2.11, 12, 4.17); both speak of Christ as the 'head' of all creation and of the church (Col. 1.18, 2.10, 19; Eph. 1.22, 4.15, 5.23); both hold that the church is a universal community, a new humanity (Col. 3.9; Eph. 2.15, 4.24), and both emphasize realized eschatology – the end-time has already broken into history (Col. 1.11–13, 2.10, 3.1; Eph. 1.3, 13, 19, 2.6) – and thus they see eschatology more often in spatial terms (here on earth/there in heaven) than in temporal terms (now/then) (Col. 1.5, 13, 3.1–4; Eph. 1.3, 20–3, 2.6). There are differences, nevertheless, particularly so in regard to the amount of attention given to Christology and ecclesiology respectively. Bruce makes the point succinctly

125

when he says, 'Colossians expounds on the cosmic role of Christ', whereas Ephesians expounds on 'the cosmic role of the church'.[1]

Colossians

The epistle to the Colossians is written to a Christian community that the apostle perceives to be under threat from false teaching, which 'Paul' considers to be a denial of the gospel Epaphras had brought them.[2] The exact nature of the Colossian heresy is not spelt out, but it clearly called into question the Lordship of Christ, encouraged speculative philosophy (2.8), and involved ascetic practices (2.16–17, 21–3).[3] Paul's rebuttal is essentially Christological, but in proclaiming Christ as the head of all creation, seen and unseen, he also speaks of him as the head of the church.

In the opening chapter, Christ's Lordship is proclaimed in the so-called 'Christ Hymn' of verses 15–20, which, as the name suggests, is thought to have been a pre-Pauline hymn or confession taken over and modified in some details by the apostle. Here the elevated status of Christ and his unique redemptive role are given equal emphasis. In speaking of his status, Paul points to his role in creation: 'He is the image of the invisible God, the first born of all creation; for in him all things in heaven and on earth were created . . . he himself is before all things, and in him all things hold together. He is the head of the body, the church; he is the beginning, the first born from the dead, so that he might come to have first place in everything . . .' (1.15–18). And when speaking of Christ's work, Paul thinks of it in terms of cosmic and personal reconciliation, having as its goal the establishment of a community at peace with God, called to be holy: 'Through him God was pleased to reconcile to himself all things, whether on earth or in heaven, making peace by the blood of his cross. And you who were once estranged and hostile in mind, doing evil deeds, he has now reconciled in his fleshly body through death, so as to present you holy and blameless and irreproachable before him' (1.20–2).

Christ stands over all, having triumphed even over the spiritual principalities and powers. As part of this bold declaration, Christ is proclaimed 'the head of the body, the church' (1.18), thereby intimately connecting Christology and ecclesiology. The church is the place, says Lohse, 'where Christ here and now realizes his world-wide Lordship'.[4] Thus while this 'hymn' is cosmic in scope, the application narrows down firstly to the church, and then to the reconciliation of men and women accomplished in Christ which makes the church a possibility. The Greek word *kephalē*, translated 'head' in this verse, clearly alludes primarily to Christ's rule over his people, but the head–body connection also highlights the organic union that exists between Christ and his church.[5] Yet the body metaphor in Colossians is understood in a quite different way than it is in 1 Corinthians 12.14–26 and Romans 12.3–8, where the unity and diversity of the members of the congregation is the point, and the head is but one member. In Colossians, the head is distinct from, and over, the church, and the church is all God's people. Paul also speaks of the church as the body of Christ in Colossians 1.24 when describing his labours for the gospel as part of the sufferings to be endured in the last days; in 2.19 when he speaks of 'the head from whom the whole body . . . grows with a growth that comes from God', and in 3.15–16, in his exhortation that peace prevail in 'the one body'.

Virtually all commentators take these references to the *ekklēsia*/church in 1.18 and 24 (and all the uses of the word *ekklēsia* in Ephesians) as referring to the world-wide Christian community, the universal church, whom God 'has rescued from the power of darkness and transferred to the rule of his beloved Son' (1.13), but a significant dissenting opinion comes from a small group of scholars who trained at Moore Theological College, Sydney, under Dr Broughton Knox and Dr Donald Robinson – later Archbishop of Sydney. In published works Robert Banks, Peter O'Brien and Bill Dumbrell, taking up the ideas of their mentors, argue that these texts speak exclusively of a heavenly church/assembly.[6] They insist that the word *ekklēsia*/church simply means an 'assembly' (in the act of meeting), and in Christian usage refers only to: (1) Christians as they meet on earth, or by extension to a local congregation who gain a corporate identity by meeting together, or (2) a heavenly assembly continuously in session – and to nothing else. As these two references do not allude to localized gatherings on earth, then the heavenly assembly must be in mind. From this, the conclusion follows that the only reality on earth that can be called 'church' is the local congregation. An exclusively congregational understanding of the church is thus found even in Colossians and Ephesians. In support of their thesis, these scholars note that in Colossians and Ephesians Christians are thought of as raised with Christ and already members of a heavenly world (1.18, 3.1; Eph. 1.3, 22, 23, 2.5–6, etc.).

However, this claim simply does not make sense of how Colossians (or Ephesians) uses the word *ekklēsia*. The difficulties with this view are brought out by O'Brien himself in his commentary, for many of his statements about the *ekklēsia/* church are inconsistent with his own thesis. For example, in his exegetical comments on the opening verses of this epistle, he admits that the title given to these Christians, 'the saints', means virtually the same as the title 'the church/*ekklēsia* of God', as both terms are in apposition in 1 Corinthians 1.2. He then adds that the saints 'are the called and elect community of the end time'[7] – that is, all Christians, I presume, since he accepts that the title 'the saints' refers to Christians generally. In his comments on 1.18, where it is said that Christ 'is the head of the body, the church', he says, 'in this context headship over the body refers to Christ's control of *his people . . .*'[8] Then in explaining Paul's sufferings for 'his body, that is the church', he says, 'though presently exalted in heaven Christ continues to suffer in his members, and not least in Paul himself'.[9] In these three places alone, O'Brien admits unreflectively that the term *ekklēsia/*church refers to 'the community of the end time' (on earth), 'the people' (of God) in this world, and all the members of the body who are even now suffering. Yet his most telling betrayal of his own thesis is made in his explanation of 1.15ff, where he says, 'Paul affirms that Christ is the head of the body, that is, *the church*. That headship, pointing to an organic and living relationship with *his people,* . . . It is the risen Christ who . . . is the founder of *a new humanity.*'[10] If the universal *ekklēsia/*church is the body of Christ, God's people and the new humanity, then it is the Christian family on earth, though it might also be thought to include some who have died and are now in heaven.

It must also be asked how a heavenly church could suffer (1.24)? Or how a heavenly church could grow (2.19)? Or why Paul should plead for love, harmony, and peace in the body – that is, the church – if he was thinking only of a heavenly gathering? Two errors are inherent in this thesis put forward by Banks and O'Brien, and others who follow them. The first is the assumption that the Greek word *ekklēsia*, as used in the New Testament, always carries the meaning 'assembly', and the second is that it is only possible to speak of 'the church' when the actual word is used. In the first instance, the substitution test for meaning alone shows that 'assembly' is an inadequate definition of the word *ekklēsia* as used in this epistle (and in most other places in the New

Testament). In Colossians 1.18 and 1.24, you can substitute for the word 'church', 'the Christian community', and it makes good sense, but substituting 'heavenly assembly' makes little sense of what Paul is saying. In the second instance, attempts to separate off one word, *ekklēsia*/church, as if it referred to a reality that is not, and cannot be, designated in any other way is called into question by the general rules of semantics. Whatever *ekklēsia*/ church means, the concept it denotes must be able to be expressed by other words, groups of words, or metaphors. One of these in Colossians is undisputedly *sōma*/body; another that O'Brien admits to is 'the saints', which in Colossians 1.2 is equated with 'the faithful brethren', but there are others. In each of the places where the word 'church', or the 'body of Christ', understood as the church, is used, other terms are found in the same context that obviously refer to the same reality. In 1.18ff, the church consists of all those reconciled to God by Christ's death. In 2.19ff, the church as the body of Christ is those who have died 'with Christ'. In 3.12ff, the church as the body of Christ are those who are 'God's chosen ones, holy and beloved' – all terms once used of Israel as the people of God. The concept alluded to in all these examples is the Christian community. The word *ekklēsia*/church speaks of this identifiable group of people on this earth, and so do all the other terms or expressions just given.

Yet besides the two so-called universal uses of the word *ekklēsia*/ church in 1.18 and 1.24, the word also appears in 4.15 and 4.16 in reference to particular churches (the so-called local usage). In 4.16, the recipients of the epistle are told to make sure it is sent on to be read 'in the church of the Laodiceans'. This church is not only 'those who assemble', but *the Christian community in Laodicea*, as the other titles given to this entity in the immediate context make clear. In verse 13, this group is called 'those in Laodicea', and in verse 14, 'the brethren in Laodicea'. The three designations all refer to the Christians in this one city. These Christians in the neighbouring city of Laodicea, as in Colossae, met in small house groups as they did elsewhere,[11] and these sub-groupings were also designated by the word *ekklēsia*/church. In these uses the word is used of a particular Christian community that meets in the home of a particular person. How many house churches existed in Colossae is not known, but two are explicitly named: the church that meets in the home of Nympha (Col. 4.16) and the church that meets in the home of Philemon (Philem. 2)

(Philemon lived in Colossae). It seems, then, that rather than *ekklēsia*/church being a word in Colossians that exclusively means 'assembly' and is used only of Christians actually assembled on earth or in heaven, the word in this epistle carries the sense 'the Christian community', and it can have three applications: to the whole Christian community, to a city-wide Christian community, and to a home-centred Christian community.

The fact that one of these house churches named is hosted almost certainly by a woman is significant.[12] It means that at this stage of the mission to the gentile world, women were allowed positions of authority and leadership. Nympha, like the men who hosted house churches, would have been a person of some social standing and wealth who had a large home. She was probably a widow who owned land or managed a business, who was the 'head' of an extended family including blood relations, employees, and slaves. It is unlikely that when the church met in her home that she would have subordinated herself to socially inferior males. In that social setting it would have been expected that she would be deferred to in the same way as her husband, if he were present. This liberated stance towards the leadership of women stands somewhat in tension with Paul's more conservative advice to women, children, and slaves seen in the so-called 'household code' given for the first time in the New Testament in this epistle (3.18—4.1).[13] Here Paul offers practical advice to those living in an extended family setting which reflects the social mores of that age but points beyond them by distinctively giving reciprocal directions to husbands, fathers, and masters. The apostle accepts that the gospel liberates, but he advises that as a general rule prevailing social structuring should be honoured so that outsiders are not offended (4.5). In our age, when different standards prevail in secular culture, the advice would need to differ if the abiding principle enshrined in these codes is a concern that Christian behaviour does not offend and become a hindrance to the acceptance of the gospel.

No doubt there was much variation in the way house churches operated, but to some extent these house church hosts, whether they were a man or woman, would have functioned analogously to the leader of house synagogue, the so-called *archisunagōgos* (synagogue ruler).[14] Those holding this position presided over meetings and invited people to participate, but did not lead worship as ordained ministers do today. There is, however, no mention of office bearers, or named leadership positions in this epistle, apart from Paul (who is called an apostle) (1.1).[15] The one little glimpse we get of house church meetings implies that informal ministry to one another characterized Christian gatherings at Colossae. After exhorting the Colossians to be kind, patient, and loving to one another (3.12ff), Paul says, 'let the word of God dwell in you richly; teach and admonish *one another* in all wisdom; and with gratitude in your hearts sing psalms, hymns and spiritual songs to God' (3.16). This mutual ministry was augmented, it seems, by the visits of itinerant Pauline associates such as Tychicus and Onesimus (4.7–9), and possibly Archippus (4.17); and, we would argue, presided over by the host of the house church.

The eschatological people of God

In Colossians, as in the earlier Paulines, lofty titles once used of Israel as God's own people are transferred to the Christian community, the church. They are called the saints (*hoi hagioi*) (1.2, 4, 12, 22, 26, 3.12), 'God's chosen ones' (*eklektoi*) and 'the beloved' (*agapēmenoi*) (3.12).[16] Yet what is new in Colossians is the thought that the Jew–gentile division has been transcended or cancelled. The apostle boldly affirms that those in Christ 'have been clothed with the new self, which is being renewed in knowledge according to the image of its creator', and 'there is no longer Greek and Jew, circumcision and uncircumcision, barbarian, Scythian, slave and free; but Christ is all, and in all!' (3.10–11). The wording of verse 11 reflects Galatians 3.28 and 1 Corinthians 12.13, but the description of the church as 'the new self' (NRSV) or 'the new man' (RSV) (v. 10), which is to be understood primarily in a corporate sense as referring to the new humanity ruled by Adam's counterpart, Jesus Christ, is a development in Pauline thought.[17] The church is a new creation replacing the old order that was characterized by the division between Jew and gentile. In Christ, there is now one people of God made up of believing Jews and gentiles.

In Colossians, as was mentioned earlier, the emphasis falls on realized eschatology. Future eschatology is not forgotten (3.4, 6, 24), but this hope recedes into the background. Paul stresses that the end-time realities have broken into history and are known in the church. In the epistle to the Romans, believers die and are buried with Christ in baptism (Rom.6.3–5), whereas in Colossians they are buried and raised with Christ (2.12). They therefore are already 'alive together with him [Christ]' (2.13), having been 'raised with Christ' (3.1) and made recipients of the life to come (3.4). As a corollary to this, Colossians speaks very starkly of the 'transfer' from the community ruled by Satan to the community ruled by Christ, even sometimes in cosmic terms. Paul says, 'He [God the Father] has rescued us from the power of darkness and transferred us into the kingdom of his beloved Son' (1.13); 'you who were once estranged and hostile in mind, doing evil deeds, he [Christ] has now reconciled' (1.21); 'these are the ways you once followed . . . but now you must get rid of all such things . . .' (3.7). This new status means that believers 'have come to fullness in him [Christ]' (2.9). Just as Christ is indwelt with the fullness of God, so the Christian community is filled with the fullness of Christ. There is a completeness in both cases. Moreover, the one who fills them is 'the head of every principality and power' (2.10), and he who has triumphed over the evil forces (2.15). The victory of Christ over spiritual forces opposed to God, which according to apocalyptic Judaism was to happen on the last day (cf. Rev. 19.11–16, etc.), is here proclaimed as an accomplished fact. The Christian community, the church, in Colossians is the eschatological people of God, the new Israel.

Ephesians

The epistle to the Ephesians was written after Colossians, reflecting many of its ideas, but also some development of thought. In Colossians, for example, the church is considered as a total entity, with all believers corporately bound together (1.18–24), but the writer can still speak of the local church (4.15, 16). In Ephesians, in contrast, the word *ekklēsia*/church, in all nine occurrences,[18] refers exclusively to all believers bound together as a total entity, as do all the many corporate images used of the reality envisaged by this word.[19] The church, which is most commonly described as the body of Christ, is part of the grand redemptive purposes of God, involving heaven and earth. Nowhere else in the New Testament do we find such a lofty ecclesiology. Some studies of the church in Ephesians proceed by considering the major ecclesiological terms and concepts thematically; but in what follows, this topic is pursued as it unfolds sequentially in the text of the epistle.[20] However, first a comment is needed about how the author saw the world.

In the earlier Pauline epistles the existence of a heavenly world is presupposed, as was noted, but in Ephesians this dimension comes into clearer focus. As in Jewish apocalyptic literature and at Qumran, the thought is that what lies in the future already exists in the heavens above. As far as the author of Ephesians is concerned, Christ's death on the cross and the Christian community on earth, the church, brought into being through this event, must be understood in relation to this unseen world. God's plan is to sum up all things in Christ, 'things in heaven and things on earth' (1.10), and the church on earth makes known 'the wisdom of God' to the 'rulers and authorities in the heavenly places' (3.10). 'In the heavenly places' is a recurring formula (1.3, 1.20, 2.26, 3.10, 6.12), which alludes to the heavenly world where God dwells, Christ rules, good and evil spirits exist, and where the believer already has a home.[21] In Christ, men and women participate here and now in the blessings of this world 'above', although they remain very much on this earth 'below'. This mode of thinking is part of the realized eschatology that dominates in Ephesians, and to a large degree determines its ecclesiology. The Christian community is where the powers of the age to come are now realized. In this epistle there are no explicit comments about the return of Christ, although there are several references to a future consummation (cf. 1.14, 4.30, 5.5, 6.13). The early Pauline 'already' and 'not yet' tension is still found, but the emphasis falls on the former, so that the new creation 'in Christ', now known in the church, takes centre stage.[22]

Communal blessings 'in Christ' (1.1–14)

Ephesians begins by addressing the Christians of Ephesus as 'the saints' (1.1), a title that we have noted in the Old Testament designated Israel as the people of God. Then follows a long benediction (1.3–14), which introduces many of the key terms and ideas basic to this epistle. In this prayer filled with praise of what God has accomplished in Christ, Paul enumerates all the blessings that have been bestowed on believers corporately; the plural is used throughout. Most of these blessings were once given to Israel, but here they are poured out on the Christian community, the church. What is more, in Christ there are added blessings.

The opening words that speak of believers being blessed in Christ possibly echo the promise to Abraham that all the nations of the earth would be blessed through him (Gen. 18.18).[23] This thought leads the apostle then to speak of the supreme blessing, the believer's election 'in Christ' (v. 4). The election of Israel stood right at the centre of Jewish self-understanding (Deut. 7.6–8, 14.2; Isa. 43.20, 65.9, etc.), and here Paul sees Christ as fulfilling Israel's destiny and the believing community standing in solidarity with him.[24] In these opening words, the existence of the Christian community is not grounded on the historic mission of Christ, or his death and resurrection, or on the giving of the Spirit, but in the eternal purposes of God, who 'chose us in Christ before the foundation of the world' (v. 4).[25] Yet this privileged status demands ethical behaviour, as was the case with historic Israel. Indeed, election in Christ has as its goal 'to be holy and blameless before him in love' (cf. Lev. 11.44–5, 19.2, 20.7–8, 26).

The expression 'in Christ' is very common in Ephesians, being found eleven times in this section alone.[26] It can be used in more than one way, but in this verse and in probably most (if not all) the other uses in this section, it almost certainly has a 'local' sense.[27] 'Christ is the "place" in whom believers are and in whom salvation is.'[28] This involves the notion of the incorporation of believers into Christ, and the identification of the believing community with its representative head. In this benediction, the writer consistently has the whole Christian community in mind, as a totality 'in Christ'. Stott says in this one little expression that Paul spells out 'a new principle of human solidarity'.[29]

Having begun with God's electing choice of the Christian community, 'before the foundation of the world', Paul then speaks of the historical redemption achieved by Christ (vv. 7–8). Like Israel, the church has been 'redeemed', but in this case it is by the blood of Christ (v. 7) (cf. Deut. 7.8, 9.26, 13.5, 15.5, 24.18; 1 Chron. 17.21). This redemption has taken place in 'the fullness of time' (v. 10), words that imply that the present is the fulfilment of Old Testament eschatological expectations.[30] This act of redemption has, however, a cosmic dimension as well. 'It is to gather up (*anakephalaioōmai*) all things in him, things in heaven and things on earth' (v. 9b). A similar idea is expressed in Colossians 1.20. The thought seems to be that Christ's death did not only provide for the salvation of the whole Christian community, the church, but also for the reintegration of the whole cosmos rent asunder by sin.[31]

Having spoken of Christ in these cosmic terms, the apostle

then returns to the believing community by adding, in whom '*we have also obtained an inheritance*' (v. 11). The verb in this sentence (*klēroun*) is in the passive form, and means 'appoint by lot', or 'assign', and calls to mind God's choice of Israel as his inheritance (Deut. 32.8–9; Ps. 33.12; cf. Deut. 4.20, 9.29; Ps. 106.40, etc.). 'So here, believers in Christ are God's chosen people, claimed by him as his portion or heritage', says Bruce.[32] A very similar idea follows in verse 14, where the gift of the Holy Spirit to believers is said to be 'the pledge of our inheritance'. The noun translated 'inheritance' (*klēronomia*) was also used of Israel (Exod. 19.5; Deut. 14.2, 26.18; Mal. 3.17), but here it is applied to believing gentiles as it is in 1 Peter 2.9 and Acts 20.28.

In this long benediction, two matters stand out. The Christian community, as a corporate entity, owes its existence ultimately to the electing will of God; and secondly, all the blessings bestowed in Christ on this community are the fulfilment of the promises made to Israel. This means that this benediction addresses the eschatological people of God, the church, who it declares to be the elect 'in Christ'.

The Christian community defined as the *ekklēsia*, Christ's body and fullness (1.22–3)

Following the opening benediction in which Paul blesses God for the benefits bestowed on those in Christ, he then expresses his gratitude for the way God is working in them (1.15–23). At the end of this section he gives the whole Christian community, which is in mind throughout chapter 1, its most distinctive name, 'the church/*ekklēsia*', which he says is 'his body' and his 'fullness' (1.22–3). These comments raise a number of exegetical questions; but it is clear, first, that when Paul says God has made Christ 'the head over all things for the church', he is speaking of Christ's rule over the whole world that benefits the church.[33] The cosmic headship of Christ, here and elsewhere in Ephesians (and Colossians), is determinative for every believer, and so the body metaphor in these epistles must refer to the universal church. No longer is the body the local church in which unity and diversity are inherent, and the head is but one member as in 1 Corinthians and Romans. The body is the believing community subject to Christ as head. And secondly, when he says the church as his body 'is the fullness of him who fills all in all' (1.23), this strange-to-our-ears expression is to be taken in apposition to 'his body', so that 'body' and 'fullness' are seen as two definitions of the church,[34] and to mean 'as Christ is filled with God [cf. Col. 1.19, 2.9], so his body is filled with Christ'.[35] In these two descriptions of the *ekklēsia*, any suggestion that 'the church' should be recognized only in specific congregations, or as but the aggregation of believers locally or universally, is excluded. It is a universal community created by God's action in Christ, and inextricably bound together in corporate solidarity. It is a community called into being by God himself, ruled by Christ its head and filled with his presence.

A third race: Ephesians chapter 2

Although commentators usually divide Ephesians chapter 2 into two main sections (vv. 1–10 and vv. 11–22), one developing argument gives unity of thought to the whole. Here Paul writes to this gentile community to remind them of how much God in Christ has done for them by bestowing on them not only all the privileges once belonging to Israel, but also extra blessings uniquely known in the one body of Christ – that is, in the church. The argument starkly contrasts their past and present status.

Once you were . . .	*Now you are . . .*
Dead (vv. 1, 5).	Alive (vv. 1, 5).
Children of wrath (v. 3).	Children of God (v. 18).
Without Christ (v. 12).	In Christ (v. 13).
Aliens to Israel (vv. 12, 19).	Fellow citizens (v. 19).
Strangers (v. 12).	Family (v. 19).
Without hope (v. 12).	With hope (v. 13).
Far off (vv. 13, 17).	Brought near (vv. 13, 17).

The great change has been wrought by the shedding of Christ's blood, which created one new community out of the two. This broke 'down the dividing wall, that is, the hostility between us' (v. 14), 'abolished the law' (v. 15), and created peace (vv. 14, 15, 17). Paul calls this unified, corporate entity the 'one new humanity' (v. 15): an expression that sounds strange to our ears, but not necessarily to the readers who would have been aware of Paul's teaching on Christ as the second Adam who, like the first Adam, is the representative leader of all those identified with him. In speaking of their new status in this way, Paul is reminding the Christians at

Ephesus that the church is a new creation that replaces the old order that was characterized by the division between Jew and gentile. The old ethnic hostilities have been abolished in Christ, and one unified, new reality has emerged. The essential oneness of the church is underlined. Christ has created 'one new humanity in the place of two' (2.15); 'made both groups into one' (2.14); 'reconciled both groups to God in one body' (2.16), so that both 'have access to God in one Spirit' (2.18). This new creation in Christ that has objectively transcended the old divisions, as far as the author is concerned, must be accepted and expressed in daily living by those to whom he writes. The reason for making these assertions is of course that the readers need to hear these things.

This thought then leads Paul to say more on the nature of this new community. Those who belong to it are 'citizens with the saints',[36] and 'members of the household of God' (v. 19), 'built upon the foundation of the apostles and prophets, with Christ himself as the corner stone' (v. 20). What he seems to be saying is that the church was constituted by the early Christian apostles and prophets who first proclaimed the gospel, thereby laying the foundation of the new community. Scholars are divided as to whether the Greek noun, *akrogōniaios*, here translated 'corner stone', which describes Christ's place in the 'household of God', is to be understood as the foundation stone or the crowning stone that completes the building.[37] Yet whatever the answer to this debate, the point is clear: 'In him [Christ] the whole structure is joined together and grows into a holy temple in the Lord' (v. 21). (The architectural metaphor is mixed with the biological.) It is no surprise that the church that is filled with Christ is now described as a temple. The depicting of God's end-time people under this image reflects Old Testament ideas, Qumran teaching, the words of Jesus,[38] and the early Pauline epistles. But in contrast to Paul's use of this metaphor in 1 Corinthians, where the apostle calls the Christians in Corinth a temple, here the temple is the world-wide Christian community where the division between Jew and gentile no longer has any significance. Nevertheless, as Paul concludes this section, he draws in the Ephesian community by reminding them that they are included in this process: '*you also* are built together spiritually into a dwelling place for God' (v. 22).

Ephesians takes us further than anything else seen so far in the Pauline corpus on the question of the relationship between Israel and the church, although some comments in Galatians stand close. The church has its origins in Israel, but it now transcends Israel. Continuity with the past is not forgotten, but in Ephesians 2.11–19 the emphasis is on discontinuity. The church is not restored Israel into which believing gentiles have been grafted, but something altogether new in which Jew and gentile are united. 'One new humanity' replaces the two old entities (2.15). The concept of the church is thus, to use an early Christian expression, 'a third race' – or, as it was commonly called in Latin, a *tertium genus*, neither Jewish nor gentile.[39]

The church as the revelation of the wisdom and glory of God: Ephesians chapter 3

The church as a substantive entity in the world again appears in the second occurrence of the word *ekklēsia*/church in 3.10. In this context, the author speaks of the mediating role of the church using the formula 'through the church', found nowhere else in the New Testament. In the preceding verse the apostle mentions 'the mystery hidden for long ages', but now revealed in Christ, which is that believing gentiles and believing Jews are one in Christ. He then goes on to say, 'that *through the church* the wisdom of God in its rich variety might now be made known to the rulers and authorities in the heavenly places'. How the church does this, we are not told. Some suggest it is through the preaching of the gospel, others that it is in worship; but in the light of the overall message of Ephesians, it seems most likely the idea is that the church as an entity in world history, where the division of Jew and gentile has been overcome, proclaims to the hostile forces in the heavens that one day cosmic divisions will also be overcome.[40] This is something the church does as one corporate entity. Its very existence on earth makes known the wisdom of God to the powers in the heavens.

The word *ekklēsia* appears again in this chapter in the concluding doxology, and once more the wording has no parallel in the New Testament: 'to him [God] be glory in the church and in Christ Jesus' (3.21). In line with the apostle's thought that the church is the place where God's presence and rule is recognized (see 1.22, 23, 2.2, 3.10), he now declares that this is where his glory is manifested. Yet what is startling is that he makes the church and Christ co-ordinates. God's glory is seen in both, and the church is mentioned before her Lord. Paul probably does this because his thinking moves from the church on earth to the Lord in heaven, but the wording is a stark reminder of the corporative thinking basic to the ecclesiology of Ephesians. Christ and the church can be seen together. Because believers are one with their Lord, God's glory is seen in 'the church *and* in Christ Jesus'. Schnackenburg commenting on this amazing statement says the author conceives of the church, 'as a partner whom we cannot imagine Christ without'.[41]

One church: Ephesians 4.1–16

This section of Ephesians says more specifically on the church than any other part of this epistle, but the focus is mainly on the unity, ordering, and goals of church life rather than on theological definition. The major images for the church in this section are ones introduced earlier: 'the body' (vv. 4, 12, 16), 'building' (vv. 12, 16), 'the fullness of Christ' (v. 13), and 'the new humanity' (v. 13). A division can be made between what is said in verses 1–6, which concentrate on the unity of the body, and verses 7–16, which concentrate on the diversity of ministries given to the body; however, this should not be pressed, for even the varied gifts are given to further the unity of the church. In this whole section, the Christian community, the church, is drawn as a living organism. The one body grows as the individual members each contribute to the developing maturity and growth of the whole, the ultimate goal being 'the fullness of Christ' himself. It is possible to apply all this to individual congregations, but here as elsewhere in Ephesians the Christian community in its entirety is in mind. This is made abundantly clear in the opening sevenfold affirmation: 'There is one body and one Spirit ... one hope, ... one Lord, one faith, one baptism, one God and Father of all' (vv. 4–6). The author consistently thinks of the church in its universal dimension. Lincoln concludes, 'The assertion of these unifying realities drives home the sense of cohesion and distinctive identity the writer wants his readers to have as members of the church.'[42] Some think the sevenfold repetition of what is 'one' for all Christians reflects an early credal formulation, but this is by no means certain. The affirmations begin by mentioning the one body, since the church is the apostle's immediate concern, then moves to the Spirit, then to Christ, and finally to God the Father. The change from the imperative 'be eager to maintain the unity of the Spirit' (v. 3) to the indicative 'there is one body and one Spirit . . .' (vv. 4ff) should be noted. The church is one; but in the realities of this world, unity is something for which the church must work. This thought again draws attention to the constant understanding of the church in Ephesians. It is not a chance collection of believing individuals, but a substantive entity in this world brought into existence by God himself, which has a unity already given: the responsibility of the members is to actualize this unity in their corporate life. Only as they do this can God make known 'through the church' his manifold wisdom to the powers in the heavens (2.10).

To further the unity of his body, the church, the ascended Christ provides a number of ministries that are exercised by particular people. 'The gifts he gave were that some would be apostles, some prophets, some evangelists, some pastors and teachers' (4.11). Whether or not pastors and teachers are one ministry or two is not an issue for this study, but most think only one ministry is implied. This comment about the leadership of the church that identifies certain ministries with particular people has led some to argue that Ephesians has a well-developed understanding of office.[43] Yet what is said here is very similar to 1 Corinthians 12.28, where three of these ministries are associated with particular people. Furthermore, Ephesians continues to emphasize that these ministries, plural in number and differing in function, are gifts given to the church. Nevertheless, what is said about the leadership of the church in Ephesians is less dynamic than that given in the earlier Paulines where the ministry of the whole body is the main focus.

The reasons why God gives these ministries to the church then follows. The RSV translates the three prepositional phrases of verse 12 as if the designated leaders were given by Christ: 'for the equipment of the saints, for the work of ministry, for building up the body of Christ'. This translation makes these three matters the sole responsibility of the leaders mentioned in verse 11. The NRSV, on the other hand, considers the second and third phrases dependent on the first, and gives the translation: 'to equip the saints for the work of ministry, for building up the body of Christ'. In this case, the leaders of the church mentioned in verse 11 have but one task: 'to equip the saints' so that they can pursue 'their ministry' by building up the body of Christ. Both translations are possible, and in recent times the latter has been preferred because it highlights the ministry of the whole church, but it is not demanded by the change of Greek prepositions in the second and third clause.[44] If it is conceded that the three ministries mentioned are probably those of the designated leaders, this is not a problem, for the ministry of all believers is safeguarded by verse 7, which speaks of the grace (to minister) given to each Christian, and verse 16, which speaks of 'each part working properly [to] promote the body's growth'.

Next the apostle speaks of the goal of Christian leadership. It is to labour in ministry 'until all of us come to the unity of the faith and of the knowledge of the Son of God, to maturity, to the measure of the full stature of Christ' (v. 13). The first Greek verb in verse 13, *katantan* (we come), expresses the thought of striving towards fulfilment. The point implied is that the church is on a journey. It is moving not so much towards an eschatological future, but rather upwards to her heavenly Lord. What the NRSV translates by the word 'maturity' is in Greek two words, *andra teleion*, which literally means 'the perfectly mature or complete man'. This has been understood as if this was the aim for each individual Christian, but the context demands that it be understood corporately. The church is seen here as a single organism, the body of Christ, and as an entity it is to grow to adult stature.[45] This maturity is defined by the next phrase, 'to the measure of the fullness of Christ'. Here the goal is not that each member be like Christ, but that the church becomes the 'fullness of Christ' (cf. 1.23, where the church has already been described as 'the fullness of Christ').[46] Bruce makes the comment: 'The glorified Christ provides the standard at which his people are to aim: the corporate Christ cannot be content to fall short of the perfection of the personal Christ.'[47] The picture is of the Christian community on earth bound together and empowered by the presence of Christ growing upwards towards Christ in all his glory in heaven. This is made explicit in what follows. The author concludes, so 'we must grow up in every way into him who is the head, into Christ, from whom the whole body, joined and knit together . . . builds itself up in love' (4.15b–16). 'The whole body' stands under Christ as its head, but at the same time Christ, the head (*kephalē*), is the *source* of growth, and, referring back to verse 13, the measure of that growth.

In this passage, Christology and ecclesiology are related closely, but one does not swallow up the other.[48] Christ remains the one Lord of the one church (v. 5), who from his exalted position gives both grace to the whole church and to its leaders. The unity of the church, the body of Christ, is emphasized (vv. 2–6, 13, 16), but this unity is not monochrome uniformity, or a static state, for within it there is manifested a variety of ministries, and growth is expected. The picture of the church is thus a robustly dynamic one. It is a growing body in which each part makes a contribution and complete unity in Christ, and the full maturity of the whole is the goal.

The church as the bride of Christ: Ephesians 5.21–33

The main purpose of this passage is to give direction on marriage, but the apostle does this by drawing parallels between the relationship of Christ, the bridegroom in heaven, and the church, the Christian community, most of whose members are on earth. The imagery comes from the Old Testament where Israel is often spoken of as Yahweh's bride (e.g. Isa. 54.1–6, 62.4–5; Jer. 2.2–3, 32; Ezek. 16.23; Hos. 2.19, 20; Mal. 2.14). The archetypal marriage, which sets the ideal, is not seen in Adam and Eve, but in the relationship between Christ and his church. The only appeal to the Genesis creation stories comes in the comment about the one flesh union consummated in marriage (v. 31). In this discussion on marriage, the word *ekklēsia*/church appears no less than six times in these twelve verses.

The section begins with an introductory call to mutual submission in the body of Christ before Paul begins to address particular people (v. 21). He first asks submission of wives. They are to submit willingly to their husbands, because 'the husband is the head of the wife as Christ is the head of the church, the body of which he is the saviour' (v. 23). Although the Greek word *kephalē* translated 'head' can mean source or origin (cf. Eph. 4.15; Col. 2.19),[49] it is not used in this sense here. Christ as the head of the church sets the model, and provides the reason why the wife should subordinate herself to her husband. In this exhortation Paul is saying what his readers would have expected. The subordination of wives was universal in the ancient world as it has been in most cultures. It is a consequence of the fall (Gen. 3.16). To make sure the nature of this subordination is understood, the apostle adds, 'Just as the church is subject to Christ, so also wives ought to be, in everything to their husbands' (v. 24). The model for wifely submission is that of the church to Christ. It is voluntary and gladly given without conditions. If this was all that was said, then Christian marriage would be but a total submission of the wife to her husband as binding and demanding as the worst of patriarchalism. However, Paul does not stop here. He goes on in a much longer section to address husbands, setting out for them a model of 'headship' unknown in the ancient world, and seldom put into practice even by those who call themselves Christians today.

The exhortation to husbands is in two parts, verses 25 to 27 and verses 28 to 32. Paul first of all asks husbands to love their wives as Christ loved the church. He uses the same word, *agapē*, to describe how husbands should relate to their wives, as he does to describe Christ's bond with the church. There are rare examples from the ancient world where male writers tell husbands to love their wives, but there are none that bear the slightest resemblance to what Paul demands. This is an entirely novel Christian perspective. Christ's love (*agapē*) for the church is seen in his self-giving in death (v. 25b). It is this kind of self-denying love that the Christian husband is to show his wife. At no point in this passage is *agapē*/love understood as an emotional feeling. It is consistently characterized in terms of self-giving: as an act of the will. Three reasons as to why Christ gave his life for the church then follow. First, it was 'to make her holy (*hagiasē*) by cleansing her by the washing of water by the word' (v. 26). The mention of cleansing by water is almost certainly an allusion to water baptism, which is seen as the point where the response to the 'word' is actualized, but possibly the pre-marriage bridal bath evoked the idea (cf. Ezek. 16.8–14).[50] Second, it was 'to present the church to himself in splendour, without spot or wrinkle or anything of the kind' (v. 27). Now the bridal imagery comes to the fore. The picture is of Christ preparing a bride, the church, for himself. Third, Christ gave himself 'so that she [the bride] might be holy and without blemish' (v. 27b). The idea here, in this the last of the three purpose clauses, is that the preparation of the bride involves moral cleansing. Because the emphasis is so strongly on realized eschatology in Ephesians, we should expect that the presentation of the church to her Lord would be something that takes place in this world of space and time, and this is made explicit in verse 32 where the present union between Christ and his bride is given as a model for the union of the Christian husband and wife. In both cases, it is a consummated union. The church is already the bride of Christ.[51]

In verses 28ff, a new paragraph begins with a renewed exhortation to husbands to love their wives. 'In the same way', Paul says, 'husbands should love their wives as they do their own bodies', . . . nourishing and caring for them, 'just as Christ does for the church' (vv. 28–9). This again is a demanding and revolutionary appeal. Because our interest is in the church, and not in Christian marriage, we must leave this point; but it must be noted that this verse gives the essence of what is to be different in Christian marriage. Paul has subtly sought to transform the marriage relationship in his own historical situation, and in doing so set a trajectory that would culminate in the modern partnership model of marriage. The climax of his argument is reached when he quotes Genesis 2.24, 'For this reason . . . and the two shall become one flesh' (v. 31). This, he says, 'is a great mystery, and I am applying it to Christ and his church'. In Ephesians, a 'mystery' is a divine truth once hidden, but now revealed in Christ (cf. 1.9, 3.3, 4, 9, 6.19).[52] This 'great mystery' is the revelation that this text speaks primarily not of the union between a man and a woman, but of the union between Christ and the church. Christian marriage is analogous to this. In this striking claim, the church as the bride of Christ is seen as intimately one with him, although subordinate to him. The unity between Christ and the church could not be more vividly described.

In this section in another image, the profound unity between Christ and the Christian community, the church, is underlined. The bride is Christian believers viewed corporately as an entity. Christ gave himself for the bride to make her holy, to present her to himself in splendour and to cleanse her from all moral impurity. His love for the church is so great that he gave his life for her, and his relationship with her is so intimate that the union of the man and the woman in marriage is a parallel. Again the apostle reminds his readers of their amazing privileged status they have as members of the church, as they struggle in the ambiguities of life here on earth.

A distinctive community

So far we have concentrated on what might be called the theological definition of the church in Ephesians, but right at the beginning of the epistle the ethical definition of the church is raised. Those chosen in Christ are to be 'holy and blameless before him in love' (1.4); this is how the Christian community is to live. As the new temple, 'joined together', the church is to grow in holiness (2.21), and as the new humanity to be 'clothed' in 'righteousness and holiness' (4.24). They are to be 'rooted and grounded in love' (3.17); 'bearing with one another in love' (4.2); 'speaking the truth in love' (4.15); building one another up in love (4.16); and living in love 'as Christ loved us' (5.1). In their ongoing relationships with one another, they are to respect traditional structures, but renew them in Christ. Wives are to be subordinate to their husbands, children are to obey their parents, and slaves obey their masters (5.21—6.4). This 'household code', which appears first in Colossians, reflects the norms of that age, but Paul adds a distinctive Christian element. He speaks first in each case to those with authority, and asks certain things of them as well. In other words, he makes it a reciprocal ethic. The redefinition of household relationships 'in Christ' is most thoroughly worked out in relation to marriage.

Paul also sees the Christian community caught up in a cosmic battle with spiritual forces (6.10–20), needing always to call on God for the resources needed. This power is found in the Holy Spirit.[53] The Spirit characterizes the life of the church on earth, and is understood as a foretaste of final redemption in heaven (1.13–14).[54] In the present time, the Spirit directs the church (1.17–18); strengthens the church (3.16); and should fill the church (5.18). When facing spiritual forces, the word of God is the 'sword of the Spirit' (6.17).

A concluding overview

The church, as the totality of the Christian community on earth, with a distinct dignity and role in the cosmos, is the unique element in the ecclesiology of Colossians, and particularly Ephesians. In both instances, the author writes to impress on his readers the dignity and privileges they have in Christ. They are to understand that as members of the church they are part of a great plan that God is working out, which has an earthly and heavenly dimension. 'They are actors in the cosmic drama with a significant part to play.'[55] In speaking of the church in these terms, soteriology, Christology, and ecclesiology are drawn together, but one does not swallow up the others. Because of the stress on realized eschatology, salvation is a present communal blessing (e.g. Col.

1.13–14, 3.1; Eph. 1.3, 7, 2.4–6), but in neither epistle is the future consummation of this salvation forgotten (e.g. Col. 1.5, 12, 22b; Eph. 1.10, 14, 4.30). The reason why the church is the place where salvation is realized on earth is because the church is the body of Christ, filled with his person. However, Christ continues as the heavenly Lord set over the church.

This ecclesiology adds important insights not seen elsewhere in the New Testament, but taken on its own it has certain limitations. Ephesians, in so concentrating on the church as the whole Christian community, eclipses the congregational aspect of the church, which must always be the concrete expression of the body of Christ in human history. Similarly, in defining the church in relation to Christ, basically as a theological entity, the sociological dimension of the church in both its world-wide, regional, and congregational aspects is also eclipsed. When these two characteristics are combined with the language of heavenly existence so common in Ephesians, it is not surprising that some have seen here but an ideal, other-worldly, church, but this is quite mistaken, as we have seen. Indeed, this thought should be combated as it encourages escape from facing the problems and responsibilities of corporate Christian existence in this world. Schnackenburg says, 'the talk of the heavenly church which people try to find in Ephesians urgently needs to be corrected. In spite of her "presence" in heaven (cf. 2.5f) which is bestowed upon her in Christ, her head, she still remains his instrument on earth.'[56]

The glimpses we do see of the church as a sociological reality in Colossians and Ephesians suggest, nevertheless, that not only in theology has some development from the early Paul taken place, but also in form and in relation to the world. The household codes found in both epistles show the Christian community working out rules of behaviour for its members, the stress on unity implies certain tensions as the church settles down to life in this world, and the more formal description of the leadership structures in Ephesians points to the association of particular ministries with particular people. These things are accepted and encouraged by what is said in these epistles. This therefore suggests that again Margaret MacDonald's argument can be accepted. In these two epistles, 'community stabilising institutionalisation'[57] is being encouraged.

The late Paulines: the Pastorals

Since the eighteenth century, 1 and 2 Timothy and Titus have been grouped together and titled the Pastoral epistles, because they are basically homogeneous in thought and style and show a common interest in defending the faith and in the ordering of the church. In their thinking on the church there is a different perspective to that noted so far. We find here no debate about the relationship between Israel and gentile believers; the Christian community are the people of God; the church is like a solid building; the dynamic metaphor of the body disappears altogether; appointed leaders with distinctive titles are set over the church; the charismatic ministry given to each member of the church is not mentioned; women are to accept the authority of men and not teach in church; the freedoms given to women in the earlier Paulines are cancelled; and 'sound teaching' and preserving the truth once given are the responsibilities of leaders. A struggle to see how the gospel applies to new situations is not in evidence.[58]

These changes are to be explained in part by the threat to the life of the church created by the social and doctrinal problems these epistles seek to redress, by the fact that they were written at the end of the apostolic age and thus reflect a situation where Christians are coming to accept that Christ will not return as soon as expected, and by the evolution of institutional forms. Yet despite these significant changes, the Pastorals find their setting in a continuum of theological and social development within the Pauline corpus rather than as a completely new departure. Thus the Pastorals still hold to the eschatological tension basic to apostolic Christianity. These are the last days (1 Tim. 4.1; 2 Tim. 3.10), and Christ is still expected to return (1 Tim. 6.13–15; 2 Tim. 4.1; Tit. 2.13).[59] Proclaiming the message about the salvation provided by Christ's death is thus an urgent task (1 Tim. 4.10; 2 Tim. 4.1–4).[60] And although authority structures are more formalized, leadership is still provided by a group of people and prophecy still known (1 Tim. 1.18, 4.1, 14).

The Christian community in the Pastorals is discussed in both its universal extension and in its local manifestation. The Christian community in the world is true Israel. Profound Old Testament designations of Israel are unambiguously applied to the church. Christians are 'God's elect' (Tit. 1.1; 2 Tim. 2.10), God's own people (*laos*) (Tit. 2.14), and 'those who are his' (2 Tim.

2.19). A comment on these last two references is needed. Titus 2.14 sees the creation of the Christian community as the counterpart of the establishment of the nation Israel. Jesus Christ 'gave himself for us that he might redeem us from all iniquity and purify for himself a people of his own who are zealous for good deeds'. This verse echoes a number of Old Testament passages that speak of God's action in making the Jews his elect people; chief among them is Exodus 19.5, but there are echoes also of Numbers 16.5, Deuteronomy 7.6, 14.2; cf. Ezekiel 37.23 (cf. 1 Pet. 2.9). So explicit is the equating of the Christian community and Israel in this text that P. Richardson, who writes a thesis to argue that in the Pauline corpus the church is not identified with Israel, admits this is the one unambiguous exception to the rule. He says, 'here a transposition has been effected from the old people [of God] to the new'. *Laos* 'applies to Christians alone, with no underlying continuity with the original people [of God]'.[61] A similar claim is made in 2 Timothy 2.19, where the church is described as 'a firm foundation' that bears the inscription: 'The Lord knows those that are his' – words taken directly from Numbers 16.5 where they apply to Israel – one of the texts reflected in Titus 2.4.

Most commentators hold that 'the firm foundation' mentioned in 2 Timothy 2.19 alludes to the church, because in 1 Timothy 3.15, 'the *ekklēsia*/church of the living God' is called 'the pillar and bulwark of the truth'. The wording is different, but the overall thought is very similar. This description of the church has no parallel in the New Testament. Instead of the church being seen as a living organism like a body, or as a growing building, as it is in the early and middle Paulines, it is here described as an unshakeable, stately edifice and the bearer of 'the truth'.[62] Hendriksen concludes that in these two passages Paul stresses 'the permanency and immobility' of the church.[63] How the church preserves 'the truth' we are not told; but as it is given this responsibility, it is clearly conceived of as an ongoing institution in this world. The contrast with the ecclesiology of Ephesians is striking. There the sociological and this-worldly aspect of the church are almost forgotten, but here they are to the fore.

In 2 Timothy 3.15, the *ekklēsia*/church is also called 'the household of God', an idea that again parallels 2 Timothy 2.19–20, where the apostle first speaks of 'God's firm foundation', and then of what is found 'in a large house' (v. 20). It has been suggested that these references view the church as the new temple,[64] but this is unlikely and is not supported by most modern commentators, for domestic household imagery pervades these epistles (cf. 1 Tim. 3.4, 5, 12, 5.4; 2 Tim. 1.16, etc.). In this metaphor for the church, ideas of location in the world, good management, prescribed ordering, and the respect of outsiders are envisaged.[65] The thought that the church has within its membership believers and unbelievers is also indicated by 2 Timothy 2.14ff. This whole section in 2 Timothy has the Christian community in mind. In the church, pictured as 'a large house', there are vessels of 'gold and silver' and 'wood and clay' (v. 20) and some have 'swerved from the truth' (v. 18).[66] This imagery suggests that the author accepted that unbelief could exist within the church and apostasy from it could take place. Again this indicates a more institutionalized church than hitherto seen in the Paulines.

In calling the church a 'bulwark of the truth' and 'a household', the whole Christian community or just the local community of Christians could be in mind. Both options are possibilities, and perhaps no distinction was intended. It seems that in the Pastorals both aspects of the church are recognized. The numerous references to houses in the Pastorals suggest that the Christians addressed met in homes. The existence of many houses in which Christians assembled in Ephesus is almost certainly implied in the introductory directives as to what men and women should do when they meet 'in every place' (1 Tim. 2.8); these words reflect Malachi 1.11, and mean 'in every meeting place' (cf. 1 Cor. 1.2). Whether or not these little communities of believers are explicitly called *ekklēsia*/church in the Pastorals cannot be answered with certainty because of a lack of clear evidence, but it seems that this is the case. In 1 Timothy 3.1ff, the qualifications to be a bishop are given, and among these there is the demand that the bishop 'manage his own household well', because 'if someone does not know how to manage his own household, how can he take care of God's church?' (vv. 4–5.) Uncertainty about what the word 'church' refers to in this passage arises because of uncertainty about the nature of the bishop's office at this time and in the place envisaged. If the singular *episcopos* (bishop) points to one man set over the churches in a given location, then *ekklēsia* in this passage would refer to the Christian community in that place. However, if the bishop in the Pastorals is an elder set over one house church, as I have argued elsewhere, then *ekklēsia*, in this context, would refer to a house church host and overseer.[67] The reality in mind in the use of *ekklēsia* in 1 Timothy 3.16 is also not clear. Is the church that is not to be burdened with the care of the widow the Christian community in Ephesus, or the house community to which she belongs? I suspect it is the former, as nothing is said about belonging to any particular group. If our preferred options are accepted, then in the Pastorals the word *ekklēsia* is used for the Christian community as an entity in the world, of the Christian community in one location, and of the Christian community that meets regularly in a home.

Church leadership

In the Pastorals, instructions are given as to the appointment of bishops, deacons, and elders, but their exact function is not explained, nor are we told how these three offices are related. In my *Patterns of Ministry Among the First Christians*, I argue that the bishop is an elder in charge of a house church (cf. 1 Tim. 3.1–7), the deacons are respected men and women who assist in the leadership of house churches (cf. 1 Tim. 3.8–13), and the elders form a governing pastoral 'council' (1 Tim. 4.14).[68] Whether or not this possible construct is accepted is not important for this study. What is important to note is that in the Pastorals we find a more institutionalized pattern of Christian leadership than seen elsewhere. The more structured understanding of church leadership matches the more structured understanding of the church already outlined. For the first time we meet with people in leadership who can rightly be called office bearers.

A special feature of this church ordering in the Pastorals is its restriction on the ministry of women. They are 'not to teach or to have authority over a man' (1 Tim. 2.11); some believe this command is given because women were the main teachers of the false doctrines denounced (cf. 1 Tim. 5.12–13; 2 Tim. 3.7; Tit. 1.11), but others argue that this instruction is simply part of the overall concern of the Pastorals to endorse the general norms of the society in which the church found itself. Women, senior people, younger people (1 Tim. 4.1–2; Tit. 2.3–6), citizens (1 Tim. 2.1–3; Tit. 3.1), and slaves (1 Tim. 6.1–3; Tit. 2.9–10) were all to accept the station in life prescribed by that culture.[69] If this is the case, then when the norms of society change, other directives are needed to ensure that the gospel is not hindered by the church being out of step with the general ordering of society. To suggest that these restrictions placed on women are timeless, transcultural law because they are buttressed by the comments that man was created first and woman was 'deceived and became a transgressor' first (1 Tim. 2.13–14),[70] is to ask far too much of these *ad hominem* arguments.[71]

Locating sociologically the ecclesiology of the Pastorals

The point has already been made that discontinuity and continuity with what can be seen in the earlier Paulines is a characteristic of the Pastorals. However, a marked development cannot be missed. Some of the dynamic features of the ecclesiology, such as seen in Romans and 1 Corinthians, with its strengths and weaknesses, has been lost. More so than even in Colossians and Ephesians, we sense that the Christian community is settling down to life in this world. Yet it is to be noted that the author of the Pastorals does not think that to stress keeping the traditions, preserving the truth, upholding the prevailing household order, and the appointment of office bearers is a negative approach. He writes to commend these very things. Whether we applaud these developments or abhor them is of no significance. The fact is that this is how the churches in the Pauline circles developed, and how the gospel was preserved. Thus Margaret MacDonald helpfully describes what we see in the Pastorals as 'community protecting institutionalisation'.[72]

Chapter 7

The Church in the Non-Pauline Epistles and the Book of Revelation

The Book of Acts and the Pauline epistles use the word *ekklēsia/* church the most frequently, but 'the church', defined as the Christian community, is of equal importance to every contributor to the New Testament – although some speak more directly on this matter than others. In every case, the particular reason(s) for writing governs what is said. This communal understanding of the Christian faith is there to be seen in the texts, and it is to be pre-supposed because every contributor to the New Testament was a person of their own age, and that age tended to see social realities primarily in communal terms – not individualistically as we moderns do. They all believed that faith in Christ insolubly bound Christians together, theologically and socially.[1]

In concluding our survey of how the apostolic writers understood the Christian community, we come to study a select number of the writings so far not covered: Hebrews, James, 1 Peter, the three epistles of John, and the Book of Revelation.

Hebrews

On beginning to read the epistle to the Hebrews, one is immediately struck by the distinctive language, style, Christology, and use of the Old Testament. It is not a surprise, therefore, to discover that this book also has a distinctive understanding of the Christian community, the church. The key to entering into the thought of this epistle lies in an appreciation of how the writer draws on the Jewish Scriptures.[2] Every chapter in the epistle to the Hebrews explicitly or implicitly alludes to one or more Old Testament text. These texts are usually quoted as if God or Jesus is speaking in the present, and they are read as if they prefigure and anticipate what has come to pass in the incarnation, ministry, and death of Christ, and the subsequent formation of the Christian community. Thus when the author of Hebrews addresses his readers, especially in chapters 2–6 and 11–13, he likens them and their situation to that of Israel in the wilderness.

The Christian community initially comes into focus in 2.1–4, in the first of a series of exhortatory passages that warn the readers not to fall back, and thus lose their salvation. After insisting again that Jesus is superior to the angels (see 2.5–9), the author returns to address the community (2.10–18). He now spells out their status as members of Christ's family, and by implication the status of all believers. The 'many children' (*huious*) of verse 10 must allude to the whole Christian community on earth.[3] The argument is built on an exposition of three Old Testament texts that are taken to anticipate and prefigure the Christian community. They speak of the solidarity between Christ and his followers. The first quote is from Psalm 22.22: 'I will proclaim your name to my brothers and sisters [*adelphoi*], in the midst of the congregation [*ekklēsia*] I will praise you.' This text establishes that the members of the Christian community are truly members of Christ's family. The use of the word *ekklēsia*, which is translated 'congregation', is significant for here the word is in synonymous parallelism with 'brothers and sisters'. The word is not included simply to complete the quotation, for the author of the epistle to the Hebrews carefully chooses his texts and only quotes them as far as they are pertinent to his argument. He is rather, by use of this quote, defining in another word the community called into existence by Christ. The Psalmist sees Jesus standing identified with his brothers and sisters, praising God 'in the midst of the church'.[4] The second quote from Isaiah 8.17b is somewhat cryptic, but it also seems to be used to show that Christ identifies himself with all Christian believers by also trusting in God. The third quote from Isaiah 8.18a again affirms solidarity between Christ and his people, not by calling them 'sons and daughters' (*huious*) (as in v. 10), or 'brothers and sisters' (*adelphoi*) (as in vv. 11, 12, and 17), but 'children' (*paidia*) (v. 13).

*The Christian community typologically
foreshadowed and identified*

In chapters 3 and 4, the Christian community again comes on to
centre stage; this section begins by comparing Moses and Jesus
(vv. 1–6). Both were faithful to the one who appointed them to
lead 'God's house', but Jesus 'is worthy of more glory than Moses'
because he is the builder of the house, whereas Moses was only a
servant in the house. ('House' here means household – Moses and
Jesus are set over people: cf. Num. 12.7.) Just as Jesus is superior
to angels, so too he is superior to Moses. This house that Jesus is
now over then becomes the Christian community, as the author
boldly declares, 'we are his house if we hold firm . . .'. It is Christ,
not Moses, who is 'over' the church as its Lord. The warning to
'hold firm' then leads naturally to a warning about falling away (vv.
7–18). Psalm 95.7–11 is quoted and applied directly to the
Christian community. 'Today, if *you* [plural] hear his voice, do not
harden your hearts . . .' This warning that originally applied to
Israel in the wilderness is now applied to the Christian community. The argument is then taken to a new stage and brought to
completion in 4.1–11; it is here maintained that the Christian
community is the heir of the promise to enter God's 'rest' since
Israel failed to enter because of disobedience.

This method of appropriating the Old Testament as if it pre-
figured Christ's advent and what followed as a consequence is
characteristic of the Book of Hebrews. This is what is called 'the
typological use of the Old Testament'. The author of Hebrews uses
this approach in speaking about the person of Christ, his sacrifice,
and the Christian community, and in each case he is claiming that
in these last days what was foreshadowed in the Old Testament
has been fulfilled in Christ and superseded.[5]

In regard to ecclesiology, his belief that Christ has inaugurated
a radically new order is best seen in Hebrews chapters 8 to 10,
where the author develops his argument by appeal to the prophecy
of Jeremiah about the new covenant (Jer. 31.31–4).[6] The prophecy
is quoted twice, once in full (8.8–12), and once in part (10.16–17),
and the word 'covenant' is used fourteen times. In this prophecy,
two groups of people are in mind, the first are the Israelites under
the Mosaic covenant who failed to keep the covenant; the second
are Christians identified as the new 'house of Israel'. The point is
emphatically made that the old covenant, including the law, was

but a shadow of things to come (10.1), which has now been superseded. The covenantal theology of Hebrews allows that both continuity and discontinuity play their part. The community of the new covenant brought into being by the one sacrifice of the perfect High Priest is a new entity, but it is the fulfilment of the Old Testament hope that God would reconstitute Israel. The sharpness of the change in epochs is brought out by the qualifying adjectives: first/second, old/new, better, and by the comments in verse 8 that speak of the 'fault' of the old covenant, and in verse 13 of the old covenant 'as obsolete and growing old . . . soon [to] disappear'. This means that the author of the epistle to the Hebrews does not see the Christian community as simply evolving out of Israel, or as restored Israel: it replaces Israel. In this unfolding of redemptive history, the Christians become God's people (*laos*),[7] who through the one sacrifice for sin offered by the High Priest, Jesus, have been sanctified as priests[8] so that in their own right they can 'draw near'[9] to God and offer worship (*latreuō*).[10] Paradoxically, this epistle that builds so much of its case by appeal to the Old Testament boldly underlines the fact that the Christian community has superseded Israel. We find here no struggle to understand the continuing significance of Israel: the author of Hebrews believes Israel and her institutions have now been left behind, as all has been fulfilled in Christ.

The contrast between Israel and the Christian community, the church, building once again on a typological use of the Old Testament, also comes to the fore in 12.18–24. Here two groups, with different mediators, are said to have 'drawn near' or 'come to' (*proserchesthai*),[11] either the earthly Mount Sinai or the heavenly Jerusalem identified as Mount Zion. The author tells his readers that they have not come to the earthly Zion in fear, as the Israelites of old did, but to a new Mount Zion which is the heavenly Jerusalem where there is a great festive gathering. Who exactly is included in this gathering is not at all clear, and it has aroused a lot of debate. Following Lane and Scholer, I take it three groups are envisaged:[12] 'innumerable angels in festal gathering', 'the assembly [*ekklēsia*] of the first born who are enrolled in heaven', understood as Christians who have died, and 'the spirits of the righteous made perfect', understood as believers under the old covenant such as listed in chapter 11. This 'drawing near' by the Christian community, the counterpart of Israel of old, to 'mount Zion, the city of the living God, the heavenly Jerusalem', where this festive gathering is in progress, requires clarification – for the readers are on earth. Again we have here the common Jewish apocalyptic idea that what lies in the future already exists above. In this present time, the author of Hebrews is affirming, Christians can think of themselves through faith as already one with all those gathered around the throne of God in heaven as they will be on the last day. In other words, this passage speaks of end-time existence as present possibility for the believer. The Qumran writings significantly also speak of the faithful on earth participating in the worship of heaven.[13] Scholer, on the basis of the cultic language used in this passage and elsewhere in Hebrews, argues that this takes place in Christian worship. He speaks of the 'proleptic participation' by believers in their worship on earth in the worship of heaven.[14] Peterson, on the other hand, argues that 'conversion' allows believers to sense that already they are part of the heavenly community that is continuously worshipping God in heaven, but he insists that this worship is not a particular activity, but the totality of Christian living.[15] It would seem that Scholer is more to the point, for in the two uses of the word *ekklēsia* in Hebrews (2.12, 12.23), the church in effect is defined as a worshipping community in the narrower sense. It is as Christians join together to pray, praise God, and listen to his word that they 'draw near' to God, and sense that they are part of a heavenly community.

At this point, a digression must be made for a moment. The thought that the Christian community on earth in some way can see itself as part of the worshipping community in heaven is an inspiring vision, but on the basis of the use of the word *ekklēsia* in this passage some have argued that we have here one sure-proof text that this word, when not geographically circumscribed, refers exclusively to a heavenly gathering.[16] However, this claim does not bear scrutiny. Even if it was agreed that the second group among those gathered in heaven, 'the assembly of the first born', included believers both living and dead, it does not follow that the word *ekklēsia* without a geographical qualifier refers exclusively to a heavenly gathering. Rather, it speaks of the church on earth, the Christian community, and the church in heaven, seen as two aspects of the one reality. Peterson correctly recognizes that the whole vision has reference to 'the ultimate, completed company of the people of God, membership of which is now enjoyed by faith'.[17] It is to this gathering in heaven that believers on earth have 'drawn near'. Yet even if the author of the epistle to the Hebrews thought that the one true *ekklēsia* was exclusively a heavenly assembly, it would say nothing about apostolic thought in general, and his thinking would not provide a key to interpreting the 'universal' uses of the word *'ekklēsia'* in the Pauline epistles.

Thus by the use of typology the author of Hebrews identifies the Christian community as Israel of 'these last days' (1.1), as the new covenant community (10.16–17), and the worshipping community (*ekklēsia*) the counterpart of the Israelites who received the law at Mount Sinai (12.23; cf. 2.12). Yet he also makes this point explicitly by designating Christians collectively with the theologically pregnant titles once the sole preserve of Israel: the people (of God) (*laos*) (2.17, 4.9, 8.10, 10.31, 11.25, 13.12), the children of God (2.10, 12.5, 6, 7), God's house (3.6), and the saints (6.10, 10.24).

The house churches

Who the recipients of this epistle were is still debated, but we may presume they belonged to possibly one house church, but more probably several house churches, in or near Rome.[18] The congregational life of these house groups comes into focus most clearly in 3.12ff, 4.16, and 10.19ff. In 3.13, the author tells his readers 'to exhort one another every day'. Lane, among others, takes these words to mean these Christians met on a daily basis (cf. Acts 2.46), but while this is possible, the evidence is not compelling.[19] The second reference speaks of their communal worship (4.16): 'Since, then, we have a great high priest. . . . Let us therefore approach the throne of grace with boldness, so that we may receive mercy and find grace to help in time of need.' In the light of the completed work of Christ as High Priest, the readers are exhorted to approach God's throne, now characterized by the grace that flows from it. The fact that communal worship is envisaged is indicated in several ways: (1) The word 'approach' in the NRSV translates the Greek word *proserchesthai*, which several other translations render as 'draw near'. In the Greek Old Testament, this word is used of Israel's worship. (2) They are told to draw near 'with boldness' (*parresia*), an expression that frequently alludes to coming to God in prayer.[20] (3) And with the expectation that they will 'find grace to help in time of need'.

The corporate prayer and praise of the local church is also

called 'worship' in 9.14 and 12.28, but in these instances another term taken from Israel's cultic vocabulary is used (*latreuein*). The third place where a glimpse of the communal life of these Christians is seen is in the exhortatory section 10.19–25, but here something of their wider responsibilities are also mentioned. On the basis of what has been accomplished by Christ the readers are called on again to confidently approach God in worship (v. 22),[21] to maintain their Christian confession (v. 23), to provoke one another to good works (v. 24), and to meet regularly, encouraging one another (v. 25). The call to meet together regularly is often taken at a popular level to be an apostolic endorsement of the view that church attendance is vitally important; this is not disputed, but the use of the unusual noun *episunagōgē*, which is translated as if it were a verb in the above quote ('to meet together'), demands comment. Schrage gives evidence for this compound form being used in the same way as the shorter form *sunagōgē*.[22] Like *sunagōgē*, *episunagōgē* could refer to the act of assembling,[23] or to the corporate body so formed.[24] He suggests it is used in the latter sense like *sunagōgē* in James 2.2. Attridge comes to the same conclusion, and says that the problem is that some 'are not coming to church'.[25]

What exactly took place in these Christian gatherings for 'worship' is not clear; but as hearing the word of God is a major theme in Hebrews, we can conclude that the sermon or homily took pride of place.[26] Prayer also seems to have been important (4.16, 10.22, 13.18; cf. 5.7), as was thanksgiving and praise (12.28, 13.15). Many would include the Eucharist, but as there is no undisputed allusion to this in Hebrews, this cannot be included with certainty.[27] However, it is hard not to believe that the comment about tasting of 'the heavenly gift', following what would seem to be a reference to baptism, does not have the Eucharist in view.[28] The author of the epistle to the Hebrews does not speak of the ministry of each member of the body as does Paul, but he is equally insistent that when Christians meet they should minister to one another. He thus frequently calls on his hearers to exhort or encourage one another,[29] and tells them that by this time they should be teaching one another (5.12). Pastoral oversight of the community was given by a group of leaders mentioned in 13.7, 17, 24 who are called *hēgoumenoi*. This word is not a title for an office, but a purely descriptive term applied to all those who collectively provided leadership to the community (cf. Luke 22.26; Acts 15.22). This functional understanding of leadership implies that institutionalization had not progressed very far.[30]

Focusing the picture

At first thought, one could think that the epistle to the Hebrews said very little about ecclesiology, but this is not the case. The author is concerned to define Christians collectively in relation to historic Israel, and all but in exact words he concludes they are Israel of the last days. This community has inherited all the blessings promised by the prophets in the past, and now realized in Christ. Socially these Christians were, it would seem, a minority in a larger Jewish and pagan city, and they had known some persecution.[31] From the limited evidence, the picture seems to be of a community with respected leaders who are not seen in any technical sense as office bearers. When the house churches met for worship, mutual encouragement, teaching, and prayer took place. In this setting, there was an awareness that they had 'drawn near' to God and were in the presence of a great heavenly company.

James

The epistle of James is possibly the most difficult New Testament book to locate on the historical, theological, and social map of the first century.[32] It is very Jewish in character, strongly pastoral in tone, and yet expectant that Christ will soon return as the Judge of all (5.8–9). It can be read as a moralistic tract, directed at individual Christians, reflecting the wisdom tradition such as is seen in the Book of Proverbs, but this does not do the book justice. The practical advice and condemnation of certain behaviour is pastorally aimed at a group of Christians. James is not trying to change the world but the Christian community to which he writes. Careful reading of the epistle supports this contention for it soon becomes obvious that so much of what James writes has a particular Christian community in view. The opening address is, however, unclear. James writes, 'to the twelve tribes scattered among the nations' (1.1b). Does he have in mind Jews, some who believe in Christ, and others who are sympathetic to the Christian message,[33] or Jewish believers in general,[34] or believers – Jewish

and gentile – seen metaphorically as the twelve tribes in the dispersion – in other words, new Israel?[35] Each position has scholarly
support, but at this stage of the debate no resolution is in sight, so
the question must be left unanswered.

Andrew Chester says, 'James has no developed ecclesiology',[36]
and, while we agree, it is also true that communal concerns can be
seen at many points in the epistle. James only once gives specific
instruction with regard to Christian gatherings for worship. He
insists that no partiality is to be shown to those who come into
'your synagogue' (2.2); the rich are not to be given special treatment. The use of the word 'synagōguē' for the local Christian
community is unexpected. This usage has one possible close parallel in the New Testament,[37] and several in the second century,[38]
but the word *ekklēsia* is elsewhere in the New Testament used in
this sense as it is in 5.14. Adamson takes the use of the word
'synagogue' at this point as confirmation of his thesis that James is
written early and reflects a point of transition between Judaism
and Christianity. However, the evidence could equally point to a
late date, for most of the uses of the word 'synagogue' for
Christian communities are found in the second century. He rejects
the suggestion that a judicial meeting of the Christian community is envisaged because the words 'court' and 'judgement' (v. 6
and vv. 12–13) are used, for he says that these words do not define
the setting. A regular church meeting, he concludes, makes most
sense of the passage, and this is the general consensus.[39]

As just mentioned, the word *ekklēsia*/church appears in 5.14,
where James advises that the sick should send for 'the elders of the
church'. In this instance the word quite clearly refers to an organized local community of Christians with their own office bearers.
This comment about elders, more than anything else in the
epistle, has led some to conclude that James has a well-defined –
and later, more institutional – view of the church, but this is to
be challenged. Christian elders seem to have originated in the
earliest Palestinian church, and in this very Jewish little epistle
they are not unexpected. They are the communal leaders who give
general oversight and provide pastoral care. The author identifies
himself as a teacher, but he allows that teaching can be undertaken by those who aspire to do so and warns of the responsibility
involved (3.1–2). This comment suggests that freedom to exercise
a teaching ministry in Christian gatherings still prevails. Hearing,

listening, and doing the word of God is seen as of great importance (1.21, 22–5, 3.1–12, 5.10); no reference to either baptism or the Eucharist is found. It may be presumed that both were known and taken for granted, but James had no reason to mention them.

Besides the emphasis on hearing the word of God, many other passing comments suggest that the author had communal gatherings much in mind as he wrote.[40] Some of these comments can be read individualistically, but a communal reference is more compelling. Thus the stress on prayer can be noted (1.5–6, 4.2, 5.13–15, 17–19), the command to confess sins to one another (5.16), the mention of praise (3.9–10) and singing (5.13), the reading of Scripture (2.8, 4.5, 5.10–11), and on the need to have good relations with one another (4.1, 11–12, 5.9). An epistle that at first thought could be taken to say little about the church, has much to say on this topic of a practical nature – but none of it of profound theological significance.

As the readers cannot be identified with any certainty, and there is no agreement as to when this epistle should be dated, locating the Christian community in mind socially, in any detail, is problematic. The epistle envisages a group of Jewish Christians who meet together (2.2), have their own elders (5.14), but are somewhat divided by anger (1.19–20), jealousy (4.1–2), slander and criticism within the community (4.11–12). It seems they were mostly poor, but some could relieve the needs of others (2.15–16).

1 Peter

The word *ekklēsia*/church does not appear in 1 Peter, nor does the communal metaphor 'the body', but ecclesiology 'permeates'[41] this little epistle. Indeed, we find here some of the most profound thinking to be seen in the New Testament about the church. In three overlapping themes, Peter spells out what it means to be the Christian community in the world.[42] He insists, first, that as a chosen race, a holy people, a priesthood, a temple, a brotherhood, a flock and a house/temple, the church has a closely defined theological status. Secondly, as believers who meet together to pray and support one another in localized expressions of the one flock, the church has a distinct common life. And, thirdly, as a socially alienated, ethically distinct and suffering group, the church has a precarious social existence in the world.

Theological status

Although many have thought in the past that 1 Peter is addressed to Jewish Christians because it addresses the recipients as if they are children of Israel (cf. 1.1, 17, 2.2–4, 12, 4.3), the 'clear consensus' of scholarly opinion today is that it is 'in fact directed to a predominantly gentile audience'.[43] The evidence need not be reiterated, but the key conclusion is that when Peter uses titles once used of Israel, he is in fact addressing Christians, and when he speaks of outsiders as 'gentiles', he is speaking of unbelievers. Both terms are metaphors. In other words, in 1 Peter, Christians are 'honorary Jews'.[44] The continuing significance of historic Israel in the purposes of God and the place of the law are issues not even raised in this epistle.

Thus the recipients of the epistle are introduced as 'God's elect, exiles in the dispersion' (1.1). The first term speaks of their relationship with God; the second speaks of their relationship with society. Divine election or choice is the essential basis of their distinct Christian identity: that they are now exiles or sojourners in the world is the inevitable social consequence of their election. Three other times in this epistle, the Christian community is designated 'the elect' (*hoi eklektoi*, see also 2.4, 6, 9). This is a common collective title for Christians in the New Testament (e.g. Matt. 20.16; John 1.34; Rom. 8.34; Col. 3.12, etc.), and for Israel in the Old Testament (e.g. 1 Chron. 16.13; Ps. 105.6; Isa. 65.9, 15, 23, etc.). Michaels says this term denotes 'the whole community of Christian believers' being the 'virtual equivalent' of the word 'church'.[45] Peter explains that their election as God's people involves three things (1.2): (1) 'the foreknowledge of God the Father' (cf. 1.15, 2.9, 21, 3.9, 5.10); this points to the ultimate cause of their election; (2) being 'sanctified by the Spirit'; this highlights their separation from the world as God's holy people (cf. 2 Thess. 2.13; 1 Cor. 6.11); and (3) being 'sprinkled with his blood'; this marks them out as the new covenant community, for these words reflect the enactment of the Sinai covenant (Exod. 24.3–8).[46] The Exodus motif returns in 1.18–21, where Jesus is depicted as the sacrificial lamb. The most important statement on the theological status of the Christian community is, however, seen in 2.4–10. Peter begins by exhorting individual Christians to come to Jesus, that 'living stone', a Christological title justified by an appeal to Isaiah 28.16, Psalm 117.22 and Isaiah 8.4, but then he moves to corporate imagery by speaking of a building process that creates 'a spiritual house' (v. 5). Because of the cultic terminology that follows, this house is to be thought of as the new spiritual temple where God now dwells (cf. 1 Cor. 3.16; Eph. 2.19–22).[47] It is 'spiritual' (*pneumatikos*) in the sense that it is not a literal house, but rather one constituted by the Spirit of God. Another metaphor shift then follows: believers who are stones in the temple now become 'a holy priesthood' who 'offer spiritual sacrifices'. The word translated 'priesthood' (*hierateuma*) reflects Exodus 19.6 (the text is quoted in 2.9), where it applies to the whole people of Israel. The point being made is that in this spiritual house, understood as the Christian community, all members have a priestly status.[48] For this reason they are 'to offer spiritual sacrifices acceptable to God through Jesus Christ'.

In the author's mind, priests offer sacrifices; and so if the Christian community is a priestly body, it too must offer sacrifices. However, as these priests are a spiritual house/temple, Peter understands that their sacrifices will be 'spiritual' – like the new temple itself. They will offer metaphorical sacrifices, for the house is a metaphorical temple. What are these spiritual sacrifices to be offered to God? Already in the later parts of the Old Testament the thought is present that what really pleases God is not literal sacrifices, but rather such things as prayer, praise, thankfulness, a broken and a contrite heart, and a life of compassion marked by a concern for justice (e.g. Ps. 50.13–14, 51.16–19, 141.2; Hos. 6.6; Mic. 6.6–8). The Qumran community, cut off from the temple in Jerusalem, developed a similar spiritual interpretation of sacrifice, arguing that 'prayer rightly offered shall be as an acceptable fragrance of righteousness, and perfection of way as a delectable free-will offering' (1QS 9.3–5). After the destruction of the temple in AD 70, orthodox Jews did the same.[49] In 1 Peter, the moral behaviour of Christians is stressed, but it is unlikely that this is the content of the sacrifice to be offered in this instance (cf. Rom. 12.1). It would seem rather that the author has Christian communal worship in mind. He insists that this offering is Godward; it is to be 'acceptable to God through Jesus Christ', and it is to 'declare the praise of him' who called them out of darkness (2.9; cf. Heb. 13.15–16).[50] In other words, the church, corporately considered, is defined as a worshipping community.

In 2.9, a similar and sometimes overlapping series of communal titles are given to the church. Peter declares: 'But *you* [plural – in

contrast to those who do not believe] are a chosen race, a royal
priesthood, a holy nation, a people belonging to God.' All four of
these titles are drawn from either Exodus 19.6 or Isaiah 43.20–1,
where they apply to Israel. In the most explicit way, Peter again
speaks of gentile Christians collectively as if they are Jews. Their
corporate identity is so profound that these gentiles of differing
nationality are called a 'race' (*genos*), as were the Jews. This is the
first recorded use of this title for Christians, which became common
in the second century (*Mart. Pol.* 3.2, 14.1; *Diog.* 1.1; *Herm. Sim.*
9.17.5) and led to them being called 'the third race' – neither Jew
nor gentile (*Preaching of Peter*, Tert. *Ad. Nat.* 1.8, etc.).[51] Also,
Peter identifies them as the people of God (*laos*) explicitly. This is
first stated (v. 11) and then spelt out. Again, using the plural 'you',
the readers are told, 'Once you were not a people, but now you are
the people of God.' The wording is drawn from Hosea 1.6, 9 and
2.1. Previously as gentiles they had not been God's people, but
now, through accepting the gospel, they had been given this
status. With this affirmation, the first major section of the epistle
concludes (1.3—2.10). Two distinct groups have been identified:
unbelievers and 'you who believe'. The latter are firmly identified
as Israel. Surprisingly, nothing at all is said about historic Israel. It
is almost as if it had ceased to exist.

Communal life

We have already noted that Peter calls the corporate praise of the
church a 'spiritual sacrifice' (2.5); but he has other things to say
about church life as well. Once he speaks of baptism (3.21), which
it is said 'now saves you – not as a removal of dirt from the body,
but as an appeal to God for a good conscience'. The sense in which
it can be said that baptism saves is explained by the parenthetical
clause. It is doubtful that Peter is saying something so obvious as
that Christian baptism is not just a washing away of dirt. The
point he is making seems to be that Christian baptism is not
simply a washing away of moral defilement (cf. Jas. 1.21). It is
rather an 'appeal'[52] to God for a good conscience, either in the
sense that it is an enacted prayer asking God for inner cleansing
and forgiveness, or a 'pledge' to God to maintain a good conscience, in the sense that it is a promise to keep from sin. What is
given more prominence than baptism is, however, conversion,
which is described in a number of ways. It is a new birth (1.3, 23),

a ransom from a former futile life (1.18), coming to trust in God (2.21), obedience to the truth (1.22), tasting that 'the Lord is good' (2.3), 'to receive mercy' (2.10), and to be 'healed' (2.24). This has been made possible by the shedding of 'the precious blood of Christ, like that of a lamb without defect or blemish' (2.19), and because 'he bore our sins in his body on the cross, so that free from sins, we might live for righteousness' (2.24). Peter understands that Christ's death has made provision for the salvation of his people. Conversion publicly witnessed to in baptism appropriates this salvation, and at the same time incorporates the believer into the Christian community, the new Israel.

In this community of the redeemed, social relationships are to be different to those seen in the world. In speaking of the qualities demanded of those in the Christian community, yet another title for the Christian community, the church, appears. Peter exhorts his readers to love 'the brotherhood' (*adelphotēs*) (2.17 and 5.9). This use of a somewhat uncommon noun to speak of the church may reflect distinctive terminology coined in Petrine circles. Closely related to this familial address is the wording in two exhortations to pursue 'brotherly love' (*philadelphoi*) (1.22, 3.8). The need to exhibit love for one another in the church again is stressed in 4.8, where Peter says, 'above all maintain love [*agapē*] for one another'. This love is in part to be shown in being 'hospitable to one another without complaining' (4.9). Another practical expression of brotherly or mutual love in the community is to 'greet one another with a kiss of love' (5.14). In regard to ministry in the community, Peter insists that God has given 'a gift [*charisma*] to each', and as 'good stewards of the manifold grace of God', believers are to minister to one another by either word or deed (4.10–11). This broad twofold division of charismatic ministries is an early functional differentiation which was possibly later formalized in the office of the bishop and the deacon (cf. Acts 6.1–6; 1 Tim. 3.1–13).[53] As Peter speaks about these ministries in the context of a discussion on the practical love of Christians for one another, it would seem that he sees them as given for the edification of the community.

Having spoken about the charismatic ministry given 'to each' believer, Peter then addresses the elders in particular (5.1–5). Apparently, in these churches charismatic and institutional forms of ministry coexisted in the same way as the Book of Acts describes.[54] Since the elders are contrasted with the younger members, it is to be understood that age was the one essential qualification for being designated an 'elder'. These elders are 'to tend' (or, more literally, 'shepherd') the 'flock of God which is in [their] charge' (v. 2). These words echo the command of Christ to Peter to 'shepherd my sheep' (John 21.15–19), and closely parallel the wording of Acts 20.28, where the words 'flock' (*poimnion*) and church (*ekklēsia*) are equated. The word *ekklēsia* is not used here or elsewhere in 1 Peter, but at this point the total community of believers (the so-called universal church) (cf. 'your brothers and sisters in all the world', 5.9) and particular congregations are distinguished in the comment about 'the flock of God'. There is only one flock, for there is only one shepherd (2.25); but wherever Christians become an identifiable group, this flock is present. Thus Peter exhorts these elders to shepherd the flock 'in your care'. The NRSV translation quoted captures well the meaning of the Greek (*en humin*). The elders are to exercise their ministry over that part of the flock that is personally known to them, and of which they are a part. This same idea appears again when Peter exhorts the elders 'not to lord it over those in your charge' (5.3).[55] Bigg, writing at the turn of this century, anticipates the recent realization of the fact that the house church was the congregational setting for the early believers. He says that these words suggest that 'particular presbyters may have had charge of a particular house-church, while for certain purposes all the presbyters met in council'.[56] These details are important in establishing Peter's conception of the church, but the reason why the elders are spoken to at this point should not be missed. Peter demands that the manner and motives of their leadership should be pleasing to 'the chief shepherd' (v. 4). In other words, he is insisting that there be distinctives in Christian communal leadership. They are to labour not for material gain: to lead, but not be domineering (5.2–3).

Social separation

Because the Christian community is the counterpart of Israel, believers are to be as separate from pagan society as were Jews in the past. The author believes there is, and there should be seen to be, a difference between those who accept or reject Christ (2.47); between those who obey the word and those who do not (2.8, 3.1,

4.17); between 'us' and 'them' (2.4, 9, 4.18). At one and the same time, faith in Christ unites and divides. Christian communal distinctiveness in the first instance, Peter insists, involves an ethical separateness. He writes, 'Like obedient children, do not be conformed to the desires that you formerly had in ignorance. Instead, as he who called you is holy, be holy yourselves in all your conduct for it is written, "You shall be holy, for I am holy."' The quoting of Leviticus 19.2, which originally applied to 'all the congregation of the people of Israel' (Lev. 17.2), illustrates how completely the church has supplanted historic Israel. Many similar exhortations to holy living follow (cf. 1.17–18, 3.1–2, 11–12, 18–25, 3.1–7, 8–17, 4.1–6, 12–19). This brief letter contains no less than fifty-one imperative exhortations, most of them of an ethical nature.[57]

The description of the Christian community as 'exiles' (1.1, 17) and as 'aliens and exiles' (2.11)[58] is also particularly important in any discussion on how 1 Peter views the church as a social entity in the world. These terms are pregnant with meaning. They first of all draw to mind Israel's sojourn in Egypt as slaves (cf. Acts 13.7), thereby once more identifying the Christian community as the counterpart of Israel. Secondly, they convey the thought that the church is not at home in this world. It is in an environment that is hostile and unwelcoming. This means that the Christian community cannot avoid standing apart from the society in which it finds itself. Elliott argues that these comments about the social standing of the Christian community addressed in this epistle go beyond theological description. They in fact allude to the actual political, legal, and social status of these Christians. The Christian community is socially marginalized, and an 'alien' group as far as the state and the local populace are concerned.[59] The many comments on suffering in this epistle support this thesis.

1 Peter speaks six times about the suffering of Christ and/or his people (1.6–7, 2.19–25, 3.13–22, 4.1–6, 12–19, 5.9–10). Far from being offended by the idea that Christ and his followers should suffer, Peter suggests that this is be expected. Almost certainly, these comments reflect a situation where the persecution of Christians was a common experience. The opponents are not specified. Most commentators think it unlikely that the persecution was motivated by any local official decree or imperial policy.[60] Elliott identifies the persecutors as both Jews and gentiles hostile to this new exclusive 'sect'.[61] This suffering comes because they are

'Christians' (4.16) and members of 'the household of God' (4.17), says Peter, but he adds that it is happening also 'to your brothers and sisters in all the world' (5.9).

The epistles of John

One of the special characteristics of the three epistles of John is the concern to define the 'true' Christian community in distinction from those who have broken away, whom the author thinks are the enemies of Christ. This means that in these epistles the main ecclesiological concern is the definition of the boundaries of the Christian community. What are the marks of the true church? The question of the relationship between the church and Israel is of no interest at all.

It is generally thought that one person is responsible for the three epistles, but the author is not named. In 2 and 3 John, the author calls himself 'the elder'. The force of this title is uncertain, but one thing is clear: he believes that he has the right to speak to these Christians with some authority. The epistles of John have a family resemblance to the Gospel of John, and many have argued that the one man first wrote the Gospel, and then some years later, in response to changed circumstances, the three epistles. However, the modern, widely held view that John's Gospel appeared in more than one edition, and that there was a community especially concerned with the transmission and preservation of the Johannine tradition, complicates things. This debate can be studied elsewhere,[62] but it is to be noted that 1 John does supply evidence for the existence of a community of Christians who looked to the apostle John as their founder and the source of their knowledge of Christ. Although the first person singular, 'I', is used with the verb 'write', the author does not claim individual or independent authority; instead he writes as if he is speaking on behalf of a group. On more than fifty occasions in 1 John, the plural 'we', 'us', or 'our' appears. In the opening prologue (1.1–4), the use of the collective 'we' is most striking.

The identity of those who have left the community, whom the author identifies as 'anti-Christs' (1 John 2.18–19, 4.3; 2 John 7), is uncertain. Once they belonged, but now they stand apart and are viewed as implacable opponents of the truth. In seeking to clarify the essentials of true belief and thereby underline the boundaries between the two communities, the author repeatedly returns to what have been called 'the tests of life'. At least nine times the readers are told how they may assure themselves that they are in fellowship with the apostolic community, and thus with the Father and the Son (1 John 1.3; cf. 1.7). In each case, these tests begin with the words 'by this we know' or 'by this we can be sure' (2.3, 5, 3.16, 19, 24, 4.2, 6). These tests, as the plural pronouns and the comment about fellowship show, are not given for personal assurance of one's standing before God, but of one's membership of the community of salvation.[63] As far as John is concerned, those who do not belong to 'the true church' are lost (1 John 2.18–23, 3.10, 14, 4.5; 2 John 9). Three tests are given the most prominence: right belief, Christlike behaviour, and love for one another.

Confidence that one belongs to the apostolic community of faith is first of all marked by a right confession of Christ. What this involves is spelt out in the Johannine epistles, mainly in contrast to what those who have gone out believe. They seem to have denied that Jesus is the Christ (5.1) who came in the 'flesh' (4.2; 2 John 7), that he is the Son of God (1.3, 7, 3.8, 23, etc.), and that he 'came by water and the blood' – that is, as an historical person (5.6). However, these people do not only fail in their confession of Christ, they also fail in their behaviour as professed followers of Christ. Thus the second test of membership is a life lived in a way pleasing to Christ. John writes, 'by this we may be sure that we know him, if we obey his commandments. Whoever says, "I have come to know him," but does not obey his commandments, is a liar, and in such a person the truth does not exist . . . whoever says, "I abide in him" ought to walk as he walked' (1 John 1.3–6; cf. 1.6–10, 3.3–10, etc.). The third test of membership is love: 'we know that we have passed from death to life because we love one another' (1 John 3.14; cf. 2.10, 3.18, 4.7–21, etc.). Many commentators have argued that love is the most important theme in 1 John, noting the repeated use of the word (noun, *agapan* 18 times; verb, *agapē*, 28 times), and that this one term can be used of God's relationship with believers, believers' relationship with God, and their relationship with one another. It is this last matter that is of interest to us. One of the most constant refrains in 1 John is, 'let us love one another', or its equivalent. This love, it is quite clear, is to be expressed to fellow believers. Even the demand to share with those in need applies only to other members of the 'true' church, for they are 'brothers' (3.17).[64] This has led to the charge that the commands to love in this epistle fall far short of the command of Christ, 'to love our neighbour as our self', for this love is only of those who are fellow 'true' believers; the opponents deserve no love, they are to be turned away if they try to make contact (2 John 10–11), and unbelievers who are in need are not even considered.[65] This charge cannot be brushed aside, for there is some truth in it; but an appreciation of the situation envisaged by these epistles helps explain why this is so. These epistles reflect a community in crisis caused by schism. This has resulted in internal questioning and dissent, and animosity from those who have left. The appeals to love one another are thus part of the 'damage control' made in response; they are an attempt to strengthen community cohesion and community identity. This is seen to be the primary need of the hour, and it is so pressing that the wider vision is eclipsed.

Closely related to what has just been discussed is the charge that these epistles are marked by a dualistic attitude to the world. In most of the twenty-three uses of the word 'world' (*kosmos*) in 1 John, and the one use in 2 John, it refers to human society opposed to God. In 1 John 2.15, believers are not 'to love the world'; in 3.1 they are not known by the world because the world does not know God; in 3.13, they are hated by the world; in 4.3, they are to be careful for the 'antichrist' is in the world; and in 5.19, they are warned that 'the whole world lies under the power of the evil one'. This is not divergent New Testament teaching: it is only the emphasis that is distinctive.[66] The reason for this is again the situation addressed. This community of Christians is very much feeling under threat from the hostile forces arrayed against them, both of a human and a supernatural kind. These comments by the author, in yet another way, seek again to strengthen community distinctiveness and solidarity.

In 1 John, collective and corporate terms for the Christian community, such as 'the church', 'the body', or 'the saints', are missing. Instead, John addresses his readers in personal forms such as 'beloved', 'children', or 'brothers', but this should not lead to the conclusion that the Christian community (the church as a corporate, theologically defined reality) is of no concern to the author. What has been said so far shows that this is not the case, and much more can be added. The author insists that true believers have been born into God's family (5.1) and are now his children;[67] in a unique way they 'know' God or Christ;[68] God abides in them and they abide in him,[69] and they have fellowship with one another (1.3, 6).

The use of the word *koinonia*/'fellowship' in the opening chapter deserves a comment. The Greek noun carries the meaning 'participate in' or 'share in', thereby differing from the English word 'fellowship', so often used to translate it, which brings to mind first of all convivial relationships.[70] John says he writes that they (the readers) may have *'koinonia* with us' (the 'us' is the apostolic community) as 'our *koinonia* is with the Father and the Son' (1 John 1.3). The writer and those who stand with him believe they participate in the divine life in a vertical *koinonia*, and their desire is that those to whom they write will also enjoy this blessing by holding to the truth as revealed in Christ. It will then be possible for them to enjoy a horizontal *koinonia* together. In verse 7, the basis of horizontal *koinonia* is predicated on walking together in the light. In this chapter, therefore, the word *koinonia* is used to describe both the believers' relationship with God in Christ that constitutes the church and the relationship believers have with one another. We conclude, then, that while the language and the imagery is different to what has been seen elsewhere, the epistles of John still conceive of the Christian community as a corporate entity. It is a family – God's family – distinguished by the fact that those who belong to it have a personal knowledge and fellowship with their heavenly Father, and his Son, Jesus Christ.

House churches

Very little is said in these epistles about the practicalities of Christian communal life, and what can be deduced about this comes mainly from 2 and 3 John.[71] Recent scholarly studies of the Johannine epistles tend to argue that what is implied is a number of house churches probably in and around Ephesus;[72] 2 John is an epistle written by the leader of one house church to another house church in the region. He calls those to whom he writes, 'the elect lady and her children' (v. 1) and his own group, 'the children of your elect sister' (v. 13). This is generally taken to be a metaphorical way of speaking of a congregation. He warns those to whom he writes of the 'many deceivers who have gone out into the world, those who do not confess that Jesus Christ has come in the flesh'

(v. 7), and tells them not to receive such people into 'the house' – which almost certainly means your house church (v. 10). These words make it plain that the threat from the world comes not from unbelievers, but from heretical teachers.

The situation envisaged by 3 John is somewhat more difficult to work out. The short letter is written by the elder to 'the beloved Gaius' (v. 1) – probably a house church leader – whom he commends for 'walking in the truth' (v. 3). He also speaks warmly of 'the brothers' (vv. 3, 5, and 10) who have spoken of Gaius' love before the church/*ekklēsia*. The three uses of this word in 3 John allude to an identifiable community of Christians. Their ongoing communal membership is seen in that the elder writes to 'the church' (v. 9), and allows that people can be excluded from membership of the church (v. 10). These 'brothers', it would appear, are 'orthodox' travelling teachers and/or evangelists. This is made plain, for the elder says, 'they have gone out for the sake of the name' (v. 7), which reflects early mission terminology.[73] The particular problem on which he instructs Gaius concerns Diotrephes, 'who likes to put himself first' and will not accept Gaius' authority (v. 9). What is more, he is 'spreading false charges against us' and 'refuses to welcome brothers' (v. 10). Is Diotrephes another house church leader who has been won over by the false teachers, or is this but a personal feud? Most think it is the former. Demetrius, who is warmly mentioned at the close of the letter, is probably yet another house church leader (v. 12). A great deal has been made of the comment about Diotrephes. In a number of ways the argument has been put that this man had assumed an office in the church, possibly that of bishop, and Gaius opposed this.[74] On this view, the problem faced in this epistle is to do with a battle over church order: Gaius representing the older charismatic ideal, and Diotrephes the emerging institutional model. This is unconvincing because too much is made of too little. Possibly, Diotrephes is simply an egotistical leader who differed from Gaius on a number of matters. He may well have seen Gaius in the same light.

The suggestion that the Johannine epistles reflect a largely informal and charismatic pattern of church leadership is nevertheless basically correct. To say this is not, however, to endorse Schweizer's thesis that in the Johannine writings we have 'the most radical' ecclesiology to be found in the New Testament:

where 'there is no longer any kind of special ministry, but only direct union with God through the Spirit who comes to every individual'.[75] In 1 John, this idea could be suggested by the comment in 2.26–7: 'I write these things to you concerning those who would deceive you. As for you, the anointing that you received from him abides in you, and you do not need anyone to teach you. But his anointing teaches you about all things.' If John intended to deny the right of any human to teach about the Christian faith, he was excluding himself and should not have put pen to paper. It is more likely therefore that what he is excluding is the right of anyone to teach otherwise than what is given by the Spirit.[76] On this interpretation, these words should be taken with 1 John 4.1, where the readers are told 'to test the spirits to see whether they are from God; for many false prophets have gone out into the world'. The obvious meaning of this verse is that every word of prophecy is to be evaluated. The test of content is then given; it is a right confession of Christ (4.2–3). There can be no doubt that these comments indicate that spontaneous, Spirit-inspired ministry still played a part in the Johannine house churches, but these epistles also show that insipient institutional leadership was also known. The author of 1 John writes as a recognized teacher; the author of 2 and 3 John calls himself 'the elder', which separates him in some ways from ordinary church members; and in 3 John, a number of recognized house church leaders are named.

Evaluation and setting

The epistles of John betray a distinctive ecclesiology as part of the Johannine tradition, and because of the context in which they arise. They are, as has been underlined, a response to painful divisions that have taken place in the community addressed. The teaching on the church is directed to meet this challenge. The emphasis falls on separation from the world, separation from those who have gone out, and close familial relationships with other 'true' believers. These epistles are rich in the language of personal communion with God and Christ; they stress that believers may know the assurance of sins forgiven; they speak the power of faith to conquer the world, and of the Christians collectively as the family of God. Yet although they have been numbered among the 'catholic epistles' (along with 1 and 2 Peter, James, and Jude) because it was thought they were originally addressed to the whole church, they are in fact somewhat narrow in outlook. There is a tendency to be inward looking and somewhat defensive.

The Book of Revelation

The final book in the Bible is addressed to 'the seven churches which are in Asia' (1.4, 11). The number seven is symbolic and signifies completion or totality. It suggests that these letters are directed not only to the churches of Asia, but also to the whole Christian community, the universal church on earth.[77] This is made clear in the refrain at the end of each of the seven letters, 'Let any one who has an ear listen to what the Spirit is saying to the churches', which means, 'Listen well, there is a word from God here for every Christian'. In its entirety, the Book of Revelation is a prophetic word to the Christian community of western Asia Minor at a given point of time, as it faces persecution and senses its social marginalization.[78] However, such is its power that it still speaks to all who listen. It proclaims that because the Lamb has triumphed, his people will triumph. In heaven the Lamb is being worshipped even now in never-ending praise, and soon heaven will come down to earth. Various suggestions have been made as to the main concern of the Book of Revelation, but if we follow those commentators who argue that the book is written to encourage the suffering Christian community on earth, then Harrington's claim that 'the church is the centre of interest of this book'[79] must be seriously considered.

The seven churches are again mentioned in 1.20, where an angel explains to John the meaning of his first vision: 'the seven stars are the angels of the seven churches, and the seven lampstands are the seven churches'. Since seven is the number of completeness, John is speaking of the whole church, of which the seven churches of Asia Minor are representative.[80] The role of the church is to bear witness, this point being made under the symbolism of light. If any individual church ceases to do this, the reason for its existence is lost (2.5).

What is meant by 'the angels of the churches' is much more difficult. As the word 'angel' usually refers to a heavenly being in Revelation, it is best to take it in this sense.[81] Possibly John understood that each church had a guardian angel (cf. Dan. 10.13, 20–1; Matt. 18.10; Acts 12.15; 1 Cor.11.10).[82] What entity John has in mind when he addresses 'the church' of a particular city is uncertain. Is he thinking of a small house church, or of a local community of Christians who meet in separate house churches? It is very doubtful whether in each of these cities there was only one house church with from twenty to a maximum of fifty members. That John uses the word *ekklēsia* of local communities of Christians seems most likely; he is writing to the Christians in Pergamum, Thyatira, and so on. His main emphasis seems to be on the witness of these believers in their own city (2.2, 9, 13, 19, 3.1, 8, 15, 17).

The church is Israel

In Revelation, the Christian community, the universal church, is, as Schweizer says, 'no longer merely the legitimate development of Israel – it is Israel'.[83] The church completely supplants the old entity. The Jews are allied with the forces of the beast and doomed to destruction.[84] This is plainly said in the letters to the seven churches, but this thought is prominent in the symbolism of the rest of the book. In 2.9 and 3.9, Jews who oppose the church are denied their national name and said to be 'a synagogue of Satan' – implying a contrast with 'the church of God'. In the first of these references, in the letter to the church at Smyrna, John speaks of the *slander* of those 'who say that they are Jews'. 'Slander' (*blasphēmia*) is a very negative word. Elsewhere in the book this term is reserved for the activities of the beast and the whore (13.1, 5, 6, 17.3). The pervasive use of the Old Testament in Revelation is widely noted, but how it is applied to the Christian community is what is most important. The Seer *typologically* makes the church the successor to historic Israel. It is the Christian community who are taking part in the second exodus, who have been redeemed from slavery by the death of the Lamb, and are now enjoying the blessings of the new covenant; and it is the enemies of the Christian community who fall under the judgement of God as he sends 'plagues' on them.[85] In this framework of thought, the earthly Jerusalem, representing Judaism, becomes 'Sodom and Egypt' (11.8), and the Christian community becomes Israel who takes over the promises once made to the Jewish people.[86] Twice the author of Revelation, quoting the great covenant passage Exodus 19.6, applies it to Christians. He says they have been made 'a kingdom, priests to God' (1.6, 5.10; cf. 20.6).[87] This is the same passage quoted in 1 Peter 2.9 ('you are a royal priesthood'), where the collective noun *hierateuma*, reflecting the *LXX*, is used; this implies that the whole Christian community is a priestly body. In Revelation, in contrast, a literal translation of the Hebrew is given, introducing the concrete specific term *hiereis*/priest. Every believer is a priest in their own right and all have royal dignity. This author is not satisfied in giving priestly status to the church in its entirety: he attributes priestly status to each believer.

Between the description of three sets of seven judgements soon to fall from heaven on the enemies of the Christian community on earth, the church, there are three interludes where the author digresses to shed light on what is happening, and will happen, to the Christian community on earth in this time. The first of these interludes is found in chapter 7 between the account of the breaking open of the sixth and seventh seals. It seeks to assure Christians that they will eventually triumph. Two visions are recounted (7.1–8 and 7.9–17), both of which apply to the Christian community. In the first, the 144,000 out of every tribe of Israel who are 'sealed' are called 'the servants of our God'. They are the whole Christian community, the church on earth, understood as Israel of the last days as elsewhere in Revelation (cf. 2.20, 11.18, 14.1, 19.2, 5, 22.3, 6). The sealing thus has a double significance: it is a mark of God's ownership and thus of his protection.[88] In the second version, the same group is in mind, but it is now seen at the climax of world history as 'a great multitude that no one could count' (v. 9).[89]

Between the sixth and seventh trumpet, another interlude occurs (10.1—11.13) that seeks to answer two questions: how long is it before the end, and what is the Christian community to be doing now? The first question is answered in the first vision: 'there will be no more delay' (10.6). The thought that the end is close at hand is consistently taught in Revelation (cf. 2.16, 3.11, 20, 22.8, 20, etc.).[90] The second vision begins with a symbolic action, the measuring of the temple. The background to this is found in Ezekiel 40–8. In this vision the temple is the Christian community, the church, and the implied thought is that God will protect his people through the present distress. God speaking through the angel then says, 'I will grant my two witnesses authority to prophesy' (v. 3). In Revelation, prophecy and witnessing are closely related (cf. 1.2, 19.10); it is in the power of the Spirit that witness to Christ is made. Who these two witnesses represent in this symbolism is much debated. Moses and Elijah, or John the Baptist and Christ are two options, but it seems that the immediate application is to the whole church.[91] Bauckham writes:

> Two individual prophets represent the prophetic witness to which the whole church is called in the final period of world history, the 1260 days (11.3). That they represent the church is shown by the identification of them as the 'two lampstands that stand before the Lord of the earth' (11.14; cf. Zech. 4.1–14) . . . lampstands which represent the seven churches (1.12, 20, 2.1).[92]

The third interlude (12.1—14.20) marks a major division in the book. Before giving an account of the seven last plagues, the bowls of wrath, John pauses to explain in rich symbolism the ultimate cause of the hostility now being experienced by the Christian community. It is part of the age-long conflict between God and Satan. Although the crucial battle was won by the Lamb on the cross, his adversary, despite his 'mortal wound', continues to struggle and oppress his servants, 'the saints'. Cast out of the heavenly realm, Satan, personified in the beast, now rages – knowing his time is short. The church is suffering; but in disclosing what is really happening, John hopes to strengthen believers on earth in these last days before the final glorious victory when they will reign with the Lamb in heaven.

In this section (12.1—14.20), the Christian community is three times called 'the saints' (13.7, 10, 14.12) – a designation frequently applied to Israel in the Old Testament, as has been pointed out repeatedly – but the church is also depicted symbolically as Israel of the last days. In 12.1, the woman crowned with twelve stars is the church, the heavenly Jerusalem, the successor to Israel,[93] which is proleptically realized in the Christian community now suffering on earth. In Jewish writings, Zion as the mother of Israel is a common motif (Isa. 54.1; 2 Esdra 10.7; cf. Gal.4.26). This interpretation is confirmed by verse 17, where, it is said, the dragon made war with the children of the woman, 'those who keep the commandments of God and hold the testimony of Jesus'. In chapter 14, the Seer comes to speak of the final victory of the redeemed, and at this point the church is again depicted under the image of the 144,000, the totality of Israel, who are standing on Mount Zion with the Lamb.

The heavenly Jerusalem

The church again comes to the fore in the concluding chapters of
Revelation. In 19.11ff, it is clear that the Seer is speaking of the
return of Christ and of the final victory, but in the thought of
Revelation this is but a disclosure of what already is a reality. Rissi
concludes, 'Since for the seer, the goal of all history has become
visible in the history of Jesus, the future will be first of all the
unveiling of the true nature of the present.'[94] For this reason, the
vision of 'the holy city, the new Jerusalem, coming down from
heaven from God, prepared as a bride for her husband' (21.2) is
both a statement of faith about what the church is in God's sight
now, and a declaration of how it will be seen by all in the near
future. In the preceding chapter, this is made plain because in the
final battle of the church on earth, Gog and Magog 'surround the
camp of the saints and the beloved city' (20.9). The 'beloved city'
is not geographic Jerusalem that is equated with Sodom and
Egypt (11.8), but a metaphorical Jerusalem, equated with the
church.

The opening verses of chapter 21 bring together a number of
key theological ideas, all having communal dimension, which in
each case are both present reality and future hope: the new creation (v. 1), the new Jerusalem (v. 2), the new temple (v. 3a), the
new covenant (v. 3b), and the new Israel (v. 4).[95] Dumbrell says,
here is 'the meeting point of heaven and earth'.[96] In 20.9–27, the
new Jerusalem is symbolically described, and it is pointed out that
in this city there will be no temple (vv. 20ff). This is because God's
presence will be ubiquitous. In this cluster of images, the Old
Testament is once more read typologically. The church takes the
place of Israel, and is seen as God's new creation in Christ. No
localized temple building is needed now, and no temple will be
needed after the final consummation.

Although the Book of Revelation is radically dualistic in outlook, constantly assuming that there is a counterpart to earthly
existence in the heavenly realm, the universal church made up of
the saints, the servants of God, is always seen as a suffering community on this earth. It has its counterpart in heaven made up of
angelic beings, and those who have been martyred (8.3–4), and it
will be revealed in all its glory as heaven comes down to earth on
the last day; but in the present, the church is Christian people on
earth. It is the community that has been redeemed by the Lamb

(1.6, 5.9–10), designated 'a kingdom and priests serving God' (5.10, 1.6, 20.6), described as new Israel (7.4ff, 14.1), symbolically named as 'a woman' with a crown of twelve stars on her head (12.10) who is persecuted and has children (12.17), which on the last day will be seen as the new Jerusalem (20.7, 21.2) and the bride of Christ (21.2).

The worship of the church

One theme of continuing significance in the Book of Revelation is the worship of God or Christ. Peterson writes:

> Visions of the heavenly realm consistently portray the offering of adoration and praise to God and the lamb and the language of worship pervades the whole book. Most significantly, the worship term *proskunein* is used twenty-four times, in ways that indicate the centrality of this theme to the author's message.[97]

John the seer was apparently in worship 'on the Lord's day' when he received this revelation (1.10). A vision of the worship in heaven commences the main part of the book (4.1–11), and the book concludes with a vision of the heavenly Jerusalem where worship will be uninterrupted (22.1–5). It is in fact the terminology of Revelation that gives us the English word 'worship' – to give someone or something their worth. In 4.11, the twenty-four elders who 'worship' (*proskunein*) the one who lives for ever and ever cry, 'You are *worthy* [*axios*], our Lord and God, to receive glory and honour and power' (4.11, 5.12). Frequently in Revelation this worship takes place in heaven (4.10, 5.14, 7.11, 11.16, 19.4, etc.), but on earth it can take two forms, false worship of the beast (9.20, 13.4, 8, 12, 15, 16.2, 19.20), or the true worship of God or the Lamb (11.1, 14.7, 15.4). The stress on worship in Revelation, which is far wider than a study of the terms suggests,[98] implies that giving worth to God in praise and prayer and adoration must have been a vital part of the experience of the Christians addressed. Liturgical language, often in the form of doxologies, is found throughout the book (1.5–6, 17–18, 4.8, 11, 5.9–10, etc.). The doxology that addresses Christ alone (1.5–6) is of particular interest, for it shows that John and his readers not only worshipped God, but also Jesus.[99] It is probable that the wording of these doxologies and hymns of praise reflect something of the worship that was characteristic of the church known to John the Seer.[100] In reading these passages one almost feels transposed into another world. Indeed, Thompson argues that Revelation implies a belief that in worship, heavenly, end-time realities break into earthly existence: eschatological reality becomes present reality.[101]

Church order

Very little is said about the leadership of the churches addressed;[102] prophets obviously were prominent. The book is called a 'prophecy' (1.3, 22.7, 10, 18, 19), and the author was very conscious that God was speaking through him in a quite distinct and authoritative way (1.3, 21.5, 22.6). There were, however, others who could be called prophets (10.7, 11.18, 16.16, 18.20, 24, 22.6, 9), and bearing witness to Jesus, something expected of every Christian, seems to be described as a manifestation of prophecy (19.10).[103] Elders are frequently mentioned, but always as heavenly figures (4.4, 10, 5.5, etc.). This suggests, nevertheless, that the leadership of elders was well known, and therefore quite possibly part of the leadership structures of the Christian communities in the cities to which the Book of Revelation was first sent.

Social setting

The theology in general (and the ecclesiology in particular) of the Book of Revelation is highly contextual, finding its setting in a specific religio-political social setting. It is a book written to Christians suffering persecution to encourage them amid their trials and to assure them that God will punish their oppressors and vindicate them. In this struggle, which has cosmic implications, there are two earthbound solidarities who represent God and the devil respectively, set in implacable opposition to one another. On one side is the Christian community, the church, and on the other is the Roman empire and all who share in its ideology, oppression, and violence. The Roman empire is seen in this light not because it persecutes the Christian community, but because it 'absolutises itself by claiming the religious loyalty due only to the ultimate power of God'.[104] It is thus described as 'the beast' who blasphemes (13.1–3).

In this setting, it is not at all surprising that we find the church completely identified with Israel of old, undertaking a second exodus, again involved in a holy war, and led by Christ as the Messiah whose work it is to establish God's reign on earth. This profound theological definition of the Christian community is matched by a demand for social separation. Those who belong to the lamb must not share with those who worship the beast. The two communities based on the allegiances given are diametrically opposed to one another. As a consequence, an ecclesiology of great clarity emerges. The church on earth is a spiritual community, a reflection of another community already existing in the heavens. It is separate from the world, but living in the world as a witness to the transcendent power of God to those blinded by Satan and his minions. Though persecuted and suffering, the church is assured of final victory. This community is intrinsically one, but Christians find themselves in particular believing communities in the cities of the empire, and John seems also to call these groupings 'the church in', and then name the city. In these localized communities, the challenge is to remain faithful, maintain a clear witness to Christ, oppose heresy, and bravely face opposition and persecution in the power God supplies.

Chapter 8

Drawing the Threads Together and the Visible–Invisible Church

One of the main goals of this book has been to bring some clarity and precision to the theological meaning of the word 'church'. We began by putting forward the almost obvious thesis that the church should be defined as 'the Christian community'. On this basis, we have undertaken a detailed study of the communal thinking of the apostolic writers. What we have found is that assuming this definition, all the relevant material in the New Testament can be explained and integrated. At every point, this thesis or theory made sense of what was given in scripture, and what was given in scripture confirmed the thesis. One significant aspect of our approach has been the argument that the word *ekklēsia* is not the right starting point, or the only issue to pursue, in seeking to discover what the New Testament says about the 'church', defined as the Christian community. The point was made that when the word *ekklēsia*, in isolation, is made the main route to establish the ecclesiology of the New Testament, so much is missed, for often 'the church idea' (the Christian community) is present although the specific Greek word is not.

However, besides confirming the basic premise on which the study commenced, we discovered not a community established and defined once for all, but a community in transition. The church brought into existence by the life, death, and resurrection of Jesus Christ is depicted as slowly realizing its true identity and slowly coming to terms with its ongoing life in the world. In the pages of the New Testament we see this community working out its beliefs in response to issues as they arose, defining itself theologically, especially in relation to its parent, the nation Israel, and gradually ordering its communal life. This was a dynamic process. Different writers often come to the same question in different ways, varied theological definitions of the Christian community are given, and church order assumed varying forms from place to place and tended to become more structured with the passing of time. This varied and developing ecclesiology seen in the New Testament was indelibly brought to the attention of Christian leaders at the 1963 Montreal conference on Faith and Order, when Professor Ernst Kasemann gave a lecture on 'Unity and Multiplicity in the New Testament Doctrine of the Church'.[1] He argued that the New Testament does not present a unified understanding of the church, but rather 'a number of ecclesiological archetypes' and 'an incessant process of change'.[2] The Roman Catholic scholar Raymond Brown[3] has come to a similar conclusion, as has the English Protestant James Dunn.[4] We need not necessarily accept the details of the differing cases they make on this matter, but the general thesis that in the New Testament we see variation and development in the theological understanding and social structuring of the church has been confirmed by this study.

Yet to admit this could suggest that no conclusions can be drawn from the New Testament about what should be believed about the church, or how it should be ordered. Once the Bible was a source of texts that were used to prove every doctrine of importance, but now only the diversity in scripture is seen; but hopefully there is some middle ground between these two extremes. The old dogmatism that proved too much must be abandoned, but within the diversity now seen so clearly in scripture there would appear to be major themes and ideas that bind together the parts.[5] It is these we must pursue as we seek for guidance from scripture for Christian living in our age. This study has proceeded on the premise that some constants and foundational beliefs can be discovered in relation to the church. It is now time to see if this premise stands. In what follows I want to draw together some key themes that could give direction and inspiration for a renewing theology of the church for our own day and age. This section will be quite short, for much of what is concluded stands on its own feet as a summary of what has been discovered by our inductive study of the communal thinking of the major contributors to the New Testament.

Some key theological insights

1 *The Christian community is one*

First of all, it is clear that every contributor to the New Testament is of a common mind on at least one issue: there is but one Christian community. The various writers may theologically define this entity in different ways and witness to more or less structuring of the corporate life of those who belong to this community, but they all agree that the exalted Christ now reigns over a world-wide company of people, which in Matthew's Gospel Jesus calls 'my church'. Jesus himself is always the primary focus of these writers, but when they come to think of those who confess him as Lord and know the presence of his Spirit, they think first of all of a great company of people who are united to him and to each other. This explains the constant emphasis on the unity of believers. The church by definition is one community in Christ; this is a given fact. The responsibility of believers is to recognize this, work to maintain it, and demonstrate it in their relationships with fellow Christians. Membership in this community is predicated on belief in Christ, characterized by the forgiveness of sins and the presence of the Holy Spirit, and realized through baptism.

This fundamental insight calls into question immediately all essentially congregational definitions of the church. Not only is the thought that the congregation is somehow primary in antipathy with the apostolic vision of the church as one world-wide community, but it is also alien to the communal thinking of the biblical writers. As important as the congregation is as the concrete expression of Christian community, the prevailing mind set of the biblical age was that people were to be understood in relation to the larger groupings to which they belonged. To say this is not to suggest a return to the fold of Rome that claims to be the one true church, or endorse the goal of creating one institutionally united church, or even to challenge the validity of independent congregations, but to suggest that much of the congregational thinking of modern Christians that sees the congregation as complete in itself and primary is misguided. It is a reflection of the values of our age rather than anything in the Bible.

2 *The Christian community is true Israel*

In seeking to define the new community called into existence by Christ, the New Testament authors begin by seeking to explain it in relation to Israel, God's own people of the old covenant. Luke is possibly the most conservative, defining the church primarily as renewed Israel, but he shows that he is finding this definition hard to maintain as he writes. In his earlier epistles, Paul also struggles with this issue. Right from the beginning he designates the Christian community with titles once the sole preserve of Israel, but in the epistle to the Romans he shows himself to be reluctant to concede that God has completely abandoned Israel as his people. He solves his dilemma by predicating a future salvation of 'all Israel'. Later writers are bolder. Matthew and John, each in their own distinctive way, claim that the Christian community, the church, is 'true Israel'. Colossians, Ephesians, the Pastoral epistles, Hebrews, 1 Peter, and the Book of Revelation make a similar claim, but in each with some variation in how the case is put.

3 The Christian community is the body of Christ

The New Testament authors consistently depict the followers of Christ in profoundly communal terms, but Paul makes this point most starkly when he identifies the church as the body of Christ. In Romans and 1 Corinthians he uses this metaphor when thinking of the congregational life of the Christians addressed. They are one body, but this body has many members, all with a ministry to contribute to the edification of the community. In Colossians and Ephesians, on the other hand, the body of Christ is a metaphor for the whole Christian community. The corporate unity of all believers is the main focus, but a diversity in ministries is still seen as an aspect of body life.

4 The Christian community is the ekklēsia

In the face of contending claims, we have concluded that for the early Christians the term 'the *ekklēsia*', when used theologically, meant the Christian community. It was a title that spoke of those bound together by their common bond with Christ. Without ever seeking to relate his different applications of this one word, Paul sometimes uses it of the world-wide community of Christians, sometimes of the community of Christians in one location, and sometimes of the community formed by those who met together in a home setting. In each case, their common union with Christ created this community, but in the third case it was realized most vividly by common association.

This threefold usage calls into question the meaning of the expression 'the local church'. Most who use this expression confidently assume a given meaning, but ecumenical encounter has disclosed major differences between church traditions on this issue. For some, the local church is the Christians in a given location, the second usage given above. Thus in the Roman Catholic Church, the Orthodox Churches and for many Anglicans, 'the local church' is the diocese or national church. For many Protestants, on the other hand, the local church is taken to be a congregation. They maintain the word *ekklēsia* has as its primary reference a group of Christians who actually gather together – the third usage of this word given above.[6] Until I began this study, I have always accepted this last position, but I am now convinced that Paul and Luke, and possibly some other New Testament writers, could speak of the Christians in one area as the church/ *ekklēsia*, although these believers did not necessarily all meet together. This suggests that perhaps Protestants also should think of all the Christians in their area, rather than just their own congregation, as 'the local church'.

5 *The Christian community creates specific communities*

Because Christians generally are a distinct community, all the New Testament writers take it for granted that believers will have a common life together wherever they are found. When there were few Christians in one place, expressing this unity and family bond would have been straightforward, as all the believers would have been able to meet together, at least on occasions. Yet once the number of Christians multiplied in a city, group identity must have been more tenuous. The main meeting places were larger homes, which determined the size of each congregation. Paul also called these household communities 'the church', as we have noted. He saw them as the most intimate expression of Christian communal existence and as the body of Christ. To be a believer and not identify with other believers in your city or town by meeting with them is such an inconceivable thought that the New Testament writers barely consider it.

6 *The Christian community always has leaders*

All the New Testament authors, each in their own way, insist that the Christian community has but one leader, Jesus Christ, who is the ascended Lord of the church, and is now present through the Holy Spirit. Nevertheless, Spirit-initiated and empowered leadership is always provided in this community. It can take many forms, but it is invariably depicted as corporate in nature. In every instance in the New Testament, leadership is given by groups of people with differing functions, and from place to place and from time to time with differing titles. In his earlier epistles, Paul develops a profound theology of corporate life in Christ. He speaks of the congregation as the body of Christ united together, but with each 'member' of the body having a contribution to make. The ministry of each person, man and woman, is made possible by a '*charisma*', or gift of grace, which had as its goal the edification of the congregation. In this conception of the church, some are leaders (the apostles, prophets, teachers, and the hosts of the home churches), but everyone has the Spirit-given ability to exercise a ministry for the benefit of the whole. Although it is only Paul who spells out this theology of the ministry of the few and the potential for ministry of all, this pattern seems to have prevailed in the apostolic church. Nevertheless, institutionalization did progress and was encouraged by the threat to the life of the church by heresy, and this brought with it some diminution of this corporate vision of ministry.

Nothing seen in the New Testament has endorsed the view that the ordering of the church was given from the start, or that the threefold order of bishops, priests, and deacons was known in the first century. This means that the church is not defined by its ministerial structures; it is defined by its communal existence given by God in Christ, and by the presence of the Spirit who provides the leaders needed.

7 *The Christian community always has institutional form*

From the time Jesus called the first disciples, some social structuring of the community thereby created was present; and after his death this developed as leaders with special names arose, set patterns of communal life and worship emerged, and rules of conduct were established. Institutional form is not something a group of people with an ongoing existence and a common life may or may not have. It is part of the givenness of social existence; groups spontaneously create structures to govern their life together and further their purposes. These structures tend to develop with the passing of time, as group life becomes more complex. This process, which we have noted at work in the New Testament age, is called 'institutionalization' by sociologists. Although the apostolic writers do not know this term and do not reflect on this process, they assume that the church will have a structured life, and, what is more important, they encourage its development. Implicitly they all accept that the church is both a theological reality and a social reality. There are always these two aspects of the church: one cannot exist without the other. Indeed, Luke and Paul would suggest that the latter is needed for the former to thrive. The problem of too much structuring and too little interest in the dynamic work of the Holy Spirit, a problem ever since the apostolic age, is not an issue for them. Yet just as they affirm the importance of institutional form, they also lay down the principle that should always be a controlling force – namely, the freedom of the Holy Spirit to renew the church by raising up Spirit-filled leaders who will call the Christian community back to its roots.

8 *The Christian community as a whole and particular Christian communities are interrelated*

It is often assumed that in the New Testament age there were no institutional structures linking individual congregations or local churches to the wider Christian community, but this is not true. The institutional forms that were needed and were appropriate for this period began to appear very early. In the Book of Acts, Luke maintains that a group of elders with general oversight of the Christian community in Jerusalem was in place by the time the church at Antioch was established. Thus when the Christians in Antioch sent a gift for the poor among the saints in Jerusalem, Luke has a group of elders receive it on behalf of the church (11.30). Later he depicts James as the chairman of this group of elders (21.18). We do not know any more than this, but on Jewish parallels it may be assumed that these elders were 'overseers' of the whole community. They were not ministers of the word, or house church leaders (although some of them may have fulfilled these roles), but a pastoral council with authority to determine issues of importance to the whole community. It was an institutional structure to link together the Christians in Jerusalem. Luke's account of the Jerusalem council is also important (Acts 15). This was a meeting between the leaders of the church in Jerusalem and the leaders of the church in Antioch to settle an issue that demanded an answer. It was a one-off meeting, but it is a model that Christians have followed by establishing synods to allow for full and frank discussion by representatives from churches in different locations. In the Pastoral epistles, the elders are quite explicitly said to form a 'council' (*presbuterion*) (1 Tim. 4.14); in writing to Titus, Paul instructs his associate to 'appoint elders in every town' (Tit. 1.5). Apparently with the growth of the church in Crete this governing structure was needed. Yet the most important link that the early Christian had with the wider Christian community was through contact with one of the leading apostles such as Peter or Paul, or their co-workers or delegates. It is never allowed that each group of Christians, or the individual house churches, were a law unto themselves. After the death of the apostles, other ways to express this interdependence between Christians and general supervision of the churches had to evolve.

9 *The Christian community is distinct from the world*

In our own age, many Christians are uneasy about drawing too sharp a line between the church and the world. They want believers to be fully involved in the great issues of our day rather than being an inward-looking, self-satisfied holy huddle, as is all too often the case. Yet the New Testament writers, in speaking of the church, do not show any interest in this matter. They in fact stress the separation between unbelief and faith, between the church and the world. They do not want Christians to withdraw from the world, but their task is not to challenge the political structures of the world, or the injustices of their day, but to win the world for Christ. Generally speaking, the apostolic writers see Christian communal life as a means of encouraging growth in Christ and evangelistic outreach by believers: the proclaiming of the good news. The demand that followers of Jesus be compassionate and caring is especially underlined in the Gospels, but it has to be admitted that the actual teaching of the New Testament does not call on Christians to challenge the political injustices of their age. This may be something Christians should do today in a totally different social context; but if this is the case, then theological motivation must come from another source.

The visible and the invisible church

In drawing the main part of our argument to a close, some comment needs to be made about the distinction between the visible and invisible church. This has been a vexed area of debate among Christians for centuries. The New Testament never speaks of the church in these terms, but the idea implied, in the better formulations of this schema, are present. In Matthew's Gospel, the Pastorals, John's epistles, and the Book of Revelation, and possibly elsewhere as well, it is acknowledged that unbelievers can be part of the 'visible' life of the church, but not have that 'invisible' relationship with Christ that makes one a true member of the community of salvation.

Eric Jay traces the origins of this ecclesiological distinction back to Clement of Alexandria (*c.* 150–215), who writes as a disciple of Plato and of Christ.[7] For him as a Platonist, reality is bipolar: there is the physical and the metaphysical. The church is not simply to be conceived of in two ways, but as having two forms: the earthly and the heavenly, the visible and the invisible. The earthly church, he argues, is 'the image of the heavenly'.[8] The same thought is present in Clement's more famous successor at the catechetical school of Alexandria, Origen (*c.* 185–255). This Platonic, heavenly–earthly conception of the church has appealed to Protestants; and, as we have seen, is still popular among some evangelicals who are generally not aware of its philosophical roots. Yet this is not the classic expression of the doctrine of the visible and invisible church.

This owes its origins to Augustine who developed his ecclesiology in response to problems of his own day. When he became bishop of Hippo in AD 396, his diocese had long been split by the Donatist schism. Both the practical and the theological repercussions of this division concerned Augustine throughout his term of office.[9] What troubled him was not only that some claimed to be members of the church although they would not accept the Catholic faith, but also even within the membership of the Catholic Church there were 'the covetous, the defrauders, the robbers, the usurers and the drunkards'. In answer, Augustine appealed to the doctrine of predestination. The true members of the Catholic Church are 'the fixed number of the saints predestined before the foundation of the world'.[10] Membership of the visible church and partaking of its sacraments was no guarantee of salvation; all that counts in the final analysis is belonging to the invisible church, known only to God.

In the late Middle Ages, Augustine's doctrine was taken up by Peter Waldo (*c.* 1140–1217), John Wycliffe (*c.* 1330–84), and John Huss (1372–1415), who all wanted to distinguish between the visible church as they knew it with all its faults, and in desperate need of reform, and the community of true believers, the elect. The sixteenth-century Reformers also appealed to this twofold understanding of the church as they sought to make sense of a society where almost everyone was thought to be a Christian. They were all too aware that not everyone who outwardly belonged to the church was directed by faith in Christ, and that some church members were flagrantly immoral. This had to be explained, and the visible–invisible categories served this end. Luther never actually uses these terms, but this distinction was very much part of his thinking about the church.[11] In Calvin, the idea and the terms are present, and the key is the doctrine of predestination. Luther and Calvin both think of the church as having two aspects, but neither of them believed there were in fact two separate churches as many have suggested. Calvin insists that every member of the invisible church belongs to the visible church.[12] Those who simply associate with the visible church, who are not 'children of God by grace and adoption and members of Christ by sanctification of the Holy Spirit',[13] are not in fact true members of either church. Yet despite this distinction, Calvin has the very highest estimation of the importance of the visible church. It is his argument that just as God redeemed human beings within the historical process, so God gives spiritual life and nurture in the same context, in the fellowship of an institutional church. This visible church exists 'wherever we see the word of God purely preached and heard, and the sacraments administered according to Christ's institution'.[14] Belonging to this church, he insists, is necessary for salvation. Speaking explicitly of the 'visible church', he writes:

> For there is no way to enter into life unless this mother conceive us in her womb, give us birth, nourish us at her breast, and . . . keep us under her care and guidance until, putting off mortal flesh, we become like the angels. . . . Furthermore, away from her bosom one cannot hope for any forgiveness of sins or any salvation.[15]

In response to the Reformers, the Roman Catholic Counter-Reformation stressed the visible, institutional aspect of the church. This was expressed bluntly in the famous words of Robert Bellarmine (1542–1621), who said: 'the church is a society as visible and as palpable as are the community of the people of Rome, or the kingdom of France, or the republic of Venice'.[16] As far as he was concerned, those who belong to this church headed by the Pope, and partake of its sacraments, are those (and those alone) who will be saved.

In the light of this debate, Ferdinand Christian Bauer, in the middle of the last century, argued that the Reformation was in fact in essence a debate about the doctrine of the church. He contended that whereas in Catholicism the 'idea' of the church involved the complete identification of the historical sociological form with the divine reality, the Reformers insisted that the relationship between the two is always a dialectical one.[17] They are to be neither separated nor identified. The essence and the form of the church always coexist in tension; the historical and sociological form of the church can never be regarded as the perfect embodiment of the gospel-created community. Bauer calls this 'the Protestant principle'. Paul Tillich, in his book *The Protestant Era*, develops this principle thematically, defining it as 'the protest against any absolute claim for a relative reality'.[18] Later, in his *Systematic Theology*, he makes this the key to a modern reformulation of the invisible–visible ecclesiological schema.[19]

Tillich believes that the sixteenth-century Reformation distinction between the visible and invisible church is the counterpart of the twentieth-century distinction between the church as an empirical sociological entity and the church as a theological reality. Both arise out of the same awareness of a tension between the church as it is experienced and as it is confessed as 'one' and 'holy'. He thus proposes a more contemporary expression of the older Protestant ecclesiology. He argues that the church is both an ambiguous social reality and a 'spiritual community'. The latter is constituted by the 'spiritual presence' (the Holy Spirit or the divine life), but this also creates the former. Tillich insists that the term 'the spiritual community' alludes neither to an other-worldly, heavenly entity, nor to an ideal conceptual projection, but to the essential behind and within the church as it is manifested in history. The 'spiritual community' does not exist as an entity separate

from the church, but as a spiritual essence at work in the outward
forms – giving them life and power and fighting against their
ambiguities.[20] It is 'the inner telos' of the church that is the source
of everything that makes the church. This alternative solution to
the problem that the Reformers were seeking to address by distinguishing between the visible and invisible aspects of the church
has potential for development. However, possibly the best alternative has arisen in modern Catholic ecclesiology.

Modern Roman Catholic ecclesiology

After long centuries of rejection by Roman Catholics of the
'Protestant principle' in ecclesiology, a big change has taken
place concerning this matter. The terms 'visible and invisible' are
generally avoided, but the important truth this dichotomy seeks
to enshrine is now widely accepted. Bruno Forte says the goal of
modern Catholic ecclesiology is the 'overcoming of the visibilist
and juridical conception of the church of the Counter-
Reformation, in the rediscovery of the Church's supernatural and
mystical elements'.[21] The church is a 'mystery', he insists, because
'it is not reducible to sociological categories', since it 'bears within
itself the signs of the amazing encounter between the world of the
Spirit and the world of humankind'.[22] I suspect the Reformers
would gladly endorse this conception of the church. Calling the
church a 'mystery' is very common in contemporary Roman
Catholic literature. The first chapter of Vatican II's most comprehensive ecclesiological statement, *Lumen Gentium*, is entitled,
'The Mystery of the Church'. Catholic theologians are not always
agreed as to what is implied by this expression, but the trend these
days is to see it as pointing to the fact that the church is far more
than that which the human eye sees – its true nature being given
by revelation.[23]

Hans Küng in fact argues that Catholic ecclesiology has never
denied that there is an invisible aspect to the church, even if at
times the visible aspect has been stressed. He says that so long as
it is recognized that the visible church is 'the real church', Catholic
theology does not deny that there is a 'hidden and invisible aspect
of the church'.[24] The Reformers' visible–invisible distinction, he
accepts, was an important reminder that, 'the church is essentially
more than what it appears to be in its all-too-human visible

aspects'.[25] He notes that this very point is affirmed even in the Tridentine catechism, which insists that 'the vital element in the Church is hidden, recognisable only with the eye of faith'.[26]

Recent Catholic ecclesiology has, however, made a significant advance in explaining this tension. Rejecting Platonic dualism and the doctrine of election as the key, it has explained these two dimensions to the church by appeal to Christian eschatology. The Christian community is a pilgrim people travelling towards the heavenly home to be realized on the last day. It exists in tension between the gift already given and the promise not yet completely fulfilled. 'This eschatological character points up the provisional nature of all ecclesial realisations.'[27] In the 1985 Bishops conference report, it is concluded that:

> The Council has described the Church in diverse ways: as the people of God, the body of Christ, the bride of Christ, the temple of the Holy Spirit, the family of God. These descriptions of the Church complete one another and must be understood in the light of the Mystery of Christ, or of the Church in Christ. . . . From the Church's connection with Christ we clearly understand the eschatological character of the Church herself. In this way the Church in its earthly wandering is the messianic people that already anticipates in itself its future reality as a new creation. Yet it remains the Church which embraces sinners.[28]

In different language to the Reformers, the Bishops speak of the invisible and visible aspects of the church of Christ.

The impossibility of final correlation

The relationship of the church as it is theologically defined in the pages of the New Testament, and the church as an historical, sociological, and visible reality known to experience, will always stand in an uneasy tension. It is not that the church of the apostles was above history, devoid of sociological form, or without 'tares' mixed in with the wheat, but with the passing of time these aspects of the church in the world became more accentuated and at times seemed almost to obscure the theological definition of the church as the body of Christ, the people of God, the community of the risen Christ. This is not a problem that can be overcome by church discipline, or any reorganizing of church structures, for the church in the world by definition has this dual aspect. It can only be overcome by God when he makes all things new. The church in the world will always share in the ambiguities of fallen existence as it waits for the consummation of all things. It is a pilgrim com- munity bound together by a common faith in Christ, comprising only forgiven sinners, who pray to God, 'Your kingdom come'.

Chapter 9

The Denomination as Church

One of the most observable and entrenched manifestations of the institutional form of the church in the world today is its denominational character. Richard Norris maintains that, 'in the contemporary world "Church" normally (though not invariably) means "denomination" – that is, an organised corporation which operates on a national or supranational level'.[1] Thus most Christians tend to think of 'the church' primarily as the centralized, denominational structure represented by the bishop, or the elected overseer with a characteristic title. In theory, it is of course generally conceded that in this ecumenical age the universal church is not to be identified with any one denomination, but in actual practice, and in the language used by many church leaders, it is clear that, for all practical purposes, 'the church' is for them their denomination seen as a single entity. In Anglicanism, for example, to speak only of my own community, it is very common to hear people speaking of the Anglican Church as 'the church of God', without any qualifications whatsoever. For those who tend to think in this manner, it is hard (if not impossible) for them to appreciate the fact that there are large numbers of Christians who reject the idea that any denomination should be considered a church, let alone *the* church of God – some of whom even question the validity of denominational structures however understood.

Because Roman Catholic and most Protestant theologians are dismissive of the congregational understanding of the church, they see no need to justify their practice of speaking of their denomination as 'the church'. As a result, there are very few discussions that attempt to justify calling a particular denomination 'church'.[2] The modern ecumenical movement also discourages reflection on the church in its denominational form, because – at

196

least until recently – the thought has been that denominational structures were a mark of human sinfulness which obscured the oneness we have in Christ. The argument was that they were essentially illegitimate. H. Richard Niebuhr speaks of 'the evil of denominationalism', describing it as the ultimate expression of the 'moral failure of Christianity'.[3] Others call it 'tribalism'. The goal of the ecumenical movement was once the overcoming of these 'man made' divisions by the creation of one visible church, confessing the one Lord with one voice. The Roman Catholic Church and the Orthodox Churches (at an official level) agree with this to some extent, but they differ on one fundamental point: they maintain that the one 'holy Catholic Church' has existed all along (they both claim to be that one church). They hold that the other so-called 'churches' need to renounce their sinful schism and return to the fold of the mother church.

Recent trends have, however, put the topic of the denomination as church back on the agenda. There has been a marked upsurge in evangelical conviction, and it is among evangelicals that the congregational understanding of the church is most commonly found;[4] Roman Catholic theologians have been more willing to recognize that their church is one denomination among many;[5] and the ecumenical movement has moved away from the ideal of one visibly united church by allowing for the continuing contribution of denominational groupings – so long as they are in communion with one another. In this chapter I want to speak mainly to my evangelical friends who cannot allow that the denomination as an entity should be called 'church', but set the discussion on a wider canvas. In doing this I hope to outline a provisional theological basis for seeing the denomination as an expression of Christian community – that is, as church. I use the word 'provisional' because I am attempting to give theological status to an historical, empirical form of the church that, like all other historical forms of the church, is transitory; and because a perfected and visible unity in Christ is of the essence of the end-time vision of the church. I also use this term because 'the Protestant principle' means that the church as God's creation in Christ can never be simply equated with any particular manifestation of the church.[6] On this premise, there is always a dialectical tension between any historical and therefore sociological form of the church and the divine reality, which forbids an absolute identification of the two. What is therefore being sought is a theological definition of the denomination as an entity that is neither equated with the church of God, nor seen as but a pragmatic federation of churches, a fully human construct, with no theological validation.

The origins of denominationalism

The idea that the apostolic church was one united community where believers were in complete harmony with one another, in one undivided family, is a myth. Not only were churches divided geographically, but also racially and theologically. These divisions were dynamic and changing, but they were very real.[7] The churches of the apostolic age as reflected in the Johannine tradition, the Book of Acts, the early Pauline epistles, and the Pastorals, to mention only the four most important witnesses, were united in their allegiance to Christ – but not in how he was to be confessed, or on how the corporate life of those who made this confession should be ordered. What is more, the earliest Christians were also conversant with rivalry and divisions. Apparently in the church in Corinth, which met in various house churches, there were divisions between the groups that looked to Paul, Cephas, or Apollos (1 Cor. 1.10–16). Ephesians 4.1–6 also alludes to divisions in the church that were to be addressed if unity was to be restored. In writing to the Philippians, Paul attempts to reconcile two church workers, Euodia and Syntyche, who were at loggerheads. Many more examples from the New Testament could be cited, but the point has been made. From very earliest days, even while the apostles were alive, there were divisions and disunity among Christians. This is never depicted as acceptable behaviour, but it is realistically acknowledged as a fact of life needing to be constantly corrected. These observations are a reminder that some divisiveness is as much a characteristic of the church as an historical and sociological entity, as is its unity as a theological entity.

In the post-apostolic age, divisions and disputes between Christians continued. Clement writes to the Corinthian church, at the close of the first century, seeking to sort out the problems that were tearing that community apart. The occasion for the letter was the removal of certain presbyters from office by a younger group, probably claiming charismatic authority.[8] Clement insists that the leadership of the older men is to be respected, as order in the church is given by God. Ignatius, the bishop of Antioch, is also concerned with unity a decade later, but the major threat he counters is doctrinal.[9] It seems that the congregations he wanted to keep united under the one bishop in each place were being tempted to break away by the inroads of false teaching. His repeated argument is that allegiance to the bishop is the basis for unity (Eph. 5.1–3; Mag. 6.1–2, 7.1–2; Trall. 2.1–3, etc.). Later writers in the second, the third, and the fourth century also speak of church disputes and breakaway movements.

Following the election of Cornelius as Pope in AD 251, a serious dispute arose in the church in the city of Rome over how to treat those who had compromised their faith during the Decian persecutions. Novatian, a Roman presbyter, espoused a rigorist stance, and Cornelius espoused a more conciliatory approach. In the end, Novatian's supporters elected him as a rival bishop of Rome. Though doctrinally orthodox, Novatian and his followers were excommunicated. This resolved nothing, and a small Novatian church continued for some centuries. A similar schism took place in North Africa, about fifty years later, known as Donatism; and again, as a consequence, two competing churches became part of the scene. After the council of Chalcedon in AD 451, yet another schism followed. Those who continued to believe in 'the one nature of Christ' broke with the Chalcedonians who confessed 'one person in two natures', and eventually this resulted in the creation of the Oriental Orthodox Churches that have existed down to this day; only in 1988 was a peace made with the Roman Catholic Church. In the Middle Ages there were other disputes and divisions, but the Papacy backed by the power of the state was able to crush these, or force them underground.

The most important and continuing pre-Reformation division looks back to 1054 when the papal legate laid a bull of excommunication on the altar of the cathedral in Constantinople against the Eastern Patriarch, Cerularius. This cemented the breach between the Orthodox Church(es) of the East and the Roman Church of the West that has continued to this day. In the sixteenth century, an even more catastrophic breach took place in a similar way. The Reformers did not set out to start a new church, but rather to reform the church. The Pope responded to their calls for reform by excommunicating them. The outcome of the Reformers' efforts was the creation of a number of national churches, a phenomenon they had never envisaged. Yet the Reformation disruption is not to be seen as the origin of denominationalism as it is known today. In each case, the Reformers assumed that there could only be one church in each nation or region. The thought that doctrinally differing groups of Christians in the one state could equally be *the* church was an abhorrent idea as far as they were concerned. Thus those who advocated a more radical reform of the church, the Anabaptists who went their own way, were as severely dealt with in the Reformation states as were those of reform mind in the papal states. The toleration of dissent from the national church in the Protestant territories and in Catholic countries took several centuries to achieve. A good example of the intolerance assumed is the well-known case of John Bunyan (1628–88) in England, who was jailed for twelve years for preaching Christ as an independent.

Denominationalism took form first in the American colonies, as dissenters, and various national church groups, along with Roman Catholics, found themselves living together. They arrived on foreign soil believing they alone were the church, and only reluctantly came to accept the reality of church plurality. In this context, it was impossible to enforce uniformity. With the passing of time, the divisions multiplied in this competitive and independent milieu. Gradually the various churches learnt to respect one another and to co-operate with each other. The same pattern occurred in other places of European migration, but in Europe the toleration of Christians not allied with the state, and not conforming to the national church, only followed after a bitter struggle.

On this explanation, denominationalism as we know it today is basically a by-product of European colonization, which placed the competing churches side by side. Now, differing historical origins and confessions are not the only basis for the institutionalized divisions between the churches;[10] there are today many other forces at work as well. The differing confessions that once gave identity to the different denominations are matched by other factors that divide Christians – such as socio-economic standing, cultural origins, styles of worship, political convictions, and conservative –liberal theological positioning.[11] This means that denominationalism is no longer just an accident of history or the expression of differing confessions that can be overcome by dialogue, but a reflection of modern pluralism; a pluralism that has taken concrete expression in a hitherto unknown degree in the contemporary denomination which is a centralized bureaucratic structure analogous to other centralized organizations of our day.[12] This means that both in essence and in form the modern denomination is how the church is for most Christians in this period of history. So pervasive is this form that attempts at creating non-denominational churches have been abject failures, only creating new denominations in their own right,[13] and even independent congregations get defined in terms of their collective character. They are grouped together and given quasi denominational status.

The ecumenical critique of the denominations

For most of this century, the goal of the ecumenical movement has been the 'organic union' or 'visible unity' of the churches: the overcoming of denominational division. The World Council of Churches has as its mandate 'to call the churches to the goal of visible unity in one faith and in one eucharist fellowship expressed in worship and in common life in Christ'.[14] The nature of this unity – and how it is to be achieved – has been much discussed, but it has been generally agreed that the formation of the Church of South India – which brought together the Anglican, the Methodist, and the United Church, which was a prior amalgamation of Congregationalists, Presbyterians, and Dutch Reformed in 1947, and then in 1977 united with five Lutheran Churches to form the Church of Christ in South India typifies what the ecumenical movement is about. Many similar unions were achieved between 1950 and 1980, but since then this approach has slowed down to a feeble trickle; this is one reason why it is now being called into question. However, the main objection is that such unions, if carried on *ad infinitum*, would create one super, monolithic church that many believe would then claim a monopoly over the consciences of all believers, and as a result do more harm to the cause of Christ than our present divisions.

Konrad Raiser, the present General Secretary of the WCC, writes:

> talk of the [organic] 'unity of the church' has now become highly questionable. It has, of course, been repeatedly emphasised in ecumenical debate that unity does not mean uniformity, but the application of the concept of unity to church politics and the difficulty inherent in holding unity and diversity together in tension brings again to mind the problematic historical ancestry of unity thinking as an instrument of domination. Again and again in the course of church history

dissidents have been excluded or violently persecuted by invoking the 'unity of the church'. Indeed, it is possible to defend the thesis that most divisions in the church have been the consequence of carrying concern for unity too far.[15]

His solution, along with many others at this time, is that the goal of the ecumenical movement should not be the eradication of the denominations by the creation of one superchurch, but rather the bringing together of the denominations so that there is a unity in diversity. This position recognizes that diversity is of the nature of the church, not a sin to be overcome. In this sense, it is a theological argument for the denominational form of the church, carefully conditioned. However, it is also a recognition of reality. In our pluralistic culture, the creation of a united – and in some ways uniform – church simply cannot be willed into existence. King Canute had more chance with the tide! The denominational form of the church is how the church is present in this period of history. Raiser speaks of a changed ecumenical paradigm in which the denominations are not viewed as something negative, but as expressions of the pluraformity that is foundational to Christian existence in the world. Instead of structural unity, Raiser says, 'the biblical concept of "fellowship" or "communion", in its vertical dimension as participation in the divine reality through Jesus Christ in the Holy Spirit, and in its horizontal dimension as sharing with one another in a life of solidarity, is better suited to give direction to the ecumenical movement'.[16] In introducing the idea of 'communion' (*koinonia* in Greek), as the expression of the unity in Christ to be pursued, he follows the growing consensus among theologians that this term takes us right to the heart of ecclesiology. It reflects the unity in diversity inherent in the divine Trinity of persons that in an analogous way should characterize the life of the church in its local, regional, international, and universal dimension. This fellowship does not aim to overcome all diversity, but rather to embrace it in a dynamic, relational, and growing bond of love and understanding.

For those who have opposed the ecumenical movement because they believed it had as its goal the organic and structural unity of the church, this is a startling development; frequently, evangelical, fundamentalist, and Pentecostal opponents have stood apart on this basis. However, now that this objection can be laid aside, this does not mean that they all will join wholeheartedly in the ecumenical quest; their commonly voiced objection to organic union is in fact secondary to their strictly theological concerns. They tend to believe that the ecumenical movement is dominated by Christians of 'liberal' persuasion who are more interested in political causes than the gospel. Their major anxiety is that the proclamation of Christ would be compromised by involvement in the ecumenical movement. Michael Kinnamon, in his book *Truth and Community*, seeks to answer just these fears and objections, but this is not a matter we need to pursue.[17] However, it is to be pointed out that many in the ecumenical movement also have their own criticisms of theological conservatives. They argue that all too often they are in error themselves, for their preoccupation with evangelism and the life of the local church so often eclipses social and political concerns. This counter-charge reminds us of the maxim 'whoever preaches half the gospel is as much a heretic as the person who preaches the other half'.

What we have said about the new paradigm and the objections to structural unity raised by some opponents of the ecumenical movement could suggest to some that ecumenism has had its day; in reality, this is far from the truth. Hans Küng is certainly right when he argues that this is the most profoundly ecumenical period the church has ever known.[18] For a number of reasons, Christians are generally more concerned about unity than ever before. The new paradigm only questions making the goal one visible institutional church. It is now widely thought that what we want to see is the minimalizing of 'tribal' distinctions, so that the oneness we already have in Christ can come to the fore amid the legitimate variety that will continue. This has been called 'reconciled diversity'. With this as the goal, Christian co-operation and conciliar action – in each place and theological dialogue between the denominations at a national and supra-national level – become the means of attaining this end.

Theological dialogue presupposes both that there is revealed truth, and that no one person or group has a monopoly on it. While it is true that many in the ecumenical movement are of more 'liberal' conviction and sometimes imply that unity and co-operation are more important than truth and doctrine, this has never been the official position taken by the World Council of Churches, and it has been repeatedly denied by leading ecumenical theologians.[19] Hans Küng, in a well-balanced comment, sums up the challenge:

A Church which truly desires to find unity with other Churches must be a lover and follower of truth, it must be a Church which knows in all humility that it is not the manifestation of the whole truth, that it has not fulfilled the whole truth, a Church which knows that it must be led anew by the Spirit of truth into truth.[20]

In sitting down to talk together, Christians from divided churches are conceding that they may have something to learn from those with whom they differ, and they are taking the offer made to them to explain what is of greatest importance to them. Only those who are absolutely certain that they alone have the whole truth, and conversely that all other Christians have nothing to teach them, can confidently remain aloof from such dialogue.

The goal of 'reconciled diversity' demands dialogue, but it raises the matter of how much diversity can be allowed. Can Christians hope to be in communion with those they disagree with most strongly? Conservatives raise the issue of orthodoxy, and liberals raise the issue of orthopraxy. The former might say, for example, 'I cannot sit down and dispassionately discuss whether or not Christ is divine as if this is an open question, let alone extend the hand of fellowship to those who deny this', while the latter might say, 'I cannot sit down and discuss dispassionately social and political injustice as if this is something only of marginal concern to Christians, let alone extend the hand of fellowship to those who ignore such issues'. This is possibly the most difficult question raised by the ecumenical process, but it is not a new problem. The first epistle of John attempts to deal with these very issues in a particular context, stressing that right confession and right behaviour go together. This linking of orthodoxy and orthopraxy, first enunciated in the apostolic age, is surely a basis to move forward; but as the contemporary protagonists will not agree on minimal essentials on either matter, it is not a complete solution. This means that no matter how committed we may be to the ecumenical cause, we have to concede that some will not enter into dialogue and not want communion with those with whom they differ. Their freedom to do this must be recognized to be as important as the quest for unity; imposed unity that denies freedom of conscience cannot be part of ecumenism.

In a strange turn of events, the ecumenical movement has ceased to reject the denominational form of the church on theological grounds, and in the process discovered an abiding theological value in the denominations so long as communion with one another is made a primary goal.

The evangelical critique of denominationalism

Many evangelicals also maintain that the denominations are human constructs with no theological warrant. They argue that the word *ekklēsia*/church in the Bible is used only of two entities: all those who are in Christ, or a local congregation.[21] On this basis, they claim that there is no scriptural warrant for calling a denomination 'a church'; thus the so-called Anglican, Presbyterian, or Roman Catholic 'Church' is wrongly named. These corporate entities should not be called 'church', they argue, for they are but an organizational structure to link together churches with the same confession or national origin. They are a federation of churches, not church.[22] John Frame, a professor at Westminster Theological Seminary, goes so far as to claim that the Bible 'requires the abolition of denominationalism'.[23] He tells us he was inclined to call his book 'the curse of denominationalism'.[24] When this position is taken to its logical conclusion, it follows that the local church must be autonomous and self-governing.[25]

Presuppositions

The congregational definition of the church rests on a number of premises, none of which can be substantiated. The most basic of these is that the word *ekklēsia*/church is *only* used in the New Testament of all Christians in the world, or of local congregations, but we have seen this is not true. The word comes to mean 'the Christian community', and in this sense has a number of applications and scope for a wider usage. Paul and Luke use the word of (1) all Christians, (2) of Christians in one location, and (3) of Christians who assemble together. In each case, believers are seen as a single entity because they constitute a community on the primary basis of their common allegiance to Christ, and secondarily, in examples two and three, because of their geographical or associational connections. However, it is important to note that Paul does not limit himself to just these three uses of the word *ekklēsia*/church. On occasions he can use the word of specific groupings of Christian communities not circumscribed by geographical or associational parameters, but by ethnic links alone. For example, he can speak of 'the churches of the gentiles' (Rom. 16.4; cf. 16.16; 1 Cor. 14.33). It is true that he uses the plural, but if the apostle can allow this wider usage then surely it is permissible to speak of Christians united together by a common heritage and confession as a distinct Christian community, a united entity – that is, as a church.

The congregational position also rests on the premise that there were no structural links between congregations in the apostolic age, but this too is to be rejected. There was nothing like the modern denominational bureaucracy, nor an exact equivalent to the modern-day bishop or superintendent, but there were precursors to both of these things. We have already noted that: (1) councils of elders with pastoral and administrative responsibilities over the Christians in one location, who would have met in several house churches, were known in the apostolic age (e.g. Acts 21.18; 1 Tim. 4.14); (2) Paul regularly asserted his authority and exercised a continuing pastoral concern over particular Christian communities; (3) in the Pastorals, Paul is depicted as delegating this ministry to others, thereby implying supra-congregational superintendence was to continue; and (4) a dispute affecting the relations between Jewish Christians and gentile Christians was resolved by representatives from both churches meeting together in a 'synod' to reach a binding agreement (Acts 15.1–29). If these things were encouraged by the apostles, then surely it is possible to allow for their extension as the church grows numerically, and as institutionalization progresses.

Yet the congregational position is flawed in other ways as well. It is predicated on a view that theology is simply a reflection of what the Bible teaches; no development is allowed. As the Bible does not conceive of anything like a denomination, a denomination cannot be considered a church, and it cannot be given any theological status. This understanding of theology that arises out of American fundamentalism is not true to the Reformation tradition, and fails to notice that many of the doctrines seen as 'fundamental' by those who hold this view, such as the credal definition of the Trinity and the person of Christ, are in fact a development on what is actually found in the Bible. Protestants standing in the Reformation tradition are committed to the supremacy of Scripture in matters of faith and practice, but not to the view that the Scriptures speak with one voice on all issues, or that Scripture alone is the source of all valid theology.[26] Reformed theologians have generally allowed for an organic development in theology; taught that other sources of information contribute to the theological quest, and that theology is to be understood as an attempt to speak to the issues facing the Christian community in its present historical context. A theology that can say nothing but what is found in the Bible offers little to the modern Christian facing all sorts of complex questions, many of which were not even contemplated by the apostolic writers. To reject the prevailing denominational form of the church simply because it is not explicitly found in the Bible speaks only of the poverty of this approach. On this premise, the consubstantial unity of the persons of the Trinity, meeting in special buildings for worship, the celebration of the Eucharist outside of a meal setting, the baptism of infants, and many other things would need to be rejected because they are not mentioned in the Bible. And Christians could have no opinion on such matters as gambling, abortion, euthanasia, and democratic government, for they are not directly spoken about in Scripture.

Finally, the consistent congregational position is to be rejected because it exhibits no appreciation of the related historical and institutional form of the church as it manifests itself in the world. The empirical Christian community is always subject to historical and social forces that dictate its form to some degree in any given age. A church completely separate from the social setting in which it finds itself cannot be conceived. In its essential nature, the Christian community is both a theological entity *and* a sociological and institutional entity existing in space and time. In the New Testament we can see the Christian community being defined theologically, and slowly developing into its institutional form. In the Book of Acts, Luke tells us a little of the early history of this empirical community that has lasted for 2,000 years in radically different social and historical contexts. The characteristic denominational form of the church today is in some measure an expression of the pluralism and the bureaucratic structures of modern life. In other ages it has had different forms, which also have been dictated to some extent by history and societal forces. For example, after Constantine made Christianity the official religion of the Roman empire, the church in its totality was organized on the model of Roman provincial government, and following the

Reformation, which was in part an expression of emerging nation-
alism, as a state church. These forms should not be given ultimate
theological validation by theologians in any age, or categorically
rejected. What is needed is an historically aware ecclesiology that
speaks of the possibilities and the pitfalls of church life as it is
manifested at any given time – a theology that neither completely
denies the theological validity of the sociological form of the
church, nor endorses it without any theological critique. In the
preliminary comments to this chapter, I called such a theology of
the church 'a provisional ecclesiology'.

Positive aspects of the denominational form of the church

In a world where Christians are divided by various forces and these
divisions have developed institutional forms, the denomination
unites together Christians who have certain things in common on
a broader basis than the congregation. It becomes in fact an
attempt to approximate the universal church on the canvas that is
available. In most of the larger denominations, the institutional
structure brings together congregations into a regional fellowship
or communion; and then through representation into a national
fellowship or communion; and finally into a world-wide fellowship or communion. In doing this, it recognizes that the Christian
community manifests itself congregationally, locally, nationally,
and internationally. In this expanding association, Christians
united by their denominational allegiance, but divided on a range
of other matters, are drawn together. They are forced into fellowship and dialogue with others with whom they differ. They are
not allowed to think that their point of view is the only one that
a Christian can hold. History shows just how important this is,
as most heresy, and all bigotry among Christians, arises when
believers cease to listen to those with whom they differ.

The denominational form of the church also enables Christians
to act co-operatively together. It provides the opportunity to cen-
tralize resources such as theological education, social services,
training, and expertise on particular things such as youth work.
The denomination also allows Christians to act together in a more
significant way when confronting the social and political chal-
lenges of the age; a combined voice and combined action has more
impact.[27]

Finally, the denominational form of the church caters for the supervision and pastoral care of the leaders and the people in particular congregations. This may often be done poorly, but the ideal embodies something that seems to have been foundational – at least to St Paul's understanding of Christian communal life. These supra-congregational ministries are a reminder that no congregation is completely independent, and none without the need of some supervision and pastoral care beyond what the congregation itself supplies.

Negative aspects of the denominational form of the church

A constant danger with the denominational form of the church is that the members of any one denomination will see themselves as the only true church. This was once the almost universally held position, but it is seldom endorsed today. Even where it is officially enunciated, such as by the Roman Catholic Church, this is rejected by many of their theologians – and in practice is not believed. The strength and the weakness of modern Christianity is its tolerance. The oft-made claim by congregationalists that denominationalism actually restricts Christian fellowship is in most cases simply not true today. Christians from the various churches have never mixed so freely together as they do at present. Instead, the truth is that, as a general rule, the most narrow and exclusive of Christians are those who belong to independent congregations. It is isolation from other believers that breeds the worst of the sectarian spirit.

Another danger inherent in the denominational form of the church is that ecclesiastical bureaucrats in denominational headquarters and some theologians are prone to claim that somehow the corporate denominational church is prior to, or more important than, the local congregation. Often this is specifically related to finance. The central administrators and their supporters see the congregations as the source of their ever-increasing demands for money. If the congregations are reluctant to give, or cannot, they are told they are parochial in outlook and failing in their support of 'the church'. Congregations do have responsibilities to the wider church community to which they belong, but this wider community also has responsibilities to them. There is no warrant for setting one body over the other. Those who see things mainly from the perspective of the corporate denomination, thought of as 'the church', need to remember that the denominational structure exists to support, facilitate, and to further the concerns and mission of the congregations it collectively embodies, and those who see things mainly from the congregational perspective need to remember that there is far more to the church than any one congregation, no matter how large and vibrant. But having said this, it is important to add that the congregation may be said to have a certain priority in the purposes of God. It is in this setting that the Holy Spirit manifests the *charisms* that enable Christian ministry, the word of God is proclaimed, the believer is built up in faith and love, and the sacraments administered. Furthermore, congregations can exist and thrive without being part of a larger community of Christians grouped into a denominational framework, but a denomination cannot exist without congregational life. In making this point I am in no way undermining a central thesis of this book, namely that believers need to always recognize that they are part of one great world-wide community of Christians, which Jesus called 'my church', and their own congregation is but a microcosm of the whole.

The relationship between the church as congregation, the church as denomination, and the church as all believers will always be a dynamic one, because three expressions of Christian community are in interplay. The key to dealing with these tensions is a full-orbed communal understanding of the church. It demands recognizing that each particular congregation/community is church in the fullest sense of the word, but there are other expressions of Christian communal life that are also church – and these play a fundamental role for they always remind particular congregations that they belong to something larger than their immediate fellowship. A congregation may be thought of as church in the fullest sense of the word,[28] but is not the church; and a denomination may be thought of as the church, a true expression of extended Christian community, but it is not the whole church.

Another more practical problem with the denominational church as it is known today is its ability to soak up human resources in its ever-increasing bureaucratic structures. Most denominations have innumerable committees and working groups; and despite all the effort, they often achieve very little. They tempt people to believe they are involved in significant Christian endeavour, but often this is highly questionable. This is not a theological critique of denominationalism, but a recognition of one of its great failings.

Summing up our case

This whole discussion takes us back to a matter raised in the first chapter of this book: how can the church be defined? Of the several competing answers, three are of significance at this point.

For the traditional Roman Catholic, the answer is crystal clear: the church is that world-wide family of Christians who are united in their allegiance to the Pope who is the vicar of Christ on earth. A congregation of Catholic Christians may rightly be called church if an ordained priest is present and the mass is celebrated, but *the* church is always the complete number of those obedient to the bishops – and ultimately to the Pope.

The consistent congregationalists can also answer categorically: the church is nothing other than a local congregation of believers united by their confession of Jesus as Lord. On this understanding, the church is found where two or three are gathered in Jesus' name (Matt. 18.20). No specific entity where Christians do not actually assemble together can be rightly called 'church'. As far as the Bible is concerned, we are told, the church is a fellowship of believers. All denominational groupings are but human constructs that most congregationalists allow as permissible, but others condemn as contrary to their understanding of the biblical doctrine of the church.

No Protestant can accept the Roman Catholic definition of the church, and very few can endorse without reserve the radical congregational definition, but a more nuanced answer is not so easy to express. I have suggested a third approach: an approach that gives to the denominational form of the church provisional theological validation.

This builds on the premise on which this book is based: the church is to be defined as the Christian community. As the denomination is a true expression of Christian communal life, it is rightly called 'church'. Nevertheless, as it is but one historical form of the supra-congregational church, and a form that expresses the divisions among Christians that will not be known in heaven, it can only be given provisional theological endorsement; yet this is all that is needed. Every aspect of the life of the church in history is provisional, a pale reflection of the communal life to be revealed on the last day.

Chapter 10

Deficiencies in Past Ecclesiology and the Promise of Trinitarian Ecclesiology

Most of this book is devoted to the study of the emergence of the Christian community in the apostolic age, and to the quest to understand how the apostolic writers theologically defined this community. In the opening chapter, however, we carefully distinguished between biblical theology as a descriptive discipline and systematic theology as a prescriptive discipline. The former attempts to capture the thought of the various biblical writers in their own literary and historical context; the latter has as its goal to address the church in the present, and while building on biblical theology, it draws on other sources as well. A theology of the church (or some other topic) can be constructed, as we have done, by following the trajectory prescribed by the biblical data, taking up issues of significance from Christian history and by interacting with present-day experience, but this does not exhaust the theological enterprise. It is possible to develop theology at a more conceptual level by beginning with what is seen to be the essential element, the very foundation on which all else stands, and then extrapolating from this point. The most profound systematic theology often comes via this route. Systematic theology of this kind is also more likely to bring to light the interconnections between doctrines. This is vitally important, for all too often Christian theology has been written as if it was made up of a number of isolated doctrines – rather than being one grand vision of God and his work in the world, which frail human beings are called on to see in its totality in so far as they are able.

Many discussions on the theology of the church follow the path

212

taken in this book so far, but usually with less interaction with the text of Scripture and the debates about its meaning. They begin with the teaching of Jesus, move to the Book of Acts, and then the epistles and Revelation, after which they note how the church has developed across the centuries; finally, they attempt to address the present situation, answering the questions of their day. A theology of the church is given, but often without sharp conceptual clarity; it is not related at any depth to other doctrines, and the fundamental importance of the church in the plan of God is not adequately demonstrated (albeit that it *is* asserted). In the end, it might be better to say that such writings produce 'a doctrine of the church', but not a systematic theology of the church. Some improvement on this basically descriptive approach to ecclesiology has been introduced in the opening chapter by clarifying the essential nature of the church 'idea' or 'concept', but now in this concluding chapter we will explore the possibility of grounding ecclesiology on the doctrine of the Trinity – arguably the most fundamental doctrine for Christians.

Ecclesiology in historical perspective

For many centuries of Christian history, little attention was paid to the doctrine of the church; most of the comments on this topic found in early Christian literature are in response to particular problems. Seldom is there any theological reflection on the nature of the church and its place in the purposes of God. Torrance, in fact, claims that from the time Cyprian penned *The Unity of the Catholic Church* in AD 251, there was no other book written on the doctrine of the church for more than a thousand years – until Wycliffe wrote *The Church* in 1378.[1] Cyprian, the Bishop of Carthage from 248 to 258, wrote on the church in answer to a schism that had taken place in his diocese following the persecution of Christians by the Emperor Decius (250–1). He insisted on the visible unity of the church, and argued that ordained clergy, outside of the 'one Catholic Church', did not have authority to administer the sacraments. He had trained in Roman law, and as a result his writings are basically authoritarian, rational, and legalistic in outlook. The church for Cyprian is an empirical, geographically extended institution. It is the spiritual counterpart of the Roman state, a well-ordered society unified under one ruler, the bishop. He likens it specifically to a military camp.[2] Although sacerdotal terminology appears in Tertullian and Hippolytus, it is generally agreed that Cyprian is the first to call the bishop, as the celebrant of the Eucharist, *sacerdos*/priest. Furthermore, he unambiguously parallels the ordained Christian ministry with the hierarchically ordered Aaronic priesthood.[3] Jay says that his thinking on the church 'prevailed in the West throughout the middle ages'.[4]

During the fourth and fifth centuries, theologians were chiefly engaged in debates about the person of Christ and the Trinity, and no attention was given to the doctrine of the church – although significant changes that impacted on this were taking place. Some of these changes were as uncongenial to biblical thought as the rejected elements in the competing doctrines of the person of Christ and the Trinity, but they went unnoticed. It was in this period that the church took on the form that went unchallenged until the Reformation, and then was only modified in some areas by the Reformers. Under the Emperor Constantine, the church was reorganized on the model of the administrative structures of the Roman empire. What Cyprian had suggested became a reality. The major ecclesiastical regions were made to coincide with the civil provinces or 'eparchies'. In the majority of cases, the capital city became the see of the bishop, who had primacy over other bishops in his eparchy. From this point on, there were enumerable disputes over jurisdiction, the powers of bishops, and precedence among clergy. In this process, the church came to see itself as analogous to the state, only differing in its primary concerns. The fraternal and communal nature of the church was almost forgotten.

Graded hierarchy

There was, however, a second counterproductive element introduced into ecclesiology in the post-apostolic age that readily blended with the legal–rational ecclesiology of Cyprian and captured Christian minds. This was the view that the church, like the state, was to be conceived of as a static hierarchy instituted by God.

The *Timaeus* is generally taken as the most mature dialogue of the great Greek philosopher Plato.[5] It deals with the creation of the world and the ordering of social life. Early Christian theologians immediately saw parallels with the teachings of the Bible, but in fact the differences were more profound than the similarities. In the *Timaeus*, metaphysical reality is a rationally organized hierarchy of forms that give shape to physical reality. As this is the foundation on which the individual and the state should be patterned, it follows that a rationally organized city-state and its virtuous citizens should organize themselves accordingly. It was only a small step for Christian thinkers to identify this metaphysical order with the divine mind. The world thus became not a reflection of eternal forms, but of the mind of the Christian God.

The hierarchical order basic to the *Timaeus* came to be part of the taken-for-granted understanding of reality held by people in the Greco-Roman empire. They accepted that between 'the supreme good' of Plato or the supreme God of the Bible, there was a host of intermediaries: a hierarchy of being in a continuum from the pinnacle of pure spirit to unspiritual humankind at the bottom. It was against this ontology that Christian theologians had to contend in their fight against gnosticism and in the debates over Christology and the Trinity. In these matters they were victorious, but in their view of society, and in particular on the ordering of the church, they unreflectively accepted the prevailing world view. The hierarchical structuring of all reality was taken as an axiom, and in the Middle Ages it was transposed into dogma. The medieval church pictured God's grace being mediated downward from the Father through the Son, to the Virgin Mary, then to the angels, and from the saints to the priests, via the sacraments, till finally it reached the sinner. Prayer and the eucharistic offering was thought to follow the same path upwards. Medieval theologians sought to order society and the church on the eternal hierarchical order they believed existed in the unseen world. The church was set over the state as the perfect society; and in this realm, 'holy order(s)' placed people in their appointed positions. It was not recognized that there was an irreconcilable tension between both the teaching of Jesus who called Christian leaders to be servants and Paul's theology of the *charismata* – which allowed that all could minister as they were enabled by the Spirit – and the Greek idea that there was a fixed order where some were permanently set over others.

The monopoly in thought of this ontology is seen in the importance given to the *Corpus Areopagiticum*, a series of writings supposedly penned by an Athenian convert of Paul, but almost certainly composed in the late fifth century. Two of Dionysius' four major works are entitled *Celestial Hierarchy* and *Ecclesiastical*

Hierarchy. These books enjoyed great esteem in both the east and west, and Thomas Aquinas frequently refers to them. In fact, he appeals to Dionysius to substantiate his case that the church should be ordered hierarchically.[6]

Reformation and Counter-Reformation ecclesiology

The doctrine of justification by faith is rightly seen as the central theological concern of the sixteenth-century Reformation. As this doctrine placed everyone on the same footing before God, it had profound implications for ecclesiology.[7] It meant there was no place for a mediatorial priesthood, and everyone in the church could think of themselves as priests with free access to God. It also meant that the church as an empirical community, an identifiable number of people in the world, could not be exactly equated with the community of salvation, a spiritual reality created solely by the justifying grace of God. In making this distinction, as has already been noted in the last chapter, the Reformers revived Augustine's categories of the visible and invisible church.

The Reformers' doctrine of the church was radical in its conception, but in actual practice it was not fully realized.[8] They assumed the prevailing hierarchical view of society, where some were set by God over others. Each congregation was to be led by an ordained man who alone was to provide the teaching and administer the sacraments. A high view of the ordained ministry as a permanent office with special powers was therefore maintained, although this ministry was defined in prophetic terms rather than priestly terms. The thought that every Christian had a ministry in the church and in the world was not considered. Closely allied to this defect in Reformation ecclesiology was a deficit in pneumatology.[9] Because the church was seen primarily as the community of those who were justified by faith in Christ, the role of the Holy Spirit in the life of the church was not developed. Here again, soteriological concerns came to the fore. The Spirit's work in salvation and personal sanctification was stressed, not his work in empowering and equipping every believer for ministry. The hierarchical ordering of the church, though challenged by the Reformation doctrine of justification by faith and associated doctrines, was not overthrown.

Although it was not the Reformers' wish or intention, a consequence of their actions was the splitting asunder of the Western church. When they were excommunicated by the Pope, their response was to argue that there could only be one true church, and they were that church – a claim also made by Rome. The result was competing claims to be the 'one Holy Catholic Church'.

In reply to the Reformers, Roman Catholic Counter-Reformation ecclesiology stressed the visible, institutional, and hierarchical aspects of the church. Robert Bellarmine, in his well-known words, sums up this view:

> The one and true church is the community of men brought together by the profession of the same Christian faith, and conjoined in the communion of the same sacraments and under the government of the legitimate pastors and, in particular, the sole vicar of Christ on earth, the Roman Pontiff. . . . We believe that to be considered a member of this church . . . one need not have any interior virtue. All that is needed is an exterior profession of faith and of the communion of the sacraments. The church, in fact, is a community of men and women as visible and palpable as the community of the Roman people, or the kingdom of France, or the Republic of Venice.[10]

This understanding of the church prevailed in the Roman Catholic Church until the middle of the present century;[11] and although other ideas are found in the documents of Vatican II, this opinion is maintained and is still definitive for many Catholics. On this view, the Roman Catholic Church is a visible society entered by baptism; certain 'powers', most importantly the power to offer the Eucharist, are given solely by Catholic ordination, and grace is conveyed by the sacraments. This suggests that the Holy Spirit is mediated by the ordained clergy through the sacraments; lay ministry in the life of the church is limited in scope, and every other church along with its ordained ministry and sacraments is invalid. Not surprisingly, many Roman Catholic scholars have criticized these views and put forward alternative proposals.

The renewal of ecclesiology

Many forces have come together since the 1960s that have shown the need for, and laid the groundwork for, a renewal in ecclesiology. The ecumenical movement, post-Vatican II Catholic theology, the growing importance of the Pentecostal churches, wider agreement on the interpretation of Scripture, a more egalitarian and democratic view of church life, the growing acceptance of the ministry of women, the house church movement, liberation theology, and secularization have all been important contributing factors. A lot has been written on the church in these years, mainly by Roman Catholics, but the tension between understanding the church on the one hand primarily as a community of faith where all have equal dignity, equal freedom to exercise God-given ministries, and all are brothers and sisters of the one family, and on the other hand, primarily as a hierarchically ordered institution in which certain men have unique powers and Christian is divided from Christian, still remains. This tension is most evident in Roman Catholic ecclesiology, but Protestant ecclesiology is often equally problematic. In response, many theologians in recent times have argued that what is needed to overcome the impasse is an ecclesiology grounded on the Trinity.

In the Fathers, the Reformers, the writings of Roman Catholic scholars, ecumenical texts, and the documents of Vatican II, the church and the Trinity are sometimes related, but it is only in the last thirty or so years that scholars have begun to develop ecclesiologies grounded in the triune revelation of God. An early indication that a change in thought about ecclesiology was under way came in 1961 at the New Delhi Assembly of the World Council of Churches, when the Christological definition that had stood from the beginning of the movement was replaced by a trinitarian definition: 'The ecumenical Council of Churches is a fraternal association of Churches which confess the Lord Jesus Christ as God and Saviour according to the Scriptures and do their utmost to respond together to their common vocation for the glory of the only Father, Son and Holy Spirit.'[12]

In the World Council of Churches, this change came about mainly through the influence of the Orthodox theologians, but even in Orthodoxy, trinitarian ecclesiology is something relatively new, stemming mainly from the work of the Russian emigré, Father Vladimir Lossky (1903–58).[13] In the Western Christian tradition, to which both Roman Catholics and Protestants belong, events in the World Council of Churches no doubt made their impact, but equally important in the flowering of trinitarian ecclesiology has been the somewhat surprising upsurge in interest in the doctrine of the Trinity, which has now become possibly the most discussed of all doctrines after centuries of neglect.[14] The rediscovery of the Trinity has disclosed the potential that this doctrine has to elucidate so much of the Christian faith, not least ecclesiology. On this basis, many theologians believe for the first time that a real advance in the formulation of a theology of the church is possible. The Trinity provides the conceptual foundation for a much-needed reformulation of ecclesiology; but what this means in practice is not so clear.

The renewal of trinitarian theology

In the Western Christian tradition, the doctrine of the Trinity is generally conceived within the terms first given in Latin by Tertullian in about the year AD 200: *una substantia – tres personae* (one substance – three persons).[15] This wording suggests that the God defined by Christian revelation is one, indivisible, divine substance, constituted as three individual persons. And the converse applies: the three persons are different from one another, but they are one in their divine substance. A common criticism of this approach is that it borders on modalism (the three persons are seen as modes of the divine being), and monarchianism (ultimate divine rule is unitary).[16] In contrast, the Cappadocian Fathers[17] in the east and their successors insisted that, by definition, God in his essential being from all eternity is triune. The starting point is not the unity of God, but his tri unity. Although the Cappodocians sought completely to exclude hierarchical ordering within the Trinity, their idea that the Father was the one supreme principle (or *arche*) was problematic, for it made the Son and the Spirit dependent on the Father. They avoid the charge that they thereby imply the subordination of the Son and the Holy Spirit by insisting that the differences between the persons lie only in the realm of the differing relations of one to the others,[18] and by taking up the thought, possibly first enunciated by Athanasius (296–373), that the communion of the divine persons with each other is so complete that each could be said to dwell entirely in the other in a complete exchange of divine life.[19] This last matter, many today believe, is to be seen as the culmination of patristic trinitarian theology, for it is the most sure safeguard against subordinationism and tri-theism. This principle was taken up by Augustine in his monumental study *De Trinitatis*, composed between 354 and 419. He wrote: 'Each [of the divine persons] is in each, all are in each, each is in all, all are in all, and all are one.'[20] However, it was the great Eastern theologian, John of Damascus

(*c*. 675–749), who established the word *perichoresis* as the technical
term to describe this mutual interpenetration of the three persons.[21] When the Trinity is understood perichoretically then the
Father exists in the Son, the Son in the Father, and both of them
in the Spirit, just as the Spirit exists in the Father and the Son.
On this principle, the divine life cannot be understood merely as
one subject. It must exist as a living fellowship or communion
(*koinonia*) of three persons who are related one to the other, exist
in one another, and act in unison. In this conception of the triune
God, a total break with pagan Greek hierarchical ontology was
achieved.[22] It was replaced by an ontology that saw the ground of
everything in a divine being who was separate from the world,
fully personal, free and communal.[23]

In what has been said so far we have been in effect talking
about what is called 'the immanent Trinity', the inner life of the
divine persons. This can be distinguished from what is called 'the
economic Trinity', the manner in which the three persons are
revealed by their activity in the world. To exclude the thought that
there could be two differing trinities, Rahner coined the axiom,
'The economic Trinity is the immanent Trinity and vice versa.'[24]
This is true in what it affirms, but demands qualification. The
revelation of the triune God in history is the self-revelation of
God, but it is not an exhaustive revelation of God.[25] What is
more, in the incarnation the second person of the Trinity comes to
us not in his full glory, but in kenotic form (his self-emptying). In
his incarnation he does subordinate himself to his Father and
humble himself in death, and by doing so reveals something of the
triune God; yet he remains the divine Son who is equal with the
Father in divinity, glory, and power.[26]

In these brief comments on trinitarian theology, only the
matters relevant to a trinitarian ecclesiology have been raised.
Much more could be said, especially on issues still contested by
theologians, but at this juncture how the doctrine of the Trinity
can inform the doctrine of the church becomes the agenda. More
than one approach can be seen in the literature, and different
theologians have the Trinity impacting on ecclesiology in different ways. Three alternatives can be distinguished. Some writers
assume one approach rather than the other two, but often all three
are in interplay without any distinction being made.

1 *The trinitarian origin and edification of the church*

In one strand of trinitarian ecclesiology, the main concern is to transcend the exclusively Christocentric definition of the church. The goal is to emphasize that all three persons of the Trinity are involved in the emergence and life of the Christian community. The Father sends the Son to redeem a people for himself, the Son dies on the cross to effect this redemption, and the Spirit is given by the Father through the Son to the redeemed community, the church. This approach is in full accord with New Testament thought. Those sent out by the risen Christ to make disciples, are to baptize 'them in the name (singular) of the Father and of the Son and of the Holy Spirit' (Matt. 28.19), thereby incorporating them into the Christian community. In the epistle to the Ephesians, the church is called into being by the elective will of the Father 'in the Son' (1.4) and 'sealed' by the promised Holy Spirit (1.13). In the church, the Father, the Son, and the Holy Spirit are all active in providing the ministries needed for the edification of community (1 Cor. 12.4); and it is the church, called 'all of you', that receives the trinitarian benediction: 'The grace of our Lord Jesus Christ, the love of God, and the communion of the Holy Spirit' (2 Cor. 13.13).

Yet while the New Testament insists that all three persons of the Trinity are involved in the emergence and continuation of the church, it has to be acknowledged that until recently ecclesiology has been related primarily to Christology. Christ instituted the church; the church comprises all those who confess Jesus as Lord, and Christ is the ever-present lord of the church. Where the Holy Spirit fits in is not altogether clear. Kilian McDonnell says all too often the Spirit has been seen as 'an extra, or addendum' in Christocentric ecclesiology.[27] In a trinitarian ecclesiology, this problem is avoided. The contribution of the Spirit in the life of the church, so much emphasized in recent times, is not an 'addendum' to ecclesiology, but a foundational principle.

When the church is discussed solely in terms of Jesus Christ, a key question becomes: did Jesus 'found' or 'institute' the church? The very words suggest the answer 'no'. The verb 'to found' implies a 'foundation', something clearly defined in shape, set in place by an historical event, fixed in form, while the verb 'to institute' implies an institution, a structured organization, something given once for all, and the Gospels do not depict Jesus as establishing the church so understood. In seeking to transcend these categories, Yves Congar distinguishes between what he calls in French the *vie* (life) of the church given by Jesus *and* the Holy Spirit, both of which he sees as primary, and the *structure* (institution, structure) of the church, which he sees as necessary but secondary.[28] He thus speaks of the Spirit as the 'co-instituting principle of the church'.[29] To understand adequately the origins of the church and its continuing and developing life, Congar insists that both Christ and the Holy Spirit must be given equal place. He says that the Spirit is not given simply 'to animate an institution that was already fully determined in all its structures',[30] but to be a continuing transforming and empowering presence in the institutional life of the church.

When this is recognized, then the church cannot be seen as a static and once-for-all given institution. Instead, the church is the place where the Spirit is ever-active in giving new life to old forms, and constituting again and again the community called into existence by Christ. The church has an historical beginning in the incarnation, death, and resurrection of Christ, but the Spirit of Christ enables it to grow as the body of Christ, and to adapt to the ever-changing circumstance of subsequent history.

In this ecclesiology where the Son and the Spirit both institute and constitute the church chosen from the foundation of the world by the Father, the Christological and pneumatological dimension are brought together. The Spirit is both the 'co-instituting principle' of the church and also the life-giving principle. It is the Spirit who brings into being the post-Easter church, and it is the Spirit who manifests the *charismata*, the graces of ministry, which provide the leadership and the edification needed for the church to grow and prosper in Christ.

In this approach, the economic Trinity is the ground on which a comprehensive and theologically developed ecclesiology is built.

2 *The trinitarian model of ecclesiology*

The more common approach, however, is to appeal to the Trinity as the model on which ecclesiology should be formulated. On this premise, the inner life of the divine Trinity provides a pattern, a model, an echo, or an icon of Christian communal existence in this world.[31] The thought is that there is an analogical relationship between the church and the triune God of Christian revelation. In this case, the immanent Trinity is of primary importance.[32] It is argued that the life of the triune God should be reflected in the life of the church, and that the church should be:

(a) Communal. In this book we have argued that the church is to be defined primarily as 'the Christian community'. Right at the heart of much trinitarian ecclesiology stands exactly the same conception of the church. The God of the Bible is not a monad, but a Trinity of persons in community, and, as such, wills to be in community with human beings and for human beings to be in community with one another. The church is therefore not something extra in the Christian life, but of the very essence of life in Christ. When expressed like this, trinitarian *communio* is seen as the perfect model of communal existence to which, by divine grace, men and women can approximate in the life of the church. This means that the church can never be considered simply as an assembly of believers, or as many isolated congregations, but rather as one community bound together in Christ, a reflection of the very life of the triune God.

In speaking of the Trinity as a community of persons, the question of how the human person should be conceived is raised. In modern thought, two competing explanations are available.[33] One defines the person as an individual, a self-determining, rational creature. The other explanation defines the person as a being in relation to others. On this view, the self is constituted in relationships with other persons. The impact of these two possibilities in regard to ecclesiology is far-reaching. The first results in an atomistic ecclesiology where the church is seen as but an assembly of believers who meet for edification, especially sound teaching to inform the mind. The second results in an ecclesiology that sees the church as essentially a community of persons, an organic unity, a dynamic interacting fellowship where each believing person finds himself or herself and Christ in the other. If ecclesial existence is to be modelled on the divine life, then the social conception of the person must be endorsed.

(b) Ecumenical. As the Trinity is three persons in dynamic unity, an ecclesiology in which the Trinity is the model or pattern will be ecumenically committed. The unity of the church will be presupposed on a theological level, but seen as needing to be realized on a practical level because the church in the world is yet to be perfected. This ecclesiology will affirm that unity among

Christians is a fundamental issue, but it will not have as its goal uniformity or institutional unity; but instead *communio* – a word that sums up the unity known by the persons of the Trinity. *Communio* ecclesiology and trinitarian ecclesiology go hand in hand. On this model, the goal of the ecumenical movement is unity in diversity: a dynamic and relational oneness of love, understanding, and mutual acceptance.[34]

(c) Egalitarian. Another characteristic of an ecclesiology patterned on the inner life of the Trinity would be equal dignity and regard for all. When a doctrine of the church builds on trinitarian thinking, there is no room for hierarchical ordering among the clergy, or between the clergy and the laity, or of one group over another. This implication is clearly seen by Leonardo Boff, who in his book *Trinity and Society*[35] grounds all human liberation on a fully communal understanding of the Trinity.

The conception of the church as a divinely ordered hierarchy is one of the oldest and most pervasive ways of viewing the church, as has been noted. It is nowadays enunciated most explicitly in the official teaching of the Roman Catholic Church, but the idea is well entrenched in the other churches as well. In the documents of Vatican II, one major section on ecclesiology is entitled 'The hierarchical structure of the church, with special reference to the episcopate'.[36] We are told that this hierarchy has been instituted by God through the agency of Jesus Christ, who appointed Peter and the apostles as the model of, and the instruments to establish, the order that God intended. First comes 'the Roman Pontiff [who] has full, supreme, and universal power over the whole church', then the order of bishops who exercise supreme power over the church, but 'only with the consent of the Roman Pontiff';[37] under them come the priests 'who on their level'[38] have the particular privilege of offering the Eucharist, and under them again come at 'a lower level of the hierarchy, the deacons'.[39] A separate section follows on the laity, which includes many affirmations of the contribution they can make; but there is no blurring of the absolute distinction between those ordained and those who are not.[40]

Major modifications to this approach appear in the Anglican– Roman Catholic 'Agreed Statement' of 1976 on *Authority in the Church*.[41] In this document, the starting point for ecclesiology is not hierarchy, but *koinonia/communio*. Hence a much more personal and communal view of the church results. Nevertheless, as the issue of the authority of the Pope and the bishops remains a central concern, hierarchical ordering is not challenged.

Yet hierarchical ordering is not only a problem for the Roman Catholic Church. It is endemic in the other churches, although it is not generally written into their constitutional documents, or so consistently practised. It appears in different forms. In episcopally ordered churches like the Anglican Church, traces of the Roman Catholic hierarchical order are often very evident. Sometimes this is explicitly stated,[42] but more often it is seen in practice. Many bishops lord it over their clergy, and many vicars or rectors set themselves over junior clergy, if they have the opportunity – and in particular over lay people. In this egalitarian age when the ministry of lay people is needed as never before, these attitudes are sadly counterproductive. Still more important, they are inimical to a trinitarian ecclesiology. They undermine the essentially communal nature of the church, hinder fraternal relationships, and divide the one body of Christ into differing camps. Bishops are set over clergy, senior clergy over junior clergy, and clergy over the laity.

However, such problems are not only found in the Anglican and other mainline churches. One of the most common problems in many fundamentalistic congregations and Pentecostal churches is the unrestrained exercise of 'charismatic authority'. Pastors claiming to speak on behalf of God set themselves above their flock and beyond criticism. One common argument to support such claims to absolute authority is that the church is not a democracy, but a theocracy – the implication being that the pastor rules on behalf of God! The strange paradox is that in such churches there is usually also a strong emphasis on lay ministry, sometimes expressed in terms of the exercise of charismatic gifts, but what we find is that the ministry of the whole body is always seen as in some way very different to that of the pastor who represents God. In these churches, teaching on authority structures in the church and the home is constantly given. It is emphasized that the pastor or pastors have been set over the flock, leadership is a male preserve, and the flock is to obey. This is seldom described as a hierarchical order, but this is what it is in reality.

Trinitarian ecclesiology does not question the need of leaders, or the exercise of authority as such in the life of the church, but it does call into question all forms of domination by those who claim some innate right to rule, and all expressions of authoritarianism.

It encourages instead the ministry of all believers, democratic and participatory decision-making, and everything that promotes the communal nature of the church. If the contribution of every believer is to be respected and facilitated, the best way to do this is to encourage the democratization of the church – as many contemporary Roman Catholics point out.[43]

(d) Non-sexist. The other area where hierarchical ordering quite contrary to an ecclesiology grounded on trinitarian theology is to be seen concerns women. For many centuries women have been set under men in the church. Various arguments have been used, but the result has been the same: women have been considered the subordinate sex. This involves more than their exclusion from ordination, but in recent years this has been the focal issue. Many Protestant churches, including the Anglican Church, have now faced this particular problem and agreed to the ordination of women. However, in the Roman Catholic Church, Eastern Orthodoxy and in many evangelical and fundamentalist churches, women are still considered to be ineligible for ordination, simply because they are women. For the two Protestant groups just mentioned, a common argument to support the case that women have been permanently set under men is based on an appeal to the Trinity. We are told that the Trinity shows that equality and hierarchical ordering are not inconsistent; and that since God is male, authority must be a male preserve.[44] In reply, it must be said, first, that the understanding of the Trinity implied is mistaken, as there is no hierarchical ordering in an orthodox trinitarianism; second, the God of Christian revelation is not the Father alone; and third, to speak of God as Father does not mean God is a male person. For Christians, God should be defined in the first place as triune. The naming of the first person of the Trinity, Father, does not imply that he is literally a male, for divinity transcends such human categories. However, it is the *perichoretic* nature of the Trinity that shows most clearly the error of such reasoning. This not only teaches that each person resides in the other; but also as a consequence of this, what one person of the Trinity does, the other does. It therefore follows that one cannot appeal to the Trinity to justify excluding women from the roles that men have traditionally reserved for themselves. Instead of supporting the permanent subordination of women and the allocation of fixed roles to men and women, the doctrine of the Trinity negates such arguments. A trinitarian ecclesiology demands a fully communal understanding of man and woman in Christ. It suggests that in our relationships we should affirm what the Athanasian creed says of the Trinity: all persons are 'co-equal', 'none is afore, or after other: none is greater, or less than another'.

Trinitarian ecclesiology does not negate the differences between the sexes – in fact, it affirms them. It recognizes both that there is a profound unity between man and woman, and that male is not female and female is not male. As in the Trinity, there are distinctions constituted by differing relations, not hierarchical ordering. What a trinitarian ecclesiology negates is the belief that God has set men over women, that he has appointed fixed social roles to each sex, and that he can only accept men for ordination. Instead, it encourages the free participation of men and women in the life of the church according to the gifts God bestows.

Colin Gunton suggests how such an egalitarian ecclesiology might operate:

> If the attribution of particular positions to particular groups or orders is to be replaced by a pattern more reflective of the free personal relations which constitute the deity, should we not consciously move towards an ecclesiology of perichoresis: in which there is no permanent structure of subordination, but in which there are overlapping patterns of relationships, so that sometimes the one person will be 'subordinate' and sometimes 'superordinate' according to the gifts and graces being exercised? And would that not more nearly echo the relationships of which Paul is speaking in 1 Corinthians 12–14?

The Trinity does provide wonderful potential for a corrective to many of the inadequacies of older ecclesiologies, but the fact that theologians can appeal to the doctrine of the Trinity to justify both hierarchical ordering and democratic ordering is a warning. This shows that human preferences can be projected on to God and then used to substantiate our values. Two controls must operate. The doctrine of the Trinity must be allowed consistently to determine ecclesiology, not vice versa, and all conclusions reached by reflection on the immanent Trinity must be congruous with theological positions soundly established by other routes as well.

3 *The trinitarian ontological basis of the church*

Yet another approach grounds ecclesiology in the being of God. John Zizioulas, the Greek Orthodox Metropolitan bishop of Pergamon, in his important book *Being as Communion*, speaks of the triune God as 'the primordial ontological concept'.[45] He maintains that as man and woman are made in the image and likeness of God, humankind is only truly human when in community. The social conception of the person is not simply a reflection of the triune God, but a statement about the being of those created by God. On this premise, he argues that 'ecclesial being is bound to the very being of God'.[46] Thus the term *communio* (*koinonia/* community) is not simply a way of describing what should be the hallmark of our life together in Christ, but what defines it. This word speaks of the 'being' – the 'ontology' – of the church. In fact, Zizioulas cogently argues that communion (*koinonia*) is the ultimate ontological category in all of reality.[47] This means, then, that to define the church as the Christian community is not one option among several possibilities, but the only definition possible if one is to ground the being of the church in the being of the triune God of Christian revelation.

Robert Jenson, an American Lutheran theologian, also maintains that the church is grounded in the being of God; but just as his understanding of the Trinity differs somewhat from Zizioulas, so too does his ecclesiology.[48] He argues that the God revealed in Jesus Christ is a God who creates and actualizes himself in sustaining and perfecting what he has created. The church is a particular and distinctive instance of the actualizing of his presence in the concrete realm of nature and history. It is distinctive actualizing because it is centred in the revelation of God's purposes in Christ, and in the subsequent gift of the Holy Spirit. For this reason, the church must be defined theologically 'as that community whose very essence consists of the explicit witness to God's being and purposes as they have been articulated in Jesus Christ'.[49] This understanding of the church follows directly from what is believed about the Trinity. However, he adds that this theological definition is not an empirical description of the church. The church in space and time, while actualizing the divine being, is part of the created order – and as such is marked by imperfection, exhibiting many 'blemishes and ambiguities'.[50]

To conclude this section, a third example of trinitarian ecclesiology that makes ontology foundational is mentioned. In contrast to Zizioulas, who reasons basically from the immanent Trinity, and Jenson, who begins with the immanent Trinity but makes the church an expression of the economic Trinity in self-actualization, Catherine LaCugna begins with the economic Trinity – insisting that only in the revelation of Jesus Christ and the Spirit can the divine life and the church be understood. It is her argument that 'God's way of being in relationship with us – which is God's personhood – is a perfect expression of God's being as God.'[51] In this claim she is concluding her argument that the triune God revealed in Jesus Christ is fully personal and relational, and as such exists in perfect communion, and wills a corresponding community on earth that is realized in the church. In this community, she argues that 'it is incongruous that a pattern of subordination between persons, having been painstakingly excised' in the trinitarian theology of east and west should be reintroduced into the church by setting clergy over laity and men over women.[52]

In what has just been outlined, the relationship between trinitarian theology and ecclesiology has been developed, but many note that what is said about the church has wider implications. If the church is that community on earth that most clearly (though always imperfectly) reflects the divine life, then this says something about the mission of the church. The Christian community is called not only to proclaim the gospel, but also to embody it in word and deed. In this last matter, trinitarian theology should be both an incentive and a broad agenda for Christian social involvement and action. Community, equality of consideration, freedom, and love are values the church should uphold, proclaim, and seek to see implemented. In other words, an orthodox trinitarian theology should not only inform ecclesiology, but also inform and motivate corporate Christian action in the world.

Excursus 1 The Meaning of the Word *Ekklēsia*: Old Testament and Intertestamental Background

How a word is actually used in a given body of writings is always the most significant issue in understanding its meaning, but the background and usage elsewhere can often elucidate this. In regard to the Greek word *ekklēsia*, translated by all modern English versions as 'church', the debate over how the early Christians understood this word, and why they adopted it as the key term to describe themselves as a distinct community, has generated a huge amount of debate – but very little consensus. Although there is a limited body of objective evidence, scholars draw diametrically opposed conclusions. This suggests that prior commitments about the nature of the church may be more significant than the actual data. The issues can be best grasped by first of all setting out the two opposing positions on the central question, before trying to separate the wood from the trees.

The opposing positions

One commonly held view is that the early Christians adopted the term *ekklēsia* because for them it signified Israel as the people of God. In using the title 'the church of God', they were claiming to be true Israel.[1] The case runs as follows. In the Septuagint, *ekklēsia* translates the Hebrew word *qahal*, which, along with the closely related term *edah*, designates Israel as the covenant people of God. Theological importance is given to the word *qahal* by its prominent use in the accounts of Israel gathered at the foot of Mount Sinai to receive the law given to Moses (Deut. 9.10, 10.4, 18.16, 31.30), and from those texts where the extended designation 'the *qahal-Yahweh/ekklēsia kupiou*' (the assembly of God/the Lord) (Deut. 23.2–8; 1 Chron. 28.8; Neh. 13.1 (*tou Theou*); Mic. 2.5) is used. This designation of Israel is the counterpart of the New Testament name for the Christian community, 'the church of God' (1 Cor. 1.2, 10.32, 11.16, 22, 15.9; 2 Cor. 1.1; Gal. 1.13; 1 Thess. 2.14, 2 Thess. 1.4, 1 Tim. 3.5, 15, cf. Acts 20.28).

In complete contrast, others claim that the word *ekklēsia* was taken over by the early Christians because it was a word with no theological content. It is argued that neither in classical Greek nor in the Septuagint does *ekklēsia* mean anything other than 'assembly'; and the Hebrew term it translates, *qahal*, also means 'assembly' and no more. The argument is as follows. In classical Greek, *ekklēsia* refers to 'an assembly duly summoned'. The word designates the citizens actually gathered to discuss political matters. Philo and Josephus regularly use the word *ekklēsia*, but they too only use it of people gathered together. The fact that Luke can use the word in this classical Greek sense in Acts 19.32, 39, 41, albeit of an unlawful assembly of citizens, is seen as very significant, for it shows that the early Christians were well aware of this meaning.[2] This meaning, we are told, exactly reflects the force of the Hebrew, *qahal*, the word it translates in the *LXX* some one hundred times. Like the Greek, the Hebrew does not allude to a society, an ongoing entity, but to people actually gathered at one time. Often the people assembled have met together for religious purposes, as we would expect in a religious society, but *qahal* can be used of any assembly, even an assembly of evil men, in both the Old Testament and in the Qumran writings (e.g. Gen. 49.6; Ps. 26.5; 1QM. 11.16, 14.5, etc.). When the Old Testament writers wish to speak of Israel as the covenant community as an entity, they use the word *edah* (147 times), which is translated in the *LXX* by *sunagōgē* (congregation), but never by the word *ekklēsia* (assembly). The conclusion is therefore reached that *qahal* never designates Israel as the people of God; *edah* and *qahal* are not synonyms.[3]

Considering the evidence

As in so many polarized debates, both sides have points that are valid; their error is in seeing only half the evidence. Both positions err in what James Barr calls 'illegitimate totality transfer' – the carrying over of the meaning of a word in one or more texts to other texts.[4] Those who argue that *qahal* (and thus in the *LXX*, *ekklēsia*) alludes to Israel as the covenant community fail to notice that neither of these two words usually bears this meaning, while those who argue that *qahal*, and *ekklēsia* in the *LXX*, mean no more than 'assembly' fail to notice that sometimes a more developed usage can be seen.

Before considering the data, the ground rules for procedure and our presuppositions need to be spelt out. The following matters are taken as axioms. First, words often develop and change in meaning, and can have different meanings at one time, or at different times. In regard to this study, it is accepted that the earliest parts of the Old Testament were written down many hundreds of years before the latter parts, and probably all the books were edited by more than one hand. Thus even in the writings attributed to a single author, more than one meaning of a word may be present for this reason alone. Secondly, most (if not all) biblical words were part of everyday usage, and as such were not technical terms. They had a range of meanings that are disclosed mainly by the context in which they are found, but one meaning sometimes gained semi-technical force by being regularly used to denote the one reality. This means that on occasions a colloquial usage and a semi-technical meaning for one word may be found even in close proximity in a given document. Thirdly, there is a widespread tendency in the development of language for abstract or verbal nouns to become concrete nouns, and often the transition is not easy to pinpoint in written texts. The Greek word *sunagōgē* is one example. The verb *sunagō*, to bring together, or gather together, gives rise to the abstract noun *sunagōgē*, which at first means simply 'a bringing together', 'a gathering', 'an assembly', and then later (as in the *LXX*), it becomes a concrete noun meaning 'those whom God has gathered together' – that is, the Jewish covenant community.[5] The difficulty of differentiating the force of such nouns is illustrated by appeal to the English word 'building'. In any sentence one must determine whether it is used as an abstract noun implying activity, or as a concrete noun – and thus alluding to the end product of this activity, a substantive entity. It is agreed that both *qahal* and *ekklēsia* begin as abstract nouns; the question is, do they develop into concrete nouns in pre-Christian Judaism?

The Hebrew word *qahal*

The Hebrew word *qahal* appears some 123 times in the Old Testament, being translated by *ekklēsia* about 73 times, and by *sunagōgē* 35 times.[6] In the older parts of the Old Testament, *qahal* can be used quite generally of people assembled for any purpose and in any number (cf. Gen. 49.6; Num. 22.4; Pss. 26.5, 89.6, etc.), but it is most commonly used of Israel assembled for one reason or another (cf. Exod. 16.1; Num. 10.3, 14.5, 16.2, etc.). In a number of passages, some of which are post-exilic, the reason for assembling is to worship Yahweh (cf. Mic. 2.5; Joel 2.16; Pss. 22.23, 35.18, 40.9, 10, 89.5, 107.32, 149.1). In the Pentateuch, with the exception of Deuteronomy, and especially in the P tradition, the term that is used to speak of Israel as the covenant community as a whole is *edah*.[7] It is virtually always translated by *sunagōgē* in the *LXX*.

In Deuteronomy, *qahal* is used eleven times, while *edah* is not found at all. Here, *qahal* becomes the special term to speak of all Israel assembled to receive and hear the law (5.22, 9.10, 10.4, 18.16), and of the worshipping community thereby constituted (23.3, 4, 9). In these passages, the event of assembling is envisaged, but the author depicts the *qahal* as a theological entity, God's covenant people, the recipients of the law, a defined community set apart to worship Yahweh.[8] In other words, *qahal* in Deuteronomy can be used as a concrete noun to refer to Israel.

The complete absence of *edah* from Ezekiel, the word so common in the priestly writings, is surprising. This is unexpected because the influence of the priestly tradition in Ezekiel is universally recognized. However, it is not just that the one word is found and not the other; *qahal* in fact takes on the same meaning as *edah*. The Jewish scholar Milgrom finds twelve examples where this occurs (16.40, 17.17, 23.3, 46, 47, 32.22, 23, 38.4, 7, 13, 16).[9] Three of these uses of *edah* are especially enlightening, for they deal with the judicial sentence of death by stoning (16.38–40, 23.44–7), which in the P tradition was decided by the *edah*, whereas Ezekiel uses the word *qahal*.

In Chronicles, Ezra, and Nehemiah, *qahal* also can replace *edah* in usage and meaning. The later term still appears in source material utilized by the Chronicler, as does the word *qahal* in the earlier, non-technical sense to denote any gathering, but in passages coming from the hand of the final redactor, *qahal* supplants *edah.* The word change by the Chronicler is important to note. In 2 Chronicles 23.1–3 we read of the covenant struck between the representatives of the people of Israel, called the *qahal*, and the newly crowned Josiah. This is the Chronicler's term. In the source he is drawing on (1 Kings 11.17), the term is *am*, 'the people', while in pre-exilic times the body that made covenants was the *edah* (Josh. 9.15ff). Again when speaking of Josiah's tax (2 Chron. 24.6), the Chronicler uses the word *qahal* to designate those who must carry this burden, although he is writing the story to parallel Exodus, chapter 35, where those taxed by Moses are called the *edah* (vv. 4, 20). In yet another instance, the officials of the city, called the *qahal* (2 Chron. 29.20, 23, 28, 30, 31), participate with the king in the hand-laying ceremony over the animals (v. 23), whereas in Leviticus 4.15 the elders of the *edah* do this.[10]

Yet the meaning given to the word *qahal* by the Chronicler is the most significant matter to observe. He is at great pains to demonstrate in the telling of his story the unanimous participation of 'all Israel' in significant cultic events surrounding the reigns of David and Solomon, such as the transfer of the ark to Jerusalem and the construction of the temple, and in Hezekiah's reforms. In all of these narratives, the word *qahal* is prominent.[11] Although in every instance the Chronicler draws the scene as if the people are actually gathered, his intent is to depict Israel, the whole nation, as a worshipping community. In other words, in these passages the word *qahal* defines Israel in terms of the Chronicler's own theology; it refers to a substantive entity.

Other examples of the use of the word *qahal*, where the note of actually being assembled is missing, are seen in Ezra 2.64, and Nehemiah 5.13 and 7.66. In these texts, the reference is to Israel as a religio-political entity. The term is used to designate the totality of the nation. Nehemiah 13.1 is another example. This text reflects Deuteronomy 23.1ff, and speaks of those who may be considered true Israelites. In this one instance, the expression *qahal Elohim* (the community of God) is found. In other instances where *qahal* is linked with the divine name, we find *Yahweh* (Lord) (cf. Deut. 23.2–8; 1 Chron. 28.8; Mic. 2.5).

In the Qumran writings, both *edah* and *qahal* are found, the former being the more common. Like the Old Testament writings, the Qumran documents come from different authors and from different times, so although there is a familial relationship, no uniformity in theology or word usage is to be expected. *Edah* is used both for the sect (1QSa 1.1, 12f) as the true people of God (1QM 4.9), and for its enemies (1QH 2.2; 1QM 15.9). *Qahal* can be used for an assembly of the sect (CD 2.22, 12.16), or for an assembly of their opponents (1QM 2.16, 14.5, 1QH 2.30), or in a more technical sense of the community itself (CD 7.17; 1QM 4.10; 1QSa 1.25, 2.4, 4QMMT).[12] In two of these references, 1QM 4.10 and 1QSa 2.4, the fuller expression *qahal elohim* is found, which, like Nehemiah 13.1, anticipates the New Testament title 'the church of God'. In 1QSa 2.4, the issue is who may be numbered among the community of God. The writer has Deuteronomy 23.2–9 in mind, which – as already noted – assumes that the word *qahal* speaks of Israel as a theological entity. This same Old Testament passage is again in mind in 4QFlor 1.4, but here it is not from the *qahal*/community that gentiles or the imperfect are excluded, but from 'God's house', which is true Israel.[13] This suggests, then, that in the Qumran documents (as in the Old Testament) some writers use *qahal* in much the same way as others use *edah*.

The Greek word ekklēsia in Hellenistic Judaism

The most important pre-Christian Jewish writing in Greek is unquestionably the Septuagint (the *LXX*). This is the translation of the Old Testament, plus the books Protestants call the apocrypha, which in most cases were written in Greek in the first place. The Septuagint was the Bible of Greek-speaking Jews, Philo of Alexandria (see below), Paul the apostle, and the other early missionaries of the gentile world. Some 600 verses in the New Testament are quoted from this source. Many classical Greek words were given new content through being used in the Septuagint, as they picked up some of the content of the Hebrew word translated. It is thus generally agreed that the most important source to elucidate the meaning of any significant term used in the New Testament is the Septuagint. If a change in meaning from the classical usage of the word *ekklēsia* did take place in pre-Christian times, then it probably originated in this work that is thought to have been completed in two or three stages over a hundred-year period, in the second and third centuries BC, almost certainly in Alexandria.[14]

In the *LXX*, the word *ekklēsia* appears about one hundred times, of which twenty-two are in the apocrypha. It always

translates *qahal*, except in three places where there is no Hebrew
equivalent, but *qahal* is not always translated by *ekklēsia*. Some
thirty-five times it is translated by *sunagōgē*, especially in Genesis,
Exodus, Leviticus, and Numbers, where *ekklēsia* does not appear
at all. It is only found once in Ezekiel (32.23), although *qahal*
appears fifteen times, and not at all in Jeremiah, where *qahal* is
found five times. The word preference of the translators may
explain these observations, but they are a reminder that a clear
distinction between the meaning of *ekklēsia* and *sunagōgē* in the
LXX is not possible.

   Almost all the hundred uses of *ekklēsia* refer to Jews, with
Psalms 26.5 and Ezekiel 32.22–3 being the notable exceptions. The
majority of the references imply that the Jewish people, or part
thereof, are actually assembled, but a large number of uses of *ekklēsia*
leave the reader wondering if this is meant, and some certainly
envisage the word being used of a substantive entity. In this last
category, the significant examples reflect those texts we have
noted in which *qahal* is used in an almost technical sense to designate Israel. Thus in Deuteronomy 9.10, 18.16, and 31.30,
ekklēsia refers to Israel as the community constituted by the giving
of the law, and in Deuteronomy 23.1ff (see also Neh. 13.1; Mic.
2.5) to the sum total of true Israelites. Even J. Y. Campbell, who
argues for a basically classical meaning for most uses of *ekklēsia* in
the *LXX*, concludes that in these Deuteronomic texts the word
refers to 'the religious community of Israel'.[15] Other examples
where it is hard not to read the meaning as Israel as a religious
community are Ezra 2.64 and 10.8, and Nehemiah 7.66 and 8.17.
Closely allied to this usage is that found in some thirty-three texts
in 1 Kings and 1 and 2 Chronicles, where *ekklēsia* refers to Israel
as a worshipping community.[16] In all these references, the writer
depicts the people as assembled, but the scene painted is an ideal
one. The *ekklēsia* is Israel theologically defined. In many of these
key texts where *ekklēsia* is used as a concrete noun of a community
of people, the context makes this explicit by defining this group
as 'all Israel'.[17] Finally, the use of *ekklēsia* to refer to a particular
group of Jews gathered for worship, possibly in a synagogue,
should be noted. This is common in the Psalms,[18] and the Book
of Ecclesiasticus.[19] In the latter case, a substantive entity with
ongoing existence is definitely envisaged. This *ekklēsia* can have
permanent office bearers (33.18) and declare the alms of the rich

man, which, says Campbell, must mean 'more than they will be declared in one particular meeting'.[20]

The possibility of added semantic development in the understanding of the word *ekklēsia* was provided also by the fact that both Hebrew words, *qahal* and *edah*, as we noted above, could be translated by the one Greek word *sunagōgē*.[21] Thus although *ekklēsia* was never used to translate *edah*, some of the content of this almost technical Hebrew term for Israel, as God's elect covenant community, passed over to the Greek word *ekklēsia*, because in Hellenistic Judaism it was equated with *sunagōgē*. Many examples can be cited from the *LXX* to show this overlapping in meaning of the two words could occur, but three instances are sufficient for our purposes. In Deuteronomy 5.22, the word *sunagōgē* is introduced to speak of the day of assembly when the law was given at Mount Sinai, but in the other four passages discussing this scene, where *qahal* needs to be translated, the *LXX* translator has *ekklēsia*. By placing the word *sunagōgē* at this focal point, the reader is encouraged to understand the subsequent uses of *ekklēsia* in terms of the initial *sunagōgē*. Proverbs 5.14 is another interesting illustration. Here the Hebrew text uses *edah* and *qahal* in parallelism to refer to the one reality, and the LXX translator noting this followed by placing *sunagōgē* and *ekklēsia* in parallelism. Similarly, in Psalm 40.11f, *qahal* is first rendered *ekklēsia*, and then following as *sunagōgē*. The two words again stand in synonymous parallelism.

If there was this overlapping in the meaning and use of these two Greek words, as all the evidence suggests, this means that there must have also been some overlapping in the understanding of the two closely related Hebrew words, *edah* and *qahal*. This is indicated by Acts 20.28, which reflects Psalm 74.2 where *edah*, not *qahal* as we might expect, is found as the antecedent to *ekklēsia*. Jeremias and other scholars also think *edah* stands behind the word *ekklēsia* as used in Matthew 16.18.[22]

Philo of Alexandria (*c.* 20 BC–AD 50) is also important in tracing the development in meaning of the word *ekklēsia*. He uses this word some thirty times, five as in classical Greek, and twenty-five in *LXX* quotations or allusions, most frequently in reference to Deuteronomy 23.1f.[23] In this Old Testament passage, certain people are excluded from the *ekklēsia* of Israel. Philo appeals to this teaching not to limit who can actually assemble for worship, but who can be numbered among God's people. In these passages, the Greek word designates true Israelites. This is quite explicit in his treatise 'On Virtue' (*De Virt.* 108), where those who form the *ekklēsia* are said to be Jewish citizens (*politeia*). In 'Questions on Exodus', a similar equating takes place in this instance between the *ekklēsia* and Israel (*Quaest. in Ex.* 1.10).[24] Several of the other quotations from the *LXX*, where Philo uses *ekklēsia*, allude to the giving of the law at Sinai.[25] In two of these quotations, the *ekklēsia* is equated with 'all the people' (*laos*) (*Quis. rer. div.* 251, *De Post Caini* 143),[26] and in another by implication with Israel, the covenant community (*De Som.* 2.187).[27] This suggests that while Philo most commonly uses *ekklēsia* as an abstract noun to refer to people in assembly, he can also use it as a concrete noun to refer to the community thereby constituted. In doing this, he follows Old Testament precedents in the *LXX*.

Josephus (*c.* AD 37–100) also uses *ekklēsia* frequently, some eighty-four times, of which eighteen are *LXX* quotations, with possibly another twelve being allusions to passages in the *LXX*. All of these references refer to actual assemblies, albeit usually of a religious nature rather than of a political nature, as in classical usage. Hort speaks of Josephus' 'ostentatious classicism'.[28] What is of particular interest is that in nine of the direct quotes from the *LXX*, Josephus substitutes the word *ekklēsia* for an original *sunagōgē*.[29] The most likely reason he did this was because for him the word *sunagōgē* designated the building in which a Jewish community met.[30]

The Greek word ekklēsia in Christian usage

The ways in which *ekklēsia* is used by the various New Testament writers is taken up in our study of their individual contributions to the biblical witness; but before we leave this discussion, a comment as to why the early Christians chose *ekklēsia* as a communal designation is needed. The case that they chose it because it was a neutral term, simply meaning 'assembly', has been excluded by the evidence just cited; and, we argue, this view makes little sense of the New Testament data. There are, however, two other widely held answers to this question that demand consideration. One opinion is that the earliest Christians understood the term *ekklēsia*, or more particularly the extended *ekklēsia tou Theou*/the church of God, as an eschatological reality. Jesus as the new Moses came to gather the community of the last days, new Israel, and this title spoke of that new entity.[31] Some scholars see this eschatological meaning foreshadowed in Deuteronomy, and in two passages in the Qumran writings (1QM 4.10; 1QSa 2.4).[32] However, this seems to read too much into the evidence. This meaning may be implied in the passages just mentioned, but this is not explicit; and other texts certainly do not suggest this sense. The early Christians may or may not have understood the full designation 'the church of God' as an eschatological reality, but neither the Old Testament nor the intertestamental writings unambiguously point in this direction. The other major view is that when the early Christians came to choose a collective title for themselves, the *LXX* provided two alternatives, *ekklēsia* or *sunagōgē*, which in the sacred text were virtual synonyms, but in actual fact were not equally acceptable options. By the first century, the word *sunagōgē* had become a self-designation for a local Jewish community, or the place where the Jewish community met. If the Christians were to distinguish themselves from Jews, and exclude denoting a building, they had but one option, *ekklēsia*. They chose it not because it had a profoundly different meaning to *sunagōgē*, but because it emphasized that they were a distinct new entity that was foreshadowed in the Old Testament. A degree of debate among the early Christians in settling on *ekklēsia* rather than *sunagōgē* is suggested by the fact that at least once in the New Testament, *sunagōgē* is used to designate Christians collectively: other examples can be found in the post-apostolic writings.[33] This seems by far to be the best explanation.

Conclusion

It seems then that while a distinction in meaning between *edah* and *qahal* can be observed, especially in pre-exilic texts, this is not so in Deuteronomy or in post-exilic texts. In Deuteronomy, the *qahal* is the community of Israel who receives and lives by the law; in Chronicles, the *qahal* is the community who worships Yahweh; and in Ezra and Nehemiah, it is the Jewish national community obedient to the law. However, the importance of the force of these two Hebrew words for the early Christians is doubtful. Their Bible was mainly the Greek *LXX*. Here they found the word *ekklēsia* at times used as we have just noted *qahal* could be used, and standing as a synonym of *sunagōgē*, which more often translated *edah*. This means that while it cannot be claimed that the word *ekklēsia* in the *LXX* simply means Israel as the people of God, to claim that it carries no more than the classical meaning of 'assembly' is equally mistaken. As the New Testament came to be written, this word in Hellenistic Judaism was a term filled with theological possibilities.

That a development in meaning took place with the word *ekklēsia* is not unexpected, for the Greek word *sunagōgē* had several changes of meaning in Greek-speaking Judaism, as we noted above. It was first the favoured word to translate *edah*, the special term designating all Israel as God's covenant community. Later, as groups of Jews began living outside of Palestine, these communities were individually called *sunagōgē*, or in the plural *sunagōgoi*; and still later, the building in which these communities met was called *sunagōgē*.[34] Finally, returning almost to its original meaning in the earlier part of the Old Testament, *sunagōgē* came to be used of Judaism as an entity. Thus in the apostolic fathers, the church (meaning Christianity) and the synagogue (meaning Judaism) are set in contrast.[35]

The path for *ekklēsia* differed in detail, but the parallels are striking. The original meaning for *ekklēsia*, like *sunagōgē*, was assembly, the event of gathering. In both the *LXX* and in the New Testament, it can be used in this way; but as with many abstract nouns, there was a movement from reference to an activity to the reality thereby constituted. Thus the word *ekklēsia* came to be used not only of people assembled, but also of the community who assembled, the people of God – which in the Old Testament is historic Israel, and in the New Testament, the Christians.

Excursus 2 Translating the Greek Word *Ekklēsia*

How best to render the Greek word *ekklēsia* has not been altogether clear to translators. In southern European languages, most have followed the earliest Latin translations and transliterated the word. Thus in French we have *église*, in Italian *chiesa*, and in Spanish *iglesia*. Northern European translators, on the other hand, have mainly chosen forms of *kuriakon*, which means 'belonging to the Lord'. Thus in German we have *kirche*, in Dutch *kerke*, in Celtic *kirk*, and in English *church*.

Luther for one would not accept the usual northern European practice, and consistently translated *ekklēsia* by the old German, *Gemeine*, meaning community or fellowship, which is now spelt in modern German as *Gemeinde*. In the 'Larger Catechism' in *The Book of Concord*, in discussing the meaning of the words 'the communion of the Saints', he rejects *kirche* as a translation of the Latin *communio*, which he sees as the basic meaning of the Greek word *ekklēsia*, arguing that the Creed is speaking of the Christian community. He says, 'I believe there is on earth a little flock, or community of pure saints under one head, Christ. It is called together by the Holy Spirit in one faith, mind and understanding.'[1] In this century, Karl Barth has followed his lead. He consistently uses *Gemeinde* for *ekklēsia*, which in the English translation of his *Dogmatics* is rendered correctly as 'community'.[2] William Tyndale (*c.* 1494–1536), who completed the first full translation of the Bible into English, used 'congregation' to translate *ekklēsia*, both when used in the so-called 'local' and 'universal' senses. Many of the English Reformers followed his lead, but never so consistently. They were uneasy with the word 'church', as

it was regularly used of the clergy as a distinct group, but it was so
well established in English usage that this word remained dominant. Here it is to be noted that in the sixteenth century the word
'congregation', like the Latin *congregatio*, was commonly used of a
collective body of people, a company.[3] It was only later that the
word came to mean primarily a local community of Christians,
through the emergence of the Congregational Churches.[4]

In the Anglican Thirty Nine Articles of Religion, the
Reformers use of the words 'congregation' and 'church' is well
illustrated. In articles 23 and 24, 'congregation' obviously refers
to a local community of Christians, but in article 19 it refers to
the Christian community of all England in its reformed state.
'The visible church of Christ is a congregation of faithful men in
which the pure word of God is preached, and the sacraments duly
administered.' In the Latin text that has equal authority, 'congregation' translates the words *coetus fidelium* – a 'community of
believers'. The English Reformers were not laying down a test so
that people could judge each parish to see whether or not it was
truly a church, as some modern-day Christians suggest, but the
marks of a reformed national church. For them, the Church of
England was the counterpart of the Church of Rome, or the
Church of Jerusalem (see the second clause in article 19). To argue
that article 19 defines the church as a local congregation and no
more is a profound mistake.[5] To do so is to read the word 'congregation' in this context anachronistically. Such an understanding
of the church by any of the Reformers is untenable. The use of
congregation to refer to the whole Christian community is common in this period.[6] For example, Bishop Hooper writes, 'I believe
and confess one catholic and universal church, which is an holy
congregation, an assembly of all faithful believers.' While in the
Belgic confession, the affirmation is: 'we believe and profess one
catholic or universal church, which is the holy *congregation* of true
believers' (art. 27). This usage is also seen in the Authorized
Version of 1611, where 'congregation' is used to translate the
Hebrew word *edah*, meaning all Israel, the covenant community.

Congregation can no longer be used in English as the usual
translation of *ekklēsia*, for the word has lost its universal sense –
having become a word used mainly of local groups of Christians.
It is unlikely in any case that any word will supplant 'church' at this
stage. The point simply needs to be made that in modern English

the best word to give the meaning of *ekklēsia*, in its Christian theological usage, is 'community'. Sometimes the word alludes to the whole Christian community; sometimes to the Christian community in a particular location; and sometimes to a community of Christian people who meet together.

Abbreviations

Dictionaries

DJG   *Dictionary of Jesus and the Gospels*, J. B. Green and S. McKnight (eds) (Downers Grove, IVP, 1992).

DPL   *Dictionary of Paul and His Letters*, G. H. Hawthorne, R. P. Martin, and D. G. Reid (eds) (Downers Grove, IVP, 1993).

EDNT   *Exegetical Dictionary of the New Testament*, H. Balz and G. Schneider (eds) (Grand Rapids, Eerdmans, 3 vols, 1990–3).

NIDNTT   *The New International Dictionary of New Testament Theology*, C. Brown (ed.) (Exeter, Paternoster, 3 vols, 1975–8).

RGG   *Die Religion in Geschichte und Gegenwart*, H. F. Campenhausen *et al.* (eds) (Tubingen, Mohr, 3rd edn 1962).

TDNT   *Theological Dictionary of the New Testament*, G. Kittel and G. Fredrick (eds) (Grand Rapids, Eerdmans, 10 vols, 1964–74).

TWZAT   *Theologische Worterbuch Zum Alten Testament*, G. Botterweck and H. Ringgren (eds) (Kohlhammer, Stuttgart, 6 vols, 1973–89).

Journals

ABR   *Australian Biblical Review*
AJT   *Asian Journal of Theology*
BTB   *Biblical Theological Bulletin*
CBQ   *Catholic Biblical Quarterly*
ExpT   *Expository Times*

EQ	*Evangelical Quarterly*
GTJ	*Grace Theological Journal*
Interp.	*Interpretation*
ITQ	*Irish Theological Quarterly*
JBL	*Journal of Biblical Literature*
JES	*Journal of Ecumenical Studies*
JQR	*The Jewish Quarterly Review*
JSNT	*Journal for the Study of the New Testament*
JTS	*Journal of Theological Studies*
LTJ	*Lutheran Theological Journal*
NovT	*Novum Testamentum*
NTS	*New Testament Studies*
RTR	*Reformed Theological Journal*
SJT	*Scottish Journal of Theology*
TS	*Theological Studies*
T Today	*Theology Today*
VC	*Vigiliae Christianae*
ZTK	*Zeitschrift fur Theologie und Kirche*

Notes

Preface

1. D. W. B. Robinson, *The Church of God* (Sydney, Jordan, 1965); D. B. Knox, *Thirty-Nine Articles* (London, Hodder & Stoughton, 1967), pp. 36–52. See also W. Dumbrell, 'An Appreciation of the Theological Work of Archbishop Donald Robinson', in D. Peterson and J. Pryor, *In the Fullness of Time: Biblical Essays in Honour of Archbishop Robinson* (Homebush, NSW, Lancer, 1992), pp. xvii–xxviii.
2. For example, R. Banks, *Paul's Idea of Community* (Homebush, NSW, Anzea, 1980); P. O'Brien, 'The Church as a Heavenly and Eschatological Entity', in D. Carson (ed.), *The Church in the Bible and the World* (Exeter, Paternoster, 1987), pp. 88–119; O'Brien's *Colossians and Philemon* (Waco, Word Biblical Commentary, 1982), pp. 57–61, and his article 'Church' in *DPW*, and most recently, W. J. Dumbrell, *The Search for Order* (Grand Rapids, Baker, 1994), pp. 266–8.
3. Sadly, Dr Knox passed away on 15 January 1994, while this book was being drafted.
4. See K. N. Giles, *Created Woman* (Canberra, Acorn, 1985).
5. Published in Melbourne by Collins-Dove, 1989.

1 Opening the Door: What Is the Church?

1. These include H. Küng, *The Church* (Exeter, Search, 1968); R. Schnackenburg, *The Church in the New Testament* (London, Burns & Oates, 1974); G. Lohfink, *Jesus and Community* (London, SPCK, 1985).
2. J. Macquarrie, *Principles of Christian Theology* (New York, Scribner, 1966), p. 346.
3. We will return to this distinction in a moment, and explain in more detail the issues involved.
4. For an attempt to clarify some of this confusion in the context of the Roman Catholic debate on ecclesiology, see H. Rikhof, *The Concept of the Church* (London, Sheed & Ward, 1981).
5. For details, see Rikhof, *The Concept of the Church*, pp. 206–10.

6. So F. J. A. Hort, *The Christian Ecclesia* (London, Macmillan, 1914); E. Brunner, *The Misunderstanding of the Church* (London, Lutterworth, 1952); L. S. Chaffer, *Systematic Theology* (Dallas, Dallas Seminary Press, 1948, vol. 4); E. D. Radamacher, *What the Church is All About?* (Chicago, Moody, 1972); R. Saucy, *The Church in God's Program* (Chicago, Moody, 1972); R. P. Lightner, *Evangelical Theology* (Grand Rapids, Baker, 1986), pp. 227–8; D. W. B. Robinson, *The Church of God* (Sydney, Jordan, 1965).

7. Published in Oxford by OUP, 1961.

8. The discussion of the relationship between justification and sanctification in *Salvation and the Church. An Agreed Statement by the Second Anglican–Roman Catholic International Commission (ARCIC 2)* (Sydney, AIO, 1987) should be consulted. In this document, a large degree of agreement is reached.

9. For more detail on the meaning and uses of the word *ekklēsia*, see the excursus on pp. 230–40.

10. This is discussed in detail in the chapters on Paul's understanding of the church.

11. The creating of so-called 'models' of the church is common today. The classic study is by A. Dulles, *Models of the Church* (Dublin, Gill & Macmillan, 2nd edn 1988). See also his essay, 'A Half Century of Ecclesiology', *TS*, vol. 50, 1989, pp. 419–42. For a critique of this approach, see Rikhof, *The Concept of the Church, passim*. An earlier important attempt at explaining the church in the framework of differing models is L. Newbigin, *The Household of God* (London, SCM, 1953).

12. 'Lumen Gentium', 1, 8, in W. Abbott and J. Gallagher (eds), *The Documents of Vatican II* (USA, Geoffrey Chapman, 1966), p. 22.

13. 'Lumen Gentium', 23.

14. 'Lumen Gentium', 39.

15. 'Lumen Gentium', 40.

16. 'Lumen Gentium', 53.

17. 'Lumen Gentium', 53.

18. Dulles, *Models*, p. 34.

19. See E. Schillebeeckx, *Ministry: A Case for Change* (London, SCM, 1981); *The Church with a Human Face* (London, SCM, 1985).

20. B. Cooke, *Ministry to Word and Sacrament* (Philadelphia, Fortress, 1980).

21. K. Osborne, *Priesthood: A History of the Ordained Ministry in the Roman Catholic Church* (New York, Paulist, 1988).

22. Published in London by SPCK, 1936 (rev. edn). For a summary of Gore's position and a criticism, see A. T. Hanson and R. P. C. Hanson, *The Identity of the Church* (London, SCM, 1987), pp. 16–18. On the Anglo Catholic position, see, in more detail, T. Bradshaw, *The Olive Branch: An Evangelical Doctrine of the Church* (Carlisle, Paternoster, 1992), pp. 41–82.

23. The title given is of the English translation (Milwaukee, Bruce, 1938).

24. L. Thornton, *Common Life in the Body of Christ* (London, Dacre, 1941), p. 298.
25. Subtitled *A Study in Pauline Theology* (London, SCM).
26. Robinson, *The Body*, pp. 24–37. Some say this is the primary definition of the church in the documents of Vatican II, but this is not true. The institutional definition of the church is given in the first chapter, and the hierarchical structure is allocated a complete section as well. Even in the chapter on the church as the people of God, Dulles points out that the discussion implies 'institutional and hierarchical structures'. See Dulles, 'A Half Century', p. 429.
27. Yet the reply could be made: but does not Paul frequently speak of 'the church of God' (e.g. 1 Cor. 1.2, 10.32, 11.16, etc.)? This is so, but he always relates the church to Christ as well. It is God's church, called into being by the death and resurrection of his Son.
28. Dulles, *Models*, pp. 89–102, calls this 'the servant model of the church'.
29. On the theology of the church in liberation theology, see Dulles, 'A Half Century', pp. 438–40; P. Lynch, 'Servant Ecclesiologies: A Challenge to Rahner's Understanding of Church and World', *ITQ*, vol. 57, 1991, pp. 277–95.
30. Rev. edn (New York, Macmillan, 1963), p. 203.
31. H. Cox, *The Secular City* (New York, Macmillan, 1965), p. 134.
32. G. Winter, *The New Creation as Metropolis* (New York, Macmillan, 1965).
33. J. A. T. Robinson, *The New Reformation* (Philadelphia, Westminster, 1965).
34. See, especially, 'The Pastoral Constitution on the Church' (*Gaudium et Spes*), in Abbott and Gallagher, *The Documents*, pp. 199–248. It is also alive and well in the Anglican Church. For details, see Bradshaw, *The Olive Branch*, pp. 205–25.
35. Dulles, *Models*, p. 99.
36. So P. T. Forsyth, *Faith, Freedom and the Future* (London, Hodder & Stoughton, 1912).
37. In detail, see A. P. Snell, *Saints: Visible, Orderly and Catholic: The Congregational Idea of the Church* (Geneva, World Alliance of Reformed Churches, 1986).
38. For details, see M. D. Williams, 'Where's the Church? The Church as the Unfinished Business of Dispensational Theology', *GTJ*, vol. 10, 1989, pp. 165–82. On Brethren ecclesiology, and in particular that of J. N. Darby, see R. Coad, *A History of the Brethren Movement* (Exeter, Paternoster, 1968).
39. Robinson, *The Church of God*; Knox, *Thirty-Nine Articles*, pp. 36–52. Both of these men grew up in clerical homes where dispensational theology was very important. On the impact of this theology on the Sydney diocese, see W. J. Lawton, *The Better Time to Be* (Kensington, NSW University Press, 1990).
40. 'Vatican 2 (1962–1964), Pueblo (1979), Synod (1985): *Koinonia/Communio* as an Integral Ecclesiology', *JES*, vol. 25, 1988, pp. 399–427.

See also the important studies: J. Hamer, *The Church is a Communion* (London, Geoffrey Chapman, 1964); J. M. Tillard, *Church of Churches: The Ecclesiology of Communion* (Minnesota, Glazier, 1992).

41. Published in London by Geoffrey Chapman, 1990.
42. Published in Crestwood, New York, by St Vladimir's Press, 1985.
43. This last point is well illustrated in the document *Church as Communion: An Agreed Statement by the Second Anglican–Roman Catholic International Commission* (London, ACC, 1991). A full list of reports taking up this motif is given in G. Vandervelde, 'Koinonia Ecclesiology—Ecumenical Breakthrough?', *One in Christ*, vol. 29, 1993, p. 128, n. 9.
44. Published in Geneva by the WCC, 1991, p. 46.
45. There are numerous studies on the uses and meaning of this word – the most recent to hand being J. Reuman, '*Koinonia* in Scripture: Survey of the Biblical Texts', unpublished paper WCC Fifth World Conference on Faith and Order, Spain, 1993.
46. This was seen in one of the first major studies on this word by H. Seesman, *Der Begriff Koinonia im Neun Testamentum*, ZNWB, 14 (Giessen, 1933). S. Brown, 'Koinonia as a Basis of New Testament Ecclesiology?', *One in Christ*, vol. 12, 1976, pp. 157–67, and Reuman, in '*Koinonia* in Scripture', reach the same conclusion, despite many less careful studies that suggest otherwise.
47. Much more could be said on this, but see the useful discussion in Avis, *Christians in Communion*, pp. 14–30.
48. In medieval Latin, *communio* can be used as a synonym of *communitas*. See C. Du Cange, *Glossarium mediae et infirme Latinitatis*, vol. 2 (Niort, 1893), p. 452.
49. On this, see the comment by Brown, 'Koinonia', pp. 155–6, and ns. 5 and 6; and in more detail, J. N. D. Kelly, *Early Christian Creeds* (London, Longman, 1972), pp. 388–97.
50. See Luther's discussion of this matter in T. G. Tappert (trans.), *The Book of Concord* (Philadelphia, Muhlenberg, 1959), pp. 416–17.
51. Published in Edinburgh by T.&T. Clark, vol. 4, 1956, pp. 653–701.
52. Published in San Francisco by Harper & Row, 1987, p. 6.
53. No contemporary, competent New Testament scholar would endorse this picture. It is agreed that Jesus and Paul see their work as the gathering of the elect people of God of the last days. There is an inherent communal goal to their ministry.
54. Lohfink, *Jesus and Community*, pp. 1–6, argues that modern individualism is the greatest obstacle to be overcome by present-day exegetes who want to understand what the New Testament says about the church.
55. On what follows, see B. J. Malina and J. H. Neyrey, 'First Century Personality: Dyadic, not Individualistic', in J. H. Neyrey (ed.), *The Social World of Luke–Acts* (Massachusetts, Hendrickson, 1991), pp. 67–96.
56. The word 'community' is an important term in the social sciences, but with no one fixed meaning; one writer gives 94 definitions. D. and J. Jary, *Collins Dictionary of Sociology* (Glasgow, HarperCollins, 1991),

pp. 97–9, say the term has 'both descriptive and prescriptive connotations in popular and academic usage'. Yet despite debate about the term, three broad meanings can be identified in the sociological literature. The first concerns geographical location; a community is a group of people in a bounded area. The second understands community to refer primarily to a network of social relationships. And the third assumes that a community is a group of people with some quality of relationship with one another.

57. See the discussion in S. J. Grentz, *Revisioning Evangelical Theology* (Downers Grove, IVP, 1993), pp. 148–62.

58. R. Bellah *et al.*, *Habits of the Heart: Individualism and Commitment in American Life* (Berkeley, University of California, 1985), p. 84.

59. The word 'catholic' is another slippery term with more than one meaning. It is used here to mean universal, inclusive, and corporate.

60. In the last twenty years, one of the most important contributions to understanding the Bible has come via utilizing sociological analysis and theory. It has been accepted that modern sociology can add a dimension otherwise missing in the exegetical and theological quest. For a brief introduction to this topic, see B. Holmberg, *Sociology and the New Testament* (Minneapolis, Fortress, 1990), and the earlier study by D. Tidball, *An Introduction to the Sociology of the New Testament* (Exeter, Paternoster, 1983).

61. I discuss these issues more fully in my essay, 'Evangelical Systematic Theology: Definition, Problems, Sources', in D. G. Peterson and J. Pryor (eds), *In the Fullness of Time* (Homebush, NSW, Lancer, 1992), pp. 255–76.

2 Jesus and the Founding of the Church

1. A. Loisy, *The Gospel and the Church* (New York, Prometheus, 1988), p. 145. This edition has a foreword by the Australian scholar R. J. Hoffman, which sets the book in its historical context and gives a brief introduction to the modernist movement.

2. This position that Loisy adopts is called 'consistent eschatology'. See also W. W. Willis (ed.), *The Kingdom of God in 20th Century Interpretation* (Massachusetts, Hendrikson, 1987), pp. 1–14 and *passim*.

3. The debate about the eschatological teaching of Jesus has produced a mass of literature. In what follows, I basically assume the majority opinion. Books that take a similar position, and on which I drew, include R. Schnackenburg, *God's Rule and Kingdom* (Edinburgh, Nelson, 1963); J. Jeremias, *New Testament Theology*, vol. 1 (London, SCM, 1971); C. Rowland, *Christian Origins* (London, SPCK, 1985); G. Lohfink, *Jesus and Community* (London, SPCK, 1985); G. R. Beasley-Murray, *Jesus and the Kingdom of God* (London, Paternoster, 1986). I was not able to utilize W. J. Dumbrell, *The Search for Order* (Grand Rapids, Baker, 1994), which only came to hand when the book was at the proof stage.

4. J. Jeremias, in *The Parables of Jesus* (London, SCM, 1963), pp. 48–63, calls these five parables 'parousia parables'. He argues that in each case the evangelists have adapted the original words of Jesus so as to make the parable speak to their own situation, but the original intent of the parable has not been changed. Jesus gave these parables to warn that the end could come at any moment.

5. See Beasley-Murray, *Jesus and the Kingdom of God*, pp. 333–4. Many have tried to weaken the force of the expression 'this generation', but Beasley-Murray says, 'on the lips of Jesus this generation always signifies the contemporaries of Jesus'.

6. Again, for further detail on the exegesis of this text, see Beasley-Murray, *Jesus and the Kingdom of God*, pp. 187–93. R. H. Gundry, in *Mark: A Commentary on his Apology for the Cross* (Grand Rapids, Eerdmans, 1993), pp. 466–70, argues that Mark understands the transfiguration as the preliminary fulfilment of this prophecy, which refers ultimately to the parousia.

7. I have not included discussion about the sayings that speak of 'the coming of the Son of Man', as this would almost be a study in itself. The tendency today is to see these words, as used in such texts as Mark 14.62, as referring to the coming of the Son of Man into the presence of God following Daniel 7.13, but Matthew 10.23 certainly seems to envisage a return to earth of the Son of Man. See Beasley-Murray, *Jesus and the Kingdom of God*, pp. 283–312.

8. So W. D. Davies and D. C. Allison, *The Gospel According to Matthew* (Edinburgh, T.&T. Clark, 1991), vol. 2, pp. 187–90. See also G. Stanton, *A Gospel for a New People* (Edinburgh, T.&T. Clark, 1992), pp. 137–8.

9. See further Beasley-Murray, *Jesus and the Kingdom of God*, pp. 333–6, 343; Jeremias, *New Testament Theology*, vol. 1, p. 139.

10. Jeremias, *New Testament Theology*.

11. Jeremias, *New Testament Theology*, p. 170.

12. See further, Beasley-Murray, *Jesus and the Kingdom of God*, pp. 75–80. However, see C. C. Caragounis, 'Kingdom of God', *DJG*, p. 423, for another opinion.

13. E.g. The sower (Mark 4.1–20 par.); the treasure and the pearl (Matt. 13.44–6); the mustard seed and the leaven (Mark 4.30–2 par.); the seed growing secretly (Matt. 4.26–9), etc.

14. See Beasley-Murray, *Jesus and the Kingdom of God*, pp. 174–80. He convincingly argues that these sayings, or at least most of them, speak of a present entry into the Kingdom.

15. Schnackenburg, *God's Rule and Kingdom*, p. 224.

16. The position taken is that Jesus came to call all Israel, and it was only Israel's recalcitrance that led in the end to the formation of a remnant – so Jeremias, *New Testament Theology*, vol. 1, pp. 170–2; Lohfink, *Jesus and Community*; B. Meyer, *The Aims of Jesus* (London, SCM, 1979).

17. E. P. Sanders, *Jesus and Judaism* (London, SCM, 1985), pp. 95–8.

18. Lohfink, *Jesus and Community*, p. 22.

19. We see the beginnings of this in Sirach. See Sir. 8.17, 9.16, 11.19, 12.4,

etc.); in 1 Maccabees the judgement on sinful Israel is taken to have broken the covenant (1.43, 52–3, 9.23–5), making it possible for God to punish the apostates (1.63–4), redeeming only the few righteous (1.62–3, 3.15–19, 9.5–6); at Qumran, the covenanters are alone Israel (1QSa 1.6; 1QM 10.9; 1QpNah 3.2–3).

20. So Jeremias, *New Testament Theology*, pp. 143, 171; J. Dunn, *The Parting of the Ways* (London, SCM, 1991), pp. 41, 106–7.
21. See Dunn, *Parting*, p. 107.
22. *From Politics to Piety* (Englewood Cliffs, Prentice-Hall, 1973), p. 83, and in other writings by him.
23. They even wore the white priestly garment.
24. Meyer, *The Aims of Jesus*, p. 130.
25. Jeremias, *New Testament Theology*, vol. 1, p. 115.
26. Jeremias, *Parables*, pp. 63–6.
27. Jeremias, *New Testament Theology*, vol. 1, p. 293.
28. Jeremias, *New Testament Theology*, p. 220.
29. Schnackenburg, *God's Rule and Kingdom*, pp. 92–104; Lohfink, *Jesus and Community*, p. 27.
30. See further, Davies and Allison, *Matthew*, pp. 603–30; Meyer, *The Aims of Jesus*, pp. 185–97; J. P. Meier, *Matthew* (Delaware, Glazier, 1980), pp. 179–83; G. Maier, 'The Church in the Gospel of Matthew', in D. A. Carson (ed.), *Biblical Interpretation and the Church* (Exeter, Paternoster, 1984), pp. 45–63.
31. See E. M. Meyers and J. F. Strange, *Archaeology, the Rabbis and Early Christianity* (London, SCM, 1981), especially ch. 4.
32. So Davies and Allison, *Matthew*, p. 603.
33. Davies and Allison, *Matthew*, p. 611, and especially Sanders, *Jesus and Judaism*, pp. 76–90, where he documents the Jewish traditions that anticipate a new temple.
34. See D. Juel, *Messiah and Temple* (Missoula, Scholars, 1977), pp. 159ff; Sanders, *Jesus and Judaism*, pp. 77–90.
35. Davies and Allison, *Matthew*, pp. 627–8.
36. See below.
37. So Jeremias, *New Testament Theology*, p. 168.
38. So K. Schmidt, *TDNT*, vol. 3, p. 525. On the force and meaning of these two words, see the excursus on 'The meaning of the Word *ekklēsia*' on pp. 230–40.
39. See excursus.
40. On this passage, see the excellent study by Juel, *Messiah and Temple*, and also Sanders, *Jesus and Judaism*, pp. 71–6.
41. Sanders, *Jesus and Judaism*, p. 75.
42. John gives his own interpretation of this saying. He says Jesus 'was speaking of the temple of his body', but this does not seem to exhaust the meaning of the synoptic prophecy or reflect the common Jewish expectation that the Messiah would rebuild the temple.
43. See Juel's full discussion, *Messiah and Temple*, pp. 122–4.
44. Gundry, *Mark: A Commentary*, p. 904.

45. Some think that Jesus probably spoke more generally about when this new temple would be built, and the 'three days' is a post-Easter modification of his wording.
46. This interpretation has very wide support. Juel, who sets out the case in greatest detail in *Messiah and Temple*, gives a selective list of commentators (see p. 145) who have understood Jesus to be speaking of the building of the church. Recently, M. D. Hooker, in *The Gospel of St Mark* (London, A. & C. Black, 1991), pp. 358–9, has endorsed this view. However, Gundry, in *Mark*, pp. 898–906, rejects this interpretation. He argues Judaism knew nothing of the rebuilding of the temple by the Messiah. To make his case, he insists that: (1) Judaism ascribed the rebuilding of the temple to God, not the Messiah, and quotes 1 Enoch 90.28–9, Jub. 1.17, 4QFlor. 1.3, 6 in support; and (2) that the words 'temple' and 'house' should not be equated. Yet the clear distinction between what the Messiah does and God does must be questioned. In any case, later Jewish texts do ascribe the rebuilding of the temple to the Messiah (Lev. Rab. 9.6, Rab. 13.2, Midr. Cant. 4.16, Tg. Is. 53.5, Tg. Neb. Zech. 6.12). Why Gundry questions the connection between temple and house is unclear. This seems to have been a common intertestamental interpretation of 2 Samuel 7.13 (cf. 4QFlor. 1.1–13), and one made in the New Testament (cf. 1 Cor. 3.10–17, 1 Pet. 2.5). In answer, see in more detail Sanders, *Jesus and Judaism*, pp. 61–116.
47. Sanders, *Jesus and Judaism*, p. 77.
48. It is outside the scope of this study to enter into all the historical and exegetical problems associated with the accounts of the Last Supper. As an introduction to the key issues, see J. Jeremias, *The Eucharistic Words of Jesus* (London, SCM, 1966); I. H. Marshall, *Last Supper and Lord's Supper* (Exeter, Paternoster, 1980); Beasley-Murray, *Jesus and the Kingdom of God*, pp. 258–73; Schnackenburg, *God's Rule and Kingdom*, pp. 249–58.
49. Beasley-Murray, *Jesus and the Kingdom of God*, pp. 264–5; Gundry, *Mark*, p. 841.
50. So N. T. Wright, *The New Testament and the People of God* (London, SPCK, 1992), pp. 259–79.
51. Isaiah 54.4–8; Hosea, *passim*.
52. Jeremiah 31.31–4; Ezekiel 11.19–21, 36.22–32.
53. Joel 2.28–9; Isaiah 32.15; Ezekiel 36.22–32; Zechariah 12.10, and in the Qumran scrolls, 1QS 1.16—2.25; 1QH 5.11–12, 7.6–7, 9.32, etc.
54. Deuteronomy 10.16, 29.6, 30.6; Jeremiah 4.4, 31.33; Ezekiel 11.19, 36.26–7. Again, see also the scrolls – 1QS 5.5; 1QpHab 11.13.
55. He regularly functions as the spokesman of the twelve, which suggests a leadership role – see Matthew 14.28, 15.15, 18.21; Mark 8.29, 9.5, etc. – and Matthew calls him 'first' as he names the twelve.
56. This matter is discussed in more detail in the next chapter, when dealing with Matthew's theological perspective.
57. On the apostles, see K. N. Giles, *Patterns of Ministry Among the First Christians* (Melbourne, Collins-Dove, 1989), pp. 151–71.

58. This Johannine passage is discussed in the next chapter.
59. There is ongoing debate over the Matthean command to baptize in the threefold name, partly because it is only found once in the Gospel tradition, but it is generally conceded that Christian baptism finds its origins in the teaching of Jesus.
60. *The Social Teaching of the Christian Churches* (London, George Allen & Unwin, 1931), p. 2. For more on the background of these terms, see Holmberg, *Sociology*, pp. 77–117; P. E. Esler, *Community and Gospel in Luke–Acts* (Cambridge, CUP, 1987), pp. 6–23, 47–52.
61. See particularly his *Magic and the Millennium* (New York, Harper, 1973).
62. 'The Earliest Christian Communities as Sectarian Movement', in J. Neusner (ed.), *Judaism and Other Greco-Roman Cults* (Leiden, Brill, 1975), pp. 1–23.
63. 'Interpretation and the Tendency to Sectarianism: An Aspect of Second Temple History', in E. P. Sanders (ed.), *Jewish and Christian Self-Definition*, vol. 2 (London, SCM, 1981), pp. 1–2.
64. See Acts 5.17, 15.5, 24.5, 14, 26.5, 28.22; 1 Corinthians 11.19; Galatians 5.20; 2 Peter 2.1. Luke uses the word of the Pharisees, the Sadducees, and the Christians.
65. He is one of the most prolific writers in this field. On this matter, see his *Sociology of Early Palestinian Christianity* (Philadelphia, Fortress, 1978).
66. *Early Christianity as a Social Movement* (Toronto, Lang, 1988).
67. B. Holmberg, *Paul and Power* (Lund, Gleerup, 1978), p. 176. On this concept in general, see Holmberg's excellent study.

3 Matthew, Mark, Luke, and John

1. This term is used with some reserve, for none of the Gospel writers is a systematic theologian. In speaking of their theology we are talking about the special emphases or concerns that can be seen consistently coming to the fore in the documents they wrote. See the useful discussion on this in G. Stanton, *A Gospel for a New People* (Edinburgh, T.&T. Clark, 1992), pp. 41–5.
2. There are numerous studies on the disciples in the Gospels, but most of them discuss the contribution of just one of the evangelists. Some of these will be noted as we progress. For an introduction to this topic, see M. J. Wilkins, 'Disciples' and 'Discipleship', *DJG*, pp. 176–82, with bibliography.
3. In the Book of Acts, this term is used some twenty times as a collective title – sometimes almost as a synonym of the word 'church'. (See Chapter 4 for further detail on this.) Note also Matthew 28.19, where the historic disciples are commissioned 'to make disciples'.
4. See the discussion of this in U. Luz, 'The Disciples in the Gospel of

Matthew', in G. Stanton (ed.), *The Interpretation of Matthew* (London, SPCK, 1983), pp. 98–112, especially pp. 115–19.

5. On discipleship in Mark, see H. Kee, *Community of the New Age* (Philadelphia, Westminster, 1977); E. Best, *Discipleship in Mark's Gospel* (Sheffield, JSOT, 1981); C. C. Black, *The Disciples According to Mark* (Sheffield, JSOT, 1989); F. J. Matera, *What Are They Saying about Mark?* (New York, Paulist, 1987), pp. 38–55; Wilkins, *DJG*, pp. 176–89 and elsewhere.

6. Kee, *Community*, pp. 116–40. Best, *Discipleship*, p. 12, says that for Mark 'a true understanding of discipleship depends on a true understanding of Jesus'.

7. Best, *Discipleship*, p. 243, says, 'For Mark the disciple is not a solitary individual but the member of a community.'

8. J. Kingsbury, *Conflict in Mark* (Minneapolis, Fortress, 1989).

9. Kingsbury, *Conflict in Mark*, p. 88.

10. The majority opinion, but several scholars have argued that Mark is polemicizing against the disciples. See, especially, T. J. Weedon, *Mark Traditions in Conflict* (Philadelphia, Fortress, 1971), who argues Mark wants his readers to reject the opinions and actions of the disciples. Black, *The Disciples*, p. 181, examines Weedon's methodology that allows him to draw this conclusion, and says that it is 'fatally flawed'. See further on this thesis, Matera, *What Are They Saying?*, pp. 42–51.

11. Best, *Discipleship*, p. 12; A. Stock, *A Call to Discipleship* (Delaware, Glazier, 1982), pp. 154–5 and elsewhere.

12. Kingsbury, *Conflict in Mark*, p. 116.

13. Kee, *Community*, p 107 Best comes to a similar conclusion in *Discipleship*, p. 243.

14. Kee, *Community*, p. 107.

15. Kee, *Community*, p. 152. Best, *Discipleship*, pp. 226–7, argues that the frequent mention by Mark of the disciples meeting in houses suggests that his church met in this setting.

16. Kee, *Community*, pp. 144–77. Several other studies that attempt to locate Marcan ecclesiology sociologically are listed in S. C. Barton, 'The Communal Dimension of Earliest Christianity: A Critical Survey of the Field', *JTS*, vol. 43, 1993, pp. 408–10.

17. On discipleship in Luke, see K. N. Giles, 'The Church in the Gospel of Luke', *SJT*, vol. 34, 1981, pp. 121–46; J. Fitzmyer, 'Discipleship in the Lucan Writings', in *Luke the Theologian* (London, Geoffrey Chapman, 1989), pp. 117–45; J. Kingsbury, *Conflict in Luke* (Minneapolis, Fortress, 1991); Wilkins, *DJG* and elsewhere.

18. On how Luke does this, see Giles, 'The Church', pp. 133–5.

19. R. Maddox, *The Purpose of Luke–Acts* (Edinburgh, T.&T. Clark, 1982), pp. 31–54.

20. Maddox, *The Purpose of Luke–Acts*, p. 36. Similarly, G. Lohfink, *Die Sammlung Israels* (Munchen, Kosel, 1975), pp. 17ff.

21. Kingsbury, *Conflict in Luke*, p. 71.

22. Thus Adam, the father of all, is at the end of Luke's genealogy (3.38);

Elisha and Elijah help gentiles (4.25–7), and Luke speaks of the mission of the seventy/seventy-two, which could be read as a prefigurement of the gentile mission.

23. J. Jervell, *Luke and the People of God* (Minnesota, Augsburg, 1972), p. 95.
24. See further, Giles, 'The Church', pp. 135–42.
25. Thus he changes the introductory words in Mark's account so as to read, 'and he said to all', thereby making it more generally applicable; he adds the word 'daily' to cross bearing as a reminder that discipleship involves continuing suffering, and leaves out the words 'for the Gospel' to make sure costly discipleship is related personally to following Jesus. See Giles, 'The Church', pp. 135–6.
26. In particular on this, see J. O. York, *The Last Shall Be First* (Sheffield, JSOT, 1991).
27. See K. N. Giles, *Women and Their Ministry* (Melbourne, Collins-Dove, 1977), pp. 17–28; B. Witherington, *Women in the Earliest Churches* (Cambridge, CUP, 1988), pp. 128–42.
28. H. Flender, *St Luke: Theologian of Redemptive History* (London, SPCK, 1967), pp. 9–10. For an up-to-date survey of the debate on Luke's view of women, see R. K. Karris, 'Women and Discipleship in Luke', *CBQ*, vol. 56, 1994, pp. 1–20.
29. See the good discussion on this in R. T. France, *Matthew – Evangelist and Teacher* (Exeter, Paternoster, 1989), pp. 95–102, and Stanton, *A Gospel*, pp. 146–68.
30. There is also another reason why Matthew's Gospel was so designated. For many centuries, Matthew was the most widely used Gospel in the church. It seems as if it was preferred because it was the longest and was located first in the early canonical collections.
31. J. P. Meier, *The Vision of Christ: Christ, Church and Morality in the First Gospel* (New York, Paulist, 1979), p. 216.
32. The idea of 'building' a community is drawn from the Old Testament, and is seen at Qumran. (See Jer. 12.16, 18.9, 31.4, 33.7, 42.10; Amos 9.11; 4QpPs 1–10, 4Q164).
33. Thus W. D. Davies and D. C. Allison, *The Gospel According to St Matthew* (Edinburgh, T.&T. Clark, 1991), vol. 2, pp. 627–8. For the view that the rock is Peter's confession, see R. H. Gundry, *Matthew: A Commentary on his Literary and Theological Art* (Grand Rapids, Eerdmans, 1982), pp. 333–5; and in more detail, C. C. Caragounis, *Peter and the Rock* (New York, De Gruyter, 1990).
34. J. Kingsbury, *Matthew: A Commentary for Preachers and Others* (London, SPCK, 1986); J. Overman, *Matthew's Gospel and Formative Judaism* (Minneapolis, Fortress, 1990), pp. 139–40.
35. Some Roman Catholics have found this thought in John 21.15–19, but see my comments on this text in the discussion of Johannine ecclesiology that follows. A less weighty commissioning is given in Luke 22.23 in another context.
36. Overman, *Matthew's Gospel*, pp. 136–40; M. Wilkins, *The Concept of Discipleship in Matthew's Gospel* (Leiden, Brill, 1988), pp. 173–216. A. J.

Nau, in *Peter in Matthew* (Minnesota, Glazier, 1992), argues that Matthew is actually attempting to minimize the importance of Peter. He sees him identifying Peter with the other disciples, accentuating his failings, and contrasting him with Jesus.

37. See W. Thompson, *Matthew's Advice to a Divided Community: Mt. 17:22—18:35* (Rome, Biblical Institute, 1970); France, *Matthew*, pp. 251–3.
38. Stanton, *A Gospel*, pp. 97, 126–31.
39. See the excellent discussion in Overman, *Matthew's Gospel*, pp. 124–36, and Luz, 'The Disciples', and the much longer monograph by Wilkins, *DJG*.
40. 'The Disciples in the Gospel According to Matthew', in Stanton, *The Interpretation*, p. 105.
41. Stanton, *A Gospel*, p. 129; J. D. G. Dunn, *The Parting of the Ways* (London, SCM, 1991), p. 214, and especially n. 23.
42. See Overman, *Matthew's Gospel*, pp. 93–4.
43. In support, it should be noted that this verse is a free rendering of Psalm 130.8, and Matthew changes the more explicit Israel for *laos*/people. See Gundry, *Matthew*, p. 23; J. P. Meier, *Matthew* (Delaware, Glazier, 1985), p. 8; R. Brown, *The Birth of the Messiah* (London, Geoffrey Chapman, 1977), p. 131.
44. So France, *Matthew*, pp. 166–205.
45. For what follows on Christology, I closely follow France, *Matthew*, pp. 279–83.
46. S. Van Tilborg, *The Jewish Leaders in Matthew* (Leiden, Brill, 1972), p. 71.
47. The best way to designate this new reality as understood by Matthew is disputed. Some have argued that for Matthew the Christian community is thought of as 'new Israel', i.e. a restored Israel. This cannot be endorsed because Matthew accentuates the breach with historic Israel and introduces a replacement motif. Another suggestion is 'the true Israel'. This title underlines that a breach with historic Israel has been made and that the Christian community is the heir of the promises made to Israel. I believe this title best captures Matthew's thought, even if this expression is not explicitly used. Stanton, in *A Gospel*, pp. 11–12, tries to transcend this debate by arguing that on the basis of Matthew 21.43 the Christian community in Matthew should be called a 'new people'. However, as the word 'new' is not in this text, and the word translated 'people' is not *laos* but *ethnos*, I cannot see that this adds any clarity to the debate. This is not to deny that the choice of the right term is not difficult. Stanton helpfully points out that Matthew is not always consistent, and we should not expect him to be. The evangelist is writing to try to sort out some of these questions as he goes along, without clear categories to work with.
48. As G. Bornkamm, 'The Stilling of the Storm in Matthew', in G. Bornkamm *et al.* (eds), *Tradition and Interpretation in Matthew* (London, SCM, 1963), pp. 52–7, suggests.

49. There has been a lively debate about the meaning of these words. Does the command refer to a mission to Jews and gentiles, or only to gentiles? For details, see Stanton, *A Gospel*, pp. 137–8. The case that a mission to Jew and gentile is envisaged seems compelling.
50. This Latin expression has been used repeatedly in discussions of Matthew's ecclesiology since Bornkamm, in *Tradition*, p. 19, first introduced it. On what follows, see again for more detail, France, *Matthew*, pp. 275–8.
51. So France, *Matthew*, p. 278, and many other commentators. I note, however, that in the definitive study of this passage by S. W. Gray, *The Least of My Brothers, Matthew 25:31–46: A History of Interpretation* (Georgia, Scholars, 1989), that he concludes that the sheep are Christians and the goats are unbelieving Israel. Stanton, in *A Gospel*, pp. 207–31, takes yet another position. He argues that the passage, as interpreted by Matthew, speaks of the judgement of the nations on the basis of how they have treated Christians.
52. The charismatic dimension in Matthew's ecclesiology is stressed by E. Schweizer, 'Matthew's Church', in Stanton, *The Interpretation*, pp. 129–55. In reply, see J. D. Kingsbury, 'The Verb *Akolouthein* ('to follow') as an Index of Matthew's View of His Community', *JBL*, vol. 97, 1978, pp. 56–73, who gives a more balanced picture.
53. See further on this, D. Hill, *New Testament Prophecy* (Basingstoke, Marshall, Morgan, & Scott, 1979), pp. 154–6. Similarly, Davies and Allison, *Matthew*, pp. 226–7. D. Orton, in *The Understanding Scribe* (Sheffield, JSOT, 1989), finds the background to these ideas in Daniel and other intertestamental writings. He argues that Matthew identifies these 'inspired scribes' with the disciples, but along with the above scholars we take them to be leaders in Matthew's community.
54. With Orton, *The Understanding Scribe*, p. 156, we agree that these three designations should be taken to speak of one group of people.
55. Giles, *Patterns of Ministry Amongst the First Christians*, pp. 131–42.
56. The expression 'these little ones' has been taken in various ways, but the context determines the meaning. In 18.1–5, every disciple is to be like a child. The title is found in Matthew 10.42, 18.6, 10, 14. Stanton, in *A Gospel*, p. 215, argues that the expression 'one of the least of these (who are members of my family)' (Matt. 25.40, 45) is to be understood in the same way. Schweizer, in 'Matthew's Church', p. 138, also maintains that 'the little ones' are ordinary disciples.
57. For more detail on this chapter and discussion of the scholarly study of it, see Overman, *Matthew's Gospel*, pp. 101–6.
58. Stanton, *A Gospel*, p. 383, points out that the Matthean account of the words of institution show the influence of 'liturgical shaping of the Marcan tradition'.
59. See P. Minear, *Matthew: The Teacher's Gospel* (London, Darton, Longman, & Todd, 1984). He takes up an idea with a long history.
60. Overman, *Matthew's Gospel*; Stanton, *A Gospel*, particularly ch. 4, pp. 85–107; W. A. Meeks, 'Breaking Away: Three New Testament Pictures

of Christian Separation from the Jewish Communities', in J. Neusner and E. Freirichs (eds), *To See Ourselves as Others See Us* (California, Scholars, 1985), pp. 108–14. See also the detailed study by M. H. Crosby, *House of Disciples* (New York, Orbis, 1988), which looks at the social setting of the first Gospel on a wider canvas.

61. G. R. Beasley-Murray, *John* (Waco, Word Biblical Commentary, 1987), pp. xliv–liii, gives an excellent summary of these issues, setting out clearly the dominant way of understanding John today.

62. Beasley-Murray, *John*, p. xlvii.

63. It is also possible to read John's Gospel as if it reflects the Johannine community at different stages in its life. For example, R., Brown, *The Community of the Beloved Disciple* (London, Geoffrey Chapman, 1979), postulated four such stages. He makes some intriguing suggestions, but the case is highly speculative. The argument that this Gospel went through more than one edition may be accepted, but in this chapter we work with the final form before us.

64. J. Painter, *The Quest for the Messiah* (Edinburgh, T.&T. Clark, 1991), pp. 326–48, gives an excellent survey of the believing motif in John.

65. 'The Concept of the Church in St John', in A. J. B. Higgins (ed.), *New Testament Essays: Studies in Memory of T. W. Manson* (Manchester, Manchester University, 1959), p. 234.

66. On this, see J. F. O. Grady, 'Individualism and Johannine Ecclesiology', *BTB*, vol. 5, 1975, pp. 227–61, and R. Brown, *The Gospel According to John* (New York, Doubleday, 1966), vol. 1, pp. cv–cxi.

67. Matthew 73 times; Mark 46 times; Luke 37 times.

68. On discipleship in John, see Wilkins, DJG; R. Schnackenburg, *The Gospel According to John* (New York, Crossroad, 1968), vol. 1, pp. 162–4, and vol. 3, 1982, pp. 203–13.

69. See R. F. Collins, *These Things Have Been Written: Studies in the Fourth Gospel* (Grand Rapids, Eerdmans, 1990), pp. 46–55.

70. Witherington, *Women in the Earliest Churches*, pp. 174–82; Brown, *The Community*, pp. 183–9.

71. R. Brown, both in his two-volume commentary on John, *The Gospel*, and in *The Community*, makes much of this. K. Quast, in *Peter and the Beloved Disciple* (Sheffield, JSOT, 1989), accepts this thesis in principle, but suggests a number of important modifications to the ways it has often been expressed in the past.

72. Brown, *The Gospel*, vol. 1, p. 396; Beasley-Murray, *John*, p. 171; J. W. Pryor, *John: Evangelist of the Covenant People* (Downers Grove, IVP, 1992), pp. 43–6.

73. On the meaning and usage of the term in John, see G. M. Burge, *The Anointed Community* (Grand Rapids, Eerdmans, 1987), pp. 6–44.

74. Schnackenburg, *The Gospel*, vol. 3, p. 83, argues that the second part of the sentence explains the first. On recalling to mind, see also 2.17, 22, 12.6, 15.20, 16.4, 21.

75. So Burge with caution, *The Anointed Community*, pp. 214–15.

76. Burge, *The Anointed Community*, p. 150.

77. See further, Burge, *The Anointed Community*, pp. 114–47.
78. On this idea, see Y. Congar, *I Believe in the Holy Spirit* (London, Chapman, 1983), vol. 2, pp. 7–12.
79. Brown, *The Gospel*, vol. 2, p. 1042. Significantly, Schnackenburg, in *The Gospel*, vol. 3, pp. 326–8, comes to a very similar conclusion. He says later church exegesis 'introduced many questions into this text which are remote from it' (p. 326).
80. Pryor, *John*, p. 183.
81. So S. Pancaro, 'People of God in John's Gospel', *NTS*, vol. 16, 1969–70, pp. 114–29.
82. Pryor, *John*, p. 157.
83. Pryor, *John*, p. 160.
84. Pryor, *John*, p. 166.
85. E.g. R. Bultmann, *Theology of the New Testament* (London, SCM, 1955), vol. 2, and in more moderate terms, E. Schweizer, *Church Order in the New Testament* (London, SCM, 1961), pp. 117–24.
86. This passage has been taken by traditional Roman Catholics as a commissioning of Peter as the one supreme pastor or Pontiff over the church. See G. R. Beasley-Murray, *Gospel of Life* (Massachusetts, Hendrickson, 1991), pp. 120–1. He argues in reply that the force of this passage is much the same as that in the charge to shepherds/pastors in 1 Peter 5.2 and Acts 20.28.
87. See also the comments about the disciples being sent to the harvest in John 4.35–8. See also John 9.4.
88. See Burge, *The Anointed Community*, pp. 190–7.
89. Beasley-Murray, in *John*, says alternative explanations 'do not do justice to the text'. Even if the comment about water refers in the first instance to John the Baptist's ministry, how John intended these words to be taken by Christian readers is the key issue. It is hard not to believe he did not want them to think of the Christian rite; but see also Burge, *The Anointed Community*, pp. 159–63.
90. Brown, *The Gospel*, vol. 1, p. cxiv. But Beasley-Murray, in *Gospel of Life*, does not agree. He does not concede that the symbolism of water usually or always implies baptism in John.
91. Again, for a good summary and list of contributors to this debate, see S. C. Barton, 'The Communal Dimension of Earliest Christianity: A Critical Survey of the Field', *JTS*, vol. 43, 1992, pp. 412–14.

4 The Church in the Book of Acts

1. In this comment, two alternative explanations as to why Luke wrote are combined. See further, R. Maddox, *The Purpose of Luke–Acts* (Edinburgh, T.&T. Clark, 1982), pp. 12–23. Maddox himself argues that the prime audience were Christians with a good knowledge of the Old Testament.
2. See K. N. Giles, 'Ascension', *DJG*, pp. 46–50.

3. The number probably is significant. In the Mishnah (M. Sanh. 1.6), the number 120 is the minimum requirement to establish a community with its own governing council.

4. See our earlier discussion on the church in the Gospel of Luke.

5. The gender-specific *andēr* should be noted.

6. See K. N. Giles, *Women and Their Ministry* (Melbourne, Dove, 1977), pp. 24–5. Thus Paul does not mention the women witnesses of the resurrection in his list of witnesses in 1 Corinthians 15.3–8, while Josephus wrote, 'From women let no evidence be accepted because of the levity and temerity of their sex' (*Ant.* 4.219). It seems, however, that in some cases a woman could be a witness in Judaism. See R. K. Karris, *Women and Discipleship in Luke*, pp. 18–19.

7. To set out this evidence would be a long digression, and I have summarized this elsewhere – see K. N. Giles, 'The Significance of the Day of Pentecost', *LTJ*, 1983, pp. 137–9. See also L. T. Johnston, *The Acts of the Apostles* (Minnesota, Glazier, 1992), pp. 45–7. The debate is well set out and a good bibliography given in R. P. Menzies, *The Development of Early Christian Pneumatology* (Sheffield, JSOT, 1991), pp. 229–44. Menzies argues against any association between Pentecost and Sinai because he thinks this interpretation would undermine his overall thesis. His case is thus a critique of the evidence with a prior agenda.

8. On this debate, see E. Haenchen, *The Acts of the Apostles* (Oxford, Basil Blackwell, 1971), pp. 191–2.

9. I follow the translation given by Johnston, *The Acts*, p. 56. 'Community' is his rendering of the Greek *epi to auto* (cf. 1.15, 2.1, 47; 1 Cor. 11.18, 20, 14.32), a phrase that in the *LXX* frequently translates the Hebrew, *yahad* (e.g. Pss. 2.2, 4.9, 33.4, 36.38), which at Qumran became almost a technical term for the community (see 1Qs 1.1, 12, 8.2, 9.2). Possibly, because a later scribe was aware of the special meaning of this expression, he changed it to *en tē ekklēsia*.

10. Many have noted the recurring parallelisms in Luke–Acts. C. H. Talbert, in *Literary Patterns, Theological Themes, and the Genre of Luke–Acts* (Missoula, Scholars, 1974), lists many parallels that should be seen, and some difficult to see. R. Brown, in *The Churches the Apostles Left Behind* (New York, Paulist, 1984), pp. 63–5, also notes this parallel commencement of the church in Luke's Gospel and in Acts.

11. See our earlier discussion.

12. On this last title, see n. 9 above, and the comment on the variant readings that adds the word *ekklēsia* at this point.

13. On this phenomenon, see H. J. Cadbury, *The Making of Luke–Acts* (London, Macmillan, 1927), pp. 213–38.

14. See further, K. N. Giles, 'Present-future Eschatology in the Book of Acts', *RTR*, vol. 40, 1982, pp. 65–71; Maddox, *The Purpose*, pp. 129–45.

15. The word 'gladness' (*agalliasis*) in Acts 2.46 is one that suggests eschatological joy given by the Lord. See Luke 1.14, 44, 47, 10.21, and in the *LXX*, Pss. 9.2, 12.5, 19.5, 20.1, 30.7, 39.16, etc.

16. Brown, *The Churches*, p. 65.

17. See P. F. Esler, *Community and Gospel in Luke–Acts* (Cambridge, CUP, 1987), pp. 201–17.
18. H. J. Cadbury, 'Names for Christians and Christianity in Acts', in F. J. Foakes-Jackson and K. Lake (eds), *The Beginnings of Christianity* (London, Macmillan, 1933), vol. 5, pp. 375–92.
19. This title is usually thought to be an early designation of the Christians, but it should be noted that Luke makes much of the word 'way' (*hodos*) himself (see Luke 9.31; Acts 16.17, 18.25, 26, etc.) and of the journey motif.
20. Acts 9.25 may be an exception, for the best texts read 'his [i.e. Paul's] disciples'.
21. In the discussion on the title 'the church' that follows, we will see that this term can be used as a synonym of 'the disciples'.
22. On the background to this title and for a critique of this argument, see O. E. Evans, 'New Wine in Old Wineskins: The Saints', *ExpT*, vol. 86, 1975, pp. 196–200.
23. This position is given definitive expression in J. Y. Campbell, 'The Origin and Meaning of the Christian Use of the word *Ekklēsia*', *JTS*, vol. 49, 1948, pp. 41–54, but is adopted by many who want to stress the congregational view of the church. For further on this, see Chapter 1, where a list is given of some of those who argue in this way.
24. See C. F. D. Moule, 'The Christology of Acts', in L. E. Keck and J. L. Martyn (eds), *Studies in Luke–Acts* (London, SPCK, 1966), pp. 159–84.
25. Cerfaux, *The Church in the Theology of St Paul* (New York, Herder & Herder, 1959), pp. 187, 95–117.
26. See pp. 237–8.
27. See further on this, D. L. Brock, *Proclamation from Prophecy and Pattern* (Sheffield, JSOT, 1987), pp. 220–1.
28. So F. F. Bruce, *The Book of the Acts* (Grand Rapids, Eerdmans, 1988), p. 142 and n. 57.
29. Luke in fact speaks of three groups of people: the small group who saw these things happen, 'the whole church', and 'all who heard these things' (5.11), who would seem to be those not belonging to the church.
30. Luke has a practice of adding emphatic words such as all, every, and whole when their inclusion contributes little to the meaning of the sentence. He uses *holos* seventeen times in the Gospel, and twenty times in Acts, while he uses *pas* 137 times in the Gospel and 172 times in Acts. On this stylistic detail, see Cadbury, *Making*, p. 216.
31. In 4.32, 'the whole group' reflects the Greek word *plēthos*, which in the *LXX* usually alludes to any multitude, but twice it translates *qahal* (Exod. 12.6; 2 Chron. 31.18). In Acts it seems to be used in two ways: of a multitude (2.6, 14.1, 17.4, 21.22, 23.7, 25.24), and almost technically of all the Christians in one place, as in 4.32, 6.2, 5, 15.12, 30. See Bruce, *Acts*, p. 159.
32. This rendering by the Jerusalem Bible captures the sense. See the former note.
33. See for more detail on these texts, K. N. Giles, 'Luke's Use of the Term

Ekklēsia with Special Reference to Acts 20:28 and 9:31', *NTS*, vol. 31, 1985, pp. 135–42.

34. The textual evidence is evenly balanced between the two possible readings, 'the church of the Lord' (*ekklēsia tou kuriou*) or the 'church of God' (*ekklēsia tou theou*). The former is preferred because the expression 'the church of the Lord' appears nowhere in the New Testament, while Paul frequently speaks of 'the church of God'; and the change can be explained because the following phrase, 'which he obtained with his own blood', does not read well if God is the subject. A scribe noting this difficulty thus changed *theou* to *kupiou*.

35. So Bruce, *Acts*, p. 393, and F. J. A. Hort, *The Christian Ecclesia* (London, Macmillan, 1914), pp. 13–14.

36. Hort, *Christian Ecclesia*, p. 13.

37. See our discussion of Paul's use of this word in Chapter 5.

38. So Cerfaux, *The Church*, pp. 114–17.

39. This is a point that Cadbury, in 'Names', p. 389, underlines.

40. H. Conzelmann, *The Theology of St Luke* (London, Faber & Faber, 1960).

41. Haenchen, *The Acts*, p. 102.

42. J. Jervell, *Luke and the People of God* (Minnesota, Augsburg, 1972).

43. Maddox, *The Purpose*, pp. 31–66.

44. G. Lohfink, *Die Sammlung Israel: Eine Untersuchung zur lukanischen Ekklesiologie* (Munchen, Kosel, 1975).

45. On house churches in Acts, see J. H. Elliott, 'Temple versus Household In Luke–Acts', in J. H. Neyrey (ed.), *The Social World of Luke–Acts* (Massachusetts, Hendrickson, 1991), pp. 215–36; B. Blue, 'Acts and the House Church', in W. J. Gill and C. Gempf, *The Book of Acts in its First Century Setting: The Greco-Roman Setting* (Carlisle, Paternoster, 1994), vol. 2, pp. 119–89.

46. See K. N. Giles, 'Is Luke an Exponent of Early Protestantism? Church Order in the Lucan Writings', *EQ*, pt 2, vol. 54, 1982, pp. 3–20; Menzies, *The Development*, pp. 244–77.

47. On the reference in Acts 27.35 to the breaking of bread, see the good discussion in Esler, *Community and Gospel*, pp. 101–4.

48. H. Kee, *Good News to the Ends of the Earth* (London, SCM, 1990), pp. 16, 72. See also Haenchen, *The Acts*, p. 98.

49. In Acts 13.1, one group of people is in mind. It is not that some are prophets and some teachers. On the teaching role of prophets, see K. N. Giles, *Patterns of Ministry among the First Christians* (Melbourne, Collins-Dove, 1989), p. 115.

50. In more detail on ministry and ordination in Acts, see Giles, *Patterns*.

51. They are not called deacons, and their qualifications are quite different to those of the deacon given in 1 Timothy 3.8–13. See Giles, *Patterns*, p. 58. For a very different understanding of the elders in Acts, see A. Campbell, 'The Elders in the Jerusalem Church', *JTS*, vol. 44, 1993, pp. 511–28. He thinks Luke is a very poor historian, and argues that the elders were in fact the leaders of the Jerusalem church all along. Luke introduces the twelve apostles for theological reasons.

52. The special feature of Menzies's argument, in *The Development*, is that the Spirit in Luke is given to enable prophecy; it is an additional gift to the gift of salvation. I am not convinced that Luke allows for this distinction, but this study does not allow for a detailed interaction with this thesis. See M. Turner, 'The Spirit and Power of Jesus' Miracles in the Lucan Conception', *NovT*, vol. 33, 1991, pp. 124–52, as a partial answer to Menzies. And also Menzies's reply, 'Spirit and Power in Luke–Acts: A Response to Max Turner', *JSNT*, vol. 49, 1993, pp. 11–20.

53. Giles, *Patterns*, pp. 188–9.

54. In the post-apostolic age, James was seen as the first Bishop of Jerusalem. See further, Giles, *Patterns*, p. 29.

55. This whole story raises important historical questions, especially in relation to the meeting Paul mentions in Galatians 2.1–10, but these do not concern us at this point. Discussions on this are found in all the commentaries. The historicity of the events Luke recounts is another issue; some support for his account can be claimed on the basis of Qumran and Jewish parallels, which several scholars have noted. See J. Fitzmyer, 'Jewish Christianity in Acts in Light of the Qumran Scrolls', in Keck and Martyn, *Studies in Luke–Acts*, pp. 244–7; B. Gerhardsson, *Memory and Manuscript* (Lund, Gleerup, 1961), pp. 245–60.

56. In Acts 20.28, the word *episcopos*/oversight refers to the function of all the elders; it is not a separate office.

5 The Church in Paul's Earliest Epistles

1. Of these epistles, the only one seriously questioned in regard to Pauline authorship is 2 Thessalonians, but the case for authenticity cannot be easily dismissed. See K. Donfield, in K. Donfield and I. H. Marshall (eds), *The Theology of the Shorter Pauline Epistles* (Cambridge, CUP, 1993), pp. 84–7. As this epistle does not figure significantly in this study, no more need be said.

2. Published in Cambridge by CUP, 1988.

3. So G. E. Ladd, *A Theology of the New Testament* (Grand Rapids, Eerdmans, rev. edn 1993), pp. 595–614; H. Ridderbos, *Paul: An Outline of His Theology* (Grand Rapids, Eerdmans, 1977), pp. 44–90; J. C. Becker, *Paul the Apostle* (Philadelphia, Fortress, 1988), pp. 11–19; L. J. Kreitzer, 'Eschatology', *DPL*, pp. 253–69.

4. On transfer terminology, see E. P. Sanders, *Paul and Palestinian Judaism* (London, SCM, 1977), pp. 463–74.

5. See further, L. J. Kreitzer, 'Adam and Christ', *DPL*, pp. 9–15.

6. C. F. D. Moule, *The Origin of Christology* (Cambridge, CUP, 1977), pp. 47–90; Becker, *Paul*, pp. 307–10, etc. See also the discussion on the 'in Christ' motif on p. 101.

7. See further on this N. T. Wright, *The Climax of the Covenant* (Edinburgh, T.&T. Clark, 1991), pp. 18–40. I do not completely reject the 'corporate personality' explanation which has come under much

criticism, but Wright's explanation is given primacy. It would seem that not only the Jews, but also other ancient societies, saw themselves as a corporate unity, especially in relation to their king.

8. See further, E. Best, *One Body in Christ* (London, SPCK, 1955); Becker, *Paul*, pp. 272–4; Moule, *The Origin*, pp. 47–89; M. A. Siefield, 'In Christ', *DPL*, pp. 433–6.

9. On Paul's conception of Jesus as the Messiah, see Wright, *The Climax*, pp. 41–55.

10. See also Galatians 6.15. This expression is drawn from apocalyptic Judaism (e.g. 1 Enoch 72.1, 90.28–9, 91.16; 2 Apoc. Bar. 32.6; Jub. 4.26; 1QS 4.25; 1QH 11.10–14, etc.), but finds its origin in Isaiah 65.17–25. Elsewhere in the New Testament, see 2 Peter 3.13 and Revelation 21.1 5.

11. See Ridderbos, *Paul*, pp. 362–76; R. Y. K. Fung, 'Body of Christ', *DPW*, pp. 77–82. L. O. R. Yorke, in *The Church as the Body of Christ* (New York, University Press of America, 1991), has recently argued that Paul simply likens the church to a human body; and that the 'of' in the expression 'the body of Christ' is possessive. This body belongs to Christ. This simply does not adequately explain Paul's language. See Ridderbos, *Paul*, pp. 371–2, who discusses this well-known opinion and rejects it.

12. The final words of verse 12, 'so it is with Christ', are much debated. Since Paul does not say 'so also is the church' or 'so also is the body of Christ', some have argued that this means that the church is Christ literally. Yet in view of 1 Corinthians 12.27–8 where this thought is not present, it is better to see this as an example of 'metonymy'. Christ is a shortened form of 'the body of Christ'. So Fung, 'Body of Christ', p. 78; G. Fee, *The First Epistle to the Corinthians* (Grand Rapids, Eerdmans, 1987), p. 603.

13. Ridderbos, *Paul*, p. 371.

14. Ridderbos, *Paul*, p. 307.

15. See further Becker, *Paul*, pp. 307–10.

16. In more detail, see Ridderbos, *Paul*, pp. 362–9; R. H. Gundry, *Soma in Biblical Theology* (Cambridge, CUP, 1976), pp. 223–44; Best, *One Body*, pp. 110–14.

17. On the nature of metaphors, and in particular in relation to Paul's use of the body metaphor, see B. Field, 'The Discourses Behind the Metaphor "the Church as the Body of Christ" as Used by St Paul and the "Post Paulines"', *AJT*, 6:1, 92, pp. 88–107.

18. 4QFlor, 5Q15, 11QTemple. See further, B. Gartner, *The Temple and the Community in Qumran and the New Testament* (Cambridge, CUP, 1965); R. J. McKelvey, *The New Temple* (Oxford, OUP, 1969), pp. 46–53.

19. McKelvey, *The New Temple*, p. 100. The temple imagery also appears in 1 Corinthians 6.19, but in this case it is applied to individuals.

20. W. J. Webb, in *Returning Home: New Covenant and Second Exodus as the Context for 2 Corinthians 6:14—7:1* (Sheffield, JSOT, 1993), gives the most detailed information on the issues raised by this passage. He

concludes that the mosaic quotation reflects Ezekiel 37.27, modified by words from Leviticus 26.11–12, Isaiah 52.11, Ezekiel 20.34, and 2 Samuel 7.14, modified by words from Isaiah 43.6.

21. Webb, *Returning Home.*
22. See the helpful discussion by O. E. Evans, 'New Wine in Old Wineskins: The Saints', *ExpT*, vol. 86, 1975, pp. 196–200.
23. It has been argued that the saints were for Paul the original believers in Jerusalem. This title may well have been used first in the Palestinian church, but Paul quite clearly applies it to all believers. All believers collectively are for Paul 'saints', because of their status in Christ. For details on this matter, see Evans, 'New Wine'.
24. J. D. G. Dunn, in *Romans 1–8* (Waco, Word Biblical Commentary, 1988), p. 467, says, 'Paul prepares in this section for the discussion of chaps. 9–11. He deliberately evokes traditional Jewish motifs' so that his 'readers understand the blessings they are inheriting are Israel's'.
25. The English, 'called to be saints', is somewhat misleading in that it could suggest that 'sainthood' is a goal to be obtained rather than a status already given. What Paul is in fact stating is that Christians are 'saints by God's call'.
26. See further, H. Strathmann and R. Meyer, *TDNT*, vol. 4, pp. 29–57. The word is found only twelve times in the whole Pauline corpus, eleven of these in the early Paulines. The twelfth reference is in Titus 2.14.
27. Dunn, *Romans 1–8*, p. 575.
28. Becker, *Paul*, p. 94.
29. Becker, *Paul*, pp. 95–108.
30. Besides Becker, see also G. W. Hansen, *Abraham in Galatians* (Sheffield, JSOT, 1989); J. D. G. Dunn, *The Theology of Paul's Letter to the Galatians* (Cambridge, CUP, 1992); R. Longenecker, *Galatians* (Waco, Word Biblical Commentary, 1990).
31. Hansen, *Abraham*, p. 156.
32. Jews by birth, or believing Jews, or Jews who walk by this rule. See Hansen, *Abraham*, p. 161. D. W. B. Robinson, in 'The Distinction between Jewish and Gentile Believers in Galatians', *RTR*, vol. 13, 1965, pp. 29–38, follows those who hold that Paul is referring to Jewish believers.
33. On this possibility, see Longenecker, *Galatians*, p. 297.
34. So Hansen, Dunn, and Longenecker; H. Ridderbos, *The Epistle to the Churches of Galatia* (Edinburgh, Marshall, Morgan, & Scott, 1961), pp. 226–7; J. A. Weima, *Neglected Endings: The Significance of the Pauline Letter Closings* (Sheffield, JSOT, 1994), pp. 172–4.
35. J. D. G. Dunn, *Romans 9–16* (Waco, Word Biblical Commentary, 1988), p. 681. However, for another view, see Wright, *The Climax*, pp. 231–56. He argues that 'all Israel' is in fact the Jewish and the gentile believers – true Israel – but I think the context disallows this interpretation.
36. So E. P. Sanders, *Paul* (Oxford, OUP, 1991), pp. 122–8.

37. So Ridderbos, *Paul*, pp. 358–61.
38. A list of those who take these opposing views is given in the excursus at the end of the book.
39. V. P. Branick, *The House Church in the Writings of Paul* (Delaware, Glazier, 1989), etc.
40. *St Paul's Corinth: Text and Archaeology* (Delaware, Glazier, 1983), p. 158.
41. Branick, *The House Church*, pp. 9–18; K. N. Giles, *Patterns of Ministry Among the First Christians* (Melbourne, Collins-Dove, 1989), p. 34; J. M. Peterson, 'House churches in Rome', *VC*, vol. 23, 1969, pp. 264–72.
42. I take it that Paul is referring to Palestine when he uses the word 'Judea'. On this and on Paul's persecuting work, see M. Hengel, *The Pre-Christian Paul* (London, SCM, 1991), pp. 68–96.
43. See, most recently, H. Merklein, 'Die Ekklēsia Gottes', in H. Merklein (ed.), *Studien zu Jesus und Paulus* (Tubingen, Mohr, 1987), p. 301. Also, R. Schnackenburg, *The Church in the New Testament*, pp. 114–17. The evidence is as follows: (1) the expression 'persecuting the church [of God]' seems to be a fixed turn of phrase, as Paul gives it three times, in three different epistles. Merklein says it sounds like a *terminus technicus* for the earliest Jewish Christians. (2) It would have been a title understood in a Jewish setting. The men at Qumran, who claimed to be true Israel, gave themselves this title (1QM 4.10; 1QSa 2.4), and it was used of Israel in the Old Testament (Neh. 13.1; cf. Deut. 23.2–8; 1 Chron. 28.8; Mic. 2.5). (4) It explains how from the earliest days of the gentile mission Paul came to use this title. As the expression had already been extended to Jews outside of Jerusalem, and for the apostle the salvation of Jew and gentile was on the same basis, he assumed that all believers could collectively be called 'the church of God' (1 Cor. 1.2, 10.32; 2 Cor. 1.1) or just 'the church'.
44. Most recently by M. E. Thrall, *The Second Epistle to the Corinthians* (Edinburgh, T.&T. Clark, 1994), pp. 89–93.
45. So Longenecker, *Galatians*, p. 28.
46. Schmidt, *TDNT*, vol. 3, p. 507; Cerfaux, *The Church in the Theology of St Paul*, p. 106.
47. Donfield, pp. 42–3. He notes the frequent locative uses of *en* in this epistle (1.1, 2.14, 4.16, 5.12).
48. So P. T. O'Brien, *Commentary on Philippians* (Grand Rapids, Eerdmans, 1991), p. 45.
49. Romans 16.23, which speaks of Gaius, 'who is host to me and the whole church', has been much discussed. Banks, *Paul's Idea of Community*, p. 38, and Dunn, in *Romans 9–16*, p. 23, believe this refers to combined meetings of the various house churches in Corinth, but most commentators think that Paul, who is enjoying the hospitality of Gaius as he writes, is commending him for his hospitality to (members of) the whole church as the need arises. Yet if Banks and Dunn are correct, it means that 'the whole church' in Corinth, when Paul writes to the Romans in the mid-fifties, numbers no more than about fifty, as it is

generally agreed that no house could hold more than this number. As this seems implausible, noting the people and the number of house churches mentioned in the Corinthian correspondence, the combined church interpretation must be questioned. In 1 Corinthians 14.23, Paul also speaks of 'the whole church', but in this case he seems to be speaking of when the (whole) church gathers. In Corinth, it would seem, this took place in the several house churches, not as one gathering. See 1 Corinthians 11.17, 20, 14.26, where in similar language and envisaging a similar thing, Paul simply speaks of 'when you come together'.

50. J. Roloff, 'Ekklēsia', *EDNT*, vol. 1, pp. 410–15.
51. F. F. Bruce, *1 and 2 Corinthians* (London, Oliphants, 1971), p. 101. For the designation 'race', see *The Epistle to Diognetus* 1, and for 'new race', see *The Preaching of Peter*, quoted in Clement, *Stromateis*, 6:5:39.
52. Roloff, *EDNT*, vol. 1, p. 413; Ridderbos, *Paul*, p. 329; Thrall, *The Second Epistle*, p. 90; Hort, *The Christian Ecclesia*, p. 117. Pace Hainz, *Structuren*, pp. 252–5, who argues that Paul is only speaking of the leadership of the church in Corinth.
53. So Hainz, *Structuren*, pp. 230–5; Thrall, *The Second Epistle*, p. 93 *et al.*
54. Merklein, 'Die Ekklēsia', p. 314.
55. R. Sohm, in a number of works published late last century, popularized this view. In English, see his *Outlines of Church History* (London, Macmillan, 1895). See also Schmidt, *TDNT*, vol. 3, p. 506ff.
56. So Robinson, Knox, Banks, O'Brien and Dumbrell.
57. D. W. B. Robinson, 'The Doctrine of the Church and its Implications for Evangelism', *Interchange*, vol. 15, 1974, pp. 156–62, and 'The Church and Evangelism', *Interchange*, vol. 21, 1977, pp. 62–3. See also, more generally, his book, *The Church of God* (Sydney, Jordan, 1965).
58. See A. T. Lincoln, *Paradise Now and Not Yet* (Cambridge, CUP, 1981), pp. 21–2.
59. I was interested to note after I had worked this out independently (or so I thought) to find that G. B. Caird in his newly published *New Testament Theology* (Oxford, Clarendon, 1994), p. 214, came to exactly the same conclusion. He writes, 'The distinctions we have been taught to make between the church and the churches, the universal and the local . . . have no foundation in Pauline usage.' This is the major weakness in Thrall's excursus (*The Second Epistle*). Her whole argument is predicated on distinguishing the local and universal usages in Paul.
60. On what follows, see in more detail, Giles, *Patterns*, and more recently, J. M. Burtchaell, *From Synagogue to Church* (Cambridge, CUP, 1992).
61. See further, K. N. Giles, *Created Woman* (Canberra, Acorn, 1985); B. Witherington, *Women in the Earliest Churches* (Cambridge, CUP, 1988), pp. 24–125.
62. See especially Fee, *The First Epistle*, pp. 699–713, who rejects the apostolic authorship of this paragraph.
63. It is important to note that Paul only conceives of adult baptism. Some care is needed in appealing to the New Testament to justify infant baptism.

64. He uses the verb in Romans 15.20; 1 Corinthians 8.1, 10, 10.23, 14.4, 17; Galatians 2.18; 1 Thessalonians 2.18; the noun in 1 Corinthians 3.9, 14.3, 5, 12, 26; 2 Corinthians 5.1, 10.8, 12.19, 13.10.
65. See further, W. Meeks, *The First Urban Christians* (New Haven, Yale, 1983).
66. MacDonald, *The Pauline Churches* (Cambridge, CUP, 1988).

6 The Church in the Middle and Later Paulines

1. F. F. Bruce, *The Epistles to the Colossians, to Philemon and to the Ephesians* (Grand Rapids, Eerdmans, 1984), p. 241. There are other major differences, but for our purposes this is not an issue. See particularly, A. Lincoln, *Ephesians* (Waco, Word Biblical Commentary, 1990), pp. xlvii–lviii. On the thought of Colossians and Ephesians generally, see the recent helpful introduction by A. T. Lincoln and A. J. M. Wedderburn, *The Theology of the Later Pauline Epistles* (Cambridge, CUP, 1993).
2. The name 'Paul' is used of the author of all the epistles ascribed to him. I am well aware that some think that the middle Paulines were written by disciples or companions of the apostle (and many believe this of the late Paulines), but this is an issue that can be left to one side in this study.
3. See further, P. O'Brien, *Colossians and Philemon* (Waco, Word Biblical Commentary, 1982), pp. xxx–xli.
4. *Colossians and Philemon* (Philadelphia, Fortress, 1971), p. 179.
5. S. Lohse, p. 68.
6. R. Banks, *Paul's Idea of Community* (Homebush, NSW, Anzea, pp 44–8; W. J. Dumbrell, *The Search for Order* (Great Rapids, Baker, 1994), pp. 266–8. O'Brien, *Colossians and Philemon*, pp. xlv, 57–61, etc. See also O'Brien's articles in D. A. Carson (ed.), *The Church in the Bible and the World* (Exeter, Paternoster, 1987), pp. 88–119, and in *DPL*, pp. 123–31. I will quote in the following only from his Word series commentary.
7. O'Brien, *Colossians and Philemon*, p. 3.
8. O'Brien, *Colossians and Philemon*, p. 40.
9. O'Brien, *Colossians and Philemon*, p. 80.
10. O'Brien, *Colossians and Philemon*, p. 62. The italic is mine. The omission of some words in the quote in no way changes the meaning.
11. O'Brien, *Colossians and Philemon*, pp. 256–7.
12. O'Brien, *Colossians and Philemon*, along with most other commentators. There is some textual confusion as to whether or not the name is masculine or feminine, but as it is hard to imagine a later scribe changing the masculine pronoun to a feminine one, the general consensus is that the apostle himself spoke here of a woman.
13. On these codes, see the summary article by D. L. Balch, 'Household Codes', in D. E. Aune (ed.), *Greco-Roman Literature and the New Testament* (Atlanta, Scholars, 1988), pp. 25–50. Recent scholarly study of the household codes in the New Testament has highlighted their

apologetic nature. They are given to restrain Christian freedom so as not to offend unbelievers. This concern first mentioned in Col. 4.5 is underlined in the Pastorals.

14. K. N. Giles, *Patterns of Ministry Among the First Christians* (Melbourne, Collins-Dove, 1989); J. M. Burtchaell, *From Synagogue to Church* (Cambridge, CUP, 1992), pp. 272ff.

15. In more detail, see Giles, *Patterns*.

16. On these titles see O'Brien, *Colossians and Philemon*, pp. 187–98.

17. O'Brien, *Colossians and Philemon*, p. 191.

18. 1.22, 3.10, 21, 5.23, 24, 25, 27, 29, 32.

19. Nine times it is also called 'the body of Christ' (cf. 1.23, 2.16, 4.4, 12, 16 (twice), 5.23, 28, 30). In addition, it is called 'one new humanity' (2.15), God's family (2.19), the new temple (2.20–2), Christ's fullness (1.23, 4.13), and Christ's bride (5.23–33), and collectively Christians are called 'the saints' (1.1, 15, 18, 3.18, 5.3, 6.18); children of light (2.10); God's work of new creation (5.8); and God's beloved children (1.5, 2.19, 5.1).

    Here more than anywhere else, the word *ekklēsia* has lost completely the classical meaning of 'assembly'. Pace O'Brien, in Carson, *The Church in the Bible*, pp. 108–15; Banks, *Paul's Idea*, pp. 44–7.

20. A large number of studies have been written on the ecclesiology of Ephesians. R. Schnackenburg, in *The Epistle to the Ephesians* (Edinburgh, T.&T. Clark, 1991), p. 293, n. 20, lists many of the more important German works and gives an interesting history of interpretation (pp. 321–31). He also has an excellent excursus on 'The Church in the Epistle to the Ephesians' (pp. 293–310). In this chapter, which is mainly exegetical, my main sources were commentaries; but where specialized studies raised important issues, they will be mentioned in notes. Besides Schnackenburg's commentary, Lincoln's *Ephesians* was invaluable. He constantly returns to the ecclesiology of this epistle. This same interest is seen in his subsequent study of the theology of Ephesians in Lincoln and Wedderburn, *The Theology of the Later Pauline Epistles*. Another small monograph with a special interest in the church in this epistle is E. Best, *Ephesians* (Sheffield, JSOT, 1993).

21. See further, Lincoln, *Ephesians*, pp. lxiii, 19–21.

22. See further, Lincoln and Wedderburn, *The Theology of the Later Pauline Epistles*, pp. 128–9; C. E. Arnold, *Ephesians: Power and Magic* (Cambridge, CUP, 1989), pp. 145–58.

23. M. Barth, *Ephesians 1–3* (New York, Doubleday, 1974), p. 77.

24. In the theological debates about election, the primary communal dimension is all too often ignored. See the excellent discussion in O. Weber, *Foundations of Dogmatics* (Grand Rapids, Eerdmans, 1983), vol. 2, pp. 411–525.

25. This section emphasizes the divine initiative in the creation of the church. Note the verbs 'chose', 'predestined', 'purposed', and 'appointed', and the nouns 'good pleasure', 'will', 'purpose', and 'plan', all of which speak of God's sovereign purposes. See Lincoln and Wedderburn, *The*

Theology of the Later Pauline Epistles, p. 112. That the church is chosen in Christ 'before the foundation of the world' is not evidence that the author of Ephesians believed in an 'ontological preexistent' church as J. C. Becker, in *Heirs of Paul* (Edinburgh, T.&T. Clark, 1989), claims.

26. T. G. Allen, in 'Exaltation and Solidarity with Christ: Ephesians 1:20 and 2:6', *JSNT*, vol. 28, 1986, pp. 103–20, finds thirty-four examples all told.
27. Lincoln, *Ephesians*, pp. 21–2; Barth, *Ephesians 1–3*, pp. 69–70; Arnold, *Ephesians*, pp. 136–7.
28. Best, *One Body in Christ* (London, SPCK, 1955), p. 8. But pace Allen, 'Exaltation'.
29. J. Stott, *God's New Society* (Leicester, IVP, 1979), p. 34.
30. Lincoln, *Ephesians*, p. 32.
31. Lincoln, *Ephesians*, pp. 32–3; Schnackenburg, *The Epistle*, pp. 60–1.
32. Bruce, *The Epistles*, p. 263.
33. Lincoln, *Ephesians*, p. 68; Schnackenburg, *The Epistle*, p. 82.
34. The Greek is difficult, but with most modern commentators, *pleroma/* fullness is taken as a reference to the church rather than Christ, and having a passive rather than an active sense so as to mean 'that which is filled by Christ rather than that which fills Christ'. Schnackenburg, *The Epistle*, pp. 80–1; Lincoln, *Ephesians*, pp. 73–8; Barth, *Ephesians 1–3*, p. 158, *et al.*
35. Lincoln, *Ephesians*, p. 76.
36. The use of the title 'saints' in this verse is unusual, and has evoked a lot of debate. Lincoln, in *Ephesians*, pp. 150–1, discusses five possibilities, and concludes that it probably carries the usual meaning of Christians in general; and Paul is simply saying 'you' have been included with all those who have already believed.
37. H. Merklein, in *Das Kirchliche Amt Nach Dem Epheserbrief* (Munich, Kosel, 1973), pp. 144–55, concludes that it is the foundation stone of the building. Lincoln, *Ephesians*, pp. 154–5, concludes that it is the head stone.
38. See our earlier discussion on Matthew 16.18.
39. So, Bruce, *The Epistles*, p. 296; Lincoln, *Ephesians*, pp. xciii, 139; Schnackenburg, *The Epistle*, pp. 109–10, especially pp. 321–5. Pace Barth, *Ephesians 1–3*, pp. 130–5, and elsewhere in this commentary and in other writings – e.g. *The People of God* (Sheffield, JSOT, 1983). He argues that in Ephesians, and in the New Testament in general, Israel, even in rejecting Christ, retains a priority in the plan of God, although at this present time the church has been placed on an equal footing. Barth seems to be so concerned with contemporary Jewish–Christian relations that he allows this issue to impact on his reading of Ephesians in its historical context.

This particular name for the church Harnack traces back to 'The Preaching of Peter', an early second-century apocryphal writing. See his excursus on this title in *The Mission and Expansion of the Christian Church* (London, Williams & Norgate, 1908), vol. 1, pp. 266–78.

40. Lincoln, *Ephesians*, pp. 185–8; Bruce, *The Epistles*, p. 321; Barth, *Ephesians 1–3*, pp. 363–6.
41. Schnackenburg, *The Epistle*, p. 295.
42. Lincoln and Wedderburn, *The Theology of the Later Pauline Epistles*, p. 94.
43. So in detail, Merklein, *Das Kirchliche*, pp. 224–31.
44. Lincoln, *Ephesians*, p. 253.
45. Lincoln, *Ephesians*, pp. 256–7.
46. Lincoln, *Ephesians*, p. 257.
47. Bruce, *The Epistles*, p. 351.
48. Pace H. Merklein, 'Paulinische Theologie in der Rezeption des Kolosser – und Epheserbriefes', in K. Kertlege (ed.), *Paulus in den Neutestamentlichen Spatschriften* (Freiburg, Herder, 1981), pp. 25–69, who argues that soteriology and ecclesiology have been combined. He speaks of, to put it in English, an 'ecclesiological Christology' (p. 62).
49. For extra biblical uses in the sense of 'source', or 'origin', see J. Fitzmyer, 'Another Look at *Kephalē* in 1 Corinthians 11:3', *NTS*, vol. 35, 1989, pp. 503–11; C. C. Kroeger, 'Head', *DPL*, pp. 375–7.
50. Lincoln, *Ephesians*, p. 375; Schnackenburg, *The Epistle*, pp. 250–1.
51. Lincoln, *Ephesians*, p. 377; Schnackenburg, *The Epistle*, p. 251. Pace M. Barth, *Ephesians 4–6* (New York, Doubleday, 1974), pp. 628, 669, 678; and O'Brien, in Carson's *The Church in the Bible*, p. 115.
52. It has been argued, however, that here we find a unique New Testament meaning for the word *mustērion*/mystery. At Qumran, it often alludes to the fuller meaning of an Old Testament text, but this does not negate the interpretation given above. See further, Lincoln, *Ephesians*, pp. 380–3.
53. See further, Arnold, *Ephesians*, p. 139 and *passim*.
54. Paul speaks of the Spirit to be exact as 'the pledge of our inheritance'. The Greek word *arrabōn* ('pledge') alludes to a downpayment, a first instalment.
55. Lincoln and Wedderburn, *The Theology of the Later Pauline Epistles*, p. 96.
56. Schnackenburg, *The Epistle*, p. 305.
57. M. Y. MacDonald, *The Pauline Churches: A Socio-historical Study of Institutionalization in the Pauline and Deutero-Pauline Epistles* (Cambridge, CUP, 1988), pp. 85–157.
58. Besides the standard commentaries, see especially P. Towner, *The Goal of Our Instruction* (Sheffield, JSOT, 1989). See also the helpful recent introduction by F. Young, *The Theology of the Pastoral Epistles* (Cambridge, CUP, 1994).
59. Towner, *The Goal*, pp. 61–74; Young, *The Theology*, pp. 47–73.
60. Towner, *The Goal*, pp. 75–119.
61. P. Richardson, *Israel in the Apostolic Church* (Cambridge, CUP, 1969), pp. 205–6.
62. The Greek words *stylos kai hedraiōma*, translated in the NRSV as the 'pillar and bulwark', emphasize stability and strength. See further, Towner, *The Goal*, p. 131.

63. W. Hendrickson, *1 and 2 Timothy and Titus* (London, Banner of Truth, 1964), p. 267.
64. So B. Gartner, *The Temple and the Community in Qumran and the New Testament* (Cambridge, CUP, 1965), pp. 66–71. G. W. Knight, in *The Pastoral Epistles* (Carlisle, Eerdmans, 1992), p. 180, considers this a possibility. But see further, R. J. McKelvey, *The New Temple* (Oxford, OUP, 1969), pp. 132–3, who rejects this option.
65. On the impact of the house setting on the whole framework of thought in the Pastorals, see D. C. Verner, *The Household of God: The Social World of the Pastoral Epistles* (Chico, Scholars, 1974).
66. See Towner, *The Goal*, p. 135.
67. Giles, *Patterns*, pp. 28–47.
68. Giles, *Patterns*, pp. 28–47.
69. K. N. Giles, 'Women in the Church with Special Reference to 1 Timothy – A Response', in A. Nicholls (ed.), *The Bible and Women's Ministry* (Canberra, Acorn, 1990), pp. 65–87; Towner, *The Goal*, pp. 209–22.
70. Knight, *The Pastoral Epistles*, pp. 142–4.
71. See again my article mentioned in n. 69.
72. MacDonald, *The Pauline Churches*, pp. 159–234.

7 The Church in the Non-Pauline Epistles and the Book of Revelation

1. On this, see our opening chapter.
2. On this, see W. Lane, *Hebrews 1–8* (Waco, Word Biblical Commentary, 1991), pp. cxii–cxix; G. Hughes, *Hebrews and Hermeneutics* (Cambridge, CUP, 1979); G. Goppelt, *Typos: The Typological Interpretation of the Old Testament in the New* (Grand Rapids, Eerdmans, 1982), pp. 161–78 *et al.*
3. The use of *polloi*, 'many', is inclusive. The writer is speaking of all those for whom Christ died. So Lane, *Hebrews 1–8*, p. 55.
4. So F. F. Bruce, *The Epistle to the Hebrews* (Grand Rapids, Eerdmans, 1974), p. 46; H. W. Attridge, *The Epistle to the Hebrews* (Philadelphia, Fortress, 1989), p. 90; P. Ellingworth, *The Epistle to the Hebrews* (Carlisle, Paternoster, 1993), p. 167.
5. For more detail, see Goppelt, *Typos*, pp. 160–78.
6. See S. Lehne, *The New Covenant in Hebrews* (Sheffield, JSOT, 1990).
7. Of the twelve uses of this term in Hebrews, six refer to historic Israel, and six address the Christian readers (2.17, 4.9, 8.10, 10.31, 11.25, 13.12).
8. J. Scholer, in *Proleptic Priests* (Sheffield, JSOT, 1991), points out that although Hebrews does not call Christians priests, as does 1 Peter and Revelation, the priesthood of all believers is assumed by the cultic privileges bestowed on them. A. Vanhoye, in *Old Testament Priest and New*

Testament Priest According to the New Testament (Massachusetts, St Bede's, 1986), pp. 221ff, carefully qualifies this claim. He argues that while Hebrews unites the believer with the priesthood of Christ, there is an important difference. Christ is priest in a unique sense, as he not only has free access to God, something he shares with those identified with him, but also mediates between humankind and God as priest, something he alone does.

9. Eight times the author calls on the readers 'to draw near', using the cultic term *proserchesthai*. Both Vanhoye and Scholer agree that as this was the special preserve of the Old Testament priest in the context of worship, a new status for believers is implied. They also agree that in Hebrews this 'drawing near' takes place in worship. So also Ellingworth, *The Epistle*, p. 269. For an extended discussion on the use of the word in Hebrews, see Scholer, *Proleptic Priests*, pp. 91–149. However, D. Peterson, in *Engaging with God* (Leicester, Apollos, 1992), consistently tries to play down the allusions to communal worship in Hebrews. He argues that drawing near 'essentially describes an act of personal faith or the appropriation of the gift of salvation' (p. 250). Scholer's study shows the inadequacy of such reasoning.

10. This cultic term is used of Christian worship in Hebrews 9.14 and 12.28.

11. In both verse 18 and verse 22, the verb is in the perfect. This indicates that the action, and the relationship it symbolizes, has begun and is still in effect.

12. Scholer, *Proleptic Priests*, pp. 142–5; Lane, *Hebrews 1–8*, pp. 464–72. The debate and the options are well set out in P. E. Hughes, *A Commentary on the Epistle to the Hebrews* (Grand Rapids, Eerdmans, 1979), pp. 552–5.

13. E.g. 1QS 11.7–8; 1QH 3.21–2.

14. Scholer, *Proleptic Priests*, p. 145.

15. D. Peterson, *Hebrews and Perfection* (Cambridge, CUP, 1982), pp. 160–1; Peterson, *Engaging*, pp. 238–43; P. T. O'Brien, in D. A. Carson (ed.), *The Church in the Bible and the World* (Exeter, Paternoster, 1987), p. 95.

16. O'Brien, in Carson's *The Church*, pp. 95–8; D. B. Knox, *Thirty-Nine Articles* (London, Hodder & Stoughton, 1967), pp. 41–7. Also commonly asserted in American dispensationalism. For details, see M. D. Williams, 'Where's the Church?', *GTJ*, vol. 10, 1989, pp. 165–82.

17. Peterson, *Engaging*, p. 282.

18. So Lane, *Hebrews 1–8*, p. liii.

19. Lane, *Hebrews 1–8*, pp. lxi, 87. So also Peterson, *Engaging*, p. 248.

20. See the LXX of Job 22.26–7, 27.9–10; 1 John 3.12, 4.17, 5.14. See Scholer, *Proleptic Priests*, p. 110. Peterson, in *Engaging*, pp. 228–60, is very reluctant to concede that communal gatherings in Hebrews should be thought of as worship. His view is somewhat reductionist.

21. The wording parallels 4.16.

22. *TDNT*, vol. 7, p. 841. Some have thought the prefix *epi* is significant,

but this is doubtful. See further, Attridge, *The Epistle*, p. 290.
23. So 2 Thessalonians 2.1. In this sense it would mean much the same as 'in *ekklēsia*/church' (cf. 1 Cor. 11.13, 14.19, 28, 34, 35).
24. See 2 Maccabees 2.7, Matthew 23.37, 24.31, and Luke 17.37.
25. Attridge, *The Epistle*. So also, B. Weiss, *Der Brief an die Hebraer* (Gottingen, Vanenhoeck und Ruprecht, 1897), p. 534, and Ellingworth, *The Epistle*, p. 528.
26. See Hebrews 1.1–4, 2.3–4, 4.1–13, 13.7, 22. Also G. Hughes, *Hebrews*, *passim*.
27. See the extended discussion on this matter in Lehne, *The New Covenant*, pp. 108–17.
28. So Bruce, *The Epistle*, p. 121.
29. See 3.13, 10.25, 13.9, 22, where the verb *parakalein*, meaning to exhort or encourage, is used, and 6.18, 12.5, 13.22, where the cognate noun *paraklēsis* is used. See Peterson, *Engaging*, pp. 247–50, and his earlier essay, 'The Ministry of Encouragement', in P. O'Brien and D. Peterson (eds), *God who Is Rich in Mercy* (Australia, Anzea, 1986), pp. 235–53.
30. Lane, *Hebrews 1–8*, p. 568.
31. So most, if not all, commentators.
32. See the helpful recent introduction by A. Chester in A. Chester and R. P. Martin, *The Theology of the Letters of James, Peter and Jude* (Cambridge, CUP, 1994).
33. So J. Adamson, *The Epistle of James* (Grand Rapids, Eerdmans, 1976), p. 51.
34. So R. P. Martin, *James* (Waco, Word Biblical Commentary, 1988), p. 8.
35. So M. Dibelius, *James* (Philadelphia, Fortress, 1975), pp. 66–7.
36. Chester and Martin, p. 41.
37. See the discussion above on Hebrews 10.45.
38. *Poly.* 4.2; *Herm. Man.* 11.9, 14; *Justin Dial.* 63.5; *Eus. Ecc. Hist.* 7.9.2, 7.11.11, 12, 17, quoting Dionysius of Alexandria.
39. Adamson, *The Epistle*, p. 105; Dibelius, *James*, pp. 132–4.
40. W. Popkes, *Adressaten, Situation und Form des Jacobusbriefes* (Stuttgart, Katholisches Bibelwerk, 1986), pp. 91–103.
41. E. Selwyn, *The First Epistle of St Peter* (London, Macmillan, 1949), p. 81.
42. The name 'Peter' is used by convention, not to suggest that the debate about authorship is settled.
43. J. R. Michaels, *1 Peter* (Waco, Word Biblical Commentary, 1988), p. xlvi. See also Chester and Martin, *The Theology*, pp. 87–133.
44. Michaels, *1 Peter*.
45. Michaels, *1 Peter*, p. 7.
46. On the new covenant motif in 1 Peter, see J. W. Pryor, 'First Peter and the New Covenant', *RTR*, vol. 45.1, 1986, pp. 1–4, and vol. 45.2, 1986, pp. 44–51.
47. For example, R. J. McKelvey, *The New Temple* (Oxford, OUP, 1969), pp. 125–32. A contrary opinion is expressed by J. H. Elliott, *A Home for the Homeless* (with new introduction) (Minneapolis, Fortress, 1990), pp.

200ff. He argues that the metaphor 'spiritual house' does not allude to the temple, but to an ordinary house.

48. In an earlier study, *The Elect and the Holy* (Leiden, Brill, 1966), pp. 149–54, Elliott argues that *basileion hierateuma* in verse 9, usually translated as 'a royal priesthood', should be rendered 'a kingdom [and] a priesthood', but this suggestion has gained little support. In reply, see Vanhoye, *Old Testament Priest*, pp. 248–58; Michaels, *1 Peter*, pp. 108–9; E. Best, *1 Peter* (London, Oliphants, 1971), pp. 102–3, 107–8.

49. Best, *1 Peter*, pp. 103–4.

50. Michaels, *1 Peter*, p. 101; Peterson, *Engaging*, p. 268.

51. As noted earlier, see the excursus in A. Harnack, *The Mission and Expansion of the Christian Church* (London, Williams & Norgate, 1908), pp. 266–78.

52. 'Appeal' translates the Greek word *eperōtēma*, which usually means 'a question', 'a request', or 'an appeal', but may also mean 'a pledge'. However the word is translated, one thing is clear: Peter sees baptism as an act by human beings directed towards God. See Michaels, *1 Peter*, pp. 216–17.

53. K. N. Giles, *Patterns of Ministry Among the First Christians* (Melbourne, Collins-Dove, 1989), pp. 54–5.

54. Giles, *Patterns*, *passim*.

55. Michaels, *1 Peter*, pp. 283–6.

56. C. Bigg, *A Critical and Exegetical Commentary on 1 Peter* (Edinburgh, T.&T. Clark, 1902), p. 189. Elliott, in *A Home*, considers this house-church experience as the context against which this whole epistle must be understood. See particularly pp. 165–234.

57. Elliott, *A Home*, p. 139.

58. In 1.1, 'exiles' translates the Greek word *parepidēmos*, which refers to a person residing temporarily in a foreign place. In 1.17, the word 'exile' translates the Greek word *paroikia*, as it does in 2.11. Both words have a very similar meaning.

59. In the new introduction to the second edition of *A Home*, pp. xxvi–xxxi, Elliott himself sets out the debate and makes some concessions to his critics.

60. Best, *1 Peter*, pp. 36–8; Michaels, *1 Peter*, pp. 28–9, 268–70; Elliott, *A Home*, pp. 78–87.

61. Elliott, *A Home*, pp. 81–2.

62. R. Brown, *The Community of the Beloved Disciple* (London, Geoffrey Chapman, 1979); his *The Epistles of John* (London, Doubleday, 1982), pp. 14–35; S. Smalley, *1, 2, 3 John* (Waco, Word Biblical Commentary, 1984), pp. xxii–xxxiv.

63. J. Lieu, *The Theology of the Johannine Epistles* (Cambridge, CUP, 1991), p. 49.

64. Brown, *The Epistles*, p. 85.

65. Brown, *The Epistles*.

66. Brown, *The Epistles*, p. 223; Lieu, *The Theology*, pp. 80–7.

67. Lieu, *The Theology*, pp. 33–41.

68. Brown, *The Epistles*, p. 250; Lieu, *The Theology*, pp. 27–31.
69. Brown, *The Epistles*, pp. 259–61; Lieu, *The Theology*, pp. 41–5.
70. See our earlier discussion in Chapter 1 on this term.
71. See the excellent study by J. Lieu, *The Second and Third Epistles of John: History and Background* (Edinburgh, T.&T. Clark, 1986).
72. Brown, *The Epistles*, p. 143; Smalley, *1, 2, 3 John*, p. xxiv.
73. Lieu, *The Second and Third Epistles*, p. 107.
74. Lieu, *The Second and Third Epistles*, pp. 149–60; Brown, *The Epistles*, p. 160.
75. E. Schweizer, *Church Order in the New Testament* (London, SCM, 1961), p. 124.
76. Giles, *Patterns*, pp. 110–11.
77. R. Bauckham, *The Theology of the Book of Revelation* (Cambridge, CUP, 1993), p. 16; R. Bauckham, *The Climax of Prophecy* (Edinburgh, T.&T. Clark, 1993), p. 35; E. Schussler Fiorenza, *The Book of Revelation* (Philadelphia, Fortress, 1985), p. 51. It is to be noted that we know of other churches in this area (Troas, Acts 20.5; Colossae, Col. 1.2; Hierapolis, Col. 4.13). Bauckham, in *The Climax*, p. 35, notes that the expression 'the seven churches' appears four times in Revelation, four being the number signifying completeness.
78. Recent studies of Revelation have stressed social factors in the emergence of apocalyptic literature in general, and Revelation in particular. This is certainly a factor, but in the case of Revelation, to say nothing of other works, theological concerns also played their part, possibly being dominant.
79. D. J. Harrington, *The Apocalypse of John* (London, Geoffrey Chapman, 1969), p. 45.
80. So Bauckham, *Climax*, p. 274. See also our discussion on pp. 176–7 on the two witnesses in Revelation 11.3–4.
81. The word is found some sixty times in Revelation.
82. So R. Mounce, *The Book of Revelation* (Grand Rapids, Eerdmans, 1977), p. 82; C. Hemer, *The Letters to the Seven Churches of Asia in Their Local Setting* (Sheffield, JSOT, 1986), pp. 32–4, examines all the options.
83. Schweizer, *Church Order*, p. 132. Goppelt, *The Theology*, vol. 2, p. 189, also argues that the author of Revelation defines the church in a more radical way than other New Testament writers.
84. Recent studies recognize that Jewish opposition to Christians is more important in Revelation than earlier commentators allowed. See A. Collins, *Crisis and Catharsis* (Philadelphia, Westminster, 1984), pp. 85–7, and A. Beagley, *The Sitz im Leben of the Apocalypse* (Berlin, De Gruyter, 1987), who argues that the main opponents of the Christians are the Jews. Beagley makes some good points, but presses his thesis too far. The main opponent, the representative of the beast, is Rome, not the Jews.
85. The details of this argument are spelt out in Goppelt, *Typos*, p. 197; and F. Mazzaferri, *The Genre of the Book of Revelation* (Berlin, De Gruyter,

1989), pp. 365–74. And in reference to chapters 21–2, see W. Dumbrell, *The End of the Beginning* (Australia, Lancer, 1985).

86. Mounce, in *Revelation*, p. 226, says this is the view of 'the majority of commentators', but he argues the allusion is primarily to Rome. Bauckham, in *Climax*, p. 172, argues that although 'Sodom and Egypt' is identified as the place where 'the Lord was crucified', and thus at one level refers to Jerusalem, this symbolic name cannot be limited to this city. It is also called 'the great city', and that is a symbol for Rome (14.8; 17.18, etc.).

87. On this, see Vanhoye, *Old Testament Priest*, pp. 279–99.

88. Bauckham, *Climax*, p. 216.

89. So G. Beasley-Murray, *The Book of Revelation* (London, Oliphants, 1974), p. 140; Beagley, *The Sitz*, p. 47.

90. Fiorenza, *Revelation*, pp. 46–50.

91. So Beasley-Murray, *Revelation*, pp. 178–9; Mounce, *Revelation*, pp. 219–20.

92. Bauckham, *Climax*, p. 273.

93. So Beasley-Murray, *Revelation*, pp. 197–8; Mounce, *Revelation*, p. 267; R. Schnackenburg, *The Church in the New Testament* (London, Burns & Oates, 1974), pp. 114–15.

94. M. Rissi, *The Future of the World* (London, SCM, 1972), p. 87.

95. These terms are studied in an historical and theological framework in Dumbrell's helpful study, *The End*.

96. Dumbrell, *The End*.

97. Peterson, *Engaging*, p. 261.

98. See Peterson, *Engaging*, pp. 261–82; S. Laws, *In the Light of the Lamb* (Delaware, Glazier, 1988), pp. 69–79; L. Thompson, *The Book of Revelation* (Oxford, OUP, 1990), pp. 53–73.

99. Bauckham, *Climax*, p. 140.

100. Thompson, *Revelation*, pp. 53–73. And with some caution, Peterson, *Engaging*, p. 276.

101. Thompson, *Revelation*, p. 64.

102. See further on this, Giles, *Patterns*, pp. 138–41, 83–4.

103. On prophecy in general in Revelation, see Bauckham, *Climax*, pp. 160–2, and in particular on the meaning of 19.10.

104. Bauckham, *The Theology*, p. 37.

8 Drawing the Threads Together and the Visible–Invisible Church

1. The lecture was published in *New Testament Questions for Today* (London, SCM, 1967).

2. Kasemann, *New Testament Questions*, p. 255.

3. R. Brown, *The Churches the Apostles Left Behind* (London, Chapman, 1984).

4. J. D. G. Dunn, *Unity and Diversity in the New Testament* (London,

SCM, 1977). Dunn's book deals in detail with this question, but covers many other matters as well.

5. Dunn's study, quoted above, emphasizes the diversity in the New Testament finding the one common unifying theme, a belief that the historic Jesus and the exalted Jesus are to be identified. In contrast, see D. Wenham, 'Unity and Diversity in the New Testament', in the revised edition of G. E. Ladd, *New Testament Theology* (Grand Rapids, Eerdmans, 1993), pp. 684–719, for a position similar to the one assumed here.

6. On this debate, see the World Council of Churches study, *In Each Place: Towards a Fellowship of Local Churches United* (Geneva, WCC, 1977). See also J. Zizioulas, *Being as Communion* (New York, St Vladimir's Press, 1985), pp. 247–60.

7. E. G. Jay, *The Church: Its Changing Image Through Twenty Centuries* (London, SPCK, 1977), vol. 1, pp. 58–9.

8. *Strom.* iv, quoted in Jay, *The Church*, p. 60.

9. Jay, *The Church*, p. 88.

10. *On Baptism*, 5:27, quoted in Jay, *The Church*.

11. For details on Luther's position, see Jay, *The Church*, pp. 161–9.

12. That is, during their earthly life.

13. J. Calvin, *The Institutes of the Christian Religion*, ed. J. McNeill (London, SCM, 1960), vol. 2, p. 1021.

14. Calvin, *Institutes*, vol. 2, p. 1023.

15. Calvin, *Institutes*, vol. 2, p. 1016.

16. *Disputations Against the Heretics of the Present Time on the Controversies Regarding the Christian Faith*, 5:3:10, quoted in Jay, *The Church*, p. 203.

17. *On the Writing of Church History* (edited and translated by P. C. Hodgson), in The Library of Protestant Theology (New York, OUP, 1968), pp. 242–3, 247–53. See also P. C. Hodgson and R. C. Williams, *Christian Theology: An Introduction to its Traditions and Tasks* (Philadelphia, Fortress, 1985), pp. 258–73.

18. Published in London by Nisbet, 1951, pp. 237–59.

19. P. Tillich, *Systematic Theology* (Herts, Nisbet, 1964), vol. 3, pp. 173–80.

20. Tillich, *Systematic Theology*, p. 176.

21. B. Forte, *The Church: Icon of the Trinity* (Boston, St Paul, 1991), p. 16.

22. Forte, *The Church*, p. 64.

23. So C. Hill, *Mystery of Life: A Theology of Church* (Melbourne, Collins-Dove, 1990), pp. 1–18.

24. H. Küng, *The Church* (Exeter, Search, 1968), p. 37.

25. Küng, *The Church*, p. 38.

26. Küng, *The Church*.

27. Forte, *The Church*, p. 86.

28. *Extraordinary Synod of Bishops: Final Report* (Rome, Vatican, 1985), p. 2.

9 The Denomination as Church

1. R. Norris, 'What is "Church Unity"?', *One in Christ*, vol. 2, 1982, p. 117.

2. By this I mean, few attempts to endorse theologically the denomina-

tional form of the church. However, see R. Banks, 'Denominational Structures: Their Legitimacy, Vocation and Capacity for Reform', in D. Peterson and J. Pryor (eds), *In the Fullness of Time* (Homebush, Lancer, 1992), pp. 255–77, and H. Uprichard, 'Response to Eryl Davies', in A. F. Gibson (ed.), *The Church and Its Unity* (Leicester, IVP, 1992), pp. 91–5. H. R. Niebuhr, in *The Social Sources of Denominationalism* (New York, Meridian, 1957) (first published 1929), does not make a contribution at this level. Niebuhr changes the Weber sect–church typology by adding a mediating form, 'the denomination', that stands between the original two. Since his time, others have sought to improve further on these sociological categories by adding other classifications. See R. Towler, *Homo-Religiosus: Sociological Problems in the Study of Religion* (London, Constable, 1974), pp. 108–27.

3. Niebuhr, *Social Sources*, pp. 21, 25.

4. However, Zizioulas points out that 'congregationalism' is supported by some Orthodox theologians. See J. Zizioulas, *Being as Communion* (New York, St Vladimir's Press, 1985), pp. 133, 247–60.

5. This is particularly stressed in C. Duquoc, *Provisional Churches* (London, SCM, 1986).

6. This principle stands in opposition to the 'catholic principle', which tends to equate the church created by God in Christ with the concrete empirical church ruled by the Pope. See further on on this, the previous chapter, and the excellent discussion in P. C. Hodgson and R. C. Williams (eds), *Christian Theology* (Philadelphia, Fortress, 1985), pp. 258–64.

7. In the previous chapter we noted that this is widely recognized by New Testament scholars today.

8. The letter is given in K. Lake (ed.), *The Apostolic Fathers* (London, Heinemann, 1912), vol. 1, pp. 1–22.

9. Which he believed led irrevocably to ethical inconsistencies. Ignatius' epistles are given in Lake, *Apostolic Fathers*, vol. 1, pp. 165–278.

10. See the important study, R. B. Mullen and R. E. Richey (eds), *Reimaging Denominationalism: Interpretive Essays* (Oxford, OUP, 1994). I am of course aware that in this brief account of the rise of the denominations I have somewhat simplified things; much more could be said.

11. Norris, in 'What is "Church Unity"?', pp. 122–5, discusses these varied causes.

12. N. T. Ammerman, in 'Denominations: What are we studying?', Mullen and Richey (eds), *Reimaging*, p. 115, says, 'If denominations began in the heat of theological battle, and were definable in terms of distinctive beliefs and practices, what they have gradually become – especially in this century – is modern organisations definable by their laws, budgets, and headquarters building.'

13. H. J. A. Bowman, *A Look at Today's Churches: A Comparative Guide* (St Louis, Concordia, 1980), pp. 45–52, lists the United Church of Christ, the Disciples, the Moravians, and the United Church of Canada as examples of such attempts.

14. D. M. Paton (ed.), *Breaking Barriers, Nairobi 1975* (London, SPCK, 1975), p. 317.
15. K. Raiser, *Ecumenism in Transition* (Geneva, WCC, 1991), p. 76.
16. Raiser, *Ecumenism*.
17. M. Kinnamon, *Truth and Community* (Grand Rapids, Eerdmans, 1988).
18. H. Küng, *Theology for the Third Millennium* (New York, Doubleday, 1988), pp. 128, 162.
19. See Kinnamon, *Truth and Community*, pp. 7–12.
20. H. Küng, *The Church* (Exeter, Search, 1968), p. 376.
21. So E. Davies, 'Independency', in Gibson, *The Church*, pp. 69–90. This congregational polity was given classic expression in Congregationalism, but is held by most Baptists, so-called 'independents', the Brethren, most Pentecostals, and often by evangelicals in the mainline churches. What is unusual about the large Anglican diocese of Sydney is that in this context, an explicit congregational view of the church is publicly expressed and theologically defended. The characteristic congregational position is, however, modified. It is argued that the universal uses of the word 'church' refer exclusively to a heavenly gathering.
22. So Davies, 'Independency'; D. B. Knox, *Thirty-Nine Articles* (London, Hodder & Stoughton, 1967), pp. 40–52.
23. J. M. Frame, *Evangelical Reunion: Denominations and the Body of Christ* (Grand Rapids, Baker, 1991), p. 31.
24. Frame, *Evangelical Reunion*, p. 46.
25. So Davies and Frame.
26. I spell out this argument and document the protagonists in my essay, 'Evangelical Systematic Theology. Definition, Problems, Sources', in Peterson and Pryor, *Fullness of Time*, pp. 255–76.
27. W. Pannenberg, in *The Church* (Philadelphia, Westminster, 1977), pp. 68–71, also sees the preserving of particular theological insights as a contribution that each denomination makes.
28. Not every congregation of Christians is, however, church in the fullest sense of the word. A congregation which excludes blacks, or a congregation made up on a very selective basis such as one consisting only of women, or men, or young students, would in some sense be an inadequate expression of Christian community.

10 Deficiencies in Past Ecclesiology and the Promise of Trinitarian Ecclesiology

1. T. F. Torrance, *Theology in Reconstruction* (London, SCM, 1965), p. 266. This assertion may however need some qualification. See K. Rahner, 'The Church' in *Encyclopaedia of Theology*, K. Rahner, ed. (London, Burns & Oates, 1975), pp. 207–8. He argues that the doctrine of church was very much a matter under discussion in the twelfth and thirteenth

centuries but he does admit that the main issue was the power of the papacy.

2. *Letters*, 46.2, 54.1.
3. *Letters*, 62.14.
4. E. G. Jay, *The Church: Its Changing Image Through Twenty Centuries*, (London, SPCK, 1977), vol. 1, p. 72. On the contribution of Cyprian and Greek hierarchical ontology in the ecclesiology of the early church, I am indebted to C. Gunton, 'The Church on Earth', in C. Gunton and D. Hardy, *On Being the Church* (Edinburgh, T.&T. Clark, 1989), pp. 53–6, but my argument is developed differently and more detail is given.
5. For a good summary of Plato's thought and its impact on Christian thinking, see D. Allen, *Philosophy for Understanding Theology* (London, SCM, 1985), pp. 1–91. More generally on hierarchical thinking among Christians, see K. Turner, *The Politics of God: Christian Theologies and Social Justice* (Minneapolis, Fortress, 1992), especially ch. 4.
6. *Summa Theologiae*, 1a.108, 4; cf. 1a.108, 2.
7. G. MacGregor, in *Corpus Christi: The Nature of the Church According to the Reformed Tradition* (London, Macmillan, 1959), p. 5, in fact argues that a case can be made for seeing ecclesiology as the central doctrine of the Reformation.
8. I speak of 'the Reformers' doctrine of the church', but it must be noted that while they were one on the doctrine of justification by faith and on the priesthood of all believers, they differed especially in regard to the ordering of the ordained ministry.
9. Torrance, *Theology*, p. 267.
10. Quoted in A. Dulles, *Models of the Church* (Dublin, Gill & Macmillan, 2nd edn 1988), p. 75.
11. So Dulles, *Models*, p. 34.
12. On this, see K. Raiser, *Ecumenism in Transition* (Geneva, WCC, 1991), pp. 91–6; H.-G. Link (ed.), *One God, One Lord, One Spirit* (Geneva, WCC, 1988), pp. 106–7.
13. So J. Zizioulas, 'The Doctrine of God the Trinity Today', in A. I. C. Heron (ed.), *The Forgotten Trinity* (London, BBC, 1991), p. 20.
14. Karl Barth, by beginning his *Church Dogmatics* in 1932 (Edinburgh, T.&T. Clark, 1956) with a reformulation of the doctrine of the Trinity, set the stage for this renewal. Then followed K. Rahner's important study, *The Trinity* (London, Burns & Oates, 1970). However, see also J. Moltmann, *The Trinity and the Kingdom of God* (London, SCM, 1981); R. W. Jenson, *The Triune Identity* (Philadelphia, Fortress, 1982); B. de Magerie, *The Christian Trinity in History* (Massachusetts, St Bede's, 1982); D. Brown, *The Divine Trinity* (London, Duckworth, 1985); L. Boff, *Trinity and Society* (London, Burns & Oates, 1988); C. Gunton, *The Promise of Trinitarian Theology* (Edinburgh, T.&T. Clark, 1991); C. M. LaCugna, *God for Us* (New York, HarperCollins, 1991), *et al.*
15. Moltmann, *The Trinity*, pp. 1–20, 174–8; C. Braaten (ed.), *Christian Dogmatics* (Philadelphia, Fortress, 1984), vol. 1, pp. 135–59; T. F.

Torrance, *The Trinitarian Faith* (Edinburgh, T.&T. Clark, 1992), pp. 302–40; Gunton and Hardy, *On Being*, pp. 48–80.

16. So Moltmann, *The Trinity*, pp. 129–90; Gunton, *The Promise*, pp. 31–57; Boff, *Trinity*, pp. 21–2.

17. These were three great theologians who lived in Cappodocia in Asia Minor: Basil – often called 'the great' (330–97), his brother, Gregory of Nyssa (*d.* 394), and their friend, Gregory Nazianzus (329–90).

18. So the peculiarity of the Father is to be 'ungenerated'; the peculiarity of the Son is to be eternally 'generated'; the peculiarity of the Spirit is to 'proceed' from the Father.

19. On the evolution of the doctrine of co-inherence, or *perichoresis*, in the patristic period, see G. L. Prestige, *God in Patristic Thought* (London, SPCK, 1964), pp. 282–300. The idea originates with Jesus' own consciousness of intimate union with his Father. In John's Gospel, Jesus is recorded as saying, 'the Father and I are one' (10.30); 'the Father is in me and I am in the Father' (10.38, 14.11) and, 'Father . . . you are in me and I am in you' (17.21).

20. *De Trinitatis*, v. 1, 10, 12.

21. The two closely related Latin terms used in translation are instructive. *Circumincessio*, from *circum-incedere*, means to move around; this captures the active sense of the Greek word. *Circuminsessio*, from *circum-insedere*, means to sit around. This takes up the passive sense of the Greek word.

22. J. Zizioulas, *Being as Communion* (New York, St Vladimir's Press, 1985), p. 16.

23. Greek philosophers frequently ask questions about 'the being' of things or people, what we could call today the 'essential character' or 'essence' of something. The Greek word for 'being' is *ontos*. The study of the being of things or persons is thus called ontology.

24. Rahner, *The Trinity*, p. 22.

25. For a critique of Rahner's axiom, see W. Kasper, *The God of Jesus Christ* (New York, Crossway, 1991), pp. 273–7; LaCugna, *God for Us*, pp. 217–32.

26. On this, see Moltmann, *The Trinity*, pp. 118–19.

27. 'The Determinative Doctrine of the Holy Spirit', *T Today*, vol. 39, 1982, p. 142.

28. See Y. Congar, *I Believe in the Holy Spirit* (New York, Seabury, 1983), vol. 2, pp. 5–14, and T. I. MacDonald, *The Ecclesiology of Yves Congar* (Lanham, University Press of America, 1984), pp. 12–23.

29. MacDonald, *Ecclesiology*, p. 7.

30. Congar, *I Believe*.

31. See P. Drilling, *Trinity and Ministry* (Minneapolis, Fortress, 1991); he prefers the term 'pattern'. B. Forte, in *The Church: Icon of the Trinity* (Boston, St Paul, 1991), prefers 'icon'. C. Gunton, in *The Promise*, prefers 'echo'. LaCugna, in *God for Us*, uses 'icon' and 'model'.

32. Moltmann's ecclesiology does not fit these categories. He tends to concentrate on the economic Trinity, but sees the triune revelation of God

in history as a liberating paradigm; and he grounds the origins of the church in the Christ event, but also quite explicitly develops a trinitarian ecclesiology. See Moltmann, *The Trinity*; his *The Church in the Power of the Spirit* (London, SCM, 1977); his *History of the Triune God* (London, SCM, 1991); and his *The Spirit of Life* (London, SCM, 1992).

33. In more detail, see Gunton, *The Promise*, pp. 86–103; and LaCugna, *God for Us*, pp. 243–305.
34. So Raiser, *Ecumenism*; P. Avis, *Christians in Communion* (London, Geoffrey Chapman, 1990); M. Kinnamon, *Truth in Community* (Grand Rapids, Eerdmans, 1988).
35. Boff, *Trinity and Society*.
36. *The Documents of Vatican II*, in W. Abbott and J. Gallagher, eds (USA, Geoffrey Chapman, 1966), pp. 37–56.
37. *The Documents*, p. 43.
38. *The Documents*, p. 53.
39. *The Documents*, p. 55.
40. *The Documents*, pp. 56–72.
41. *The Three Agreed Statements* (London, CTS/SPCK, 1973), pp. 27–46.
42. As, for example, in *Episcopal Ministry: The Report of the Archbishops' Group on the Episcopate 1990* (London, Church House, 1990). From the premise that the church has to have order, the false conclusion is reached that order implies hierarchy. See n. 4 on p. 8. To make the point, I give a simple illustration. The chairs carefully set out around a round table may be said to be in order, but hierarchy is not implied.
43. See, for example, A. Dulles, *A Church to Believe in* (New York, Crossroad, 1982).
44. This argument is frequently put in J. Piper and W. Grudem, *Recovering Biblical Manhood and Womanhood* (Wheaton, Crossway, 1991); see especially pp. 103–4, 129–30, 196, 394, 456–7.
45. Zizioulas, *Being as Communion*, p. 17.
46. Zizioulas, *Being as Communion*, p. 15.
47. See n. 10 above.
48. In C. Braaten (ed.), *Christian Dogmatics* (Philadelphia, Fortress, 1984), vol. 1, pp. 187–91.
49. Braaten (ed.), *Christian Dogmatics*, vol. 1, p. 189.
50. Braaten (ed.), *Christian Dogmatics*, vol. 1, p. 190.
51. LaCugna, *God for Us*, p. 305.
52. LaCugna, *God for Us*, p. 397.

Excursus 1 The Meaning of the Word *Ekklēsia*: Old Testament and Intertestamental Background

1. F. J. A. Hort, *The Christian Ecclesia* (London, Macmillan, 1914), pp. 1–31; L. Cerfaux, *The Church in the Theology of St Paul* (New York, Herder & Herder, 1959), pp. 95–117; T. F. Torrance, 'The Israel of

God', *Interp.*, vol. 10, 1956, pp. 305–22; R. Schnackenburg, *The Church in the New Testament* (London, Burns & Oates, 1974), pp. 56–60; A. T. Hanson and R. P. C. Hanson, *The Identity of the Church* (London, SCM, 1987), pp. 5–7; H. Merklein, 'Die Ekklēsia Gottes', in H. Merklein, *Studien zu Jesus und Paulus* (Tubingen, Mohr, 1987).

2. Some arguments for the non-technical meaning of the word *ekklēsia* in the New Testament are based mainly on the thesis that the classical meaning of the word prevailed. See particularly J. Y. Campbell, 'The Origin and Meaning of the Greek Word *Ekklēsia*', *JTS*, vol. 49, 1948, pp. 130–54. But see also D. W. B. Robinson, *The Church of God* (Sydney, Jordan, 1965); R. Banks, *Paul's Idea of Community* (Homebush, NSW, Anzea, 1979), pp. 44–8; Hainz, Ekklēsia: *Strukturen paulinischer Gemeinde, Theologie und Gemeinde – Ordnung* (Regensburg, Prustat, 1972), pp. 229–55.

3. This position is spelt out in detail by W. J. Dumbrell, 'The Meaning and the Use of *Ekklēsia* in the New Testament with Special Reference to its Old Testament Background', unpublished MTh. thesis, London University, 1966. So also in more cautious terms, W. Schrage, '"Ekklēsia" und "Synagoge": Zum Ursprung des Urchristlichen Kirchenbegriffs', *ZTK*, vol. 60, 1963, pp. 178–86, and L. Coenen, *DNTT*, vol. 1, pp. 291–6. In relation to New Testament ecclesiology, see particularly E. D. Radamacher, *What the Church is About* (Chicago, Moody, 1972); P. T. O'Brien, *Colossians and Philemon* (Waco, Word Biblical Commentary, 1982), pp. 58–9; O'Brien, 'Church', *DPL*, p. 124.

4. J. Barr, *The Semantics of Biblical Language* (Oxford, OUP, 1961), p. 218.

5. There was also another development as the word came to be used of the building where a local community of Jews met, but this final step is not an issue at this point.

6. The most recent summary of the evidence is in the article on *qahal* by F. L. Hossfeld, E. M. Kindl, and H.-J. Fabry, in *TWZAT*, vol. 6, 1989, pp. 1203–22. They give a good bibliography.

7. Most of the uses of *edah* are found in the Pentateuch (123 out of 147 occurrences, 81 in Numbers alone), with only two in the prophets (Jer. 6.18; Hos. 7.12) and ten in the Psalms.

8. P. Craigie, *Deuteronomy* (Grand Rapids, Eerdmans, 1976), p. 296. Hossfeld, Kindl, and Fabry, *TWZAT*, p. 1212, maintain that the technical meaning is introduced in Deuteronomy 5.22, where *qahal* alludes not simply to an actual gathering, but rather to the specific community who receive the law. See also Merklein, *Studien*, p. 309.

9. J. Milgrom, 'Priestly Terminology and the Political and Social Structure of Pre-Monarchic Israel', *JQR*, vol. 69, 1978–9, p. 73.

10. Milgrom, 'Priestly Terminology', p. 74. Hossfeld, Kindl, and Fabry, in *TWZAT*, p. 1219, also conclude that for the Chronicler, *qahal* has taken on the meaning of *edah*.

11. In reference to David's reign: 1 Chronicles 13.2, 4, 28.8, 29.1, 10, 20, 30; Solomon's reign: 2 Chronicles 1.3, 5, 6.3, 12, 13, 7.8; Hezekiah reforms: 2 Chronicles 29.23, 32, 30.2, 30.4, 13, 17, 23, 24, 25. This

usage is foreshadowed in 1 Kings 8.14, 22, 55, 65. See R. Braun, *1 Chronicles* (Waco, Word Biblical Commentary, 1986), pp. xxxii–xxxvii, 174–5.

12. Hossfeld, Kindl, and Fabry, in *TWZAT*, p. 1219; M. Knibb, *The Qumran Community* (Cambridge, CUP, 1987), p. 260.
13. This can be seen from the text. See Knibb, *Qumran Community*, pp. 258–9.
14. K. Berger, 'Volksversammlung und Gemeinde Gottes', *ZTK*, vol. 73, 1976, pp. 167–207, gives a good outline of the use of the word *ekklēsia* in Jewish–Hellenistic writings. His main point seems to be that this word in these texts ceased to refer solely to political gatherings. It became a term mainly used of religious gatherings, often to hear what God had to say and to offer praise. He argues that when these gatherings were convened by the High Priest, the *ekklēsia* constituted was not thought of as just a random part of the holy community, but as representing Israel (p. 173).
15. Campbell, 'The Origin', p. 47.
16. 1 Kings 8.14, 22, 55, 65; 1 Chron. 13.2, 4, 28.2, 8, 29.1, 10, 20; 2 Chron. 1.3, 5, 6.3, 12, 13, 7.8, 20.5, 20.14, 23.3, 28.14, 29.23, 32, 30.2, 4, 13, 17, 23, 24, 25.
17. Compare Deuteronomy 31.30 with 32.44–5; 1 Kings 8.14, 22, 25 with 8.5, 14, 26; 1 Kings 12.3 with 12.1; 1 Chronicles 13.2, 4, with 13.6; 2 Chronicles 1.3, 5 with 1.2, etc. In other texts, the *ekklēsia* is equated with the *laos*, the people of God. Compare 2 Chronicles 6.3, 12, 13 with 7.3, 4, 6, 8; 2 Chronicles 29.1, 10, 20 with 29.9, 14, 18, etc. A longer list, not all of equal relevance, is given in Merklein, *Studien*, p. 309, n. 77 and 78.
18. Pss. 22.22, 25, 26.12, 35.18, 40.9, 68.26 (in the plural), 107.32. Similarly, Job 30.28; Prov. 5.14.
19. 15.5, 21.17, 24.2, 38.33, 39.10, 44.15.
20. Campbell, 'The Origin', p. 50.
21. As already noted, *qahal* appears some 123 times in the Old Testament; seventy-three times it is translated by *ekklēsia*, and some thirty-five times by *sunagōgē*. *Edah* occurs some 147 times, and is almost always translated by *sunagōgē*.
22. On these two texts, see the more detailed discussion on their background in the relevant sections in the body of the text. It should also be noted that some scholars have in fact argued that as *ekklēsia* in the New Testament takes on more of the meaning of *edah*, this is the word the Greek term reflects, not *qahal*. So Schnackenburg, *The Church*, pp. 56–60, and n. 10, p. 208.
23. *Leg. Al.* 3.8, 81; *De Post* 177; *De Eb.* 213; *De Confus. Ling.* 144; *De Mig. Ab.* 69; *De Som.* 2.184; *De virt.* 108; *Quod. Deus* 111.
24. This is somewhat complicated by the fact that this writing is only found virtually intact in Armenian, so we are dependent on translation. See the discussion in G. Johnston, *The Doctrine of the Church in the New Testament* (Cambridge, CUP, 1943), pp. 38–9.

25. *De Dec.* 9. 32, 11.45; *Quis Rer. Div.* 251; *De Post. Caini* 143.
26. 'Those who speak' are in Exodus 20.18 'all the people'.
27. In this allegory, the high priest constitutes the *ekklēsia*. He is seen as the representative embodiment of the community (cf. Lev. 16.7ff).
28. Hort, *The Christian Ecclesia*, p. 7.
29. *Ant.* 3.188 (Lev. 8.1f), 3.292 (Num. 10.1f), 3.306 (Num. 14.1), 4.22 (16.1f), 4.24 (Num. 16.4–11), 4.35 (Num 16.18), 4.142 (Num. 25.14f), 5.72 (Josh. 18.1), 5.111 (Josh. 22.21).
30. *Ant.* 19.300, 305; *Wars* 2.285, 289, 7.44.
31   Cerfaux, *The Church*; J. Roloff, *EDNT*, pp. 411–12.
32. Roloff, *EDNT*; K. Stendahl, 'Kirche', *RGG*, 3rd edn, H–K, p. 1299; P. Stuhlmacher, *Gerechtigeit Gottes bei Paulus* (Gottingen, FLANT, 1966), pp. 210–12.
33. *Ign. Pol.* 4.2; *Ign. Tr.* 3; *Herm. Mand.* 11.9, 13, 14, etc.
34. For references, see Schrage, *TDNT*, vol. 7, pp. 806–8.
35. First in Justin's *Dial.* 134.3.

Excursus 2   Translating the Greek Word *Ekklēsia*

1. *The Book of Concord*, p. 417.
2. K. Barth, *Church Dogmatics* (Edinburgh, T.&T. Clark, 1936–69).
3. The etymology of this word is worth noting. *Congregatio* is derived from the verb *congrego*, which literally means 'to gather together into a flock or herd'.
4. On this, see A. P. Snell, *Saints, Visible, Orderly and Catholic: The Congregational Idea of the Church* (Geneva, World Alliance of Reformed Churches, 1986).
5. So D. B. Knox, *Thirty-Nine Articles* (London, Hodder & Stoughton, 1967), pp. 45–7.
6. Quoted in P. E. Hughes, *Theology of the English Reformers* (London, Hodder & Stoughton, 1965), p. 227.

Select Bibliography

Abbott, W. and Gallagher, J. (eds), 'Lumen Gentium', in *The Documents of Vatican II* (USA, Geoffrey Chapman, 1966).

Adamson, J., *The Epistle of James* (Grand Rapids, Eerdmans, 1976).

Allen, D., *Philosophy for Understanding Theology* (London, SCM, 1985).

Allen, T. G., 'Exaltation and Solidarity with Christ: Ephesians 1:20 and 2:6', *JSNT*, 1986, pp. 103–20.

Ammerman, N. T., 'Denominations: What Are We Studying?', in R. B. Mullen and R. E. Richey (eds), *Reimaging the Church: Interpretive Essays* (Oxford, OUP, 1994).

Aquinas, T., *Summa Theologiae* (London, Blackfriars, 61 vols, 1964–81).

Arnold, C. E., *Ephesians: Power and Magic* (Cambridge, CUP, 1989).

Attridge, H. W., *The Epistle to the Hebrews* (Philadelphia, Fortress, 1989).

Aune, D. E. (ed.), *Greco-Roman Literature and the New Testament* (Atlanta, Scholars, 1988).

Avis, P., *Christians in Communion* (London, Geoffrey Chapman, 1990).

Balch, D. L., 'Household Codes', in D. E. Aune (ed.), *Greco-Roman Literature*.

Banks, R., *Paul's Idea of Community* (Homebush, NSW, Anzea, 1979).

——, 'Denominational Structures: Their Legitimacy, Vocation and Capacity for Reform', in D. Peterson and J. Pryor (eds), *In the Fullness of Time* (Homebush, NSW, Lancer, 1992).

Barr, J., *The Semantics of Biblical Language* (Oxford, OUP, 1961).

Barth, K., *Church Dogmatics* (Edinburgh, T.&T. Clark, 1936–69).

Barth, M., *Ephesians, 1–3* (New York, Doubleday, 1974).

——, *Ephesians, 4–6* (New York, Doubleday, 1974).

——, *The People of God* (Sheffield, JSOT, 1983).

Barton, S. C., 'The Communal Dimension of Earliest Christianity: A Critical Survey of the Field', *JTS*, vol. 43, 1992, pp. 399–427.

Bauckham, R., *The Theology of the Book of Revelation* (Cambridge, CUP, 1993).

——, *The Climax of Prophecy* (Edinburgh, T.&T. Clark, 1993).

Bauer, F. C., *On the Writing of Church History* (New York, OUP, Library of Protestant Theology, 1968).

Beagley, A., *The Sitz im Leben of the Apocalypse* (Berlin, De Gruyter, 1987).
Beasley-Murray, G. R., *The Book of Revelation* (London, Oliphants, 1974).
——, *Jesus and the Kingdom of God* (London, Paternoster, 1986).
——, *John* (Waco, Word Biblical Commentary, 1987).
Becker, J. C., *Paul the Apostle* (Philadelphia, Fortress, 1988).
——, *Heirs of Paul* (Edinburgh, T.&T. Clark, 1989).
Begg, C., *A Critical and Exegetical Commentary on 1 Peter* (Edinburgh, T.&T. Clark, 1902).
Bellah, R., *Habits of the Heart: Individualism and Commitment in American Life* (Berkeley, University of California, 1985).
Berger, K., 'Volksversammlung und Germeinde Gottes', *ZTK*, vol. 73, 1976, pp. 167–207.
Best, E., *One Body in Christ* (London, SPCK, 1955).
——, *Discipleship in Mark's Gospel* (Sheffield, JSOT, 1981).
——, *1 Peter* (London, Oliphants, 1971).
——, *Ephesians* (Sheffield, JSOT, 1993).
Black, C. C., *Discipleship According to Mark* (Sheffield, JSOT, 1989).
Blasi, A., *Early Christianity as a Social Movement* (Toronto, Lang, 1988).
Boff, L., *Trinity and Society* (London, Burns & Oates, 1988).
Bonhoeffer, D., *Letters and Papers from Prison* (New York, Macmillan, 1963).
Bornkamm, G. *et al.* (eds), *Tradition and Interpretation in Matthew* (London, SCM, 1963).
Bowman, H. J. A., *A Look at Today's Churches: A Comparative Guide* (St Louis, Concordia, 1980).
Braaten, C. (ed.), *Christian Dogmatics* vol. 1 (Philadelphia, Fortress, 1984).
Bradshaw, T., *The Olive Branch: An Evangelical Doctrine of the Church* (Carlisle, Paternoster, 1992).
Branick, V. P., *The House Church in the Writings of Paul* (Delaware, Glazier, 1989).
Braun, R., *1 Chronicles* (Waco, Word Biblical Commentary, 1986).
Brown, D., *The Divine Trinity* (London, Duckworth, 1985).
Brown, R., *The Gospel According to John* (New York, Doubleday, 2 vols, 1966).
——, *The Birth of the Messiah* (London, Geoffrey Chapman, 1977).
——, *The Community of the Beloved Disciple* (London, Geoffrey Chapman, 1979).
——, *The Epistles of John* (London, Doubleday, 1982).
Brown, S., 'Koinonia as a Basis of New Testament Ecclesiology?', *One in Christ*, vol. 12, 1976, pp. 155–67.
Bruce, F. F., *1 and 2 Corinthians* (London, Oliphants, 1971).
——, *The Epistle to the Hebrews* (Grand Rapids, Eerdmans, 1974).
——, *The Epistles to the Colossians, to Philemon and to the Ephesians* (Grand Rapids, Eerdmans, 1984).
——, *The Churches the Apostles Left Behind* (London, Chapman, 1984).
Brunner, E., *The Misunderstanding of the Church* (London, Lutterworth, 1952).
Bultmann, R., *Theology of the New Testament* (London, SCM, 2 vols, 1952, 1955).

Burtchaell, J. M., *From Synagogue to Church* (Cambridge, CUP, 1992).
Cadbury, H. J., 'Names for Christians and Christianity in Acts', in F. J. Foakes-Jackson and K. Lake (eds), *The Beginnings of Christianity* (London, Macmillan, 1933), pp. 375–92.
——, *The Making of Luke–Acts* (London, Macmillan, 1927).
Caird, G. B., *New Testament Theology* (Oxford, Clarendon, 1994).
Calvin, J., *The Institutes of the Christian Religion*, J. T. McNeil (ed.) (London, SCM, 1960).
Campbell, J. Y., 'The Origin and Meaning of the Christian Use of the Word *Ekklēsia*', *JTS*, vol. 49, 1948, pp. 41–54.
Caragounis, C. C., *Peter and the Rock* (New York, De Gruyter, 1990).
——, 'Kingdom of God', *DJG*, pp. 417–30.
Carson, D. A. (ed.), *Biblical Interpretation and the Church* (Exeter, Paternoster, 1984).
——, *The Church in the Bible and the World* (Exeter, Paternoster, 1987).
Cerfaux, L., *The Church in the Theology of St Paul* (New York, Herder & Herder, 1959).
Chaffer, L. S., *Systematic Theology* (Dallas, Dallas Seminary Press, 1948), vol. 4.
Chester, A. and Martin, R. P., *The Theology of the Letters of James, Peter and Jude* (Cambridge, CUP, 1994).
Coad, R., *A History of the Brethren Movement* (Exeter, Paternoster, 1968).
Collins, A., *Crisis and Catharsis* (Philadelphia, Westminster, 1984).
Collins, R. F., *These Things Have Been Written: Studies in the Fourth Gospel* (Grand Rapids, Eerdmans, 1990).
Congar, Y., *I Believe in the Holy Spirit*, vol. 2 (New York, Seabury, 1983).
Conzelmann, H., *The Theology of St Luke* (London, Faber & Faber, 1960).
Cooke, B., *Ministry to Word and Sacrament* (Philadelphia, Fortress, 1980).
Cox, H., *The Secular City* (New York, Macmillan, 1965).
Craigie, P., *Deuteronomy* (Grand Rapids, Eerdmans, 1976).
Crosby, M. H., *House of Disciples* (New York, Orbis, 1988).
Dassmann, E., 'Hausgemeinde und Bischofsamt', in *Viviarium, Festschrift Theodor Klauser zum 90 Geburtstag* (Munster, Aschendorffsche, 1984), pp. 82–97.
Davies, W. D. and Allison, D. C., *The Gospel According to St Matthew* (Edinburgh, T.&T. Clark, vol. 1, 1988, vol. 2, 1991).
de Magerie, B., *The Christian Trinity in History* (Massachusetts, St Bede's, 1982).
Dibelius, M., *James* (Philadelphia, Fortress, 1975).
Donahue, J. R., *The Theology and Setting of Discipleships in Mark* (Milwaukee, Marquette, 1981).
Donfield, K. and Marshall, I. H. (eds), *The Theology of the Shorter Pauline Epistles* (Cambridge, CUP, 1993).
Drilling, P., *Trinity and Ministry* (Minneapolis, Fortress, 1991).
Du Cange, C., *Glossarium mediae et infirme Latinitatis*, vol. 2 (Niort, 1893).
Dulles, A., *Models of the Church* (Dublin, Gill & Macmillan, 2nd edn 1988).

——, 'A Half Century of Ecclesiology', *TS*, vol. 50, 1989, pp. 419–42.

——, *A Church to Believe in: Discipleship and the Dynamics of Freedom* (New York, Crossroad, 1982).

Dumbrell, W., *The End of The Beginning* (Australia, Lancer, 1985).

——, 'The Meaning and Use of *Ekklēsia* in the New Testament with Special Reference to its Old Testament Background', unpublished MTh. thesis, London University, 1966.

——, 'An Appreciation of the Theological Work of Donald Robinson', in D. Peterson and J. Pryor, *In the Fullness of Time* (Homebush, NSW, Lancer, 1992), pp. xvii–xxviii.

——, *The Search for Order: Biblical Eschatology in Focus* (Grand Rapids, Baker, 1994).

Dunn, J. D. G., *Unity and Diversity in the New Testament* (London, SCM, 1977).

——, *Romans 1–8* (Waco, Word Biblical Commentary, 1988).

——, *Romans 9–16* (Waco, Word Biblical Commentary, 1988).

——, *The Parting of the Ways* (London, SCM, 1991).

——, *The Theology of Paul's Letter to the Galatians* (Cambridge, CUP, 1992).

Duquoc, C., *Provisional Churches* (London, SCM, 1986).

Ellingworth, P., *The Epistle to the Hebrews* (Carlisle, Paternoster, 1993).

Elliott, J. H., *The Elect and the Holy* (Leiden, Brill, 1966).

——, *A Home for the Homeless* (Minneapolis, Fortress, 1990).

Esler, P. E., *Community and Gospel in Luke–Acts* (Cambridge, CUP, 1987).

Evans, O. E., 'New Wine in Old Wineskins: The Saints', *ExpT*, vol. 86, 1975, pp. 196–200.

Fee, G., *The First Epistle to the Corinthians* (Grand Rapids, Eerdmans, 1987).

Field, B., 'The Discourses Behind the Metaphor "The Church as the Body of Christ" as used by St Paul and the "Post Paulines"', *AJT*, vol. 6, 1992, pp. 88–107.

Fiorenza Schussler, E., *The Book of Revelation* (Philadelphia, Fortress, 1985).

Fitzmyer, J., 'Discipleship in the Lucan Writings', in J. Fitzmyer, *Luke the Theologian* (London, Geoffrey Chapman, 1989).

——, 'Another Look at *Kephalē* in 1 Corinthians 11:3', *NTS*, vol. 35, 1989, pp. 52–9.

——, 'Jewish Christianity in Acts in the Light of the Qumran Scrolls', in Keck and Martyn, *Studies in Luke–Acts*, pp. 233–57.

Flender, H., *St Luke: Theologian of Redemptive History* (London, SPCK, 1967).

Forsyth, P. T., *Faith, Freedom and the Future* (London, Hodder & Stoughton, 1912).

Forte, B., *The Church: Icon of the Trinity* (Boston, St Paul, 1991).

Frame, J. M., *Evangelical Reunion: Denominations and the Body of Christ* (Grand Rapids, Baker, 1991).

France, R. T., *Matthew – Evangelist and Teacher* (London, Paternoster, 1989).

Gartner, B., *The Temple and the Community in Qumran and the New Testament* (Cambridge, CUP, 1965).

Gibson, A. F., *The Church and its Unity* (Leicester, IVP, 1992).

Giles, K. N., *Women and Their Ministry* (Melbourne, Dove, 1977).

——, *Created Woman* (Canberra, Acorn, 1985).

——, *Patterns of Ministry Among the First Christians* (Melbourne, Collins-Dove, 1989).

——, *The Making of Community: Acts 1–12* (Albatross, Sutherland, 1992).

——, 'Ascension', *DJG*, pp. 46–50.

——, 'The Significance of the Day of Pentecost', *LTJ*, 1983, pp. 137–40.

——, 'Present–Future Eschatology in the Book of Acts', *RTR*, vol. 40, 1981, pp. 65–71; vol. 41, 1982, pp. 11–17.

——, 'Luke's Use of the Term *Ekklēsia* with Special Reference to Acts 20:28 and 9:31', *NTS*, vol. 31, 1985, pp. 135–42.

——, 'The Church in the Gospel of Luke', *SJT*, vol. 34, 1981, pp. 121–46.

——, 'Women in the Church with Special Reference to 1 Timothy – A Response', in A. Nicholls (ed.), *The Bible and Women's Ministry* (Canberra, Acorn, 1990), pp. 65–88.

——, 'Evangelical Systematic Theology: Definition, Problems, Sources', in D. G. Peterson and J. Pryor (eds), *In the Fullness of Time* (Homebush, NSW, Lancer, 1992).

Goppelt, G., *Typos: The Typological Interpretation of the Old Testament in the New* (Grand Rapids, Eerdmans, 1982).

Gore, C., *The Church and the Ministry* (London, SPCK, 1936).

Gray, S. W., *The Least of My Brothers, Matthew 25: 31–46: A History of Interpretation* (Georgia, Scholars, 1989).

Grentz, S. J., *Revisioning Evangelical Theology* (Downers Grove, IVP, 1993).

Gundry, R. H., *Sōma in Biblical Theology* (Cambridge, CUP, 1976).

——, *Mark: A Commentary on his Apology for the Cross* (Grand Rapids, Eerdmans, 1993).

——, *Matthew: A Commentary on his Literary and Theological Art* (Grand Rapids, Eerdmans, 1982).

Gunton, C., *The Promise of Trinitarian Theology* (Edinburgh, T.&T. Clark, 1991).

Gunton, C. and Hardy, D. (eds), *On Being the Church* (Edinburgh, T.&T. Clark, 1989).

Haenchen, E., *The Acts of the Apostles* (Oxford, Basil Blackwell, 1971).

Hainz, J., *Ekklēsia: Structuren paulinischer Gemeinde–theologie und Gemeinde–Ordnung* (Regensburg, Prustet, 1972).

Hamer, J., *The Church is a Communion* (London, Geoffrey Chapman, 1964).

Hansen, G. W., *Abraham in Galatians* (Sheffield, JSOT, 1989).

Hanson, A. T. and Hanson, R. P. C., *The Identity of the Church* (London, SCM, 1987).

Hanson, P. D., *The People Called* (San Francisco, Harper & Row, 1987).

Harnack, A., *The Mission and Expansion of the Christian Church* (London, Williams & Norgate, 1908).

Harrington, D. J., *The Apocalypse of John* (London, Geoffrey Chapman, 1969).

Hemer, C., *The Letters to the Seven Churches of Asia in their Local Setting* (Sheffield, JSOT, 1986).

Hengel, M., *The Pre-Christian Paul* (London, SCM, 1991).

Herron, A. I. C., *The Forgotten Trinity* (London, BBC, 1991).

Hill, C., *Mystery of Life: A Theology of Church* (Melbourne, Collins-Dove, 1990).

Hill, D., *New Testament Prophecy* (Basingstoke, Marshall, Morgan, & Scott, 1979).

Hodgson, P. C. and Williams, R. C. (eds), *Christian Theology: An Introduction to Its Traditions and Tasks* (Philadelphia, Fortress, 1985).

Holmberg, B., *Paul and Power* (Lund, Gleerup, 1978).

——, *Sociology and the New Testament* (Minneapolis, Fortress, 1990).

Hooker, M. D., *The Gospel of St Mark* (London, A.&C. Black, 1991).

Hort, F. J. A., *The Christian Ecclesia* (London, Macmillan, 1914).

Hossfeld, F. L., Kindl, E. M., and Fabry, H.-J., '*Qahal*', *TWZAT*, vol. 6, 1989, pp. 1203–22.

Hughes, G., *Hebrews and Hermeneutics* (Cambridge, CUP, 1979).

Hughes, P. E., *Theology of the English Reformers* (London, Hodder & Stoughton, 1965).

——, *A Commentary on the Epistle to the Hebrews* (Grand Rapids, Eerdmans, 1979).

Jary, D. and J., *Collins Dictionary of Sociology* (Glasgow, HarperCollins, 1991).

Jay, E. G., *The Church: Its Changing Image Through Twenty Centuries: The First Seventeen Centuries*, vol. 1 (London, SPCK, 1977).

——, *The Church: Its Changing Image Through Twenty Centuries: 1700 to the Present Day*, vol. 2 (London, SPCK, 1978).

Jenson, R. W., *The Triune Identity* (Philadelphia, Fortress, 1982).

——, 'The Church', in C. Braaten (ed.), *Christian Dogmatics*, vol. 1 (Philadelphia, Fortress, 1984), pp. 135–60.

Jeremias, J., *The Parables of Jesus* (London, SCM, 1963).

——, *The Eucharistic Words of Jesus* (London, SCM, 1966).

——, *New Testament Theology*, vol. 1 (London, SCM, 1985).

Jervell, J., *Luke and the People of God* (Minnesota, Augsburg, 1972).

Johnston, G., *The Doctrine of the Church in the New Testament* (Cambridge, CUP, 1943).

Johnston, L. T., *The Acts of the Apostles* (Minnesota, Glazier, 1992).

Juel, D., *Messiah and Temple* (Missoula, Scholars, 1977).

Karris, R.-K., 'Women and Discipleship in Luke', *CBQ*, vol. 56, 1994, pp. 1–20.

Kasemann, E., *New Testament Questions for Today* (London, SCM, 1967).

Kasper, W., *The God of Jesus Christ* (New York, Crossroad, 1991).

Kee, H., *Community of the New Age* (Philadelphia, Westminster, 1977).

——, *Good News to the Ends of the Earth* (London, SCM, 1990).

Kelly, J. N. D., *Early Christian Creeds* (London, Longman, 1972).

Kingsbury, J. D., *Matthew: A Commentary for Preachers and Others* (London, SPCK, 1986).

——, *Conflict in Mark* (Minneapolis, Fortress, 1989).

——, *Conflict in Luke* (Minneapolis, Fortress, 1991).

——, 'The Verb *Akoloouthein* ('to follow'), as an Index of Matthew's View of His Community', *JBL*, vol. 97, 1978, pp. 56–73.

Kinnamon, M., *Truth in Community* (Grand Rapids, Eerdmans, 1988).

Knibb, M., *The Qumran Community* (Cambridge, CUP, 1987).

Knight, G. W., *The Pastoral Epistles* (Grand Rapids, Eerdmans, 1992).

Knox, D. B., *Thirty-Nine Articles* (London, Hodder & Stoughton, 1967).

Kreitzer, L. J., 'Eschatology', *DPL*, pp. 253–69.

——, 'Adam and Christ', *DPL*, pp. 9–15.

Kress, R., *The Church, Communion, Sacrament, Communication* (New York, Paulist, 1985).

Kroeger, C. C., 'Head', *DPL*, pp. 375–7.

Küng, H., *The Church* (Exeter, Search, 1968).

——, *Theology for the Third Millennium* (New York, Doubleday, 1988).

LaCugna, C. M., *God for Us* (New York, HarperCollins, 1991).

Ladd, G. E., *A Theology of the New Testament* (Grand Rapids, Eerdmans, rev. edn 1993).

Lake, K. (ed.), *The Apostolic Fathers* (London, Heinemann, 1912), vols. 1 and 2.

Lane, W., *Hebrews 1–8* (Waco, Word Biblical Commentary, 1991).

——, *Hebrews 9–13* (Waco, Word Biblical Commentary, 1991).

Laws, S., *In the Light of the Lamb* (Delaware, Glazier, 1988).

Lawton, W. J., *The Better Time to Be* (Kensington, NSW, University Press, 1990).

Lehne, S., *The New Covenant in Hebrews* (Sheffield, JSOT, 1990).

Lieu, J., *The Second and Third Epistles of John: History and Background* (Edinburgh, T.&T. Clark, 1986).

——, *The Theology of the Johannine Epistles* (Cambridge, CUP, 1991).

Lightner, R. P., *Evangelical Theory* (Grand Rapids, Baker, 1986).

Lincoln, A. T., *Paradise Now and Not Yet* (Cambridge, CUP, 1981).

——, *Ephesians* (Waco, Word Biblical Commentary, 1990).

Lincoln, A. T. and Wedderburn, A. J. M., *The Theology of the Later Pauline Epistles* (Cambridge, CUP, 1993).

Link, H. G. (ed.), *One God, One Lord, One Spirit* (Geneva, WCC, 1988).

Lohfink, G., *Die Sammlung Israel: Eine Untersuchung zur Lukanischen Ekklesiologie* (Munchen, Kosel, 1975).

——, *Jesus and Community* (London, SPCK, 1985).

Lohse, E., *Colossians and Philemon* (Philadelphia, Fortress, 1971).

Loisy, A., *The Gospel and the Church* (New York, Prometheus, 1988).

Longenecker, R., *Galatians* (Waco, Word Biblical Commentary, 1990).

Luther, M., *The Book of Concord* (T. G. Tappet, trans.) (Philadelphia, Muhlenberg, 1959).

Luz, U., 'The Disciples in the Gospel of Matthew', in G. Stanton (ed.), *The Interpretation of Matthew* (London, SPCK, 1983).

Lynch, P., 'Servant Ecclesiologies: A Challenge to Rahner's Understanding of Church and World', *ITQ*, vol. 57, 1991, pp. 277–95.

MacDonald, M. Y., *The Pauline Churches: A Socio-historical Study of*

Institutionalization in the Pauline and Deutero-Pauline Writings (Cambridge, CUP, 1988).

MacDonald, T. I., *The Ecclesiology of Yves Congar* (Lanham, University Press of America, 1984).

MacGregor, G., *Corpus Christi: The Nature of the Church According to the Reformed Tradition* (London, Macmillan, 1959).

Macquarrie, J., *Principles of Christian Theology* (New York, Scribner, 1966).

Maddox, R., *The Purpose of Luke–Acts* (Edinburgh, T.&T. Clark, 1982).

Maier, G., 'The Church in the Gospel of Matthew', in Carson (ed.), *Biblical Interpretation.*

Malina, B. J. and Neyrey, J. H., 'First Century Personality: Dyadic, not Individualistic', in J. H. Neyrey (ed.), *The Social World of Luke–Acts* (Massachusetts, Hendrickson, 1991), pp. 67–96.

Marshall, I. H., *Last Supper and Lord's Supper* (Exeter, Paternoster, 1980).

Martin, R. P., *James* (Waco, Word Biblical Commentary, 1988).

Matera, F. J., *What Are They Saying about Mark?* (New York, Paulist, 1987).

Mazzaferri, F., *The Genre of the Book of Revelation* (Berlin, De Gruyter, 1989).

McDonnell, K., 'The Determinative Doctrine of the Holy Spirit', *T Today*, vol. 39, 1982, pp. 140–56.

———, 'Vatican 2 (1962–4) Synod (1985): an Integral Ecclesiology', *JES*, vol. 25, 1988, pp. 399–427.

McKelvey, R. J., *The New Temple* (Oxford, OUP, 1969).

Meeks, W. A., *The First Urban Christians* (New Haven, Yale, 1983).

———, 'Breaking Away: Three New Testament Pictures of Christian Separation from the Jewish Communities', in J. Neusner and E. Freirichs (eds), *To See Ourselves as Others See Us* (California, Scholars, 1985).

Meier, J. P., *The Vision of Christ: Christ, Church and Morality in the First Gospel* (New York, Paulist, 1979).

———, *Matthew* (Delaware, Glazier, 1980).

Menzies, R. P., *The Development of Early Christian Pneumatology* (Sheffield, JSOT, 1991).

Merklein, H., *Das Kirchliche Amt Nach Dem Epheserbrief* (Munich, Kosel, 1973).

———, 'Paulinische Theologie in der Rezeption des Kolosser – und Epheserbriefes', in K. Kertlege (ed.), *Paulus in den Neutestamentlichen Spatschriften* (Freiburg, Herder, 1981).

———, 'Die Ekklesia Gottes', in H. Merklein (ed.), *Studien zu Jesus und Paulus* (Tubingen, Mohr, 1987).

Mersch, E., *The Whole Church* (Milwaukee, Bruce, 1938).

Meyer, B., *The Aims of Jesus* (London, SCM, 1979).

Meyers, E. M. and Strange, J. F., *Archaeology, the Rabbis and Early Christianity* (London, SCM, 1981).

Michaels, J. R., *1 Peter* (Waco, Word Biblical Commentary, 1988).

Milgrom, J., 'Priestly Terminology and the Political and Social Structure of Pre-Monarchic Israel', *JQR*, vol. 69, 1978–9, pp. 65–81.

Minear, P., *Matthew: The Teacher's Gospel* (London, Darton, Longman, & Todd, 1984).

Moltmann, J., *The Church in the Power of the Spirit* (London, SCM, 1977).

——, *The Trinity and the Kingdom of God* (London, SCM, 1981).

——, *History of the Triune God* (London, SCM, 1991).

——, *The Spirit of Life* (London, SCM, 1992).

Moule, C. F. D., *The Origin of Christology* (Cambridge, CUP, 1977).

Mounce, R., *The Book of Revelation* (Grand Rapids, Eerdmans, 1977).

Mullen, R. B. and Richey, R. E. (eds), *Reimaging Denominationalism: Interpretive Essays* (Oxford, OUP, 1994).

Nau, A. J., *Peter in Matthew* (Minnesota, Glazier, 1992).

Neusner, J., *From Politics to Piety* (Englewood Cliffs, Prentice-Hall, 1973).

—— (ed.), *Judaism and Other Greco-Roman Cults* (Leiden, Brill, 1975).

Newbigin, L., *The Household of God* (London, SCM, 1953).

Neyrey, J. H. (ed.), *The Social World of Luke–Acts* (Massachusetts, Hendrickson, 1991).

Niebuhr, H. R., *The Social Sources of Denominationalism* (New York, Meridian, 1957).

Norris, R., 'What Is "Church Unity?"', *One in Christ*, vol. 2, 1982, pp. 117–32.

O'Brien, P. T., *Commentary on Philippians* (Grand Rapids, Eerdmans, 1991).

——, *Colossians and Philemon* (Waco, Word Biblical Commentary, 1982).

——, 'The Church', *DPL*, pp. 123–31.

——, 'The Church as a Heavenly and Eschatological Entity', in Carson (ed.), *The Church in the Bible and the World*.

O'Connor Murphy, J., *St Paul's Corinth: Text and Archaeology* (Delaware, Glazier, 1983).

O'Grady, J. F., 'Individualism in Johannine Ecclesiology', *BTB*, vol. 5, 1975, pp. 227–61.

Orton, D., *The Understanding Scribe* (Sheffield, JSOT, 1989).

Osborne, K., *Priesthood: A History of the Ordained Ministry in the Roman Catholic Church* (New York, Paulist, 1988).

Overman, J., *Matthew's Gospel and Formative Judaism* (Minneapolis, Fortress, 1990).

Painter, J., *The Quest for the Messiah* (Edinburgh, T.&T. Clark, 1991).

Pancaro, S., 'People of God in John's Gospel', *NTS*, vol. 16, 1969–70, pp. 114–29.

Pannenberg, W., *The Church* (Philadelphia, Westminster, 1977).

Paton, D. M. (ed.), *Breaking Barriers, Nairobi 1975* (London, SPCK, 1975).

Peterson, D., *Hebrews and Perfection* (Cambridge, CUP, 1982).

——, *Engaging with God* (Leicester, Apollos, 1992).

Peterson, J. M., 'House-churches in Rome', *VC*, vol. 23, 1969.

Piper, J. and Grudem, W., *Recovering Biblical Manhood and Womanhood* (Wheaton, Crossway, 1991).

Popkes, W., *Adressaten, Situation und Form des Jacobusbriefes* (Stuttgart, Katholisches Biblewerk, 1986).

Prestige, G. L., *God in Patristic Thought* (London, SPCK, 1964).

Pryor, J. W., *John: Evangelist of the Covenant People* (Downers Grove, IVP, 1992).

——, 'First Peter and the New Covenant', *RTR*, vol. 45, 1986, pp. 1–4.

Quast, K., *Peter and the Beloved Disciple* (Sheffield, JSOT, 1989).

Radamacher, E. D., *What the Church is All About* (Chicago, Moody, 1972).
Rahner, K., *The Trinity* (London, Burns & Oates, 1970).
——, 'The Church', in K. Rahner (ed.), *The Encyclopaedia of Theology* (London, Burns & Oates, 1975), pp. 205–27.
Raiser, K., *Ecumenism in Transition* (Geneva, WCC, 1991).
Reuman, J., '*Koinonia* in Scripture: Survey of the Biblical Texts', unpublished paper WCC Fifth World Conference on Faith and Order, Spain, 1993.
Richardson, P., *Israel in the Apostolic Church* (Cambridge, CUP, 1969).
Ridderbos, H., *The Epistle to the Churches of Galatia* (Edinburgh, Marshall, Morgan, & Scott, 1961).
——, *Paul: An Outline of His Theology* (Grand Rapids, Eerdmans, 1977).
Rikhof, H., *The Concept of the Church* (London, Sheed & Ward, 1981).
Rissi, M., *The Future of the World* (London, SCM, 1972).
Robinson, D. W. B., *The Church of God* (Sydney, Jordan, 1965).
——, 'The Distinction between Jewish and Gentile Believers in Galatians', *ABR*, vol. 13, 1965, pp. 29–48.
——, 'The Doctrine of the Church and its Implications for Evangelism', *Interchange*, vol. 15, 1974, pp. 156–72.
——, 'The Church and Evangelism', *Interchange*, vol. 21, 1977, pp. 62–3.
Robinson, J. A. T., *The Body: A Study in Pauline Theology* (London, SCM, 1952).
——, *The New Reformation* (Philadelphia, Westminster, 1965).
Rolof, J., 'Ekklēsia', *EDNT*, vol. 1, pp. 410–15.
Sanders, E. P., *Paul and Palestinian Judaism* (London, SCM, 1977).
——, *Jesus and Judaism* (London, SCM, 1985).
——, *Paul* (Oxford, OUP, 1991).
Sanders, E. P. (ed.), *Jewish and Christian Self-Definition*, vol. 2 (London, SCM, 1981).
Saucy, R., *The Church in God's Program* (Chicago, Moody, 1972).
Schillebeeckx, E., *Ministry: A Case for Change* (London, SCM, 1981).
——, *The Church with a Human Face* (London, SCM, 1985).
Schnackenburg, R., *God's Rule and Kingdom* (Edinburgh, Nelson, 1963).
——, *The Church in the New Testament* (London, Burns & Oates, 1974).
——, *The Gospel According to St John* (New York, Crossroad, 3 vols, 1968, 1980, 1982).
——, *The Epistle to the Ephesians* (Edinburgh, T.&T. Clark, 1991).
Scholer, J., *Proleptic Priests* (Sheffield, JSOT, 1991).
Schrage, W., '"Ekklēsia" und "Synagōgē" Zum Ursprung des Urchristlichen Kirchenbegriffs', *ZTK*, vol. 60, 1963, pp. 178–202.
Schweizer, E., *Church Order in the New Testament* (London, SCM, 1961).
——, 'Matthew's Church', in Stanton (ed.), *The Interpretation of Matthew*, pp. 129–55.
——, 'The Concept of the Church in St John', in A. J. B. Higgins (ed.), *New Testament Essays in Honour of T. W. Manson* (Manchester, Manchester University Press, 1959), pp. 230–45.
Seesman, H., *Der Begriff Koinonia im Neun Testamentum*, ZNWB, 14 (Giessen, 1933).
Selwyn, E., *The First Epistle of St Peter* (London, Macmillan, 1949).

Siefield, M. A., 'In Christ', *DPL*, pp. 433–6.

Snell, A. P., *Saints: Visible, Orderly and Catholic: The Congregational Idea of the Church* (Geneva, World Alliance of Reformed Churches, 1986).

Sohm, R., *Outlines of Church History* (London, Macmillan, 1985).

Stanton, G., *A Gospel for a New People* (Edinburgh, T.&T. Clark, 1992).

—— (ed.), *The Interpretation of Matthew* (London, SPCK, 1983).

Stendahl, K., 'Kirche', *RGG*, H–K, pp. 1296–1303.

Stock, A., *A Call to Discipleship* (Delaware, Glazier, 1982).

Stott, J., *God's New Society* (Leicester, IVP, 1979).

Stuhlmacher, P., *Gerechtigeit Gottes bei Paulus* (Gottingen, FLANT, 1966).

Talbert, C. H., *Literary Patterns, Theological Themes and the Genre of Luke–Acts* (Missoula, Scholars, 1974).

Thiessen, G., *Sociology of Early Palestinian Christianity* (Philadelphia, Fortress, 1978).

Thompson, L., *The Book of Revelation* (Oxford, OUP, 1990).

Thompson, W., *Matthew's Advice to a Divided Community: Mt. 17.22–18.35* (Rome, Biblical Institute, 1970).

Thornton, L., *Common Life in the Body of Christ* (London, Dacre, 1941).

Thrall, M. E., *The Second Epistle to the Corinthians* (Edinburgh, T.&T. Clark, 1994).

Tidball, D., *An Introduction to the Sociology of the New Testament* (Exeter, Paternoster, 1983).

Tillard, J. M., *Church of Churches: The Ecclesiology of Communion* (Minnesota, Glazier, 1992).

Tillich, P., *The Protestant Era* (London, Nisbet, 1951).

——, *Systematic Theology* (Herts, Nisbet, vol. 3, 1964).

Torrance, T. F. (ed.), *Theological Dialogue Between Orthodox and Reformed Churches* (Edinburgh, Scottish Academic, 1985).

——, *Theology in Reconstruction* (London, SCM, 1965).

——, *The Trinitarian Faith* (Edinburgh, T.&T. Clark, 1992).

——, 'The Israel of God', *Interp.*, vol. 10, 1956, pp. 305–22.

Towler, R., *Homo-Religiosus: Sociological Problems in the Study of Religion* (London, Constable, 1974).

Towner, P., *The Goal of Our Instruction* (Sheffield, JSOT, 1989).

Troeltsch, E., *The Social Teaching of the Christian Churches* (London, George Allen & Unwin, 1931).

Turner, K., *The Politics of God: Christian Theologies and Social Justice* (Minneapolis, Fortress, 1992).

Vandervelde, G., 'Koinonia Ecclesiology – Ecumenical Breakthrough?', *One in Christ*, vol. 29, 1993, pp. 126–42.

Vanhoye, A., *Old Testament Priest and New Testament Priest According To The New Testament* (Massachusetts, St Bede's, 1986).

Van Tilborg, S., *The Jewish Leaders in Matthew* (Leiden, Brill, 1972).

Verner, D. C., *The Household of God: The Social World of the Pastoral Epistles* (Chicago, Scholars, 1974).

Webb, W. J., *Returning Home: New Covenant and Second Exodus as the Context for 2 Corinthians 6:14—7:1* (Sheffield, JSOT, 1993).

Weber, O., *Foundations of Dogmatics* (Grand Rapids, Eerdmans, vol. 2, 1983).
Weedon, T. J., *Mark Traditions in Conflict* (Philadelphia, Fortress, 1971).
Weima, J. A., *Neglected Endings: The Significance of the Pauline Letter Closings* (Sheffield, JSOT, 1994).
Weiss, B., *Der Brief an die Hebraer* (Gottingen, Vanenhoeck und Ruprecht, 1897).
Wenham, D., 'Unity and Diversity in the New Testament', in Ladd, *A Theology of the New Testament*.
Wilkins, M. J., *The Concept of Discipleship in Matthew's Gospel* (Leiden, Brill, 1988).
——, 'Discipleo' and 'Discipleship', in *DJG*, pp. 176–82.
Williams, M. D., 'Where's the Church? The Church as the Unfinished Business of Dispensational Theology', *GTJ*, vol. 10, 1989, pp. 165–82.
Willis, W. W. (ed.), *The Kingdom of God in 20th Century Interpretation* (Massachusetts, Hendrikson, 1987).
Wilson, B., *Magic and the Millennium* (New York, Harper, 1973).
Winter, G., *The New Creation as Metropolis* (New York, Macmillan, 1965).
Witherington, B., *Women in the Earliest Churches* (Cambridge, CUP, 1988).
Wright, N. T., *The Climax of the Covenant* (Edinburgh, T.&T. Clark, 1991).
——, *The New Testament and the People of God* (London, SPCK, 1992).
York, J. O., *The Last Shall Be First* (Sheffield, JSOT, 1991).
Yorke, L. O. R., *The Church as the Body of Christ* (New York, University Press of America, 1991).
Young, F., *The Theology of the Pastoral Epistles* (Cambridge, CUP, 1994).
Zizioulas, J., *Being as Communion* (New York, St Vladimir's Press, 1985).
——, 'The Doctrine of God the Trinity Today', in A. I. C. Heron (ed.), *The Forgotten Trinity* (London, BBC, 1991), pp. 19–32.

Reports

In Each Place: Towards a Fellowship of Local Churches Truly United (Geneva, WCC, 1977).
Extraordinary Synod of Bishops: Final Report (Rome, Vatican, 1985).
Salvation and the Church: An Agreed Statement by the Second Anglican–Roman Catholic International Commission (Sydney, AIO, 1987).
Church as Communion: An Agreed Statement by the Second Anglican–Roman Catholic International Commission (London, ACC, 1991).
Baptism, Eucharist and Ministry (Geneva, WCC, 1982).
Fifth Forum on International Bilateral Conversations (Geneva, WCC, 1991).
Anglican–Roman Catholic International Commission: Three Agreed Statements (London, SPCK, 1978).

Index of Names and Subjects

abiding 67
Abraham 108–10, 133
Adam/Christ 100–1
American colonies 200
Anabaptists 13
angel 174
Anglican 2, 3, 4, 9, 12, 14, 205
Anglo-Catholics 9, 10
anti-Christs 168
Apostle's Creed 17
Athanasius 219
Augustine of Hippo 190, 219
Avis, P. 15

Banks, R. 127
baptism 53, 72, 92, 122, 131, 161, 164, 207
Barrett, C. K. ix
Barr, J. 5, 232
Barth, K. 18, 241
Bauer, F. C. 192
Beasley-Murray, G. R. 63, 72
Becker, C. 104, 108
Belgic confession 242
believers (the) 79–80
believing 60, 65, 66
Bellah, R. 21
Bellarmine, R. 192, 217
beloved (the) 106
binding and loosing 54, 61
bishops 122, 149–50, 172, 187, 207
Blasi, A. 44
Blenkinsopp, J. 43
Boff, L. 224
Bonhoeffer. D. 12
Brown, R. 69, 183
Bunyan, J. 200

Cadbury, H. J. 79
called (the) 107
Calvin, J. 191
Cappadocian Fathers 219
Chalcedon (council) 199

charisma/mata 165, 187, 210, 215
charismatic order 71, 97, 165,
172–3, 215
Chester, A. 160
Christ as head 126, 141
Christology 53, 67, 71, 126, 141, 145,
152
Church (the): as the body of Christ
9–11, 103–5, 129, 135–6, 139–40, 185;
the bride of Christ 10, 142–3, 178; a
corpus mixtum 60–1; a flock 37, 160,
166, 225; the fullness of Christ 135,
139; a household 148–9; an institution
8–9; an organization 41–2, 61–2, 95–6;
the people of God 11–12; a servant
12–13; a temple 11, 37–8, 105, 137,
163, 178; a third race 117, 136, 164;
building of 11, 36–8, 148; birthday of
78; congregational view ix, 3, 13–14,
54, 119, 207; differences in doctrine of
1; heavenly existence 13–14, 119–21,
126–7; local 87–8, 115, 186, 205–6,
268n; universal 37, 53, 118–19, 132,
135, 139, 174
Church of South India 201
Clement of Alexandria 190
Clement of Rome 198
conflict in Mark 48–9
conflict in Matthew 52
Congar, Y. 9, 222
congregatio 242
congregationalism 13, 206–7, 242, 281n
Constantine, Emperor 214
Conzelmann, H. 88
communalism 19–22
communio 15–17, 202, 223, 224, 228
communitas 17
community 15–17, 20
Cooke, B. 9
Cornelius Pope 199
covenant 39–40, 71, 154–5, 162
Cyprian, Bishop 213–14

300

Darby, J. N. 14
deacons 8, 122, 150, 187
Decius (emperor) 213
denomination(s) (the) 14, 184, 196–211
Dionysius the Areopagite 215–16
disciples (the) 31–4, 46–7, 47–9, 50–1,
    55–6, 65–6, 81, 89
Donatism 199
Donfield, K. 115
Dulles, A. 8, 13
Dumbrell, W. J. 127, 178
Dunn, J. D. G. 111, 183

edah 24–5, 37, 86, 230–7
edification 123, 223, 275n
ecumenical movement 197, 201–3, 217
egalitarian 43, 224–5
ekklesia 5–8, 13–14, 23–5, 37, 53, 54, 78,
    83–8, 98, 112–14, 116, 120–1, 127–8,
    156–7, 182, 185, 205, 230–40, 241–3
elders 94, 96, 150, 161, 165, 166, 173,
    181, 188, 263n
elect (the) 100, 162
election 133–4, 148, 162
Elliott, J. H. 167
eschatology 27–31, 78–9, 102, 125,
    131–3, 193–4
Essenes 33–4, 177
eucharist 39–40, 72, 93, 103, 122, 161,
    207, 217

family 19, 45, 80, 153, 170
footwashing 72
forgive sins 55–6, 59, 69, 78
Forte, B. 193
Frame, J. 205
fulfilment 56–9

Gemeinde 17, 241
generation (this) 58–9, 281
gentiles 29, 34, 51, 59, 89–92, 107,
    108–12, 131, 136–8, 162
Gore, C. 9
grace 29, 34, 110
Gundry, R. H. 38
Gunton, C. 227

Haenchen, E. 89
Hanson, P. D. 18
Harrington, D. J. 174
hierarchy 8, 214–15, 224–7
Hippolytus 214
holy orders 215
Hooper, J., Bishop 242
Hort, F. J. 86

house churches 113, 117–18, 121–2, 130,
    157, 171–2, 186, 267n, 268n
household code 130, 145
Huss, J. 191

Ignatius 198
in Christ 17, 101, 115, 134
in the heavenlies 133
individualism vii–viii, 3, 14, 19–22, 64
institutionalization 43–4, 63, 73, 96–7,
    99, 123, 146, 149, 150–1, 172, 187–8
Israel: historic 32–4, 45, 58, 106–7, 112,
    131, 136, 155, 162, 167–8, 175, 180;
    new 132, 136–7, 147, 166, 175, 185,
    257n; reconstituted 32, 51, 57–8, 75,
    89; restored 41, 51, 82, 155, 257n; true
    40, 63, 70, 157, 164, 175

Jay, E. 190, 214
Jeremias, J. 29, 35
Jerusalem: earthly 119, 175; heavenly
    155, 177, 179
Jervell, J. 51, 90
Jesus: the founder of the church 8–9, 26,
    45, 221–2
Jews (the) 64, 70, 110, 111, 162
John of Damascus 217
Josephus 238
Judaism 63, 70–1, 109
judgement 32, 58, 64, 156, 176
justification by faith 216

Kasemann, E. 183
Kee, H. 49, 93
Kingdom of God 27–31, 38, 42
Kinnamon, M. 203
Kingsbury, J. 49, 50
Knox, D. B. ix, 14, 127
koinonia 15–17, 171, 202, 220, 228
Kung, H. 193, 203

LaCaguna, C. 229
laos 11, 50, 56, 88, 105, 107, 148, 155
Last Supper 39–40
leadership 94–5, 121–2, 140–1, 150–1,
    159, 187, 225
liberation theology 12
Lohfink, G. 32, 91, 92
Loisy, A. 26, 28, 41
Longenecker, R. 109
Lossky, V. 218
love 143, 165, 169–70
Luther, M. 191, 241
Luz, U. 55

MacDonald, M. 99, 124, 151
Macquarrie, J. 2
McDonnell, K. 15, 221
McKelvey, R. J. 105
Maddox, R. 50, 90, 92
marriage 142–4
Matthias 75
Meier, J. P. 53
Mersch, E. 10
methodology 3, 22–3
Messiah 36, 51, 57–8, 71, 100, 102, 107
Michaels, J. R. 162

Neusner, J. 33
Nicene creed 1
Niebuhr, H. R. 197
Norris, R. 196
Novatian 199

oneness 6
ordination 8–9, 95
Origen 190
Orthodox (Church) 186, 197, 199, 218
Osborne, K. 2
Overmann, J. 62

Paraclete 69
Peter 8, 36–8, 40–1, 47, 54, 71–2
Peterson, D. 156
Pentecost 69, 75–7
perichoresis (doctrine of) 219–20, 226
Pharisees 33, 85, 105
Philo 24, 84, 225, 237–8
Pius X 26
Pius XII 10
Plato 14, 19, 190, 194, 214
preaching 93–4
prophets 29, 60, 61, 95, 180
prophetic fulfilment 56–7
Protestant 2, 5, 6, 11, 72, 117, 196, 211
Protestant principle 192–3, 197
priesthood 165
priests 8, 175–6, 187, 276n

Qahal 24, 37, 230–7
Qumran 33–4, 38, 137, 156, 163

Rahner, K. 220
Raiser, K. 201–2
reconciled diversity 203–4
Reformation (the) 206, 216
Reformers (the) 199, 214, 216, 218, 242
religion 20
remnant 32, 33, 110
repentance 59

reversal 51–2
Richardson, P. 148
Rissi, M. 178
Robinson, D. W. B. ix, 14, 119, 127
Robinson, J. A. T. 10

saints 81–2, 106, 133, 177, 266n
salvation 5, 30, 34, 145, 147
sanctification 6, 162
Schillebeeckx, E. 9
Schnackenburg, R. 31, 139
Scholer, J. 156
Schweizer, E. 64
sect 43, 45, 49, 63, 73
sheep 66–7, 166
shepherd (the) 66–7, 160, 166
Spirit (Holy) 68, 76, 77, 145, 169, 173,
    191, 216, 221–2
suffering 51, 167, 174–7, 181
synagogue (*sunagōgē*) 24–5, 158, 160,
    175, 230–9

temple: building 34, 38, 55, 176; new 38,
    102, 105, 144, 163
Tertullian 219
tests of life 169–70
theophany 75
third race 117, 136–8, 164
Thornton, L. 10
theology: biblical 2, 22; systematic 2, 22,
    207
Thiessen, G. 44
Tillich, P. 192
Timaeus 214–15
tongues 75–6
Torrance, T. F. 213
Trinitarian ecclesiology 217–19
Trinity (doctrine of) 206–7
Troeltsch, E. 42, 45
twelve (the) 28, 31–4, 75–8
Tyndale, W. 241
typology 154, 157, 175

unity 79, 139–40, 144, 183, 184, 201–2,
    207

Vatican II 8, 15, 193, 217, 224
visible-invisible church 61, 149, 169,
    190–5

Waldo, P. 191
Webber, M. 43
Wycliffe, J. 191, 213

Zizioulas, J. 228–9

Index of Biblical References and Ancient Sources

The Old Testament

Genesis
2.7 68
2.24 144
3.16 142
18.18 133
19.16–19 75
49.6 231, 233

Exodus
12.6 107
16.1 233
19.5–6 82
19.6 33, 105, 163
23.16 76
24.3–8

Leviticus
11.44–5 106, 134
19.2 134, 167
20.7–8 134
20.26 134

Numbers
10.3 233
12.7 154
14.5 233
16.2 233
16.3 82, 106
22.4 233
34.10 8

Deuteronomy
5.22 233, 237
7.6 148
7.6–9 107, 134
7.8 134
9.10 231, 233, 236
9.28 134
9.29 135

13.5 134
14.2 134, 135, 148
15.5 134
16.9–12 76
18.16 84, 231, 233, 236
23.2–8 231, 233, 234, 235, 267n
24.18 134
26.18 135
31.30 231, 236
32.8–9 155
32.43 107
33.3 82, 106

Joshua
9.15 234

2 Samuel
7.13 253n
7.14 36, 266n

1 Kings
11.17 234
19.11–12 75
19.18 32

1 Chronicles
16.13 107, 162
17.1–5 36
17.1–15 36
17.21 134
23.1–3 234
28.8 231, 234, 267n

2 Chronicles
24.6 234
29.20 234
29.23 234
29.28 234
29.30 234

29.31 234

Ezra
2.64 236

Nehemiah
5.13 234
7.66 234, 236
8.17 236
10.8 236
13.1 231, 234, 235, 267n

Job
2.2–6 274n
27.9–10 274n

Psalms
16.3 106
22.22 153
22.23 233
26.5 236, 231, 233
26.12 116
33.12 135
34.9 82, 10
35.18 233
40.9 233
40.11 237
50.13–14 237
51.16–19 163
60.5 107
74.1–2 32
74.2 86, 237
79.13 13
89.3 107
89.5 106, 233
89.6 23
95.7–11 154
99.6 82
100.3 32
105.6 107, 162

106.40 135
107.32 233
108.6 107
117.22 162
141.2 163
149.1 233

Proverbs
5.14 237

Isaiah
2.2 76
2.2–3 3
4.3 105
5.1–7 59, 67
6.9–10 58
8.4 162
8.17 153
10.21 33
25.6 27
28.16 33
28.11 108
28.16 162
29.13 58
32.15 76, 253n
32.23 236
35.5–6 30
40.11 3
41.9 107
42.1 107
42.6 107
43.1 107
43.20 134
45.3 107
45.54 107
48.1–11 58
53.11–12 39
54.1 177
54.1–6 142, 253n
60.2–3 35
60.9 134

303

61.1 30
62.2–4 142
65.9 162
65.15 162
65.17–25 265n

Jeremiah
2.21 67
2.23 142
2.32 142
9.7–11 58
11.19–21 253n
12.16 256n
12.18 256n
13.20 32
18.9 256n
23.1–8 32
23.3 32
23.20 76
31.4 256n
31.31–4 40, 71, 154

Ezekiel
7.1–14 58
15.1–5 67
16.8–14 143
16.23 142
16.40 233
17.1–21 67
17.17 233
19.10–15 67
23.3 233
23.46 233
23.47 233
32.22–3 233
34.1–31 32
34.23 32
36.22–32 253n
36.27 76
37.1–28 32
37.9 68
37.14 76
37.23 148
37.26 105, 266n
38.4 233
38.7 233
38.13 233
38.16 233
38.16 76
39.27–9 32
39.40–8 32
40.1 105

Daniel
7.13 101, 251n

7.18 105
7.18–27 82
7.21–7 105
10.20–1 174

Hosea
1.6–9 164
2.1 142
2.19–20 142
6.6 163
10.1–2 67
11.1–4 107

Joel
2.16 233
2.1–30 58
2.28–32 76, 253n

Amos
5.18–20 58
8.9–12 58
9.11 256n

Micah
2.5 231, 233, 234, 267n
4.1 76
4.1–2 35
4.6–7 32
6.6–8 163

Zephaniah
3.12 33

Haggai
2.9 105

Zechariah
10.2–12 32
11.27 32
12.10 76

Malachi
1.11 149
2.14 142
4.1–6 58

Apocrypha

1 Maccabees
1.43 252n
1.52–3 252n
16.3–4 252n
3.15–19 252n
9.23–5 252n
9.5–6 252n

2 Maccabees
2.72 275n

Baruch
4.36–7 31, 32
5.5–9 31

2 Esdras
10.7 177

Ben Sira
(Ecclesiasticus)
33.18 236
36.11 32

Pseudepigrapha

1 Enoch
51.5–8 82, 106
62.6–8 82, 106
62.14 27
72.1 265n
90.28–9 105, 253n, 265n

Syrian Baruch
29.5 27

4 Ezra
5.22 76
13.39–47 31

Psalms of Solomon
17.1 82, 106
17.28–31 32

Jubilees
1.17 105, 253n
1.29 105
4.26 265n

T Job
1.23 76

T Levi
18.11 76

Apoc Baruch
32.6 265n

Dead Sea Scrolls

Damascus Document
CD
1.4 33
2.6 33
2.22 235
3.12–4.12 34

4.3 33
6.19 33
7.17 225
12.6 225

Thanksgiving
Hymns 1QH
2.2 235
2.30 235
3.21–2 274n
5.11–12 253n
6.8 33
6.26ff 37
7.6 76, 253n
7.8–9 33
7.11 253n
7.20 33
11.7–8 274n
17.26 76

War Scroll 1QM
2.2 32
2.7 32
2.16 235
4.9 235
4.10 235, 239, 267n
6.6 82, 106
10.9 33, 252
11.16 231
13.8 33
14.5 231, 235
14.12 106
14.22 82
15.9 235

Rule of the
Community 1QS
1.16 253n
4.25 265n
5.22 33
8.4 33
8.13 82, 106
8.21 82, 106
9.3–5 163
11.7–8 274n

Rule of the
Community,
Appendix 1QSa
1.1 235
1.6 33, 252n
1.12 235
1.25 235
2.3–9 34
2.4 235, 239, 267n

Florilegium 4QFlor
1.1–7 34
1.3 253n
1.4 235

Prayer of Nabonidus
4QPNab
3.2–3 252n

Josephus

Antiquities
3.18 287n
3.292 287n
3.306 287n
4.22 287n
4.24 287n
4.35 287n
4.142 287n
5.72 287n
5.111 287n
13.6 33
20.200–1 33

Jewish Wars
1.108–9 33
2.162 33

Philo

De Confusione
Linguarum
144 286n

De Decalogo
9.32 286n
11.15 287n

Quod Deus Sit
Immutabilis
111 296n

Legum Allegoriae
3.8.81 286n

De Migratione
Abraham
69 286n

De Posteritate Caini
143 238, 287n
177 286n

De Praemiis et
Poenis
28 31

Quis Rerum
Divinarum Heres sit
251 238, 287n

De Somnis
2.187 238
2.184 286n

De Ebrietate
213 286n

De Virtutibus
108 238, 286n

Rabbinic Tractates
B. Pes. 68 76

New Testament

Matthew
1.21 5, 57
1.16 57
1.17 57
1.21 5
1.23 55
2.1–4 57
2.2 62
2.11 62
3.9 56
4.17 59
4.23 30
4.26–9 251n
4.32 30, 54
5.1–10 56
5.12 61
5.20 33, 56
5.19 54, 62
5.22 23, 24, 47, 56
5.48 56
6.10 27, 56
6.15 55
6.19 32, 62
7.3 56
7.4 56
7.5 56
7.15–23 62
7.15–27 60
8.2 62
8.5–13 60
8.12–13 35
8.25 5
9.8 55
9.18 62
9.35 30, 54
10.2 41

10.2–4 41
10.6 32
10.4 61
10.5–6 60
10.6 56
10.16 45, 56
10.17 54
10.23 32, 251n
10.25 45
10.32 30
10.41 61
11.5–6 30
11.12 30
11.16 58
11.17 57
11.19 35
11.20–4 59
11.25 45
11.44–5 56
12.6 55
12.9 54
12.28 29, 30
12.38–41 59
12.39 58
12.45 58
12.41–2 58
12.46–50 80
13.14 58
13.16–17 30
13.17 61
13.24–30 60
13.44–6 251n
13.47–50 60
13.52 55
13.54 54
14.22–33 60
14.30 5
14.33 62
15.7 58
15.13 45
15.21–28 60
15.26 56
15.24 32, 56, 60
15.25 62
16.4 58
16.12 55
16.13–20 36, 37
16.16 53, 57
16.18 11, 36, 38,
   45, 53, 54, 60
16.19 55, 56, 61
16.19–20 54
17.13 55
17.17 58
18.1–4 62

18.2 56
18.3 30
18.5–9 62
18.10–14 62, 211
18.15 56
18.15–20 62
18.16 61
18.17 53, 54
18.18 41, 54, 55,
   56, 61
18.21–34 62
18.22–35 59
19.2 56
19.28 32, 41
20.7 56
20.16 106, 162
20.20 62
20.26 62
20.30 57
20.31 57
21.15 57
21.23 58
21.28–32 58
21.33–43 58
21.43 60
21.29 59
22.1–14 27, 60
22.1–10 35
22.10 59
22.11–14 60
22.14 106
22.45 57
23.8–12 62
23.9 45
23.21 55
23.28–9 33
23.29 61
23.29–36 58
23.34 61
23.37 56
23.38 55
24.6 59
24.22 22, 56
22.24 56, 106
24.31 56, 106
24.34 58
24.42 27
24.43–50 27
25.1–13 27, 60
25.14–30 27, 60
25.46–60
25.32 56
26.1 38
26.26–9 62
26.30 62

26.31 56
28.9 62
28.17 62
28.19 28, 41, 55,
  60, 62, 221
28.20 55, 60

Mark
1.1 48
1.8 103
1.11 48
1.12–13 48
1.15 28, 49
1.16–20 48
1.17 48, 49
1.20 49
1.34 30
2.15–17 35
2.16 33
2.17 33, 34
3.13–19 31
3.16–19 41
4.1–20 251n
4.10–12 30
4.30–2 251n
4.34 48
4.40 48
6.7 48
6.13 30
6.30 41, 48
6.31 48
6.34 32, 49
6.51–2 48
7.1–8 35
7.6–13 22
7.18 48
7.27 35
8.17–18 48
8.18 50
8.24 50
8.27–32 48, 49
8.31 48, 49
8.32 49
8.34–8 51
9.1 28, 32, 49
9.5–6 48
9.13–14 48
9.20 50
9.28 48
9.31 49
9.34 48
9.35 41
9.38–40 48
9.43 30
10.27–31 48, 49
10.28–31 48

10.33–4 49
10.35–44 49
10.44 41
10.45 42
10.52 5
13.1–2 38
13.10 35
13.20 106
13.22 106
13.27 106
13.28–30 48
13.27 45
13.30 28
13.32 19, 45, 48
13.33–7 27, 48
14.9 35
14.17–21 49
14.22–25 39
14.24 45, 49
14.25 39
14.27 45, 49
14.42 49
14.58 36, 37
14.61–4 48
14.60–72 49
15.9 38
15.39 48
14.58 37, 105
14.62 251n

Luke
1.27 5
2.4 20
2.11 50
2.32 51
2.50 52
4.16–30 30
4.18 30
5.29 93
6.3 50
6.13–16 41
6.15 50
6.17 50
6.43
7.3 94
7.36–59 92
8.48 5
9.10 50
9.11–17 93
9.23–7 51
9.27 28
9.32 52
9.45 50
9.48 41
10.23–4 30
10.38–42 52, 93

11.2 27, 56
11.20 29, 30
11.27–28 4
11.37 79
12.32 32, 33, 45
12.35–38 27
12.39–40 27
13.1–5 28
13.22–30 27
13.23 79
13.28–9 35
13.37–39 27
14.13 34
14.15–24 27, 35, 60
14.17 27
15.1–2 35, 93
15.3–7 32
14.25–33 51
16.16 30
16.19–31 52
17.5 50
17.19 5
17.20–1 30
17.24 27
17.26 27
17.28–33 27
18.9–14 52
18.14 33
18.34 50
19.1–10 93
19.12–27 27
19.37 50
22.6 159
22.14 50
22.14–23 93
22.15–20 39
22.19 40
22.20 39, 45
22.26 41
22.27 42
24.10 50
24.13–35 93
24.30 93
24.34 50
24.47 50, 91, 93
24.47–8 41
22.30 32, 41

John
1.11–12 70, 71
1.34 162
1.35–42 65
1.43–51 65
1.49 62, 65
2.1–12 65
2.21 38

3.5 72
3.14–16 64, 70
3.16 64, 68
3.18 64
3.19 64
3.34 64
4.7–42 65
4.13–14 72
4.21 72
4.22 64
4.23 72
4.24 72
4.34 64
4.42 64
5.1 70
5.21 64
5.22 64
5.36 64
6.1–14 70
6.4 78
6.35–59 72
6.37 66
6.39 66
6.41 70
6.52 70
6.63 68
6.69 65
7.2 70
7.15 70
7.35 70
7.37–9 72
8.12 64, 66
8.17 70
8.28 64
8.44 70
8.47 70
9.4 64
9.22 66, 70
9.38 68, 72
10.1–21 70, 66
10.1–30 32, 45
10.3 68
10.10 64
10.12 68
10.14 68
10.16 67, 68
10.26–9 66
10.28 64
10.30 64, 68
10.33 70
10.34 70
10.37 64
11.1–44 65
11.27 65
11.52 67, 68
12.1–8 65

12.19 68
12.31 68
12.35 64, 68
12.46 64
12.47 64
12.48–9 64
12.50–2 70
13.1 68
13.1–20 42, 72
13.23–4 71
13.32–3 71
13.34 67
13.41 66
14.1–14 65
14.15 67
14.16–26 68
14.18–20 68
14.21 67
14.23 67
14.24 67
14.26 68, 71
14.30 68
15.1–17 67
15.9 67
15.10 67
15.16 72
15.25 70
15.26–7 68
16.2 66, 70
16.7–15 68
16.13 68, 71
16.14 68
17.2 64
17.6 68
17.6–11 66
17.8 64
17.10 68
17.11 68
17.14 64
17.15 68
17.18 62, 72
17.20 66
17.21 68
17.22 64, 68
17.23 68
17.26 67
19.19–22 64
19.25–7 65
19.38 66
19.37 71
20.1–8 65
20.19 66
20.19–23 41, 68
20.21 68, 72
20.23 69
20.29 65, 66

21.15–19 71, 166
21.17 8

Acts
1.4 93
1.8 91
1.9–11 74
1.12–15 74
1.13 41
1.15 77
1.15–25 96
1.16 50
1.22 75
2.1 36, 84
2.1–4 75
2.4 92
2.12 75
2.17–21 76, 95
2.27 75
2.29 80
2.36 77
2.38 77, 92
2.41 78, 79, 84, 90,
   91
2.42 77, 93, 94
2.44 77, 78,
2.44–5 77, 79
2.46 79, 90, 92, 93
2.47 78, 79
3.1 90
3.12 75
3.20 78
3.22–3 84
3.23 88
3.25 20
4.4 84, 90
4.5 94
4.8 75
4.28 79
4.32 78, 79, 84
4.32–7 77
4.34 79
5.11 78, 84
5.12 79
5.14 90
5.17 254n
5.17–42 79
5.29 75
5.42 92
6.1 78, 87
6.1–6 94, 96, 165
6.4 94
6.6 95
6.7 81, 87
6.8–7 60 79
6.12 94

7.2 80
7.38 6, 83, 87
7.54–60 83
7.60 79
7.57 79
8.1 84, 85
8.1–4 79
8.3 85, 120
8.4 94
8.6 79
8.11 87
8.12 92
8.16 92
8.36 92
8.38 92
9.1 81
9.2 80, 82
9.3 114
9.10 81
9.13 78, 82, 92
9.14 79, 82
9.17 92
9.19 87
9.21 79, 82
9.23 79
9.25 82
9.26 81, 82
9.30 81, 82
9.31 85, 86, 87
9.32 78, 82
9.36 81
9.38 82
9.41 78, 82
10.2 92
10.34 75
10.41 93
10.43 80
10.44–8 92
11.2 87
11.14 92
11.22 85
11.26 81, 85, 87, 94
11.29 81
11.30 94, 96, 188
12.1 85
12.2 75
12.5 85
12.12–17 92
12.15 175
12.20 79
13.1 87, 94
13.1–3 95
13.3 95
13.7 167
13.26 80
13.38 80

13.39 80
13.44–6 89
13.48 80
14.1 90
14.2 80
14.19 79
14.22 79, 94
14.23 87, 94, 95
14.27 83, 85, 87
15.1 80
15.1–29 206
15.2ff 94
15.3 87
15.4 11
15.5 79, 85, 254n
15.6 96
15.7 80
15.10 81
15.12 96
15.14 88
15.16–8 91
15.19 96
15.20 80
15.22 84, 94, 95,
   159
15.25 79
15.30 85
15.35 94
15.36 80
16.1 81
16.3 90
16.5 85, 87
16.7 83
16.15 92
16.31–4 92
16.34 79
17.5 79
17.10 90
17.31 78
18.5–6 89
18.8 92
18.10 11, 88
18.12 79
18.23 87
18.27 79, 81
19.9 80
19.5 92
19.18 79
19.23 80
19.29 79
19.32, 39, 41 6, 23,
   83, 231
19.42 90
20.7 93
20.7–12 94
20.11 93

20.17–35 94
20.28 51, 78, 85,
  86, 87, 92, 94,
  112, 135, 166,
  231, 237
20.30 81
20.32 82
21.18 188, 206
21.16 78, 87
21.18 96
21.20 79, 90
21.25 79
22.3 33
22.16 79, 92
22.19 79
23.14 94
24.22 80
24.35 93
26.6 33
26.19 78, 82
26.18 6, 82
27.20 5, 83
27.31 5, 80
27.34 5
28.16 88
28.17 88
28.21 80
28.23–8 89
28.27 88
28.31 78

Romans
1.7 82, 106, 107,
  115
1.8ff 100
1.9 123
1.18–3.20 110
5.12ff 100
5.12–21 100
5.18ff 100
6.3 102
6.3–5 131
6.60 102
7.1–12 101
7.5 101
8.1 101
8.9 101
8.17 102
8.27 106
8.28 107
8.33 106
8.34 162
9.6–7 110
9.6–29 110
9.25 107
9.30–10.21 110

10.1–13 100
10.18 111
11.1–10 111
11.11–24 111
11.25–32 111, 112
12.1 163
12.2 6, 123
12.3–8 103
12.5 101
12.13 106
15. 10 107
15.16 123
15.25 106
15.26 16
16.1 115, 122
16.3 122
16.3–4 118
16.4 116
16.5 7, 117
16.6 122
16.12 122
16.15 82, 122
16.19 117
16.23 7

1 Corinthians
1.2 6, 7, 82, 107,
  115, 118, 128,
  149, 231
1.24 107
3.7 105
3.9 10, 105
3.16 10, 105, 163
3.18 6
6.4 116
6.11 162
10.6 16
10.14–16 122
10.14–22 103
10.16 17, 103
10.32 7, 116, 118,
  120, 231
11.5 122
11.10 174
11.16 114, 116, 231
11.17 268n
11.18 6, 113, 118
11.21–2 122
11.23 40
11.23–6 39
11.24–6 122
12.4 221
12.12–13 103, 104,
  118
12.13 101, 103,
  123, 131

12.15–26 103
12.27 103
12.28 7, 112, 117,
  120, 140
14.5 116
14.9 6
14.12 116
14.18 111
14.19 113, 118
14.23 268n
14.26 122, 268n
14.28 6, 118
14.34 6, 118, 122
14.35 6, 112, 118
15.9 7, 86, 112,
  113, 114, 120,
  231
15.20–9 100
15.22 101
16.9 118
16.19 7

2 Corinthians
1.1 7, 82, 107, 115,
  231
1.17 16
5.17 102
6.16 10, 105, 107
6.16–18 105, 107
8.1 116
8.4 16
9.13 16
13.12 82

Galatians
1.2 116
1.13 86, 113, 114,
  120
1.22 114
1.23 114
2.21 33
3.7 109
3.19 109
3.15–18 109
3.20–21 119
3.27 102
3.27–8 104
3.28 101, 131
3.28–9 109
4.21–31 109, 119
4.26 119, 177
4.30 109
5.6 109
5.15 109
6.16 109

Ephesians
1.1 133
1.3 125, 127, 133,
  145
1.3–14 133
1.4 133, 144, 221
1.9 134, 144
1.10 13
1.11 134
1.13 125, 221
1.14 133
1.18–25 132
1.19 125
1.20–3 125, 133
1.22 7, 125, 127,
  136, 138, 270n
1.23 127, 135, 138,
  141, 270n
2.1 136
2.2 136
2.5 136, 146
2.5–6 127
2.6 125
2.10 140
2.11 125
2.11–19 137
2.12 125, 136
2.14 136, 137
2.15 125, 136, 137,
  138
2.17 136
2.18 137
2.19 136, 137, 163,
  270n
2.20 10, 137, 270n
2.22 137
3.3 144
3.4 144
3.9 144
3.10 17, 133, 138,
  270n
3.15 20
3.16 145
3.17 145
3.21 7, 138, 270n
4.3 139
4.4 139
4.1–6 6, 139, 198
4.4–6 139
4.11 140
4.12 139, 140
4.13 141
4.15 142
4.15–16 132, 141,
  145
4.16 139

4.17 125
4.24 125, 144
4.30 133, 145
5.1 145
5.5 133
5.18 145
5.21–33 142, 270n
5.21–6.4 145
5.23 125, 142, 270n
5.24 142
5.25 10, 143, 270n
5.26 142
5.27 143
5.28 143
5.31 142, 144
5.32 143, 270n
6.10–20 145
6.12 133
6.13 133
6.17 145
6.19 144

Phillipians
1.1 8, 115
1.5 16
2.5–11 100
3.3 123
3.3–6 105
3.6 113, 114, 120
3.8 101
3.10 17
4.2–3 122

Colossians
1.1 130
1.2 131
1.4 131
1.5 125, 145
1.11–13 125
1.12 131
1.13 125, 127, 132
1.15–20 126, 127, 128, 129
1.18 125, 126, 128, 129
1.20–2 126, 132
1.21 132
1.24 127, 128
1.26 131
2.8 126
2.10 125, 132
2.11 125
2.12 131
2.13 125, 131
2.15 132
2.16–17 126

2.19 125, 127, 128, 129, 142
2.21–3 126
3.1 125, 127, 131, 145
3.1–4 125
3.4 131
3.6 131
3.7 132
3.9 125
3.10–11 131
3.12 131, 162
3.15–16 127
3.16 131
3.18–4.1 130
3.24 131
4.13 129
4.14 129
4.15 7, 129
4.16 129
4.17 131

1 Thessalonians
1.1 7, 115
1.4 107, 116
2.14 114
5.12 121
5.19–20 122
5.32 6

2 Thessalonians
1.1 7, 115
1.4 114
2.1 275n
2.13 107, 162

1 Timothy
1.18 147
2.1–3 150
2.8 149
2.11 150
2.13–14 151
3.1 149
3.1–7 150
3.1–13 165
3.4 148
3.4–5 148
3.5 231
3.8–13 150
3.12 148
3.15 148
3.16 149
4.1 147, 150
4.10 147
4.14 147, 150, 189, 206

5.4 148
5.12–13 150
5.22 95
6.1–3 150
6.13–15 147

2 Timothy
1.16 148
2.10 147
2.14 149
2.18 148
2.19 147, 148
2.19–20 148
2.20 149
3.7 150
3.10 147
4.1–4 147

Titus
1.1 147
1.5 87, 189
1.11 150
2.3–6 150
2.9–10 150
2.13 147
2.14 11, 147
3.1 150

Philemon
2 118, 129

Hebrews
1.1 157
2.1–4 153
2.5–9 153
2.10 153, 157
2.10–18 153
2.11 153
2.12 153, 156, 157
2.13 153
2.17 153, 157
3.6 154, 157
3.2 157
3.13 157
4.1–6 154
4.1–11 154
4.9 157
4.16 157, 158
5.7 158
5.12 158
6.10 82, 157
8.8–12 154
8.10 157
9.14 158, 274n
10.1 155
10.10 6

10.16–17 154, 157
10.19 157
10.19–25 158
10.22 158
10.23 158
10.24 157
10.29 6
11.25 157, 158
12.5 157
12.18–24 155
12.23 156, 157
12.28 158, 274n
13.7 158
13.12 6, 157
13.15 158
13.15–16 163
13.17 158
13.18 158
13.24 82, 158

James
1.1 159
1.5–6 161
1.21 161, 164
1.22–5 161
2.2 6, 158, 160, 161
2.6 160
2.9–10 11
2.12–15 160
2.15–16 161
3.1–2 160
3.1–12 161
3.9–10 161
4.1 161, 162
4.2 161
4.11–12 161, 162
5.8–9 159, 161
5.10 161
5.13 161
5.14 160, 161
5.16 161
5.17–19 161

1 Peter
1.1 162
1.2 162
1.3 164
1.6–7 167
1.15 162
1.17 162, 167
1.17–18 167
1.18 165
1.18–21 162
1.22 165
1.23 164
2.2–4 162

2.3 165
2.4 162, 167
2.4–10 162
2.5 164
2.6 162
2.9 135, 148, 162,
  163, 167, 175
2.10 164, 165
2.11 167
2.12 162
2.17 165
2.19–25 167
2.21 165
2.24 165
2.25 166
3.1 166
3.1–7 167
3.8 165, 166
3.11–12 167
3.13–22 167
3.21 164
4.1–6 167
4.3 162
4.9 165
4.10–11 165
4.12–19 165
4.17 167
4.18 167
5.1–5 165
5.2 166
5.3 166
5.4 166
5.9 165, 166
5.9–10 167
5.14 165

2 Peter
3.13 265n

1 John
1.1–4 168
1.3 169, 171
1.2–3 16
1.6–7 16
1.6–10 169
1.7 169
2.3 169
2.5 169
2.6–7 173
2.10 169
2.15 170
2.18–19 168, 169
3.1 170

3.3–10 169
3.8 169
3.10 169
3.12 274n
3.13 170
3.14 169
3.16 169
3.17 169
3.18 169
3.19 169
3.23 169
3.24 169
4.2 169, 173
4.3 168, 170
4.5 169
4.6 169
4.7–21 169
5.1 170
5.6 169
5.19 170

2 John
1 171
7 168, 169, 172
9 169
10 172
10–11 170
13 171

3 John
1 172
3 172
5 172
7 172
9 172
10 172
12 172

Jude
3 82

Revelation
1.3 180
1.2 176
1.4 174
1.5–6 179
1.6 175, 179
1.10 179
1.11 174
1.12 177
1.17–18 179
1.20 174, 177
2.1 177

2.2 175
2.5 174
2.9 175
2.13 175
2.16 176
2.20 176
3.1 175
3.8 175
3.9 175
3.11 176
3.15 175
3.17 175
3.20 176
4.1–11 179
4.4 180
4.8 179
4.10 179
4.11 179
5.5 180
5.9–10 179
5.10 175
5.12 175
5.14 179
7.1–8 176
7.4 179
7.9 176
7.9–17 176
7.11 179
8.3–4 178
8.4 82
9.20 179
10.1–11; 13 176
10.6 176
10.7 180
11.1 179
11.3–4 277n
11.8 178
11.16 179
11.18 176, 180
12.1 177
12.1–14.20 177
12.10 179
12.17 179
13.1 175
13.4 179
13.5 175
13.6 175
13.7 177
13.8 179
13.15 179
14.1 176, 179
14.7 179
14.12 177

15.4 179
16.2 179
16.16 180
17.3 175
18.20 180
18.24 180
19.2 176
19.4 179
19.5 176
19.10 176, 180
19.11–16 132, 178
19.20 179
20.6 175, 179
20.7 178
20.9 178
20.9–27 178
21.2 178, 179
21.3 178
21.5 180, 265n
22.1–5 179
22.3 176
22.6 176, 180
22.7 180
22.8 176
22.10 180
22.20 176

**Post-apostolic
writings**

Ignatius'epistles
Eph 5.13 199
Mag 6.1–2 199
    7.1–2 199
Trall 2.1–3 199,
  287n
Poly 4.2 287n

*Martyrdom of
Polycarp*
3.2 164
14.1 164
4.2 275n

*The Shepherd of
Hermas*
Sim 9.17.5 164
Man 11.9, 13, 14
  275n, 287n

*Justin Dialogue with
Trypho*
63.5 275